PROBLEMS AND PROSPECTS
IN INTERNATIONAL EDUCATION

David G. Scanlon/James J. Shields/Editors

Teachers College Press
Teachers College, Columbia University, New York

CONTENTS

Introduction: Scope and Purposes of International Education

*T*he accelerated pace of man's quest for knowledge in the twentieth century has been accompanied by an effort to bring the benefits of new knowledge to all men. This revolution has touched every continent and has left few institutions unchanged. By any measure, the impact of education has been significant, and there are many who predict that the ultimate consequences will reshape the world.

This phenomenon has caused the wholesale expansion of popular schooling in nearly all the nations of Europe and North America and the extension of educational opportunity in Africa, Asia, and Latin America. As a result new institutions have been created, such as the community college in the United States. In addition, out-of-school programs in mass literacy and community development have grown and multiplied.

These developments have been promoted by local initiative and in some instances by the interchange of people and educational materials among cultures in all parts of the world. Rapid and efficient means of communication and travel have intensified the processes involved in the sharing of beliefs, attitudes, and skills across cultural lines. These are some of the conditions that have brought international education into focus as a major field of study.

The Question of Definition

As international education has grown in importance, the need to establish a working definition accurately encompassing the broad range of activities within the field has become more apparent. Beyond this, a definition is required that supplies a basis for distinguishing between international education and the various subject fields to which it is allied, such as the history of education, international relations, and comparative education.

Of late, questions of definition are receiving the attention of the specialists in these fields. At the 1965 meeting of the Comparative Education Society in Europe, held in Berlin, there were renewed attempts to define *Auslandspädagogik* (comparative education proper) and international education.[1] The two fields have traditionally been linked. Thus, a precise and comprehensive definition is required to establish the uniqueness of international education.

Relatively few international educators have addressed themselves to the problem of definition. Among those who have, however, there is substantial agreement. "International education" is generally defined as "the various types of educational and cultural relations among nations."[2]

This definition accounts for most of the activities in the field; however, it does not incorporate all. For example, it blurs the important distinction between the roles of practitioner and theorist. As a practitioner, an individual is actually engaged in the process of transmitting knowledge, attitudes, and skills across national or cultural boundaries. Those who teach abroad, advise laborers in new nations on the formation of unions, work as consultants in every type of foreign ministry, write scripts for radio programs intended for overseas consumption, advise students from other lands, or establish libraries abroad have all assumed the role of practitioner. On the other hand, while an individual who studies international education may have worked in a practical situation, as a theorist he is more interested in chronicling events; in conceptualizing processes; and in examining the cultural, philosophical, political, and sociological implications of programs in international education. In effect, then, this definition does not do full justice to international education as an evolving academic field for the study of the processes of transmitting and fostering beliefs, skills, attitudes, and knowledge across national boundaries.

The theoretical side of the field is growing in importance. Over the past few years, an international institute for the study of educational planning has been founded in Paris, and a number of American universities, including Harvard, Syracuse, Pittsburgh, Chicago, Stanford, and Teachers College, Columbia University, have established centers for the study of educational development in the new nations.[3]

The Meaning of "Education"

The term "education" is used by some to designate all learning experiences. John Dewey, for example, once defined it as "the social continuity of life."[4] However, contemporary educators, who are concerned with building the discipline of education into a more precise and manageable area of study, reject this view in favor of a much narrower one. They limit the term to those modifications in behavior that occur because a teacher or a learner or both make a *deliberate* effort to transmit and foster knowledge, skills, attitudes, and beliefs.[5] Thus, learning experiences that take place merely because an individual is in a particular place at a particular time are not defined as education. In the context of this definition, the unintentional acquisition of learning by an individual does not qualify as international education.

The value of applying this narrower definition to the field of international education is that it clearly separates the field from the broad, formless, and almost limitless areas of acculturation and general cultural contacts. In addition, it establishes reasonableness and order at a time when the field is burgeoning. Far too large a proportion of the current literature consists of breezy travelogue, sentimental reminiscence, or pamphleteering for a favored cause or project – and far too little concentrates on the specific processes of systematically educating individuals along national frontiers.

"Educational and Cultural"

Moving from a discussion of the term "education" to the complete phrase "educational and cultural relations," one runs into yet another obstacle to the attainment of a clear idea of what international education means. At first glance, the phrase conveys the impression that activities in the field of international education can be bifurcated into "educational" and "cultural." However, everything related to the field is by definition educational, and all educational activities by their very nature have cultural dimensions.

The word "culture" has numerous meanings. Anthropologists define culture as the entire way of life of a society or, in a complex society, of each particular distinguishable subgroup within the society. And they define education as the cultural process by which the newborn infant is transformed into a full member of society. In this sense, education and culture are not discrete, but interrelated, entities.

"Culture" is also used to refer to the fine and performing arts alone. However, unless the arts are used to teach something, "culture" as used here is not related to international education. In *The Fourth Dimension of Foreign Policy,* Philip Coombs discusses yet another use of the term "cultural relations," that is, a form of diplomacy practiced in various periods by European nations.[6] Obviously, this type of cultural relations is a matter for political scientists and not for educationists. Thus, when an enterprise is classified as international education, it is because it is an educational activity and not because it is cultural in scope.

In sum, the shorter phrase "educational relations" conveys a clearer idea of the content of the field than does the widely used phrase "educational and cultural relations." In light of the foregoing comments, the standard definition of "international education" should be rewritten to read: *The study and the practice of various types of educational relations across national boundaries.*

The Literature of International Education

What are the various types of educational relations among nations? Since international education can be traced to antiquity, it would seem that the literature of the field would provide an excellent starting point for resolving the question. However, the state of documentation is such that there is little accessible material for the period before World War II and too much material for the period after the war to handle easily. Both periods present the serious scholar with complex research problems.

The research problem is intensified because so few historians are interested in international education. Thus, even where documents do exist, there has been almost no one to synthesize their contents. At the moment, there is no general history of international education, and data have to be sought in a variety of widely scattered sources. Consequently, the field of international education does not have at its command historical studies to fix the lineage, design a fitting methodology, or define its content. Because international education has not had the benefit of self-examination in the perspective of history, it has been hindered from developing into a *bona fide* field of study.

However, there is good reason to believe that many of the gaps in the history of international education will be spanned in the not-too-distant future. William Brickman, a leading historian of international education, is doing a prodigious amount of research in the field. His article in the 1950 edition of the *Encyclopedia of Educational Research* is particularly valuable and constitutes a significant milestone in this literature. In addition to outlining the foundations of the field, the article contains a list of more than two hundred references.[7]

In the 15-year period since Brickman wrote his article, a significant number of books, reports, and pamphlets have been issued that add to the historical resources of the field. It is difficult to compose a representative list that is both fair and brief. However, the following publications should have a place in all bibliographies: David G. Scanlon, *International Education: A Documentary History* (1960); F. P. Walters, *A History of the League of Nations* (1952); Walter H. C. Laves and Charles A. Thomson, *UNESCO: Purpose, Progress, Prospects* (1957); Jean Thomas, *U.N.E.S.C.O.* (1962); George N. Shuster, *UNESCO: Assessment and Promise* (1963); and Guy S. Métraux, *Exchange of Persons: The Evolution of Cross-Cultural Education* (1952) — all of which deal with multilateral programs of international education — and the U.S. Congress, *Government Programs in International Education* (1959); Merle Curti, *American Philanthropy Abroad: A History* (1963); Merle Curti and Kendall Birr, *Prelude to Point Four: American Technical Missions Overseas, 1838–1938* (1954); Walter H. C. Laves and Charles A. Thomson, *Cultural Relations and U.S. Foreign Policy* (1963); Norman Dawes, *A Two-Way Street: The Indo-American Fulbright Program, 1950–1960* (1962); Foster R. Dulles, *Americans Abroad: Two Centuries of European Travel* (1964); and Robert S. Schwantes, *Japanese and Americans: A Century of Cultural Relations* (1955) — which deal with United States activities in the field of international education.

At first glance, the literature suggests a basic outline of the broad range of topics embraced by the field of international education. Although this is true, closer examination reveals the shifting emphasis with which the separate subjects are discussed and the importance assigned to each in different periods. The early postwar literature that Brickman discusses deals primarily with war-devastated Europe, the re-education of the Axis nations, intellectual cooperation among scholars, and the role of the school in promoting international understanding and in teaching about the United Nations. Subsequently, some of these enterprises were dropped and others were added. For instance, in the 1950's and 1960's, the focus of the literature shifted to a discussion of the use of education to contain Communist aggression and to modernize the new nations of Africa, Asia, and Latin America. However, regardless of the period discussed, educational relations across national boundaries fall roughly into three categories. These are activities that are designed (1) to promote the self-image of the donor; (2) to promote international understanding and world peace; and (3) to promote human knowledge and competence.

Promoting a Self-image Abroad

Most international programs established by national governments, religious bodies, and business firms are constructed to promote the image or the purposes of the donor. R. Freeman Butts discussed this situation when he reviewed the history of contacts between Africans and the outside world for a group of young Americans who were preparing to teach in Africa. After categorizing the true reasons for which an expatriate went to Africa in the early days as missionary, proprietary, military, or plenipotentiary, Butts stressed that these young Americans would be going to Africa for selfless reasons to become "educationaries" who would help Africans achieve their own goals.[8]

Current bilateral technical assistance and intellectual relations programs provide ample evidence of the importance that the promotion of selfish interests has in international educational affairs. More and more, nations believe that they must implant their political beliefs abroad or at least defend them intellectually, whether the challenge takes place in the Assembly of the United Nations or in a remote village in Borneo.

These vents have introduced a new diplomacy that has extended beyond the diplomat and the conference room to include the average citizen and the public forum. As a result, the ordinary man has assumed new importance in world affairs. Today, the objective is to speak past governments directly to the people in an effort to win their favor and ultimately the support of their governments. Radio Free Europe is a particularly dramatic outgrowth of this climate in foreign affairs. Another noteworthy development is the creation of elaborate overseas information services, including libraries, exhibits, film showings, lectures, and concerts, by nations of every political persuasion. The United States alone has 174 libraries in 87 countries to make available to selected audiences information about this country.[9] Two provocative sources on United States programs are Wilson Dizzard's *The Strategy of Truth: The Story of the United States Information Service* (1961) and Arthur Meyerhoff's *The Strategy of Persuasion: The Use of Advertising Skills in Fighting the Cold War* (1965).

Yet another dimension of this trend is reflected in the expansion of exchange programs to include artists, housewives, and workers as well as students, teachers, and scholars. The Soviet Union and the United States signed an agreement in January 1965 to exchange visits of each nation's most accomplished performing artists.[10]

The growth of these programs in the last two decades has given added importance to the role of journalism, radio, television, library science, psychology, and the fine and performing arts in international education. It also has generated considerable discussion on the nature of propaganda and its relationship to education and diplomacy, and it has raised the question of whether the integrity of the arts, or indeed their vitality, can be maintained if they are used as instruments of political education. Alberto Moravia, in an essay entitled "When Art Becomes Propaganda," discusses this and related questions in a somewhat perplexing but penetrating manner. In the concluding paragraph of his essay he states:

> Healthy and direct art is born of an encounter between society and the artist on equal terms. We find such an encounter in the classical writers of the great epochs of art, whereas art for art's sake and propaganda art avoid the encounter, the first out of pride and the second out of a spirit of oppression.[11]

If today's programs are taken as a basis for a definition, then propaganda is the educational component of a goodly number of the intellectual-relations programs sponsored by individual nations. Theodore Sands' definition of propaganda encompasses much of the activity that goes under the heading of intellectual relations:

> In propaganda there is no exchange of views or explanation of the reasons for them. There is no listening, for the intent is not mutual understanding or agreement, but the presentation of a position.[12]

We all accept the current uses of propaganda as a reality of life in the latter half of the twentieth century. Propaganda gives the hearer no opportunity to hear alternatives. Although it is widely used in programs in international education, propaganda is poorly understood and rarely studied by academicians.

A few hopeful observers of the world scene find consolation as well as distress in these trends. The events signal for them the beginning of an era when words and ideas will replace soldiers and armies in world conflicts. However, there is little evidence that their views have validity. The total cost of all cultural-relations programs sponsored by the United States, for instance, does not add up to 1 per cent of its total military budget.

Promoting International Understanding and World Peace

A second aim of international educational activities is to promote international understanding and world peace. Efforts to implement this goal can be found in the work of the United Nations and its affiliated agencies, for example in UNESCO's Major Project on Mutual Appreciation of Eastern and Western Cultural Values and in the work of such foundations as the Carnegie Endowment for International Peace, founded to hasten "the abolition of international war, the foulest blot on our civilization." But, as indicated in the *Report on the Fiftieth Anniversary* of the Endowment, progress toward

Andrew Carnegie's aim had been small indeed. The Endowment has therefore revised its purpose. Instead of aiming for "unconditional" peace, it is working to realize some demonstrable progress toward peace and toward development of institutions that will allow humanity not only to survive, but to prosper in a less-than-perfect world.[13]

These sentiments are much more modest than those voiced by most professional peacemakers. But they represent an honest confrontation with the realities of our age of competitive coexistence. The truth is that few nations engage in more than token projects in this area. And, even when they do, the weight of other foreign-policy decisions frequently negates whatever effort they do exert to promote international understanding. Speaking to this point, William Patterson says:

> In 1965, proclaimed International Cooperation Year by the United Nations, the United States government is mobilizing a vast program of projects for international cooperation, while at the same time stifling one of the most basic contemporary expressions of cooperation: world travel, and tourism.[14]

Promoting International Understanding at Home. Not all international programs are directed to an audience beyond national boundaries. All nations engage, officially and unofficially, in activities to extend among their own nationals an understanding of other nations. Unfortunately, either out of ignorance or by design, the image presented is in most instances distorted. However, there are hopeful signs of change. In the past 20 years, many of the Western nations, the United States included, have made an honest effort to acquaint their citizens with the cultural patterns of other nations.

In the United States, the growth of foreign-language training has been a great boon in promoting knowledge about other cultures. Also, increased attention has been given to the revision of textbooks and the broadening of curriculums to include studies of African and Asian as well as Western cultures on all levels of schooling. One of the most hopeful developments is the work being done to "globalize" liberal arts programs and university training in general. Two publications distributed by Education and World Affairs, *The College and World Affairs* (1964) and *The University and World Affairs* (1960) have played a significant role in accelerating these changes.

These enterprises are friendly, humane, and fine as far as they go. However, even when they do quicken the awareness by individuals of cultures other than their own, they by no means necessarily result in understanding or a peaceful disposition toward the cultures studied. This comes, if it comes at all, in concert with the development of *critical thinking,* which is nurtured in every phase of the curriculum and not merely in one very specialized area such as geography or history.

The purposes here will not be served until international understanding is viewed in the broader context of developing men with highly cultivated rational abilities who examine all events critically. Prejudice and indifference, which are the major offenders, run too deep in the fabric of most cultures to be touched by a class assignment or a series of international conferences. Suspicion, hostility, and intolerance will persist as long as men neglect to put every attitude they have about individuals to the test of rationality. This, then, is where the emphasis must be in programs designed to promote international understanding – not in a proliferation of activities built on the assumption that "even strange people can be friendly."

Promoting Human Knowledge and Competence

The third aim, to advance human knowledge and competence, has become more important in the past ten years with the increasing number of fellowships and travel grants and with the encouragement of private international organizations, science cooperation offices, seminars, symposiums, conferences, clearinghouse activities, yearbooks, journals, art reproductions, television, radio, press, and museum programs.

However, by far the most important reason for the new significance of international educational activities related to the advancement of human knowledge and competence has been the growing awareness among individuals in all nations and at every stratum of society of the imbalance in the distribution of the world's wealth. As a result, the more advanced peoples of the world have developed a myriad of technical-assistance programs to help the nationals of developing nations realize a better life.

A whole new vocabulary and a new way of looking at the world's masses have accompanied this phenomenon. The phrases "rising expectations," "the silent revolution," and "the take-off stage" have found their way into the language of average citizens and statesmen alike. Nations are no longer spoken of as "underdeveloped," but as "developing"; their people themselves are no longer spoken of as "natives," but as "nationals"; and they are no longer given "charity," but "technical assistance." There is change on all sides as thoughtful men seek to understand what is sometimes a threat and is always a challenge.

Technical assistance and education are related in two important ways. The first is seen in programs involving the planning, the financing, the expansion, and the improvement of elementary, secondary, and vocational schools, teacher-training colleges, and universities. Nigeria well illustrates the way in which technical-assistance programs in education are developing. Shortly after Nigeria achieved independence in 1960, it identified education as a major priority item for development. To help Nigeria attain its goals, more than 50 per cent of United States technical assistance to Nigeria that year was given in the field of education. This aid was instrumental in the reorganization and expansion of the facilities of the University of Nigeria. The university increased its enrollment from 220 in 1960 to 1,200 in 1962 and has become a "land-grant" type of institution that produces graduates in agriculture, education, public administration, and business.[15]

Technical assistance and education are related in a second way, for, by definition, technical assistance is an educational process. Simply, technical assistance has come to be defined as the transmission of skills, attitudes, and knowledge that lead to development. The relationship is often overlooked because education is usually identified with formal schooling, when it is, before anything else, a process. Thus, schools are no more than the accidental and expendable institutions where education takes place. Educational processes can just as easily be found in an informal agricultural scheme or an intellectual-relations program as they can be in the formal program of an academic high school.

Thus, whenever knowledge, skills, and attitudes are transmitted, the processes of education have been activated, whether the transmission takes place in a Western-style classroom, a village marketplace, or the office of a government employee. One United States technical assistance administrator was so convinced of this that he maintained that there was no need for a separate educational branch in the Washington office of the United States technical assistance program because every technician is an educator.[16]

A good case in point is to be found in the work of the Community Development Division of the United States' former technical-assistance agency, the International Cooperation Administration. The division evaluated its programs in terms of the changes that took place in the people inhabiting the areas it aided because it believed that new schools or roads or an increase in crop yields were important only insofar as they provided tangible evidence of the development of persons. Jack Mezirow, speaking from his experience as a community-development adviser with the division, said that community development is an educational process and that the work of the community-development practitioner is essentially educational.[17]

Technical assistance differs from all other activities in international education in that its objectives are to improve the technical, professional, and managerial skills and knowledge of those assisted. The programs are geared primarily to introducing attitudes, skills, and knowledge that are essential to social and economic development. The programs are usually geared to specific development activities, such as the establishment of a local training school or an agricultural extension system, the overhaul of fiscal operations, or the setting-up of an industrial-productivity center.

What is sought is a total modernization of social and economic institutions in the assisted nations. Thus, international educators are confronted with the question of the role of technical assistance in achieving this modernization. Over the past few years, economists, political scientists, and sociologists have become more interested in this topic. Some of the significant studies that have grown out of this interest are Gabriel Almond and James Coleman, *The Politics of the Developing Areas* (1960); Frederick Harbison and Charles Myers, *Education, Manpower and Economic Growth: Strategies of Human Resource Development* (1964); L. J. Lewis, *Education and Political Independence* (1962); Lucian Pye, *Politics, Personality and Nation Building: Burma's Search for Identity* (1962); and Walter Rostow, *The Stages of Economic Growth* (1960).

The Selection and Training of Personnel for Overseas Work

The realization of economic viability and political stability requires a complicated series of changes in the cultures of the nations assisted. To date, the literature on the question of cultural change and the problem of transfer is severely limited. This is particularly unfortunate because technicians find that stimulating change in individuals and institutions alike is an extremely complex process.

Related to the question of cultural change is the problem of the selection and training of technicians for overseas work. Technical assistance personnel must, for all practical purposes, act as agents of cultural change, and their selection and training should take this role into account. Technical competency is not enough in the actual field situation. Technicians find that they have to shift from the diagnostic role appropriate to the early phases of the advisory process to the more active training role necessary for the successful completion of their overseas assignment. Specifically, in terms of selection and training, the technician needs a deep understanding of human be-

havior and how it is changed. He needs a broad knowledge of the
learning processes and their application to teaching situations. Finally,
since much of the adviser's work has to be done through groups, he
should be adept in planning for, participating in, and leading groups.

Recently, a number of studies have been published that deal with
the problem of selecting and training personnel for overseas work.
These studies include: Harlan Cleveland and Gerard Mangone, *The
Art of Overseasmanship* (1957); Harlan Cleveland, Gerard Mangone,
and John C. Adams, *The Overseas Americans* (1960); the Committee
on Foreign Affairs Personnel, *Personnel for the New Diplomacy*
(1962); the Council on Social Work Education, *Interprofessional
Training Goals for Technical Assistance Personnel Abroad* (1959);
Clarence Thurber and Richard Spencer, *American Professions and
Overseas Technical Assistance* (1965); and Mattram Torre, *The
Selection of Personnel for International Service* (1963).

International education also embraces the variety of programs in
American universities and colleges, government agencies, commercial
institutes, and business firms that develop scholars and practitioners
in international affairs. These enterprises range from one-day orientation programs provided by large business firms for employees going
overseas through twelve-week training programs for Peace Corps
trainees conducted by universities to full-fledged degree programs in
international relations. Programs offered by Georgetown University
in its School of Foreign Service, by Syracuse University in its Maxwell
School, and by Harvard and Tufts in the Fletcher School of International Law and Diplomacy represent some of the older and better-
known programs in this area.

.   .   .   .

In the selections that follow, an effort has been made to identify
the six major areas currently of importance in international education: (1) Education, Technical Assistance, and Development; (2)
The Economic and Political Aspects of Education and Development;
(3) Technical Assistance—The Problem of Transfer; (4) Cultural
Relations and Education; (5) Exchange of Persons: The Promise
and the Reality; and (6) The Response of the United States—The
New International Education Program.

The selection of these topics emphasizes the dramatic shift that has
occurred in international education since the close of World War II.
The center of interest is no longer in promoting "understanding"
among Western nations but rather in the complicated process of assisting nations in modernization. Education is viewed by the leaders of
the newly independent nations as the major vehicle for political sta-

bility and economic development. For a variety of reasons, political as well as humanitarian, Western nations, at the invitation of the developing nations, are assisting in this mass process of cultural and social transformation. But assistance must be based on a realistic "understanding" of the dynamics of the developing nations.

Unfortunately, in the rush to provide the mechanics of assistance, there has been little time or money for basic research. Assistance has been viewed for many years as an ad hoc, emergency undertaking. Today, however, it is evident that many newly independent countries will need aid for at least a decade, perhaps longer. All who have been involved in this field agree on the danger of transferring institutions, but the process of building a new institution—not simply a carbon copy of the Western model, but one based on the culture of the country—requires an emphasis on research that has been lacking. In the many branches of international education, the answers to most of the fundamental questions have to be found in the disciplines of history, sociology, anthropology, economics, and political science. With the support of research in these areas, it should be possible to make even more effective the accomplishments and goodwill that have been achieved by international education.

Since World War II, the United States has been engaged in the most extensive assistance effort the world has ever seen. In more recent years, European countries and Japan have increased their technical cooperation with the so-called emerging nations. The motives for helping are often obscure. Lucian Pye has written that "even the decision makers of the West cannot tell what mixture of self-interest and self-sacrifice, of hard calculation and human charity, have inspired their acts." [18]

Whatever the motivation, selfish or humanitarian, there is the underlying knowledge that the days of "splendid isolation" are over. And if in the past there was the belief that the oft-quoted "no man is an island" belonged to the idealists and romantics, there is the realization today that it is the very bedrock of political reality and survival.

August 1967

David G. Scanlon
James J. Shields, Jr.

Notes

[1]*Comparative Education Society Newsletter,* 2 September 1965, p. 5.
[2]U.S. Congress, House Committee on Government Operations, *Government Programs in International Education,* Forty-second Report (Washington, D.C.: Government Printing Office, 1959), pp. 2, 20.

[3]"International Institute for Educational Planning," *UNESCO Chronicle,* 9 (1963), pp. 30–31; *Center for Développment Education* (Syracuse, N.Y.: Syracuse University School of Education, n.d.); Center for Studies in Education and Development, *Annual Report* (Cambridge, Mass.: Graduate School of Education, Harvard University, n.d.).

[4]John Dewey, *Democracy and Education* (New York: The Macmillan Co., 1923), p. 3.

[5]Examples of this approach are found in the field of history in Lawrence A. Cremin, *The Wonderful World of Ellwood Patterson Cubberly* (New York: Teachers College Press, 1965), and in the field of philosophy in Kingsley Price, *Education and Philosophical Thought* (Boston: Allyn and Bacon, 1962).

[6]Philip Coombs, *The Fourth Dimension of Foreign Policy: Educational and Cultural Affairs* (New York: Harper & Row, 1964), p. 18.

[7]William W. Brickman, "International Education," *Encyclopedia of Educational Research,* Rev. ed. (New York: The Macmillan Co., 1950), pp. 617–627.

[8]Remarks from a speech given at the opening session for the first group of trainees for the Teachers for East Africa program at Teachers College, Columbia University, June 1961.

[9]U.S. Department of State, *Educational and Cultural Diplomacy—1964* (Washington, D.C.: Government Printing Office, 1965), p. 109.

[10]"U.S. and Russians Agree to Widen Cultural Links," *The New York Times,* January 31, 1965, p. 1. Also consult *International Understanding through the Performing Arts,* "A Report on the Cultural Presentations Program of the Department of State, July 1, 1963–June 30, 1964" (Washington, D.C.: Government Printing Office, 1965).

[11]Alberto Moravia, "When Art Becomes Propaganda," *Saturday Review,* April 17, 1965, p. 63.

[12]Theodore Sands, "Propaganda vs. Diplomacy," *The Nation,* May 30, 1959, pp. 488–489.

[13]Carnegie Endowment for International Peace, *Fifty Years in the Service of Peace and Justice: Report on the Fiftieth Anniversary Program of the Carnegie Endowment for International Peace* (New York: The Endowment, 1961), p. 7.

[14]William D. Patterson, "Keeping Faith with the Traveler," *Saturday Review,* September 18, 1965, p. 30.

[15]U.S. Agency for International Development and U.S. Department of Defense, *Proposed Mutual Defense and Assistance Programs, FY 1964* (Washington, D.C.: Government Printing Office, 1963), pp. 127–129.

[16]Jonathan B. Bingham, *Shirt-Sleeve Diplomacy: Point 4 in Action* (New York: John Day Co., 1954), p. 21.

[17]Jack D. Mezirow, "Community Development, Extension of the Village Aid Synthesis," *Community Development Information,* 2 (January-February 1961), p. 8.

[18]Lucian W. Pye, *Politics, Personality, and Nation Building: Burma's Search for Identity* (New Haven: Yale University Press, 1962), p. 4.

PART I

Education,
Technical Assistance,
and Development

E ducation has an indispensable role in all technical-assistance programs geared to the development of the new nations of Africa, Asia, and Latin America: aid for the development of schools and of education in general is an important part of all technical-assistance programs, and the principal donors define technical assistance as essentially an educational process. Thus, as the readings that follow demonstrate, the terms "education," "development," and "technical assistance" are used interchangeably by international educators.

The readings in this section, with the exception of George Gant's "The Ford Foundation Program in Pakistan," were written by government officials. For the most part, the selections define the extent to which the agencies described are involved in technical assistance, and, in some instances, they explore the purposes of the programs. They offer a perspective on the wide variety of activities carried on in the name of technical assistance and on the range of agencies that conduct these programs.

Three levels of technical-assistance agencies are represented in this section: bilateral governmental, multilateral governmental, and non-governmental programs. The bilateral programs described are those of the United States, the United Kingdom, and Israel. The readings on the United States include one issued by the Agency for International Development, which is entrusted with major responsibility for United States technical assistance activities overseas; one on the ever growing role of United States universities in foreign-aid programs; and one on America's most dramatic venture overseas, the Peace Corps.

Unesco was selected as a model of a multilateral program today. The source reproduced here summarizes Unesco's goals for the years 1960–1970, which have been designated as the Development Decade. These goals emphasize the importance Unesco attaches to educational planning and research. The section concludes with an article on the work of the Ford Foundation in Pakistan. If space had permitted, additional articles would have been added on the activities of religious bodies and industry to give a broader perspective on the role of private agencies in technical assistance.

The selections in this section tend to be descriptive rather than critical of the issues surrounding the topic of technical assistance; they delineate the significant principles and important practices in the field. Also, they have historical value when read in conjunction with documents on international education published before World War II, and they demonstrate the change in emphasis that has taken place in the field of international education.

1
The United States
and Technical Assistance Overseas

In most countries aided by the United States today, the development of human resources remains the priority need and technical assistance the heart of our development assistance program.

Technical assistance helps create the human resources necessary for development. It helps build the wide variety of institutions needed to make trained people effective: schools and universities, agricultural extension services, public health systems, trade associations, labor unions, and cooperatives.

Technical assistance projects also play a key role in assisting countries to carry out needed self-help and reform measures. In addition to determination, these measures require administrative skill, planning techniques, land surveys and agricultural research and extension services, savings and credit institutions, and new educational approaches. The countries themselves must provide the spirit of determination, but we can help them develop the skills and institutions crucial to effective self-help. In Latin America, for example, increased technical assistance for agricultural extension work, the development of cooperatives, and public administration are a direct response to the need for institutions that can make reforms effective.

Development of human resources, modern institutions, and the ability to carry out self-help measures contribute to more than economic growth. Technical assistance also affects the social and political character of the development process. It serves the dual role of speeding economic growth and helping to create a free and open society.

The Role of Technical Assistance in Foreign Aid (Washington, D.C.: U.S. Agency for International Development, 1963), pp. 1–8.

AID [Agency for International Development] technical assistance activities are financed by development grant and technical cooperation funds. Out of these funds come the salaries and support costs of United States technicians working overseas; the costs of sending key host country personnel to the United States or other countries for advanced training; the costs of the supplies and equipment technicians need to carry out their jobs; and, to a limited degree, the costs of construction connected with technical assistance, such as demonstration schools or rural clinics.

Technical Assistance and Levels of Development

The need for technical assistance, like the ability to make effective use of capital assistance, varies with each country's stage of development.

In countries in the early stages of development, lack of administrators, technicians, skilled workers, and professionals of all kinds sharply limits the usefulness of capital assistance. Recognizing this, the 1961 Act for International Development provided that in such countries

. . . programs of development of education and human resources through such means as technical cooperation shall be emphasized and the furnishing of capital facilities for purposes other than the development of education and human resources shall be given a lower priority until the requisite knowledge and skills have been developed.

In 40 countries, most in the early stages of development, development grant and technical cooperation programs account for more than 50 per cent of total United States assistance. In 18 of these countries, United States aid is wholly technical assistance.

In more advanced countries, such as India and Pakistan, where AID has major loan programs, development grant financing for technical assistance may amount to less than a twentieth of the total AID program. Technical assistance projects, however, remain of crucial importance, helping to develop new or additional institutions or skills required to maintain and to increase the momentum of growth.

As countries develop the ability to train professionals and skilled workers, and as they develop their own institutions to maintain satisfactory economic and social progress, United States technical assistance can be reduced and finally halted. AID technical assistance was ended in Japan in fiscal year 1961, in Israel, Spain, and Greece in fiscal year 1962, and will be ended in Lebanon in fiscal year 1963. It is currently being cut back in the Republic of China.

The Focus of Assistance

A country's stage of development determines its needs for technical assistance, but need alone does not determine the level and composition of assistance from the United States.

Like over-all AID strategy, the development grant and technical cooperation programs in each country reflect not only that country's stage of development but also the primary goals of United States assistance and the availability of aid from other free-world sources.

In countries where AID programs support broad development goals, technical assistance is directed to the most serious obstacles to growth —lack of necessary skills and supporting institutions. For example, in Nigeria, the United States maintains the largest development grant program in Africa. Nearly half is concentrated on strengthening the educational institutions. Teams from four American universities, under contract with AID, are working to expand higher education facilities, develop Nigerian institutions, and train engineers, nurses, agricultural technicians, and business administrators. Assistance is also going to demonstration secondary vocational schools in each region and to teacher training schools to expand primary education in the northern region.

Agricultural development is the second major focus of the development grant program in Nigeria. Over a hundred United States agricultural specialists are training Nigerian agricultural extension workers and establishing a network of rural agricultural centers from which they can operate. The balance of the AID program in Nigeria is devoted to improving public administration and to stimulating the growth of the private industrial sector.

In countries where United States assistance is focused on urgent security needs, technical assistance may be used to improve services and to increase production in depressed and politically restless areas. In the case of Thailand, development grant projects finance a substantial part of the large-scale program to improve living standards, win the allegiance of the border people, and integrate the strategically located Northeast more closely with the rest of the country. Technical assistance and supporting commodities and equipment are being provided to develop agricultural extension services, to promote community development programs, to survey land use, and to improve public health services and sanitation. These efforts are tied in with a major feeder road construction program, financed from supporting assistance funds, to link critical border areas with the Thai highway network.

Where the United States assistance goal is a more limited contribution to development in a country where other donors are providing the bulk of assistance, technical assistance is often the most effective form of participation—evidence of support without requiring heavy expenditures. Small development grant programs in over two dozen African countries are designed to serve this purpose. In the Malagasy Republic, to give one example, the major share of aid is provided by France and the European Economic Community's Development Fund. The modest United States development grant program provides instructors to help the Agricultural College of Madagascar establish an agricultural extension department, a well-driller, a sanitary engineer, and drilling equipment and supplies to help set up a program to improve the rural water supply in regions where people must now walk as much as fifteen miles for water.

Carrying Out Technical Assistance

Technical assistance under AID has grown out of the Point IV program. Its primary goal remains the development of skills among people in the host country. Its basic tools remain the sending of American specialists overseas and the training of key host country people in more advanced countries.

At present, about 3,500 AID employees and experts loaned to AID by other federal agencies are at work overseas on technical assistance missions. In addition, 1,500 nongovernmental experts from American industries, businesses, nonprofit organizations, colleges, and universities are abroad under AID contracts.

During fiscal year 1962, about 5,900 participants from host countries arrived in the United States for advanced training at American business firms and industries, colleges and universities, hospitals, or units of municipal, state or federal governments. An additional 2,100 participants were sent for training to third countries, where conditions were similar to those in the participants' home countries.

Although the primary goal and the basic tools of technical assistance remain the same, 15 years of experience have led to some changes in emphasis and approach. Under AID, a major effort has been made to plan all assistance, capital and technical, as an integrated program concentrated on priority needs. Among other changes are . . . [the following].

Use of Other Federal Resources

In some cases, the best man for a technical assistance job is to be found not in AID but in another specialized federal agency. The Department of Agriculture, the Bureau of Public Roads, the Department of the Interior, the Bureau of the Census, the Public Health

Service, and the Housing and Home Finance Agency are among the
agencies whose personnel participated in AID programs during the
past year [1962].

Under an amendment to Section 621 of the Foreign Assistance Act,
AID in 1962 signed interagency agreements with the Housing and
Home Finance Agency and the Department of Labor, under which
experts from these agencies might be loaned to AID on a reimbursable
basis, without break in the expert's career record with his agency.

An interagency agreement with the Federal Home Loan Bank Board
is expected to be signed early in 1963, and several other agreements
are in preparation.

TABLE I   Fiscal Year 1962 AID Project Commitments in Selected
Fields of Activity by Category of Funds
(Millions of dollars)

Field of activity	Total all funds	Develop- ment grants	Supporting assistance	Develop- ment loans
Grand total, all fields	1,000.8	355.3	102.7	542.8
Food and agriculture	134.4	54.7	6.0	73.8
Research, agriculture, education, and extension	25.7	25.7	(*)	—
Land and water resources	24.0	9.9	2.0	12.1
Crop and livestock development	38.1	6.2	.3	31.7
Agricultural economics, farm organization, and credit	33.3	3.1	.2	30.0
Forestry	1.0	.9	(*)	—
Fisheries	.8	.8	—	—
Other	11.5	8.0	3.5	—
Industry and mining	347.3	27.6	3.9	315.8
Mining and minerals	9.4	5.0	.2	4.2
Power and communications	211.1	6.1	3.3	201.8
Manufacturing and processing	113.7	3.9	(*)	109.8
Engineering and construction	5.1	5.1	—	—
Other	8.0	7.6	.5	—
Transportation	173.3	23.4	54.3	95.7
Highways	53.9	6.3	46.4	1.3
Railways	96.7	1.3	2.2	93.2
Port facilities and harbor improvement	8.7	8.7	—	—
Air transport	10.6	4.1	5.3	1.2
Other	3.3	3.0	.4	—
Labor	3.4	3.4	—	—
Health and sanitation	60.4	45.6	4.8	10.0
Control of specific diseases	28.6	27.4	1.2	—
Environmental sanitation	14.4	4.3	.1	10.0
Health training and education	6.5	6.5	—	—
Health facilities, construction, remodeling, equipment	4.0	2.2	1.8	—
Other	6.8	5.1	1.7	—

TABLE I   Continued

Field of activity	Total all funds	Develop- ment grants	Supporting assistance	Develop- ment loans
Education	**90.6**	**80.5**	**10.1**	—
Technical education	11.6	10.9	.7	—
Elementary education	13.7	12.8	.9	—
Secondary education	9.1	9.1	—	—
Professional and higher education	24.0	22.5	1.4	—
Other	32.2	25.1	7.1	—
Public safety	12.8	7.1	5.7	—
Public administration	20.5	20.1	.4	—
Community development and social welfare	7.9	3.1	4.9	—
Housing	2.0	1.5	.5	—
General and miscellaneous	147.9	88.4	12.0	47.5
Private enterprise	(53.5)	(6.0)	—	(47.5)
Development banking and investment credit facilities	45.7	1.2	—	44.5
Other private enterprise	7.8	4.8	—	3.0
Communications media	3.6	2.8	.8	—
Technical support	36.6	32.8	3.9	—
Other general and miscellaneous	54.2	46.8	7.4	—

*Less than $50,000.

State Participation

In early 1963, the state of California sent a mission to Chile to explore ways in which California could use its resources to help Chile achieve economic growth, particularly in agriculture. A number of other states have expressed interest in similar arrangements with other Latin American countries.

Greater Use of Nongovernmental Resources

AID has attempted to make greater use of nongovernmental resources for technical assistance overseas: American businesses, industries, colleges and universities, and service organizations.

During the past year [1962], for example, the agency signed contracts with seven nongovernmental organizations to carry out nine major technical assistance programs to spur the growth of cooperatives for housing, savings, agricultural credit, rural electrification, and marketing of consumer goods.

The contractors, in Africa and Latin America, include the Credit Union National Association, the National Rural Electric Cooperative Association, the Cooperative League of the U.S.A., the Foundation for Cooperative Housing, the Farmers Union, the National Grange and the National Council of Farmer Cooperatives, and the American Institute for Free Labor Development.

American colleges and universities are another growing source of technical assistance under AID contracts. By the beginning of 1963, more than seventy American colleges and universities had teams overseas carrying out technical assistance for the agency in education, agriculture and agricultural extension, public administration, public health, and industrial development.

The Association of State Universities & Land-Grant Colleges established in November 1962 an executive secretariat and a supporting committee to work with AID and the Assistant Secretary of Agriculture for International Affairs. The committee will try to channel more qualified agricultural specialists into technical assistance and to use the facilities of American land-grant universities and colleges more widely.

Greater Emphasis on Institution-building

One of the lessons of the first Point IV experience was that technical assistance cannot take place in an institutional vacuum if the people trained are to have a significant effect on their country's development.

Therefore, a public administration program in Thailand includes the training of key government officials, assistance in reorganizing and modernizing government administrative structure, and in-service training for thousands of lower-echelon Thai civil servants.

In India, a technical assistance program which helped create a vigorous fertilizer manufacturing industry worked not only to improve production techniques in the plants themselves but to establish an industrywide trade association which has helped to enforce quality control and has promoted wider use of fertilizer by Indian farmers.

Coordination with Other Aid-givers

The growing foreign assistance programs of Canada, Japan, and the western European countries and the more recent entry of Israel and the Republic of China into the technical assistance field offer resources in many cases more appropriate to host country needs than those the United States could supply.

The Development Assistance Committee of the Organization for Economic Cooperation and Development has assumed the job of finding the nation best equipped to provide a specific kind of technical assistance in a specific country. The Committee's Technical Cooperation Working Group directs its entire efforts to improving the coordination and quality of free-world donors' technical assistance programs.

2
United States Colleges and Universities and the Foreign Aid Program

The United States university is a key weapon in the nation's foreign aid program. The long-range battle of the Agency for International Development (AID) is against darkness and disease, against ignorance and misery and inhumanity, against hunger of the body and the soul all over the world—wherever they afflict our brother men, and thus ourselves. Some of the most telling blows have been struck in this battle, some of the most crucial skirmishes won, by engineers, chemists, agriculturists, nurses, professors of law or labor, and other educators carrying the banners of such American universities as Cornell, California, Ohio, Harvard, Wisconsin, Tennessee, Montana State, and the Massachusetts Institute of Technology, in such distant places as India, Brazil, Nigeria, Thailand, Iran, Chile, and the Philippines.

The universities' role is threefold. First, they are a prime source for the recruitment of overseas technicians in all fields—education, engineering, agriculture, housing, public health, law, and medicine, to name but a few. University administrators cooperate by stretching sabbaticals and leaves of absence, or by rearranging classroom schedules on their home campuses in order to enable key faculty members and graduate students to take on crucial overseas jobs.

Edward C. Fei, "New Frontiers in Education: The Universities and the Foreign Aid Program," *Higher Education,* Vol. 18 (July 1962) pp. 8–11.

Second, the universities and colleges — large and small, each according to its academic capabilities and physical plant — provide training resources for people from the various underdeveloped countries brought to the United States by AID for specialized training. This includes both academic and nonacademic training, for some come as regularly enrolled students for specific courses and degrees and others as short-term or long-term observers in classrooms, seminars, laboratories, and field projects. From southern California and Oregon to Maine and Georgia, there is hardly a major university in the land today that does not have at least one AID-sponsored student somewhere on its campus.

Last year, the Agency was directly responsible for bringing over some 6,500 foreign students for university training. In addition, the individual universities themselves brought over 405 foreign students under their AID-oriented university-to-university contracts; and the African-American Institute, acting in concert with AID, was responsible for the enrollment in United States universities of 31 students from Guinea. All this, of course, does not take into account the many hundreds of other foreign students brought to the home campuses by universities and other educational institutions as a part of their independent, nongovernmental aid projects overseas.

The third, and by far the largest, contribution from the universities is in connection with the projects which they undertake for the AID program overseas. As of March 31, 1962, the United States government had awarded 103 foreign aid contracts, totaling almost $120 million, to 62 American universities operating in 37 separate countries. These contracts vary widely in the amounts, periods, and fields involved, but all have this in common: they are carried out in parts of the world and in areas of endeavor that are absolutely basic to the social development aspects of foreign aid that the United States government is stressing unflinchingly today. The aim here is a revolutionary change — though, in most cases, many years will have to pass before their benefits will become apparent. These contracts cover projects that range from the training of teachers and writing of textbooks to the installation of American assembly line methods in a steel mill, from working with farmers out in the field to redirecting or developing curriculums in colleges and technical schools, from the creation and training of an entire government department or ministry in an underdeveloped country to the establishment of a completely new technical school or university there, often starting with the preblueprint stage and going right on through to the construction of the buildings, teaching of students, and graduation of the first matriculated class.

Agricultural Projects

Perhaps the most important field in which the universities are operating under AID contracts is agriculture. In this field, as in the foreign aid program in general, India is of decisive importance. And it is, thus, in India that there is in operation the largest number of university contracts financed by AID in any one country. The total so far is 19, of which all but three are still under way. Agriculturally, the entire country is divided on a regional basis among five separate United States universities: These are the University of Tennessee in the southern region; Kansas State University in the central region; Ohio State University in the northwest region; the University of Missouri in the northeast; and the University of Illinois in the north central region. Altogether, the 20 faculty members of these institutions engaged on these projects work with 43 separate Indian colleges, as well as with research institutions and with the governments of the states to which they are assigned. One agricultural project being carried on in India today by the University of Tennessee began in the spring of 1956 and will end in the winter of 1963. At a total cost of $1,715,000, the faculty members of the university's school of agriculture, assigned on a rotating basis, have been acting as advisers to three state governments in the southern region of India. Their ambitious and exacting task is simply to revolutionize agriculture in the States of Mysore, Madras, and Kerala. Kerala, incidentally, is the only place in the world where the Communists came to power legally by ballots, not bullets (in 1957) and were voted out of power (in 1960). During this period when the Communists held the reins of state government, the University of Tennessee's foreign aid contract continued in operation; its people went on providing training for professors of agriculture and giving equipment and books to the various agricultural schools, went on with their seminars and extension methods, and continued to send students to the United States. (As one of the Americans involved said: "We'd like to think that we had some effect in bringing about the defeat of the Communists in Kerala.")

In addition to this regional agriculture contract, the University of Tennessee also has a nationwide home economics project under way in India. This began in the fall of 1958, involved some $1,050,000, and was scheduled for completion by June 30, 1962. Under this contract, agriculture faculty members from the university work with 40 different Indian colleges in the development of home economics courses. This involves setting up a training program and courses of study and sending many Indian home economists to Knoxville and surrounding areas to take special courses and observe classes.

Each institution may, like the University of Tennessee, be involved in more than a single AID contract in India alone. For example, the University of Illinois has three contracts: (1) to advise on agriculture at the Allahabad Institute and in the north central region (an eight-year program, totaling almost $2 million); (2) to work with the Indian Institute of Technology at Kharagpur on an engineering project (for four years, $600,000); and (3) to develop an agricultural university for the state of Uttar Pradesh. The university contract for the buildings, the curriculum, and the training of faculty came into effect in November 1959 after 20,000 acres of land had been hacked out of the jungle. It is scheduled for completion in November 1963 at a total cost of some $930,000.

Comparable projects, to spark an agricultural revolution (and the necessary affiliated revolutions) by creating a land-grant style college on the American model, where a vacuum had existed before, are being carried out by Oklahoma State and the University of Kentucky. The Oklahoma project, at Aramia, in Ethiopia, is a $7.3 million agricultural college that has been 11 years building (starting in 1952 and due for completion at the end of next year [1963]). The Kentucky project is at Bogor in Indonesia—where a school of agriculture is being added to the already existing University of Indonesia. This is a seven-year project and will be completed in summer 1963, at a total cost of $2.5 million.

Under a contract now being negotiated, Iowa State University will sign a contract to provide all the technical assistance in agriculture to be made available to Uruguay under AID, through the Alianza Para El Progreso. This will be an unusual type of project since no AID personnel will be involved at all in the agriculture technical assistance program in Uruguay. Everything—training, advisory work with the Ministry of Agriculture, development of institutions—will be carried out by university people sent out from Ames.

The emphasis in these university contracts has always been, of necessity, on long-term planning and development. An example of this is the contract signed in early May of this year [1962] between the University of Wisconsin and AID Administrator Fowler Hamilton. This contract covered the most ambitious university project perhaps ever undertaken in agriculture and deals with land reform in the entire Latin American region.

Land reform is the greatest need of the underdeveloped countries, particularly in Latin America. It is the key that unlocks any revolution, whether ours or the Communists'. It is also a key that fits much more naturally into our hands than theirs. The United States is a country where farmers are not peasants, where owning land is as natural to our way of life as going down to the supermarket, while the Communists can promise private ownership of land, if they promise it at all, only as a step along the way to collectivization.

The first part of the contract with the University of Wisconsin covers three years' operation at a cost of $1.25 million; the second part, which will be signed later, will cover the remaining two years. Faculty field-workers from the university will range all over Latin America feeding back research on every aspect of land reform to the missions, to the Alianza, to AID in Washington, and to various international agencies occupied with Latin America. "These studies will not just be 'narrowly' agriculture," one of the men in AID's Office of Educational and Social Development said. "They will be going into the matters of language, legal education, anthropology, and history as well."

Multifield Projects

A number of the university projects undertaken for AID cover more than one field. For example, Colorado State University has been engaged, since the middle of 1958, in a combined engineering, agriculture, education, and home economics program with Peshawar University in Pakistan. By the time it is completed at the end of 1963, $1.5 million will have been spent. The University of Nebraska has a four-year program under way at Ataturk University in Turkey combining agriculture, education, business administration, and engineering; and the University of Minnesota has a similar four-year program with Seoul National University of Korea, in agriculture, medicine, nursing, public administration, and engineering.

Probably the most important university contract in the entire foreign aid program is for a combined engineering and educational project that started in India on February 21, 1962. This is scheduled for completion by the end of 1964 at a cost of $3.5 million and calls for nothing less than the creation of the equivalent of an "MIT" for India, a complete college of engineering created from the ground up. Since this was considered too vast a job for a single university to handle, an organization called Educational Services, Inc., was formed among nine institutions: Massachusetts Institute of Technology, Purdue University, California Institute of Technology, Carnegie Institute of Technology, Princeton University, Ohio State University, University of Michigan, Case Institute of Technology, University of California.

Educational Projects

The largest number of university projects for AID is, logically, in the field of education. At least 44 educational or educational-plus-other contracts are currently in operation throughout the under-developed world. Some of these are regional—as, for example, the $1.7 million contract with the University of Michigan for teaching English in Laos, Thailand, and Vietnam. The underlying purpose of this program of schooling Asians in English is practical, not a matter of whimsy or chauvinism. Before people can become enrolled in American universities or can read technical journals printed in English, both of which may be essential to their lifting their national economies up by the bootstraps, they have to know the English language.

The program began in August 1958 and should be completed by the end of June 1963. The Michigan academic contingent of nine men and women set up its Southeast Asia Regional English project headquarters in Bangkok and its administrative offices at the College of Education at Prasarnmitr, also in Thailand. From there, national headquarters and staff were set up in the two other member countries, with auxiliary branch offices in local communities. The situation varied from country to country. When the first members of the team arrived at Vientiane in Laos, for example, they discovered that there was not a single Lao teaching English in secondary school. Thus, it became their immediate aim to train Lao teachers of English for secondary schools. However, when they discovered that most of the prospective teachers lacked the required educational background, having had only about six years of elementary or, at most, one or two years of secondary education, they set up a program that consisted not only of specialized courses in English but also general subject-matter courses. The result was the establishment of a National Education Center with an English section providing a three-year curriculum.

The first class of 30 students began in January 1960. As of the end of 1961, 51 students were enrolled in all three years of the English section—with classes conducted on a local level in six separate cities.

In Vietnam, things were somewhat simpler. Prospective English teachers, generally, had a firmer academic background, and a faculty of pedagogy was in existence at the University of Saigon. A three-year course almost completely on the teaching of English (except for three semester hours per week in Comparative English and Vietnamese) was established. To date, 31 Vietnamese have received secondary teaching certificates in English, and it is expected that by the end of the project approximately 200 will have graduated.

In Thailand itself, with courses arranged through the Prasarnmitr College of Education and with ten Thai educators on the English teaching staff, a much more ambitious program was instituted. This consisted of special three-month inservice courses for existing teachers of English and a system of follow-up visits by staff members to see how student teachers who had returned to their local schools were putting their newly learned lessons into practice. For those who could not spare the time for the regular three-month course, there were intensified two-week seminars for teachers of English at the Bangkok teachers' college and at 11 regional centers. To date, an average of 82 teachers have attended each of these short seminars during the past three years, and a total of about 160 have graduated from the longer course.

Meanwhile, other American universities have carried on other educational programs in Southeast Asian nations. In Thailand itself, for example, Indiana University has conducted a college-level teachers' training program at Chulalongkorn University and at the Prasarnmitr College of Education. Started in September 1958, it should be completed by September 1962 at a cost of almost $3 million. In Cambodia, a rural teachers' training program will soon be started at Seim Reap, where the fabulous Ankor Wat ruins are located. The university to conduct this program has not yet been chosen. The program calls for the development of a new teacher education center in this northern region that will follow the pattern of a recently completed AID project at Kompoug Kantuot in the southern region. The latter, however, under the direction of the Unitarian Service Committee and the University of Pittsburgh, was confined to the training of rural elementary school teachers, 200 of whom were selected each year out of 5,000 applicants for four-year courses. The new project will train teachers on both the elementary and the secondary school level and, in addition, will set up a school for vocational training.

In Pakistan, two teacher-training programs have been started from absolute scratch. Before the students could be enrolled and trained, the physical plants of the schools they were to go to had to be established. Both projects began around November, 1959, one under the direction of Texas Agricultural and Mechanical College System working with the University of Dacca in East Pakistan, the other conducted by Indiana University with the University of the Punjab in West Pakistan. In each case, the United States university officials took part in the design of the buildings and the purchase of equipment as well as in the setting up of curriculums and training of students. Both projects should be completed by November 1963, when a sufficient number of teachers will have been trained to staff the faculties completely with native-born Pakistanis. The East Pakistan project will cost $660,000; the West Pakistan project, $966,000.

A university contractor is now being selected for a teacher-training program in the French-speaking West African nation of Mali. There are complications here because the teacher-training specialists must be bilingual in French and English. According to latest AID thinking, some kind of arrangement involving several United States universities will probably be worked out, and the program may be extended to the nation of Senegal, which is also French speaking. The joint program will probably take from five to seven years. Here, again, the job will have to be done from the ground up, starting with the construction of buildings (and perhaps, even before that, the clearing of the jungle) before a single student can be enrolled.

Projects in Other Fields

Although education, agriculture, and engineering are their major fields of endeavor in this program, United States universities are engaged overseas in many other AID-sponsored projects. The University of Michigan, for example, started an approximately $250,000, two-and-one-half-year public administration project in June 1961 in the Republic of China. Cornell University has a four-year, $300,000 labor affairs program under way at the University of Chile, and it also has a two-year program costing $24,000 in the health field with the Government of Peru. The University of Chicago has an eight-year economics project under way at the Catholic University of Chile, mainly having to do with the development of a faculty of economics there, and under Alianza Para El Progreso thinking, which stresses Latin American regionalism, this project is being expanded to include Argentina as well. The University of Buffalo has a program of medical education at the National University of Asunción in Paraguay; Carnegie Institute of Technology has an intensive two-year, $700,000 program, started in February 1962, in industrial training with the Hindustan Steel Company of India; Spring Garden Institute, of Philadelphia, has an eight-year, $1.5 million program in automative mechanics under way with the Ministry of Education in Turkey; Northwestern University has a public administration program in Liberia; Indiana University has a half-million-dollar audiovisual program with the government of the Western Region of Nigeria. And there are hundreds of others, scattered all over the underdeveloped world.

All these university projects, the technical sinews of the foreign aid program, are today becoming integral parts of the American people-to-people diplomacy. Certainly, the calls AID makes on the colleges and universities will not diminish in importance or magnitude. Rather, the programs themselves are sure to grow and the number of projects to increase and with them the cooperation between the faculty and AID, as the developing countries all over the world continue to expand and to take their places in the ranks of free people.

3
The United States Peace Corps

While the concept of voluntary service abroad did not begin with the
United States Peace Corps, it has been given a major boost which
should stimulate countless Americans, as well as others, to devote a
portion of their talents and energies to the service of their fellow man.
Certainly, the response to the Peace Corps idea has been heart-
warming to educators in the United States and throughout the free
world.

Forerunner of the Peace Corps

Over the past century in the United States, many private organizations, religious and secular, have engaged in the recruitment and placement of volunteers to work in many countries which suffered from the
devastation of war, poverty, and underdevelopment. Because of space
limitations only a few of the many can be mentioned, but it is perhaps
illustrative to cite the American Friends Service Committee, Inc.,
organized by the Quakers in 1917 to provide relief services and now
engaged in a variety of voluntary assistance projects in the newly
developing nations.

International Voluntary Services, Inc., founded in 1953, is a more
recent example and is regarded as a forerunner of the Peace Corps. It
has supplied volunteer teachers and technical assistance workers to
several nations, receiving financial support for such activity from the
United States government and private foundations.

Summer service in Africa on works projects is available for American college students through *Operation Crossroads Africa,* a private

Joseph F. Kauffman, "The United
States Peace Corps," *The Year Book
of Education* (New York: Harcourt,
Brace & World, Inc., London: Evans
Brothers, Ltd.), pp. 380–384.

organization created and directed by Rev. James H. Robinson. Paying their own expenses and committing themselves to speak to their local community groups about their experiences upon return, "Crossroaders" have contributed a great deal to the understanding of Americans and Africans.

One further illustration that will relate us once again to the creation of the Peace Corps is to recall the large number (over 1,000) of American teachers who, some sixty years ago, sailed to the Philippines to help start that country's public school system. Known as "Thomasites," they introduced English as the medium of instruction and are remembered today by the citizens of that country with gratitude and affection.

The Origin and Aims of the Corps

The concept of the Peace Corps, as a government-supported agency to promote and facilitate international voluntary service for Americans, was introduced late in the United States Presidential campaign during the fall of 1960. The then Senator from Massachusetts, John F. Kennedy, received favorable responses from college and university audiences to his challenge to American youth to serve the cause of peace by devoting a portion of their lives to service in the newly developing nations of the world.

Immediately following the 1960 elections, President-elect Kennedy established a task force to study how best to implement the Peace Corps idea. On March 1, 1961, a few weeks after taking office, he issued Executive Order 10924, establishing the Peace Corps on a pilot basis and naming Robert Sargent Shriver, Jr. as its Director.

Subsequent legislation by the United States Congress in September 1961 authorized the establishment of the Peace Corps on a permanent basis, declaring as its purpose "to make available to interested countries and areas men and women of the United States qualified for service abroad and willing to serve, under conditions of hardship if necessary, to help the peoples of such countries and areas in meeting their needs for trained manpower, and to help promote a better understanding of the American people on the part of the people served and a better understanding of other peoples on the part of the American people."

United States Peace Corps service is open to any United States citizen 18 years of age, or older, who is single. If married, both husband and wife must qualify for service in the same program. Married couples with dependents under age 18 are not eligible for service.

Selection, Training, and Work of the Volunteers

A rigorous selection and training program (twelve to fourteen weeks) is applied in order that only those suitable and prepared for a two-year period of service will be sent overseas.

On the basis of last year's experience, only one out of six applicants was invited to enter a Peace Corps training program. The selection process continues throughout the training program, with each trainee thoroughly evaluated as to his suitability for a two-year period of overseas service. On the average about 15 per cent of the trainees are screened out during the training program. Such procedures appear to be valid in light of the less than 3 per cent attrition rate overseas for all causes.

The goal of a successful Peace Corps training program, stated simply, is the preparation of a volunteer for effective service overseas. He must, therefore, take to his assignment the skill to do the job required, a knowledge of, and respect for, the culture and sensitivities of the people with whom he will work, an ability to communicate in the language of the host country, an understanding of his own country and heritage, and, finally, the physical and emotional strength to sustain his desire to serve for a two-year period in a difficult job.

This chapter is being written as the Peace Corps completes its second year of operations. More than 5,000 Peace Corps volunteers are now serving in forty-five countries of Asia, Africa, and Latin America. Some 60 per cent are men. The average age of the Peace Corps volunteers is 26 for women, 24 for men. Approximately 80 per cent are college graduates. It is expected that there will be more than 10,000 Peace Corps volunteers overseas by the beginning of 1964.

Peace Corps volunteers are not salaried. They receive free training for their assignments and, once overseas, a living allowance sufficient to maintain them at the living level of their co-workers in the host nation. At the end of their service they receive a readjustment allowance of $75 for each month of completed service.

While Peace Corps volunteers are engaged in a wide variety of jobs abroad (community development, agriculture, health, construction, etc.), approximately one-half of them are engaged in education—formal teaching on the primary, intermediate, secondary, or university levels. Teaching assignments range from serving as teacher-aides in the elementary schools of the Philippines to teaching in the intermediate schools of Somalia, the secondary schools of Ethiopia, and the universities of Venezuela.

While the largest single project of Peace Corps volunteer teachers is in the Philippines, it is in Africa where we find the greatest number of requests and the majority of volunteers teaching. There are thirteen African countries in which Peace Corps volunteers are teaching in the secondary schools, and their impact is of great significance both quantitatively and qualitatively.

In Ethiopia, which is desperately seeking to expand educational opportunities for its youth, there are 277 Peace Corps volunteer teachers in the secondary schools. This may be contrasted with the total of 470 secondary school teachers in that country, including expatriates. The advent of the Peace Corps program in Ethiopia enabled that country to double the capacity of its secondary schools. In examining the significance of this service, one must bear in mind that Ethiopia's Ministry of Education estimates that no more than 1 per cent of the appropriate age group actually attends secondary school today.

In Nyasaland, forty-two Peace Corps volunteer teachers have nearly doubled the secondary school enrollment. They are teaching a full range of subjects in thirteen of that nation's schools.

A massive educational effort is under way in Liberia, and Peace Corps volunteer teachers are playing a major part, both on the elementary and secondary levels. One hundred and forty volunteers are serving as teachers in Liberia now, and an additional 150 are scheduled to arrive in September 1963.

In Nigeria, 300 Peace Corps volunteer teachers are serving in secondary schools in all regions, and some thirty are assisting the faculty at the University of Nigeria. The Ashby Commission Report, issued in 1960, delineated that country's educational needs, and volunteer teachers are playing a crucial role in moving forward plans for expansion of secondary school opportunities for Nigeria's youth.

The writer has mentioned but a few illustrations of the educational service and interchange that is taking place as the Peace Corps starts its third year of operation. A special responsibility is placed on all volunteers to participate in the life of the community to which they are assigned by the respective ministries of education. During their free time they have started clubs, coached athletic teams, engaged in adult education and a multitude of other community activities.

All such Peace Corps volunteer teachers are college graduates, although no more than one-fourth have had prior experience as classroom teachers. Nevertheless, through Peace Corps training programs they have become sufficiently prepared to make a significant contribution. American universities participating in the effective preparation for such teaching service have included Teachers College of Columbia University, Harvard University, University of California at Los

Angeles and Berkeley, Syracuse University, Lincoln University, New York University, University of Michigan, and others.

A total of sixty United States universities have participated in this endeavor during the first two years of the Peace Corps' existence.

A Peace Corps training program to prepare volunteers to teach in Nigerian secondary schools was conducted in the fall of 1962 by Teachers College of Columbia University. Twelve weeks in length, it included African area studies under a distinguished faculty including Nigerian guests; an introduction to Nigerian education under the direction of Professor Karl W. Bigelow; classroom observation and practice teaching; and subject seminars. In addition to the above, trainees received health and first-aid instruction, American studies, physical education, and general orientation to their role as Peace Corps volunteers.

The Implications for International Life

The implications of this program for broadening the interest and competence of American educational institutions in the international education area is, of course, obvious. There is no question but that the fields of comparative education, area studies, cultural anthropology, and linguistics have been spurred on by this major United States effort.

Less obvious, perhaps, but of equal importance, will be the impact of returning Peace Corps volunteers, many of whom will take up teaching positions in United States schools. The experience and new understanding brought back will undoubtedly add a new dimension to international relations and discussions of foreign affairs on the community level. Thousands of American school children will benefit.

The potential value to American education has not been overlooked by United States school authorities. The National Education Association, the American Association of Colleges for Teacher Education, and other professional organizations have participated in the recruitment of Peace Corps volunteers. Local community school boards have permitted leaves of absence to career teachers who seek the opportunity to grow through teaching abroad. Such experience can only serve to enhance their career status in the future.

Writing in the *Cyprus Mail,* March 8, 1962, Professor Arnold Toynbee stated it this way: "If the Peace Corps makes a success of its job abroad, it will also serve as a leaven at home. It may revolutionize the American people's attitude towards the non-Western majority of mankind. If it succeeds in doing this, it will have made history at home as well as abroad. It will have given history a turn for the better, and it will have done this in the nick of time."

4
United Kingdom Assistance for Overseas Development

The Aims

The Queen's speech on 27th October, 1959, contained the following passage:

The improvement of conditions of life in the less-developed countries of the world will remain an urgent concern of my Government. They will promote economic cooperation between the nations and support plans for financial and technical assistance.

The Government of the United Kingdom has thus reaffirmed its continuing interest in the welfare of the poorer countries overseas and its intention to go on helping them and to cooperate in international plans directed to that object.

Malnutrition is the common lot of millions in the poorer countries of the world. Housing is frequently primitive, transport and communications are very limited, basic social services that we take for granted are almost nonexistent. Two-thirds of the world's population live in countries which face problems like these. In India, for example, there are eight times as many people as in this country: their average income per head, about £25 a year, is one-sixteenth of ours. There is a growing determination in the poorer countries to rise out of poverty through economic development. They are making great efforts themselves, and the larger part of the money they are spending on capital development comes from their own resources. But additional resources, and, in particular, foreign exchange to buy plant and materials from abroad, are an essential supplement. There is a challenge to the advanced countries to help them to help themselves.

Assistance from the United Kingdom for Overseas Development (London: H. M. Stationery Office, 1960), pp. 5–13.

The purpose of this Paper is to describe the part which the United Kingdom is playing in the provision of assistance for overseas development. Although private capital has been, and in general still is, the main source of finance from the United Kingdom, many of the poorer countries cannot under present conditions attract all the private capital they need. They are looking increasingly for help from governments and from the international institutions which have been established with government funds. The Paper is therefore concerned partly with private investment but primarily with the assistance provided from the United Kingdom Exchequer—sometimes directly and sometimes through these international institutions—for the less-developed countries of the world.

Private Investment

The United Kingdom is prominent among the small group of industrially advanced nations from which funds for investment abroad are provided by private individuals and companies. These funds are invested through a variety of channels, and one organisation, the Commonwealth Development Finance Company, has been specially established to facilitate the investment of private capital in the Commonwealth. Information about the extent of United Kingdom private investment overseas is at present not precise, and measures have recently been taken to improve our knowledge. On the information at present available it is estimated that the total has averaged, over the last seven years, £300 million a year.[1] This estimate includes sums averaging about £55 million a year that have been raised on the London market by the governments of independent Commonwealth and colonial countries and by public corporations and companies.

The investment of this money is frequently accompanied by the availability of United Kingdom knowledge and experience of industrial and commercial business. Intangible assistance of this kind cannot be evaluated, but it is an important additional contribution.

A large amount, in total, of commercial credit is extended by United Kingdom exporters to overseas importers of United Kingdom goods in accordance with normal trade practice. Much of this is under guarantee by the Export Credits Guarantee Department; and much of it is in respect of goods supplied to the less developed countries. Such credit is, in general, however, of a short- or medium-term nature and is not, therefore, included in the estimate of £300 million for the amount of private investment overseas.

A large part of the £300 million is invested in the more developed Commonwealth countries, where a basis for industrial expansion already exists and where their rate of growth – influenced, for example, by immigration – is more rapid than they can finance from their own resources and offers an attractive prospect for investment. It is estimated that something of the order of £100 million a year has been invested in less developed areas. This includes some reinvestment of locally earned profits, but information about such reinvestment is incomplete, and the figure of £100 million may be too low.

Government Assistance

The aid given from the United Kingdom Exchequer for overseas development is authorised by Parliament in its approval of the annual Accounts and Estimates. Excluding military assistance and refugee relief, the total amounts paid from the United Kingdom Exchequer for this purpose over the eight financial years from 1st April, 1951 to 31st March, 1959, and the estimate for 1959–1960, are as follows:

TABLE I   Growth of United Kingdom Government Assistance

Year	Total (£ million)
1951–52	61
1952–53	49
1953–54	52
1954–55	77
1955–56	83
1956–57	76
1957–58	81
1958–59	110
1959–60 (Estimate)	138

This assistance takes the form of:

a. grants and loans, and payments for technical assistance, under arrangements made directly with the recipient country ("bilateral assistance");
b. contributions to international bodies working in this field ("multilateral assistance").

For the last three financial years the figures in Table I may be subdivided as in Table II below. The figures show the actual or estimated disbursements and represent entirely assistance to less developed countries, with the exception of sums of £3.7 million in 1957–1958, £2.2 million in 1958–1959, and £3 million in 1959–1960, which represent disbursements to the Union of South Africa under International Bank loans for which part of the United Kingdom subscription was used.

United Kingdom emergency assistance to Malaya, Kenya, and Cyprus is shown separately in Tables II and III. This does not include the basic pay and allowances of the United Kingdom armed forces which were involved, since these have been met from the Defence Departments' Votes. A substantial part of this assistance has been used for strengthening the local administration and relieving the local budget of expenditure in various forms, thus enabling them to devote their own resources to economic and social expenditure.

TABLE II Make-up of United Kingdom Government Assistance*
(£ million)

Bilateral assistance	1957–58	1958–59	1959–60 (Estimate)
Grants	35.0	33.3	39.6
Loans	10.9	36.7	60.4
Technical assistance	4.1	4.4	5.2
Total	50.0	74.4	105.2
Emergency assistance	13.3	11.7	12.5
Total bilateral assistance	63.3	86.1	117.7
Multilateral assistance			
Disbursements from the United Kingdom subscription to I.B.R.D.	16.0	21.1	18.0
U.N. Expanded Program of Technical Assistance (and U.N. Special Fund after 1959)	0.7	0.8	1.2
Subscriptions to U.N. agencies (see paragraphs 38–41)	1.4	1.5	1.5
Total multilateral assistance	18.1	23.4	20.7
Total economic assistance	81.4	109.5	138.4

*These categories and the sums involved differ from the presentation given in the White Papers on the United Kingdom Balance of Payments. The differences arise (a) because the Balance of Payments' estimates do not make a precise distinction between economic assistance and other types of government current expenditure, (b) because of timing (disbursements from Exchequer Funds are on a Financial Year basis), and (c) because some types of transactions included as Exchequer aid do not enter into the balance of payments.

Bilateral Assistance

Independent Commonwealth Countries

For independent countries of the Commonwealth the primary source of United Kingdom capital has been private investment, including sums raised on the London Market. More recently, some of them (especially some that have only recently become independent) have been unable to raise enough money in this way. The importance of helping them (and the Colonial territories) was recognized at the Commonwealth Economic Conference in 1958, when the intention of the United Kingdom to introduce a new policy of Commonwealth Assistance Loans was announced. These loans are now available to help to provide capital for programs of sound economic development which cannot be financed in other ways.

There are no formal rules governing the circumstances in which Commonwealth Assistant Loans are granted to independent Commonwealth countries. The amount depends on the particular country's needs and on the means that the United Kingdom has from time to time for meeting them. The loans are made to independent Commonwealth countries under the provisions of Section 3 of the Export Guarantees Act, 1949 (as since amended). Loans have so far been made to India (£28.5 million in December 1958; £3 million in June 1959; and £19 million in November 1959), Pakistan (£10 million in February 1959), and Malaya (£2.25 million in February 1960). In addition, loans have been approved in principle for Ceylon (£2.5 million) and for Nigeria (£12 million) for use after independence. Figures for drawing on these loans, together with drawings on a Section 3 loan of £10 million made to Pakistan in 1954 and on a Section 3 loan made in July 1958 to India in connection with the Durgapur steelworks, are included in the tables.

Colonial Territories

The United Kingdom Government has a special responsibility for the Colonial territories, and financial assistance to them is provided on capital account for economic development and, where necessary, on current account to help their general budgetary position. Under Section 1 of the Colonial Development and Welfare Act, both grants and loans are provided, mainly for public development programs, and altogether £220 million was made available for the period 1946–1960. Of this, about £45.5 million was unspent by 31st March, 1959, and recent legislation has provided for an additional £95 million for the period up to 31st March, 1964, giving a total of £140.5 million for expenditure in the years 1959–1964. In addition, grants and loans from Departmental Votes are made available to Colonial Governments which need help either to balance their current budgets or for specific purposes such as emergency expenditure or hurricane rehabilitation.

Colonial territories have also been able to raise loans in the London Market; but to the extent that this is not possible, loans from the Exchequer have been made available to them also since the Montreal Conference to help to fill the gap. Powers to make such loans have been taken in Section 2 of the Colonial Development and Welfare Act, 1959, under which such loans can be approved up to a ceiling of £25 million a year within a total of £100 million for the five-year period 1959–1964. It is expected that loans up to £20 million will be approved during the current financial year·[1960], but it is not expected that the whole of this sum will be spent in the period. An estimate of £10 million has been included in Table III below. Loans made include £1.5 million to Kenya, £1.5 million to Sierra Leone, and £3 million to Nigeria before independence.

United Kingdom Government funds are also used to assist the economic development of the Colonial territories through the medium of the Colonial Development Corporation, set up by the Overseas Resources Development Act, 1948. The Corporation undertakes agricultural, industrial, and other types of projects on a commercial basis, generally in partnership with private enterprise or Colonial Governments. It has powers to borrow up to £150 million long-term (£130 million from the Consolidated Fund) and £10 million short-term. Its capital requirements have so far been supplied entirely by issues from the Consolidated Fund which at present [1960] total £68 million. Issues of £3.1 million in 1957–1958, £5.8 million in 1958–1959, and £4.2 million in 1959–1960 have been included in the tables.

Newly Independent Members of the Commonwealth

Colonial territories which become independent members of the Commonwealth continue to receive, as required, sums equivalent to the amounts outstanding in respect of projects already approved under the Colonial Development and Welfare Act. The Colonial Development Corporation is able to continue projects approved before independence and, if necessary, to invest additional funds in them. The countries in question cease to be eligible for Colonial Exchequer Loans but become eligible for Commonwealth Assistance Loans on the same basis as other independent Commonwealth countries, and technical assistance continues to be available. Ghana has received, since she became independent, £350,000 outstanding under the Colonial Development and Welfare Act, and also technical assistance. Malaya is receiving the unexpended balance of her Colonial Development and Welfare allocations amounting to £3.7 million, the Commonwealth Assistance Loan of £2.25 million mentioned . . . above, grants totalling

£7.6 million for emergency expenditure, and £310,000 for the University of Malaya. A Commonwealth Assistance Loan of £12 million has, as also mentioned . . . [above], been agreed upon for Nigeria for use after independence.

Education

Education is an indispensable condition of development; it is essential not only for material prosperity through technological changes but for the training of leaders and led in government, industry, the professions, and other aspects of a nation's life. In this sphere, even more important than money is the personal contribution of trained men and women — the supply of teachers and other educational experts from the United Kingdom and the provision here of facilities for training teachers and others from overseas.

About 2,500 teachers from this country go annually to serve in Commonwealth countries and some 500 to foreign countries, on interchange schemes, short-term contracts, or permanent emigration. An important element in the work of United Kingdom teachers abroad is the teaching of English. The work of the British Council in this field has been expanded in recent years, and further proposals for strengthening their activities are now being carried out.

The United Kingdom provides substantial numbers of places for overseas students at universities, technical colleges, teacher-training institutions, and other training establishments, including places for training in both private and nationalized industry and in commerce, nursing, and many other occupations. There are at present approximately 40,000 students from overseas, most of them from the less developed countries of the Commonwealth, undergoing a full-time course of instruction in the United Kingdom. Only a small proportion of these students are financed directly by scholarships from H. M. Government, but the United Kingdom Exchequer meets a large part of the cost of their education here in other ways.

The Commonwealth Economic Conference at Montreal gave a new impetus to plans for assistance by the United Kingdom in this field. As part of a coordinated new effort, a number of fresh proposals were worked out at the Commonwealth Education Conference at Oxford in July 1959. These include the Commonwealth Scholarship and Fellowship Plan under which the United Kingdom government has agreed to make available for students from other Commonwealth countries, including colonial territories, 500 scholarships tenable at any one time in United Kingdom universities, etc. With the cooperation of local education authorities, teachers' associations, and others concerned, the United Kingdom also proposes to provide in 1960 some 400 additional places, with fees and maintenance paid from United Kingdom funds, at teacher-training establishments; to make available a proportionate share of the new places provided under the current plan to increase the total number of places in technical colleges by some 70 per cent by 1970; and to encourage industry to accept yet larger numbers of overseas students for training. Financial and other measures are also being taken to promote the recruitment of additional United Kingdom teachers for service overseas. It is expected that the United Kingdom government will spend £6 million over the next five years on this form of assistance.

Technical Assistance

In all less-developed countries, technical assistance in the form of the provision of experts, advisory services, training facilities, and technical equipment is necessary both as a preliminary to and in conjunction with capital investment. Technical assistance given by private enterprise to the less-developed countries usually forms an integral part of investment or trading projects, and its full extent, though very great, cannot be assessed separately or accurately.

The United Kingdom Government provides technical assistance for Colonial territories through the Colonial Office and to independent countries of the Commonwealth and to other countries under arrangements made direct, under the Colombo Plan, and through the Foundation for Mutual Assistance in Africa South of the Sahara and the Central Treaty Organization.

An example of the technical assistance provided by the Colonial Office is the training of officers in the public services of the Colonial Territories. Out of 2,181 such officers attending training courses in the United Kingdom in 1959, the cost of training 473 was met from Colonial Development and Welfare Funds.

Other United Kingdom government departments provide a wide range of free services to overseas territories. For example, in the last five years the Post Office has trained over 1,000 people from overseas in postal, telephone, and telegraph operations and in telecommunications engineering. The Post Office also gives specialist advice and information to many countries on request, and in engineering matters it not only advises but often acts in a liaison capacity between the overseas territory and British industry.

In the field of scientific research, there are advisory bodies dealing with many subjects, including medicine, agriculture, forestry, social science, roads, tropical products, and pesticides. The Colonial Medical

Research Committee, for example, advises the Colonial Office and the Medical Research Council jointly. The Tropical Products Institute advises the Colonial Office on matters concerning the greater use of colonial plant and animal products. There is, in addition, the recently established Overseas Research Council, which is an advisory and co-ordinating body exercising a general oversight of the United Kingdom's scientific research in and for all overseas countries and in particular the newly independent countries of the Commonwealth.

In the field of surveys, the Directorate of Overseas (Geodetic and Topographic) Surveys and the Directorate of Overseas Geological Surveys undertake surveys in the colonial territories and advise the Colonial Office on all related matters.

In addition, the Colonial Office has a large number of professional advisers and advisory bodies dealing with such subjects as education, health, labor, cooperative societies, housing, engineering, fisheries, and tropical agriculture who are able to give expert advice in each field of activity. Among the advisory bodies the Inter-University Council for Higher Education Overseas and the Council for Overseas Colleges of Arts, Science, and Technology occupy a somewhat special position in that they are concerned with autonomous institutions of higher education in the Colonial territories and operate with a large measure of independence.

. . . .

The Colombo Plan

The Colombo Plan is the name given to the whole sum of the co-operative effort which the countries of South and Southeast Asia, helped by capital aid and technical assistance from member countries outside the region, are making to develop their economies and raise the living standards of their peoples. There is no master plan, but each country of the region in carrying out its own development program has the benefit of the consultation which takes place in the annual meetings of the Colombo Plan Consultative Committee; and it makes its own bilateral arrangements with other member countries of the plan for giving and receiving assistance. The cumulative total of assistance given by the United Kingdom Exchequer to Colombo Plan countries since 1951 has reached nearly £150 million, an amount which has been taken into account in drawing up the tables in this paper. An integral part of the Colombo Plan is the Technical Co-operation Scheme and the amounts provided by the United Kingdom under this Scheme in the form of technical assistance are included under the heading Technical Assistance in Tables II and III.

Distribution of Bilateral Assistance

The following table shows how much economic assistance from United Kingdom Government funds has been given in the form of grants, loans, and payments for technical assistance to Colonial territories, the independent Commonwealth, and other countries. The figures represent actual or estimated disbursements. The table does not, however, include loans made out of the United Kingdom's subscription to the International Bank. . . .

TABLE III   Distribution of United Kingdom Bilateral Assistance
(£ million)

	1957–58	1958–59	1959–60 (Estimate)
Colonial territories			
Grants	28.1	26.8	31.8
Loans	3.9	10.9	18.2
Technical assistance	3.0	3.0	3.1
Emergency assistance	10.3	8.7	9.6
Total colonial territories	45.3	49.4	62.7
Independent Commonwealth			
Grants	1.1	1.4	1.3
Loans	2.8	20.8	35.5
Technical assistance	0.7	0.8	0.9
Emergency assistance	3.0	3.0	2.9
Total Independent Commonwealth	7.6	26.0	40.6
Other countries			
Grants	5.8	5.1	6.5
Loans	4.2	5.0	6.7
Technical assistance	0.4	0.6	1.2
Total other countries	10.4	10.7	14.4
Total grants	35.0	33.3	39.6
Total loans	10.9	36.7	60.4
Total technical assistance	4.1	4.4	5.2
Total grants, loans, and technical assistance	50.0	74.4	105.2
Total emergency assistance	13.3	11.7	12.5
Grand total	63.3	86.1	117.7

Note

[1]This figure differs from the figure usually quoted for balance of payments purposes where a *net* figure, allowing for the investment of overseas funds in this country, is relevant. The net figure in recent years has averaged £200 million.

5
Technical Cooperation between Israel and the Developing World

From the beginning of its efforts in the field of international technical cooperation, Israel has considered that such assistance should first of all contribute to accelerating the training of skilled workers, having realized from its own experience that if skilled labor is the key to economic development and progress, vocational training is the key to skilled manpower.

TABLE I   Distribution of Trainees in Israel

Year	Students and trainees	Courses and Seminars	Subjects taught	Countries
1958	137	3	3	25
1959	213	5	3	25
1960	672	17	10	50
1961	1250	38	20	64
1962	1621	74	30	83
1963	2272	85	40	79
1964*	1350	55	24	60

*First six months only.

Thus it is that during the past four years over 6,000 students and trainees—more than 2,000 in 1963 alone—from more than 75 countries have taken part in over 200 courses, seminars, and study visits, devoted to over 40 subjects. The distribution for the years from 1958 to 1964 . . . [is shown in Table I above].

Ya'acov Yannay, "Technical Cooperation Between Israel and the Developing World," *International Development Review,* Vol. 6 (September 1964), pp. 10–12, pp. 14–15.

Moreover, during this same period approximately 1,300 Israeli experts (500 in 1963 alone) were scattered throughout most of the countries of the developing world, as follows:

TABLE II   Israeli Experts in Developing Countries

Year	Experts	Countries
1958	40	7
1959	80	10
1960	163	28
1961	280	40
1962	395	52
1963	544	58
1964*	450	40

*First six months only.

The breakdowns of these figures by continents and by field of service and continent appear in Tables III and IV.

TABLE III   Israeli Experts Abroad
(By continent)

	1957–1958	1959	1960	1961	1962	1963	Total
Total	40	80	163	280	395	544	1502
Africa	25	51	122	211	265	424	1098
Asia	15	25	31	44	52	43	210
Mediterranean region	–	2	7	14	59	40	122
Latin America	–	2	3	11	19	37	72

The main purpose of Israeli technical assistance (which is coordinated by a Department for International Cooperation within the Ministry for Foreign Affairs) is to train technicians and instructors and to prepare them to assume posts as supervisors. Drawn up by mutual agreement, the programs for cooperation are frequently the direct result of investigations previously carried out on the spot by Israeli experts. The next stage — vocational training — takes place either in Israel or in the country concerned. The curriculum is drawn up in relation to the trainees' level of knowledge and the general development plans of the country from which they come. The courses are usually given in English, French, or Spanish, although in certain special cases courses are also taught in Parsi, Turkish, Greek, Portuguese, and Japanese. The curriculum generally includes both a theoretical part and visits, on-the-job training, and practical work with Israeli workers or farmers, thus enabling the trainees to witness at first hand the results achieved through occupational proficiency and the pioneering spirit.

TABLE IV   Israeli Experts Abroad, 1958–1963
(By field of service and continent)

	Africa	Asia	Mediter-ranean	Latin America	Total
Agriculture	226	69	74	26	395
Education and youth	285	3	10	11	309
Health	166	26	2	–	194
Public administration, social services, and management	115	32	17	16	180
Industry, technology	140	37	16	15	208
All other	166	43	3	4	216
Grand total	1098	210	122	72	1502

Types of Training

As a general rule most courses concern fields in which the State of Israel has acquired broad experience during its own development and in which it has successfully trained specialized supervisors. A brief description of the activities carried out in some of the fields is given below. Other fields in which training courses have been organized include banking, town planning, telecommunications, radio, and industrial techniques.

Agriculture: Israeli farmers have had to tackle many problems similar to those now faced by the newly emergent nations. And, because of the pride they feel for their cooperative and collective villages, their moshavim and kibbutzim, these farmers are quite prepared to share the fruits of their experience. By having created such forms of land settlement—which have been cited as the highest examples of a democratic way of life—they have literally and completely revolutionized the Israeli rural economy, turning formerly uncultivated land into fertile regions. Thus agriculturists from all parts of the developing world come to see and learn how they too can bring about such a revolution in the rural economy of their own countries.

Courses, usually of short duration, have been organized in various branches of agriculture: agricultural planning and regional development, organization of producers' and consumers' cooperatives, aviculture, sheep and cattle-breeding, poultry-farming, soil conservation, and agricultural economics. Special mention should be made of the Ruppin Institute of Agronomy where young agronomists are taught the methods by which the dry soil of their own countries can be irrigated. Constantly on the alert to discover new and efficient ways to derive the fullest possible use from its own potential agricultural resources, Israel has become one of the world's largest training centers for irrigation experts.

Training of Vocational Instructors: In collaboration with the Organization for Rehabilitation through Training (O.R.T.), the Government of Israel established in 1961 the Israel Technical Centre for students from developing countries where courses are designed to train technical instructors for developing countries. The courses offer from two to three years of advanced training in carpentry, metallurgy, electricity, and agricultural mechanics.

Youth Leadership: To give the lives of adolescents a purpose and a direction and to instill in them a sense of civic responsibility is a primary task of developing countries. Israel has rightly appreciated the decisive role that its own youth are called on to play in building and defending their country. Its many youth facilities have attracted the attention of leaders, educators, and social workers throughout the developing world. The NAHAL [Fighting Pioneer Youth] and GADNA [Youth Divisions], cadet corps in Israel that, over the years, have revealed their value as educational organizations, act as hosts in the youth movement leadership courses given to instructors from many a developing country. These courses, each lasting four months, bring young people together from everywhere in the developing world for the purpose of teaching them how to guide youth movements, conduct athletic and recreational activities, and create a civic spirit among young people.

Many efforts have been carried out in Africa as well to train community and youth leaders. Pioneer youth training centers have been set up in the Ivory Coast, Togo, Congo, Ghana, and the Central African Republic with Israel's assistance. Still other countries, such as Malawi, plan to set up similar centers.

Public Administration: Israel receives many requests, most of them from African countries, for training in every field of municipal and government administration. After completing their theoretical studies, students in these courses receive on-the-job training in various state or municipal departments in Israel, where courses for police officers have also been organized. In addition a number of Israeli experts are engaged abroad as advisers in such government departments as finance, revenue, economic development, and social insurance.

Trade Unionism and Cooperatives: The Histadrut (General Federation of Labour in Israel) has established at Tel Aviv an Afro-Asian Institute for Labour Studies and Co-operation. Coming from over forty countries, several hundred students and trainees have already attended the four-month Institute courses where they are trained in the theory and practice of the cooperative way of life, prepared for trade union leadership, and schooled in various aspects of social and economic planning and development.

Community Development: During six weeks in April and May, 1961, women teachers and social workers from practically every newly emergent country in Africa and from many in Asia gathered in Haifa to discuss and define the role that they are destined to play in building their respective countries. During the conference—the first ever devoted to the subject of "The Role of Women in a Developing Society"—the participants studied undertakings organized and run by Israeli women, who play a decisive role in nearly every aspect of the country's national life.

Owing to the great success of this seminar, an International Centre for Community Services was subsequently set up in Haifa. Great importance is attached by this center to problems of family and community life and to the emancipation of women in changing societies. It offers courses designed to train women as officials, social workers, and community leaders and to prepare them in a general way to take an active part in the social life of their countries.

Public Health: Training courses for midwives, head nurses, nursing instructors, and sanitorium nurses have also been given under Israel's program of cooperation. At present a postgraduate course in social medicine and public health is being organized by the School of Medicine of the University of Jerusalem in collaboration with medical schools in East Africa.

Israeli medical experts have also played a leading role in the field of public health abroad. The Israeli team recently entrusted with opening the ophthalmologic clinic of the Monrovia state hospital is one of many such teams working in Ghana, Mali, Nigeria, Ethiopia, and elsewhere.

Academic Studies: Aside from the specialized accelerated courses already described, some schools at the university level have enrolled students who will remain there throughout their entire undergraduate or postgraduate studies. Thus the School of Medicine of the Hebrew Hadassah University, in collaboration with the WHO, is organizing a six-year medical curriculum in English for students from developing countries. The Technical Institute of Israel, Technion, now gives a full course for training agricultural engineers for English-speaking students from these countries. And this year the Faculty of Agriculture of the Hebrew University will introduce a postgraduate course in rural planning.

Training Overseas

A large place in Israel's 1964 program for international cooperation has been made for so-called on-the-spot courses, a recent innovation intended especially for African countries, although some courses of this type have already been planned for Latin American countries as well. The results achieved by a series of mobile courses organized in several African countries and offering a large number of persons technical, social, and vocational training adapted to the specific needs of each country, have been most encouraging. These courses, which dealt with many subjects, such as building techniques, engineering, community services, and the training of agricultural instructors, were carried out with the help of audiovisual materials, adapted to local conditions but prepared beforehand in Israel. Part of each course was devoted to theory and part to training of a practical nature. They were conducted, after very careful preparation, by a team of instructors who first gathered in Israel and then traveled from center to center, taking with them all the necessary equipment.

Multilateral and Regional Assistance

Israel takes an active part in both multilateral and regional programs of technical assistance.

A team of Israeli experts, for example, has set up an agricultural training center in Upper Volta under FAO auspices, and Israeli experts in many capacities are retained by the U.N. specialized agencies. Under an agreement recently concluded with the Organization of American States, Israel will give vocational training to 200 young Latin Americans, particularly in agriculture and cooperatives. In the Far East, Israel collaborates, *inter alia,* in the "Mekong" project, a large-scale river development scheme carried out under the supervision of the United Nations Economic Commission for Asia and the Far East.

Another international organization with whom Israel also cooperates is the Organization for Economic Cooperation and Development. Thus, for example, the OECD organized last year in Israel an international seminar on agricultural planning and regional development for some twenty nationals of its Mediterranean member-countries. Another seminar in this field will be held in Israel during 1964. Israeli experts participate in the OECD's program of assistance for regional development and planning of Crete.

Participation of the Private Sector

The execution of Israel's program for cooperation largely depends on the collaboration of all sectors of its society. There is no Israeli institution that has not been consulted on one or another question concerning the projects carried out in developing countries. Professional organizations, such as the Association of Engineers and Architects and the Medical Association, private institutions and companies, universities and other major schools, all place their knowledge, their experience, and quite often, on a temporary basis, their personnel at the disposal of the Programme for International Cooperation.

A particularly effective form of such cooperation is the establishment of joint enterprises whose partners are composed, on the one side, of Israeli private undertakings and, on the other, of the government departments or public bodies of underdeveloped countries. Such joint companies have been set up in agriculture, hydrology, and various industries, including construction, shipping, and retail trade.

In each of these enterprises the local partner controls the financial part of the undertaking, while the role of the Israeli partner is to train local staff and prepare them gradually to take over the entire management of the company. As an example, a building company set up by Israel on a basis of mutual collaboration in one of the developing countries employs 5,000 from the country itself and only 50 Israelis. Under the agreement concluded between the two parties, at the end of five years only local personnel will be employed in all the company's departments.

Assessing the Effectiveness of Israel's Program

The Government of Israel has developed several steps in assessing the effectiveness of its training programs. There are, first, summing-up talks between trainees and teaching staff; anonymous questionnaires are used to encourage trainees to comment freely. The conclusions reached in these discussions are carefully analyzed and are transmitted to the sending countries. Here Israeli representatives keep in touch with the trainees' superiors for further evaluation. Follow-up contact is also maintained with the trainees themselves.

As part of this continuing evaluation, a questionnaire was recently sent to a number of Israel-trained students. . . .

Although the great majority of trainees found that their training helped them in their work (even, it would appear, those who had shifted to another field and even though training in Israel was no guarantee of promotion upon return home), and although practically everyone thought the courses well planned and the lectures effective, there was much less satisfaction with the length of the courses and the amount of practical work.

In accompanying responses, some complained that the limited stay in Israel left insufficient time for relaxation (even though every program of courses includes some outings, many evenings of recreation, and free evenings). But most of those critical of the courses' length regretted that they had had time only to skim the surface of subjects which they had hoped to explore thoroughly. These were, for the most part, young people, just out of school, and still without professional or family responsibilities.

The impression of inadequacy that many graduates derived from their studies was intensified in certain cases by the absence of professional literature in French or English, and many asked to help them improve their knowledge by sending them material on the subjects they had studied.

All these suggestions have been turned over to the planners and directors of the courses. Some of the observations and notions are well taken; others seem to be less justified. For example, in regard to the length of studies, the decision to make courses short and intensive was only taken after careful study and because such training seemed most suitable for countries desperately short of trained manpower. Trainees in responsible positions simply could not be spared for long; many had family responsibilities as well. Moreover, large-scale programs of longer training would put a strain on Israel's educational institutions.

Complaints about the inadequacy of practical work experience seem to reflect the divergent membership of training courses. Some are technicians eager for on-the-job experience while others are civil servants whose interests are essentially administrative. More than one of these participants indeed, particularly in the agricultural courses, have found the practical work too difficult. Recently, these divergent interests have been resolved by reducing the practical parts of courses, but also providing supplementary practical experience for those interested in prolonging their stay.

The lack of professional literature was largely a complaint of graduates of the earlier courses; since then, the situation has been much improved; documentary materials have been collected and published, and lectures printed and distributed to the students.

Assessing the success of experts serving abroad is much more complex. Here let it only be said that three criteria apply:

a. To what degree, besides doing his job, does the expert succeed in preparing, in the shortest possible time, a replacement for himself, so that his period of secondment may be minimized and the necessity of sending out another expert avoided?

b. How successful is he in winning the confidence and trust of his fellow-workers? This is important in improving work-methods and engendering a team-spirit which reduces dependence upon the expert to a minimum.

c. Is he successful not only in inspiring his wards to do their work at a reasonable level of specialization, but in imbuing them with self-assurance so that they can carry out their work more and more independently even while he is still with them?

The "Integrated Project"

Wherever it is possible, Israel likes to assist in projects where (a) the planning of the training program is Israel's and (b) the duties of the Israeli expert overseas and the absorption of trainees at the end of their course are coordinated in advance: in other words, the syllabus of training in Israel and the plans for the project in which trainees are to be employed have been prepared and interlocked well ahead. A trainee should know exactly what he will do when he is back home and that he will be working alongside an Israeli expert whom, eventually, he will have to replace.

With the expert beside him, the trainee can prove, as well as check, the knowledge he acquired in Israel. This link between training in Israel and the project in action affords an ideal method of follow-up. This program of coordinated technical cooperation is known in Israel as the "Integrated Project."

The group training courses organized by Israel and its program for cooperation are based on the principle that mutual aid in the field of science and constant exchange of experience constitute an important factor in raising standards of living and in increasing mutual understanding. Israel's assistance entails no commitments of a political nature; it is available to any country that is willing to accept it in a spirit of mutual comprehension and on the basis of friendly relations.

The examples here given of the growing cooperation between

Israel and other developing countries are a clear indication that a lack of material resources in no way prevents large-scale projects from being carried out, provided that the necessary technical knowledge is available and the will to share it with others exists.

6
UNESCO,
Educational Development,
and the Newer Nations

The General Conference of UNESCO, at its twelfth session . . . adopted unanimously a resolution which, after "recalling the action taken by the General Assembly of the United Nations and the Economic and Social Council concerning the Development Decade and reaffirming its adherence to the objectives of the Decade," defines the nature and modalities of UNESCO's participation in this program.

This resolution . . . spells out the principles on which UNESCO's participation in the Decade should be based and invites the Director-General to inform the Secretary-General of the activities of UNESCO which will constitute its contribution to the Decade for the years 1963–1964.

The detailed "phased proposals for action" . . . concerning activities of UNESCO for the two-year period 1963–1964, as approved by the General Conference at its twelfth session, are contained in this document.

. . . .

The activities selected are those that are considered to contribute most directly to attaining the general objectives of the Decade in terms of a regular increase in the national product of developing countries. These activities, as may be expected, are mostly of an oper-

U.N. Economic and Social Council, *United Nations Development Decade: Activities of the United Nations and Related Agencies in the Immediate Future,* (Thirty-sixth Session, Agenda Item 6[a], N.Y., The U.N., 1963), pp. 103–118.

ational character. However, special mention should be made of the emphasis put by the General Conference "on the action taken by the Organization to focus attention on the vital part played by education and human resources as factors in a balanced economic and social development"; such action, conducted by analysis work, studies, and publications, may play an important role in inspiring the investment policy of developing countries and has a multiplying effect in the process of development. This type of activity has, therefore, also been included among the priorities within the two-year program under the Development Decade.

The Educational Prerequisites to Development

Over-all targets

UNESCO's action for educational development in 1963–1964 will continue to be based on the conclusions and recommendations of the regional conferences and meetings held from 1960 to 1962, at which long-term plans were established or reviewed by the member states concerned, as follows:[1]

AFRICA (Addis Ababa Plan, 1961, as reviewed and complemented in 1962) (In percentages)

	1964 Enrollment target	1960 Enrollment	Increase
Primary education	44*	38	6
Secondary general and technical education	9	4	2
Higher education	(percentages not available)		

ASIA (Karachi Plan, 1960, reviewed in 1962) (In percentages)

	1964 Enrollment target	1960 Enrollment	Increase
Primary education	11†	8	3

*The above figures represent percentages of the age group considered – primary education: 4 to 14 years; secondary education: 15 to 19 years; higher education: 20 to 24 years.

†Percentage of total population; the percentage of age groups will be established in the course of the next two years.

The meeting of Ministers of Education of Asian member states held in Tokyo in April 1962 decided that the governments of all countries participating in the Karachi Plan should prepare by mid-1964 twenty-year plans of balanced educational development covering all fields and levels of education, fully integrated into national programs of social and economic development, which will be reviewed at a similar meeting in 1965. In 1963–1964, UNESCO will assist its Asian member states in the preparation of such plans.

LATIN AMERICA (Santiago Conference, 1962)
(In percentages)

	1964 Enrollment target	1960 Enrollment	Increase
Primary education	88	78	10
Secondary general and technical education	20.5	15	5.5
Higher education	3.35	3.1	0.25

It should be noted that, of the primary school children now enrolled, only a more limited percentage actually complete their primary education. Major attention has to be given, therefore, to improving the quality of education so that this percentage can be substantially increased and so that all primary schools can provide a full six-year course.

The planning of education

In order to assist member states in attaining the above targets, as well as their specific national targets considered in the perspective of further development, a major effort will be made by UNESCO during 1963–1964 in the field of educational planning. Activities will consist in: providing direct expert advice to governments, developing training facilities, and promoting the basic research.

Advisory services to governments. In Africa, educational planning groups consisting of international specialists and of national officials and educators will be established in a minimum of seven countries, while a team of experts in educational planning will study in three to four countries specific problems previously identified. In addition about 30 experts will be provided under EPTA [Expanded Program of Technical Assistance] to assist education ministries in this field.

With respect to school buildings, a UNESCO School Construction Bureau established at Khartoum will complete the building and experimental research work initiated in 1961–1962. It will increasingly lay stress on the preparation of model plans for schools at various levels, giving due regard to the use of various building materials, means of reducing building costs, and the establishment of national school construction programs.

In Asia, two regional educational planning teams will be established in cooperation with ECAFE [Economic Commission for Asia and the Far East]; each team will consist of an educational planner, an economist, and a statistician. These teams will assist Asian countries in the preparation of their long-term over-all educational plans (six in 1963). In addition, eleven experts will be provided under EPTA to six countries.

In Latin America, a four-man team of experts in educational planning, financing, statistics, and school building will provide advisory service to governments, at their request, and 15 experts will be provided under EPTA to 15 countries.

In 1963–1964 there will be educational investment programming missions (each consisting of an economist and two or three educators of various specializations) to approximately 14 member states to advise governments on priority projects for investment—internal and external—in education.

Training facilities. The International Educational Planning Institute, Paris, will be established in July 1963. By the end of 1964, it tutions. Further, UNESCO and the Institute will provide on a continuing basis advice and training material to regional institutions.

Arrangements are currently being made with ECLA [Economic Commission for Latin America], ECAFE, and ECA [Economic Commission for Africa] for establishing educational planning branches within the framework of the regional development and planning institutes at Santiago, Bangkok, and Dakar, in order to train personnel for the national educational planning services. The organization of training courses at the Santiago Institute was initiated in 1962 and will continue on a regular basis in 1963–1964.

A regional center for the advanced training of educational administrators and senior educational personnel of Arab states was opened in Beirut in 1961. Its yearly output is of 48 trainees having followed an eight-month course, and of 24 trainees attending a short-term course of seminar type. By 1964, some 200 senior educational officials will have been trained at this center.

In Asia, the regional center for the training of educational planners, administrators, and supervisors, created in 1962 at Delhi, will organize in 1963–1964 two three-month training courses for educational planners, and two courses of the same duration for supervisors. The total number of trainees during the two years is expected to reach 120. Close links were established between this center and the ECAFE Institute at Bangkok.

In addition, UNESCO will assist in a minimum of 12 training or study seminars, international and national, concerned with problems of educational planning.

Research. Research will be conducted in support of the above activities, in particular as regards the relationship between educational systems and manpower structure, educational problems related to land reform, and the improvement of educational administration.

Primary and secondary education

The activities planned for 1963–1964 with respect to developing primary and secondary education are of three main types: teacher training, particularly through the establishment of teacher-training institutions and the improvement of teaching methods; revision and adaptation of curricula; and improvement and supply of teaching materials, both textbooks and other teaching aids, in particular audiovisual aids.

In Africa, the key to the solution of most of the educational problems is the training and supply of teaching staff. UNESCO plans to offer in 1963–1964 the services of not less than 130 technical assistance experts (excluding 109 experts in the Congo [Léopoldville] under U.N. Civilian Operations) to assist its member states and associate members to promote their educational services at all levels. In addition, about 50 fellowships will be awarded for further training of teaching personnel.

In order to remove the bottleneck in secondary education, a scheme has been worked out systematically to provide Africa with a rapidly increasing number of secondary school teacher-training institutions. Not less than 13 such institutions (Special Fund projects) are scheduled to be in operation by the end of 1964, each with a teaching staff of 10 to 18 experts and an enrollment ranging from 120 to 500 trainees per institution. The total enrollment will be of 4,120 trainees when the projects are fully developed, of whom 1,615 will leave each year after completing a three- to four-year training period.

Training courses for professors of teacher-training colleges will be organized (one in English and one in French). By the end of 1964, 150 professors will have attended such courses.

In the field of curriculum research and improvement, an African Committee of Experts will be set up to initiate and promote a program of adaptation and revision of school curricula. The UNESCO Regional Centre in Africa, already at work in Accra, will translate this program into an improved system of exchange of information, school textbooks, and teaching techniques and aids, using for printing national presses available or UNESCO-sponsored regional ones.

It is planned to reinforce this work by at least two research training and development projects for educational materials and techniques, one in an English-speaking country and a second in a French-speaking country. These projects will be closely linked to the programs of the new higher teacher-training institutions which are being set up by UNESCO with the assistance of the Special Fund.

The training of secondary school teachers is also one of the major problems of Arab states. The two training institutions created recently (Special Fund projects in Sudan and Morocco) will keep developing in 1963–1964. The total enrollment of 300 in 1962–1963 will reach 500 in 1964. The number of teachers having completed their training will be in the future 234 each year.

Additional facilities in secondary education will be provided to Arab refugees from Palestine under the UNRWA/UNESCO scheme. The enrollment, which is of 35,450 in 1962–1963, is expected to be of 42,000 in 1963–1964.

A total of 25 experts and 10 fellowships will be provided under EPTA for the improvement of primary and secondary education in the region.

In Asia, the main effort will be concentrated on the implementation of the Karachi Plan which aims at achieving by 1980 compulsory and free primary education of at least seven years duration. Credits amounting to $160,000 were voted by the General Conference at its twelfth session for providing in 1963–1964 assistance to member states in the implementation of their national educational programs. In addition, 28 experts will be sent to 11 countries under EPTA. The Regional Centre for the Training of Teacher Educators in Quezon City (Philippines) will organize two nine-month training courses in 1963–1964, which are expected to have an enrollment of 60 trainees. For each course, UNESCO, UNICEF, and the Asia Foundation will provide a number of fellowships.

The Asian Regional Institute for School Building Research in Bandung (Indonesia) will organize two short-term training courses in school building.

In Latin America, the main activities of UNESCO to assist member states in the region to attain their targets in primary education will be carried out mainly by the following means:

Training of specialists and directors of education through the Associated Universities of São Paul (Brazil) and Santiago (Chile) and at the Inter-American Rural Education Centre, Rubio (Venezuela) (total enrollment in 1963–1964: 390).

Improvement of teacher training, mainly through the action of the five Associated Normal Schools in Colombia, Ecuador, Honduras, and Nicaragua (total enrollment in 1963–1964: 2,800).

Ten special courses at the national and regional levels for the improvement of in-service staff (total enrollment in 1963–1964, approximately 630).

Revision of curricula through assistance of experts (36 experts, mainly under EPTA, to 14 countries).

Introduction of new teaching techniques through seminars, conferences, publications and research.

Award of fellowships for study within and outside the region (approximately 350 fellowships).

Publication of manuals and monographs.

In the field of school libraries, which are a necessary part of both primary and secondary schools, the following is planned – the establishment of a pilot project in school libraries development on a national scale in Africa and provision of experts to aid in the development of school libraries in various countries.

Seven existing *UNESCO/UNICEF* projects will be further developed in 1963–1964 in six countries, and another ten projects are under consideration. These projects, which are carried out under the supervision of experts recruited by UNESCO, involve mostly equipment provided by UNICEF.

.   .   .   .

Technical and vocational education

In this field the major emphasis will be put in 1963–1964 on the development of technical and vocational education for engineering, industry, and trade as well as of agricultural education, in consultation and cooperation with ILO and FAO.

The International Recommendation on Technical and Vocational Education, adopted by the General Conference of UNESCO at its twelfth session (December 1962) provides the necessary guidance in this respect.

Assistance will be provided to member states, upon request, in the form of experts' services, for the organization of technical and vocational education, for the development of technical and agricultural schools. UNESCO will also help them in the production of technical textbooks in their national language.

Forty-two experts will be provided to these ends under EPTA (Africa: 15; Arab states: 10; Asia: 10; Latin America: 7).

For 18 Special Fund projects, for which UNESCO is acting as executing agency, the number of trainees expected to complete their training in 1963 is 762 and in 1964 is 1,103.

Among the projects which are still under discussion with national authorities and with the Special Fund, five are expected to become operational by the end of 1964. The total number of fellowships provided under all programs in this field will rise to 107 in 1963–1964.

. . . .

Adult Education Programmes and Eradication of Illiteracy

In response to General Assembly Resolution 1677 (XVI), UNESCO will submit through the Economic and Social Council to the United Nations General Assembly, in 1963, a review of the question of the eradication of mass illiteracy throughout the world, together with recommendations for national literacy programmes, estimates of the cost of a world literacy campaign, and a proposed programme of international action.

During 1963 and 1964 UNESCO will take a series of measures to assist its member states in their programmes for the eradication of illiteracy. These would constitute a preparation for a world literacy campaign which might be launched in 1965 if the recommendations forwarded to the United Nations General Assembly are accepted and put into effect.

The main activities proposed for the achievement of these aims will be as follows:

1. *Two Regional Planning Conferences* in Africa and the Arab states on the planning and organization of literacy programmes. These will bring together for ten days ministers and senior officials of ministries from African member states of UNESCO and Arab member states of UNESCO respectively.

2. UNESCO will carry out with the aid of specialist consultants a series of *studies,* the results of which will be widely disseminated, on the methods and media used in countries which have established successful literacy programs and on the results achieved; the use of the mother tongue for literacy, and the preparation of alphabets for unwritten languages (particularly in Africa); the employment and training of school teachers for adult literacy and mass education; methods and techniques for continuing education for adults by radio and correspondence courses.

3. A six-week *workshop* will be organized for specialists concerned in the establishment and operation of national services needed for adult literacy. This will bring together some 20 participants and will be held in a country of Africa or Asia where effective literacy services have been established.

4. *A regional conference* for Southeast Asia on the role of universities and schools in adult education will be organized in Australia in 1963.

5. Two *training courses on adult education* for persons from developing countries will be organized in Denmark in collaboration with the Danish National Commission for UNESCO. Fellowships will be provided to some 48 participants.

6. Assistance will be given to member states upon request for the *promotion of mass education and literacy,* especially for the organization of regional or national training courses (fellowships for the staff of national adult education and literacy services, as well as expert missions of technical assistance).

7. UNESCO will provide *assistance to national centres* for research and the production of teaching and reading materials for literacy and adult education.

8. UNESCO will continue to operate and develop, in cooperation with the United Nations, the specialized agencies, and other organizations concerned, the two *Regional Training Centres for Education for Community Development* in the Arab states (ASFEC, at Sirs et Layyan, UAR) and in Latin America (CREFAL, Patzcuaro, Mexico). In 1963–1964, ASFEC will provide two regular courses of nine months' duration for administrators, planners, supervisors, and trainers of local staff for community development, as well as two special courses (three months), one of which will particularly aim at training specialists for national literacy programs. It is expected that some 200 officials or specialists will have been trained at the centre during this period. At CREFAL, two regular courses and four special courses will be attended by some 210 trainees. Both centres will produce prototype teaching and reading materials for adult literacy, and their staff will undertake a number of short missions to the member states of their region to advise on literacy and community development projects.

9. *The reading materials project,* which aims at a better production and distribution of reading texts for a new and steadily increasing public of readers, was initially developed in five Asian states (Burma, Ceylon, India, Iran, and Pakistan). In 1963–1964, it will be extended to another three countries of the region (Afghanistan, Nepal, and Thailand). The regional center established at Karachi for the implementation of the project will pursue its promotional activities, particularly by assisting national book centres and appropriate professional associations.

10. In the field of *public libraries,* which are an essential tool in the development of adult education and literacy, the following activities are planned:

> Establishment of a regional centre for training librarians from French-speaking African member states (Senegal); a first class of 20 students from 18 countries will graduate in 1964.
>
> Course for training librarians from East Africa at Makerere College, Uganda (ten students to graduate in 1964).
>
> Experiment in planning library development on a national scale in a Latin American country and provision of advisory services in library development to a number of countries.

11. Increased attention will be given to the use of *mass media* in adult education, literary programmes, and community development.

It is expected that a total number of 37 experts in literacy and adult education programmes will be active in the regional centres or provided to member states in 1963–1964 and that 607 fellowships will be granted or administered by UNESCO in this field.

Higher Education and the Supply of Highly Qualified Personnel

Development of universities and institutions of higher learning

The efforts on the part of the Organization in the field of higher education have received new impetus, particularly in regard to Africa, following the Conference on the Development of Higher Education held in September 1962 at Tananarive (Madagascar).

The action to be taken by the Organization relates to both the material and intellectual aspects of the development of higher education. In regard to the organization and reform of higher education as well as the creation of new institutions, high-level advisory services will be made available.

Africa. According to the Tananarive Conference, student enrollment in institutions of higher education in Middle Africa should increase from 25,700 in 1961 to 284,000 in 1980. The first target (1965) is 31,700. It was agreed that during the 20-year period for the implementation of the Addis Ababa plan, Middle Africa's needs in university institutions should be covered by 32 institutions. During the same period, 14,000 African university staff are to be trained and 7,000 expatriate staff be recruited.

In 1963–1964 the Organization will continue to provide, on request, advisory services for the organization and administration of higher education in the region and within the framework of the Joint UNESCO-IAU Research Programme in Higher Education undertake a study of the equivalence of degrees among university institutions in Africa.

The Organization will also explore, in collaboration with other United Nations agencies, governments, and private bodies, possibilities of obtaining funds to meet the excess of required expenditure over available resources for the development of higher education in Middle Africa.

Southeast Asia. In cooperation with the International Association of Universities and within the framework of the Joint UNESCO-IAU Research Programme in Higher Education, the Organization undertook a study on the role of institutions of higher education in the development of countries in Southeast Asia. This study will be completed in early 1965 and should be a basis for concerted action on the part of the Organization and for the development of higher education in the region.

Latin America. The Organization will examine in collaboration with other United Nations agencies, the Organization of American States, the Inter-American Development Bank, and competent private bodies the problems relating to the development of higher education in 1965.

Advisory missions will be made available on request for the reform and organization of higher education; UNESCO will collaborate, in particular, with the Inter-American Development Bank in providing advisory services to institutions which are receiving assistance from the Bank.

University studies and training of highly qualified personnel

1. *Natural Sciences.* In continuation of the comparative studies carried out in 1961–1962 on scientific curricula, laboratory equipment, and teaching methods in physics and chemistry, three new surveys will be undertaken in 1963–1964 concerning botany, zoology, and geology with a view to the improvement of basic science teaching at universities. Comparative surveys will also be undertaken in civil engineering, mechanical engineering, and electrical engineering at the undergraduate level in selected technological universities and institutions. In view of the great success of the "UNESCO Source Book for Science Teaching," a series of UNESCO Source Books for the teaching of the five basic sciences at the university level will be prepared in collaboration with the competent international scientific unions.

Besides, UNESCO will promote the creation and diffusion of new teaching aids at universities (films, teaching machines and their derivatives, such as programs for "self-instruction" and inexpensive laboratory and demonstration equipment). Existing centers already devoted to these tasks will be used as focal points for these activities.

In order to develop a few highly specialized scientists to serve as the professors of the future to train the larger number of scientists and technologists needed for the general scientific development of member states, UNESCO will continue to support the training of a limited number of such specialists through fellowships and training courses. In particular, the Organization will support international postgraduate training courses and schools established for the benefit of scientists from the developing countries by other member states in selected disciplines such as: experimental physics (Sweden), mathematics (Hungary and Poland), chemistry (Federal Republic of Germany), biology and technology (Czechoslovakia), plant biology and soil science (Spain), cartography methods (Netherlands).

Support will also be given to the organization of international conferences on problems of teaching mathematics, chemistry, and biology at the university level organized by scientific unions. A number of regional training courses and seminars will be set up on various aspects of science teaching.

2. *Social Sciences.* In the field of social sciences, the main efforts in relation to higher education will also be concentrated on the preparation of teaching materials, on assistance to universities, and on higher schools of public administration as well as on the organization of training courses and seminars for specialists.

In consultation with appropriate international bodies, including the United Nations Industrial Development Centre, the Secretariat will make a study of the preparation of reference works and other teaching materials suited to the needs of the developing countries. It will arrange for the preparation and publication, with the assistance of appropriate international nongovernmental organizations, of a collection of annotated texts and of translations of two or three representative modern works, together with a teacher's handbook, the arrangement and content of which will take account of the features of those countries for which it is to be prepared. The findings of two international surveys on the teaching of business management and the adaptation of the teaching of economics to the needs of developing countries will be published in the series "The University Teaching of Social Sciences." A new survey will analyse the social science teaching provided in engineering colleges and other advanced technical education establishments.

As regards field programmes, UNESCO will continue to send advisory missions and experts, to organize scientific meetings and seminars and to award fellowships for the training of specialists in order to participate, at the request of member states, in the activities undertaken by them for the development and promotion of teaching, research, and documentation in the various branches of the social sciences. An effort will thereby be made to supply higher educational establishments and research centers in the process of expansion or reorganization with appropriate facilities for their development.

As a result of the surveys conducted in 1961–1962 on the problems raised in Africa by the training of middle-ranking personnel with managerial responsibilities in the public and private sectors connected with economic and social development, UNESCO will consider, in consultation with the United Nations, the possibility of setting up or appropriately strengthening, through extra-budgetary resources, institutions (schools or institutes of public administration, social development institutes, extramural departments, etc.) responsible for improving and, if need be, speeding up the training of such personnel.

Two training courses to supplement the training of teachers and research workers will be organized: one in Africa for young economists, and the other in Asia for specialists in political science and public administration.

3. *Other activities regarding higher education.* The development of university teaching of the humanities, to which developing countries attach the greatest importance, will run parallel to that of teaching in natural and social sciences. A number of projects will also be conducted regarding higher education in journalism; collaboration will be continued with the two centers at Strasbourg (France) and Quito (Ecuador) at which it is expected that 160 journalists will attend study courses in 1963–1964. In addition a seminar on training methods in journalism will be held in Asia and a training course on journalism in Africa.

A special effort will be made to strengthen university libraries, which are the very core of the modern university's teaching program. Most projects planned for 1963–1964 will aim at providing institutions of higher learning established under the Special Fund with adequate library services.

Note

[1]The regional meeting of Arab states held at Beirut in 1960 did not establish specific enrollment targets.

7
The Ford Foundation's Technical Assistance Program in Pakistan

Pakistan is unusual among nations in two major aspects — its chief unifying force is religion, Islam, and its two wings, East and West, are a thousand miles apart, separated by India. The acts by which India and Pakistan achieved independence from Great Britain in 1947 at the same time partitioned the subcontinent. East Pakistan, essentially the deltas of the Ganges, Brahmaputra, and Meghna Rivers, is a wet country heavily overpopulated by 45 million Bengalis of whom over three-quarters are Muslim and one-fifth Hindu. West Pakistan is primarily a dry and comparatively sparsely populated area of 35 million Sindhi, Punjabi, Pushtu, and Baluchi speaking peoples, over 90 per cent of whom are Muslim. The economic factor common to both wings in 1947 was that they represented the outlying and least developed areas of the underdeveloped subcontinent of India. Although it has large reserves of natural gas, prospects of oil have not been realized and mineral deposits have not been found or exploited in any significant quantities. Pakistan's resources are chiefly agricultural. It exports jute, cotton, tea, and skins and hides, but in most years it has had to import rice and wheat for food.

Need for Trained Personnel

At Partition and Independence, Pakistan and India engaged in what was perhaps the largest exhange of populations known to history.

George Gant, "The Ford Foundation Program in Pakistan," *The Annals* (American Academy of Political and Social Science), Vol. 323 (May 1959), pp. 150–155, 157–159.

Probably 12 million people migrated from one country to the other. The influx of 7 million refugees into Pakistan added one more burden to the new nation already occupied in establishing a government, a currency, and international connections. Perhaps more seriously, Pakistan lost most of the trained professional leaders and staff from its government departments, banking and commerce, and universities and schools. Before 1947 these positions had been held preponderantly by Hindus, almost all of whom moved to India. Most of the immigrating Muslims were farmers and artisans. Furthermore, since most of the subcontinent's research and specialized training institutions were in the area that became India, Pakistan came into being with a critical shortage not only of trained leadership and manpower, but also of the institutions to produce the scientists, engineers, teachers, entrepreneurs, civil servants, and other professional and skilled personnel necessary to its survival and development. Not without reason did the Pakistan Planning Board identify the trained manpower shortage as a major barrier in fulfilling its Five Year Plan—a barrier as formidable as the shortage of economic resources and foreign exchange.

The Ford Foundation's Role

The Ford Foundation established its Overseas Development program in 1951 on the basis of recommendations made by some of its officers after an exploratory trip to South and Southeast Asia and to the Middle East. The largest part of this program has been expressed in South and Southeast Asia; Representatives are stationed in Burma, India, Indonesia, and Pakistan. Grants have been made to institutions in several countries of the Near East and the program is now being extended gradually to Africa and to Latin America.

In Pakistan the question considered by the Foundation in 1951 was whether a private philanthropy could make any contribution to a country receiving technical and economic assistance from the United States Government at the rate of over $100,000,000 per year, from the United Kingdom, Canada and Australia under the Colombo Plan at the rate of over $20,000,000 per year, and from the United Nations and its affiilates. The answer was clearly affirmative, from the point of view of both Pakistan and the Foundation. Most aid from the United States and from the Colombo countries is economic; it went for physical development—for the construction of dams, fertilizer plants, roads—or for underwriting the general economy. Only a comparatively minor portion is for technical assistance in developing research and training institutions. Assistance from United Nations agencies on the other hand, is chiefiy for consultants who can help make development plans but who do not have the funds needed to carry them out. Also, the policy and procedural limits of the programs of these governmental and international agencies fall short of some of Pakistan's major needs.

It takes a long time to create new institutions anywhere in the world. The process is particularly complex in a country like Pakistan where teaching and research skills in many new fields must be started from scratch. Annually budgeted programs of assistance, especially when designed to meet immediate economic urgencies, do not lend themselves well to institutional development. The Foundation and the Government of Pakistan agreed that they could fruitfully cooperate in the establishment or strengthening of institutions vital to Pakistan's long-range development. In addition, the Foundation could assist Pakistan in sensitive fields in which Pakistan might be reluctant to receive assistance from a foreign government. Above all, the Foundation's interest in Pakistan would symbolize the private, nongovernmental concern of Americans for the welfare of humanity everywhere. This effort to increase the ability of the peoples of the new nations to deal effectively with their problems reflects the spirit of the Foundation's Overseas Development program.

First Foundation Projects

The Foundation's first grants, in 1952, were designed to help establish three polytechnic institutes and a college (later increased to three colleges) of home economics. The polytechnic institutes offer a three-year post-high school course to fill the gap between trade schools and apprenticeships on the one hand and engineering colleges on the other. The home economics colleges will be key points in Pakistan's expanded and enriched education program for girls and women. The Foundation has financed the costs of foreign advisers, staff training abroad, and the foreign exchange requirements for equipment and construction. Oklahoma State University has provided the advisory and training services in both fields.

A few months after the first grants, others were made to assist the Village Agricultural and Industrial Development program and the Government of Pakistan Planning Board. The V-AID program was designed to encourage and assist villagers to organize themselves to deal locally with as many of their problems and opportunities as they could in agriculture, small industry, cooperatives, education, and health and sanitation, and to tap more effectively the technical assistance of the government's nation-building departments in carrying out their plans. To encourage local self-government and to marshall the villagers' interests and energies behind the nation's development program, Pakistan gave V-AID first priority. The International Co-operation Administration provided the foreign advisers and much of the equipment for village-worker training centers, and the Foundation provided funds to help Pakistan set up the training centers more rapidly than its budget would otherwise permit. There are now nine centers, training over 1,200 village workers a year.

One of the most difficult problems faced by a new nation is to plan its program of development so that the priorities it selects fit realistically the available resources. Aware that priorities had to be selected to make the most of limited money and manpower, Pakistan established a Planning Board in 1953 to draft a five year plan. Since then, planning organizations have been set up in each of the two provinces, and the Planning Board has been made a permanent organization. The Ford Foundation made a series of grants that enabled the Planning Board to obtain advisers from Harvard University. Harvard's major assistance at this stage is to help the Planning Board strengthen its staff and its procedures and techniques of planning toward the day when foreign advisers will not be needed. The Harvard–Planning Board Project is noteworthy in two respects. First, in a sensitive and intimate function of government Pakistan has benefited from assistance it would have been reluctant to accept from another government. Second, the Harvard experts have worked as advisers so anonymously and effectively that there has never been criticism of their role although such criticism, in so controversial a process as planning, could certainly have been expected.

Exploring and Selecting New Projects

For several years the four areas mentioned above – polytechnic education, home economics, V-AID, and the Planning Board – attracted the major grants of the Foundation in Pakistan. In late 1955 and in 1956, however, the Foundation's Representative initiated a process of exploration which culminated in several new projects. The framework of the exploration consisted of the priorities of Pakistan's Five Year Plan, the interests of the Foundation in key institutions – chiefly educational – and the gaps in other foreign assistance programs. Within these limits and the limits of Foundation funds available to Pakistan, a wide range of opportunities remained. This range was narrowed in conferences with the Central and Provincial Ministries and with many heads and staff members of universities, colleges and government departments and agencies. The selection process was guided by the suggestions of the chairman of the Planning

Board and by the Secretary of Economic Affairs, who coordinates foreign aid. The possibilities emerging from this process were discussed in detail with the officers and staff of the Foundation in New York. Several were selected for fuller exploration. . . .

.   .   .   .

Approval of schemes

Any foreign-aided project that involves Pakistan's funds must be through the slow but thorough process involved in the preparation, consideration, approval, and financial sanction of a scheme. This elaborate procedure is a major factor in the administration and effectiveness of foreign assistance. It means that schemes must be carefully drafted and that Pakistan's financial and administrative participation cannot be assured until the process is complete. If this fact is not taken into account. foreign contributions of expert personnel and equipment will be premature and frustrated. Much misunderstanding and unhappiness about foreign assistance in Pakistan is due to unfamiliarity on the part of aid-giving agencies with Pakistan's system of administration. Many a foreign expert has sat out his two-year term helplessly because he arrived in Pakistan before his scheme had been approved or given financial sanction. And much equipment has rusted on the docks or in storage bins.

Having failed in the early years to understand and then to follow Pakistan's system of planning and budgeting, the Ford Foundation made grants which also languished. It has since learned to relate its process of project exploration and assistance to that of Pakistan. The first and most important consideration is the quality of a scheme. When Pakistan and the Foundation have explored an idea for a new project to a point which warrants the project's translation into a scheme, the Foundation, at Pakistan's request, often provides consultants to collaborate with Pakistani officers in drafting the details. Consultants are sought particularly in connection with projects that involve institutions or skills not yet available in Pakistan. After the scheme is drafted, the consultants leave Pakistan during the six- to eighteen-month period it takes to move the scheme to approval and financial sanction. In the meantime, the scheme provides the Ford Foundation with a full and detailed statement upon which to judge its own potential contribution. Also, the Foundation's Representative, in his advisory capacity, consults with the several Pakistani departments and ministries as they consider the scheme.

A major factor in Foundation consideration of projects is their priority in Pakistan's program of development. The Foundation does not have a kitful of projects it is urging upon Pakistan. Rather, it selects from among the many suggested that also coincide with the Foundation's area of interest. The clearest evidence of Pakistan's intent about a project is not only its inclusion in the Five Year Plan, but also its inclusion in the budget on the basis of an approved scheme. The Foundation's path is clear once Pakistan decides to devote to a project such local currencies and skills as are needed. The Foundation can than make a grant to supplement Pakistan's investment with foreign exhange and specialized advice and training.

Before the Five Year Plan was approved and the annual development budget system was established, there was a tendency for well-wishing aid-giving agencies to press upon Pakistan projects that were not related in time, and in terms of Pakistan's ability to operate or maintain them, to a more rational plan of development. Pakistan's needs are great and many projects are "good," but it was a disservice to Pakistan to encourage the commitment of a large part of its future budgets to projects which were taken up not because they fitted into the sequence of Pakistan's requirements, but because some foreign aid was available.

Methodology of Assistance: Use of Grant Funds

The Foundation's Overseas Development program constantly faces the challenge of making the best use of available funds to assist projects once they have been selected. This problem has four aspects:

1. How many institutions of the same type in one country should the Foundation assist?

2. To what uses should grant funds be put to assist an approved project?

3. Under what arrangements should foreign advisers be provided?

4. Should foreign experts establish, administer and staff a new institution at the outset, or should nationals?

Because the Foundation's resources are limited, it confines its assistance to amounts necessary to help a country to set up and test new kinds of institutions or programs. The Foundation's aid is further limited to those cases needed to demonstrate the validity and effectiveness of new undertakings. Pakistan's program for polytechnic institutes, for example, calls for a series of such institutes throughout the country, but the Foundation is assisting with only the first three; perhaps two would have been sufficient to give Pakistan the "know-how" to establish others on its own. It is true that Pakistan needs economic assistance in constructing and equipping additional institutes, but neither the nature nor the resources of a private philanthropy are adapted to these purely economic needs.

The Foundation has evolved a pattern of assistance in Pakistan that is broad enough to cover all the foreign-aid needs of its projects but narrow enough to rely on Pakistan for local funds and staff. In this way, the Foundation can devote its resources to meeting each project's total dollar requirements – construction, equipment, foreign advisers, and foreign training of staff. Some other aid-giving agencies can provide only part of the foreign aid needed and sometimes must help find supplementary assistance from one or more other foreign agencies. More than one foreign-aid project has failed because all the components were not available or, if available from several sources, became hopelessly entangled in procedural confusion and conflicts in policy and methodology.

The Foundation assists Pakistan with projects which Pakistan intends to support but for which foreign technical help is needed. In most cases this means that Foundation funds provide foreign advisers; scholarships for the foreign training of staff members; and import of equipment, books, and construction materials. . . .

· · · · · · · · · · · · · ·

Case Study of a Grant: Education Extension Centers

The evolution of the Foundation's relations with Pakistan's Education Extension Centers and pilot schools of secondary education illustrates the specifics of institutional planning. Major educational objectives of Pakistan's Five Year Plan are to broaden and enrich its secondary schools, which have been heavily literary in emphasis, and to improve teaching methods. The Plan calls for five education extension centers for the reorientation and in-service training of school inspectors, headmasters, and teachers as a primary means of accomplishing this objective. It also calls for the experimental and demonstration use in forty secondary schools of new curricula, with emphasis on science and vocational subjects, and new teaching and examination methods. In the fall of 1956 it was suggested to the Foundation's Representative that the Foundation might assist these projects. Discussion and exploration over several weeks convinced both Pakistan and the Foundation that the Foundation could be helpful, but that detailed schemes were needed upon which both could make firmer judgements. The Government of Pakistan asked the Foundation to provide consultants to assist in preparing schemes.

Anticipating that, if the schemes were well drawn and approved, the Foundation would be asked to arrange advisory services from an American university to help implement them, the Foundation asked the University of Chicago to provide the initial consultants. The University, by participating in the planning stage, could form its own judgment about a continuing advisory role later. University of Chicago consultants studied Pakistan's education situation for three months in the spring of 1957. They formed a team with a group of Pakistani educators which, during the summer of 1957, studied in-service teacher training and secondary education in the Near East, Europe, and the United States. Then the joint team drafted schemes for two education extension centers and the pilot secondary schools to suit Pakistan's particular needs and education system. The Ford Foundation financed the dollar cost of this process of study and planning.

In the fall of 1957 the schemes were started on the long process of review and consideration in the Provincial and Central governments. In the meantime, the Foundation considered how it might assist with the projects, if requested, and the University of Chicago considered whether it would provide advisory services. The schemes were approved in the spring of 1958, early enough to be included in the budget year beginning April 1. Pakistan asked the Ford Foundation for funds to finance consultation and foreign advisers from the University of Chicago, the training of key extension center staff, and the import of equipment and construction materials. Pakistan indicated its intent by sanctioning the schemes and by budgeting local costs of construction, equipment, and operation. The University of Chicago accepted Pakistan's invitation and the Foundation made two grants — one to finance the services of the University of Chicago and one to finance the dollar cost of equipment and construction.

Foundation-assisted Projects in Pakistan

Much the same process of exploration and grant making has been followed in other major projects—with Oklahoma State University in the fields of home economics and polytechnics, with Harvard University for the Planning Board, and with Michigan State University for the establishment of two Academies of Development Administration. Other projects include assistance to Teacher-Student Centers at the Universities of Dacca and Punjab, the President's Commission on Education, the Inter-University Board, a new College of Agriculture at the University of Peshawar, and an Institute of Personnel Training. Under exploration now is a major project of research and demonstration in rural industry; schemes are being drafted with the assistance of the Stanford Research Institute.

It takes years to get a new institution on its feet, especially in a country where the subject is new and key staff has to be trained abroad. The Foundation has decided to assist with a relatively small number of such institutions in Pakistan so that it can help each to the extent and for the duration necessary. It is now in its sixth year of assistance to the Planning Board and in its seventh year of assistance in home economics and polytechnic education. The Foundation has been making grants for projects in Pakistan at the rate of 2.5 million dollars a year. These funds support the Foundation's contributions to the projects already in hand; they can assist new major projects only as older ones mature and no longer require the Foundation's assistance.

Implementation and Perspective

The Foundation has completed much of its program planning in Pakistan, although planning must continue in phasing out assistance to maturing institutions and exploring a limited number of new projects. The most demanding task now for the Foundation's Representative is the effective implementation of grants. This task consists chiefly of encouraging and assisting the American universities able and willing to provide the services Pakistan needs.

Considerable help and information can be given foreign advisers and their families in connection with the local living conditions — housing, health, schools, and others — that plague the newcomer to any environment. The answers for more basic problems of implementation, however, are more difficult to provide, although experience is fast accumulating. Little is known about the methodology of technical cooperation: What works and what does not, particularly over a span of time? The Foundation and the cooperating universities plan to evaluate specific Pakistan projects to shed more light on this question and perhaps to suggest some answers to it.

Since this review was first drafted, Pakistan has passed through a bloodless revolution and is now operating under what is called the "new regime." The Constitution was abrogated, and political parties were abolished. Pakistan is technically under martial law, although the civil servants and the regular officers of the government departments remain in immediate charge of law and order, collection and disbursement of revenues, and the development program. Although deploring the failure of its first efforts at constitutional government, perhaps most people in Pakistan welcome the new regime for its immediately successful efforts in halting corruption, slowing and perhaps reversing the serious economic decline, and improving the morale and efficiency of government. The first effect of the "new regime" was to improve the environment for development. The lasting effects will depend, of course, on whether repressive methods of control are instituted or whether sound foundations and processes for representative government are laid.

The Foundation has received many indications that the institutions it is assisting, not only in Pakistan but in other new nations, are well regarded by changing political forces except the Communists who are its continuing critics. Projects which receive Foundation aid are not political in nature. They are devoted to the long-time development of competence through which people will become more and more able to shape, control, and stabilize their political, economic, and social forms. The Foundation's assistance at this level of development, rather than at the level of current political and economic pressures, makes it welcome and free of suspicion as an expression of its pervading purpose — to advance human welfare.

PART II

The Economic
and Political Aspects
of Education and Development

T he strategems of waging peace and winning the cold war have brought the rich, developed nations of the West into the poor, vastly underdeveloped nations to combat the forces of poverty, ignorance, hunger, and disease. Whereas in the 1950's and the early 1960's these foreign-aid activities were often approached with a smug romanticism, today they are characterized by a hard-headed realism that has shifted the focus from proposals for increasing technical-assistance activities to efforts to build programs that are efficient, cooperative, and related to social and economic objectives.

This change in mood has grown out of the awareness that the available resources, even under the best of conditions, can meet but a small portion of the needs of the developing nations and that the high cost of technical assistance limits the broad application of these resources. For instance, the cost per year of maintaining one Peace Corps volunteer in the field is about $8,000, and the Peace Corps operation is one of the least expensive governmental aid activities in existence.

Two important assumptions underlying much of the discussion of the relationship of economic development and educational aid are: (1) educational growth leads to economic growth; and (2) educational systems can be structured to meet successfully the projected manpower needs. On the basis of these assumptions, studies of the manpower needs of the newer nations have been undertaken, and national plans have been constructed to guide educational development.

H. M. Phillips and M. J. Bowman, the authors of the first two selections in this section, review economic theory and methodology as they relate to education. Bowman is particularly critical of current thinking. She states that generalizations about education as a panacea can be dangerous demagoguery. She also believes that when manpower assessments are taken too seriously they are likely to lead to waste in overtraining and in training that is in fact inappropriate in light of limited resources. The comments of both authors reflect a new attitude of caution and, in some instances, disenchantment with manpower planning.

Obviously, there is more to national growth than economic development, and there is more to economic development than educational expansion. Adam Curle, in the final article in this section, deals with another aspect of the development picture—a nation's attitude toward human beings and the character of its politics. Curle found that the three countries in Europe that most markedly combine non-competitive politics with a nonegalitarian society have the lowest per capita expenditure on education. Also, he found that, of the 20 independent Latin American states he studied, the seven that were relatively more competitive and egalitarian had an average per capita expenditure on education of $15.4; the other 13 states had an average per capita expenditure on education of $3.9.

Curle's findings raise many questions about the relationship between the political climate of a nation and its readiness to effectively utilize overseas aid. The author's purpose, however, is not to answer these questions, but to demonstrate that there are factors beyond economics that affect educational growth and national development.

8
Economic and Social Aspects
of the Planning of Education

In what follows, planning means the process of setting out in advance a
pattern of action to bring about given over-all national policies by the
closest possible articulation of means and ends. It refers to what
supreme commanders do before battle is joined, and does not cover the
instructions they receive from their political masters, or the detailed
operations of battalions or even whole corps, after the plan is launched.
That is a separate subject of study, though the two are frequently
mixed. The word "operations" is used for the latter activities, though
they too require careful consideration and forecasting as part of the
over-all plan. Indeed the essence of a good over-all plan is that it
evaluates as many operational alternatives as possible. Similarly every
plan must contain it it a substantial margin for manoeuvre. In the
economic perspective there is always some Blücher on the horizon
advancing with a new piece of technology that may change the order
of battle.

The need for planning arises from two basic reasons. First, that
education is the main means in the hands of a society for influencing its
future value system and its stock of knowledge and skills. Economic
and social development requires certain basic values and attitudes and
and ever-increasing application of skills both productive and social.
The extent to which these requirements are met depends greatly on the
manner in which the educational system fulfills its role. Secondly, the
operation of the educational system utilizes a large proportion of a
country's existing stock of educated talent and, in developing countries,
a major part of public expenditure. Since both the use of talent and the

H. M. Phillips, "Economic and Social
Aspects of the Planning of Education,"
International Social Science Journal,
Vol. 14 (1962), pp. 706–718.

distribution of public expenditure are major problems of resource allocation, questions concerning the size of the educational system, as well as its nature, enter into the heart of over-all economic and social planning.

Within these two broad considerations, there are a number of allied facts with important implications which are touchstones on which planning measures have to be tested. The first is that in its task of forming future values and skills, the educational system is functionally interlocked with its socio-economic environment through such factors as job opportunities, the role of the teacher in the community and the influence of the community on the teacher. Thus any plan must be economically and socially oriented. The second is that the educational system should be a coherent whole with a functional interrelation between its sectors if it is to work efficiently. Thirdly, although there exist certain necessary technological relations between its sectors, there are substantial areas of choice as to the size, composition, and interrelation of those parts; that is, resource allocation is an internal as well as an externally conditioned problem for educators. Fourthly, since educational planning deals with people and not commodities, it cannot be assumed that they will be passive. The preferences of parents and pupils in the end govern entry into the different educational sectors and subjects of study. Besides, education is inalienable and cannot be sold by the individual possessor of it. Planning therefore involves taking into account psychological factors and incentives. The fifth is that the demand for education falls into two parts, the one productive and the other of a "consumption" or social nature. When Professor Schultz made his calculations of the returns on education in the United States of America, he assumed that 50 per cent of education was consumption and halved the cost to take this into account.[1]

Measures of educational planning have to be tested against this set of facts. For example, the fourth fact (parents' and pupils' preferences) means that the manpower approach to educational planning can never be sufficient. It is not possible to envisage a world in which preferences happen to be identical with needs. So long as freedom of choice of profession exists and academic freedom in respect of subjects of study, plans cannot be based on the hypothesis that educational supply and economic and social demand can be identical. Education must therefore always be planned to a certain extent in excess of occupational demand, just as full employment has to be planned to allow for frictional unemployment.

There exists no long-standing tradition of close application of the principles of resource allocation to education. If educational systems are viewed as "industries" or "services" in the economic sense, it emerges that there is substantial room for an increase of output by rearrangements of physical facilities, adjustments of curricula, increased vocational guidance, etc. without a reduction of standards. These inefficiencies in resource allocation are not due to lack of social conscience on the part of educators, but rather the opposite; they are an accurate reflection of the demands which society has hitherto placed upon them. The new factor is the belated "discovery" in the last few years of the extraordinarily important role education plays in national policy, whether it is a matter of economic and social development or one of maintaining a particular ideology and level of scientific development in a competitive struggle of ideologies. The suddenly revealed demands for education go so far beyond what has ever been experienced over the same periods of time before, that the objectives can only be reached by new means. Few people are in favor of planning in itself. Equally, few societies (except those which have reached affluence and perhaps not even those) can be sure of obtaining the direct results without the foresight and articulation of means and ends which planning involves, though the means used in planning will be adapted to the ideology of each society. Even people who are uncertain about the notion of planning as applied to their own societies are frequently exponents of educational planning in countries operating with very limited resources.

The need for planning can be illustrated by the following examples. Three vast areas (Africa, Latin America and Asia) are engaged in trying roughly to double the proportion of their gross national product spent on education over periods ranging from ten to twenty years. The sums involved are huge, and the danger of waste is commensurate. One larger European country is planning to double its university population in twenty years. These cases show the magnitude of the operations involved. Another example, illustrating the constraints on educational expansion which cannot be overcome except by planning, is the following. One country found it needed to increase its supply of scientific and technical personnel by about 70 per cent. It ascertained that about one-third of its student population at present took the necessary basic studies so as to be able to enter this category, and wished accordingly to increase the proportion of students in those subjects to 50 per cent by 1970. But the greater the increase in students, the greater the number of teachers required, thus threatening to curtail the existing insufficient supply of such personnel for industry. When a balance was found between the constraint represented by the supply of teachers and that represented by maintaining the minimum requirements of industry, a target of a proportion of 40 per cent of the student population was arrived at. Other constraints which need evaluation are the size of the class, the teaching methods, the physical plant, the minimum size of the student body, the allowance which has to be made for "dropout" and wastage, and, as we saw above, the imbalance between students' preferences and a country's occupational needs. The planning process involves the projection of requirements and their evaluation in terms of such constraints.

The task for the technician in the science of planning is to assemble the data and show their implications under various political, social and economic hypotheses. Planning of any kind is impossible, however, unless objectives are reasonably clearly specified, can be regarded as given for a suitable period of time, and are of a kind that can be achieved by planning. Specification of the objectives arises at the early forecasting stage, since the technician has to have a number of minimum political assumptions on which to proceed. The final objectives should be fixed when the forecasts have been produced on alternative hypotheses and their consequences estimated. At present the precision of definition of educational ends required for detailed planning is frequently absent at both the forecasting and the decision stages.

As regards the time period for planning, five years is usual for economic planning on the basis that, apart from a crisis, electoral opinion and world conditions can be expected to remain foreseeable during that time. The planning of education, however, requires a time perspective of fifteen years, since this is the time it takes to create the human and physical resources for the operation of educational systems. This awkward difference in time period is partially offset by the modern tendency of economic plans to survive changes of government and to be carried on by civil services and technocrats leading to "perspective planning" based on long-term forecasting. A further offset is that both the number of young people who will enter the labour force in fifteen years' time and those who will enter it at the end of their higher education at the age of twenty-one (this year's babies and this year's school entrants at six) can be determined in advance, since both groups are already born. The time period does not therefore present an insoluble problem in relating education to economic and social development, though it presents some special difficulties.

The question arises as to the feasibility of achieving the aims of educational policy by planning, since clearly not all of them can be so achieved. Fortunately there is room for many different degrees of educational planning according to the nature of the society involved, and it is not necessary to envisage the calamity of a vast bureaucratic control of the scholastic profession. Some will rely on more technocratic or centralized methods of collecting information, others may base themselves on past experience, or on data obtained from new surveys regarding regional and local preferences of pupils, parents, school leavers and the demands of employers. The area which has been least studied, despite a certain burst of activity in the last two or three years, is the means of relating educational planning to economic and social development. In this area the economist can help on two levels of analysis. First, as regards the problems of cost and financing and the impact of the educational system on the national output of goods and services, that is, cost benefit relationships falling under "the measuring rod of money." Secondly, insofar as educational planning involves "a relationship between a multiplicity of ends and scarce means that have alternative uses" (Lionel Robbins' definition), the economist can aid the educator to determine the interrelationships which will maximize the use of educational resources for educational ends. Both levels of analysis are dependent upon there being substantial areas of alternative use of resources and of choice and substitution.

The educational system itself is not, of course, substitutable. Every society must have an educational system, and no civilized society is known today to spend less than about 1 per cent of its gross national product on education, and none more than about 6 per cent. Between these two percentages, however, important possibilities of resource substitution arise, not only as regards the size of the educational effort as compared with other programmes, but inside the educational system itself. In terms of social development, education is in competition for scarce resources with health and housing programmes. On the economic side it competes with other infrastructure services like transport, and with the formation of physical capital. A *prima facie* area of substitution is the amount of training to be undertaken in the formal education system, as compared with the amount to be undertaken in employment in industry.

In the United States, a sample survey by the U.S. Department of Labor[2] has revealed that the average period of workers' formal schooling was 10.1 years in 1950 while the average period spent on in-service training was 1.72 years at that time. These proportions have changed slightly since 1940 and there is no reason to suppose that they are invariable. There are, however, serious limitations as to the extent of substitution possible without loss of efficiency. This is demonstrated by Professor Strumilin's figures[3] . . . which indicate the large superiority in productivity of workers who have had adequate formal schooling plus vocational training in industry, as compared with those who have had an insufficient number of years of school but longer training on the job. Equally, once a man has received his formal education and his on-the-job training, there is no substitute for the experience acquired over the years in his work.

There is an important area of possible substitution in respect of teaching methods, techniques, and aid. These items cover the technology of education — radio and television as compared with direct teaching, the cost of facilities, the use of buildings on a shift basis, etc. In respect of the financing of education also, alternatives of choice arise as to sources to be tapped — central or local, governmental or private, voluntary or compulsory, or both. Then there is a crucial choice facing the over-all economic planner, that is, the industrial technology to be introduced to carry out the development plan: whether this should be labour-intensive or capital-intensive, and whether (of particular interest to the educational planner) it should be "education-intensive" or otherwise. In coming to decisions on such choices clearly the planner must know the potentiality of the educational system of his country and the cost of remodeling it, since this will affect the cost benefit ratios of the different alternatives. The educational planner has to contribute to the making of this choice.

Finally there are many choices as to selection procedures and criteria for admission to the different educational levels which will influence the supply of students, costs, and standards required for economic purposes to respond to the social demand for education. Choices exist also as to the extent to which each level may be treated as an end in itself, or should be regarded as a stepping-stone in a selection process. Is primary education ever an end in itself for the majority of people in a poor country, or must there always be provision for those who wish to and can go on to higher levels? The economic and social consequences of such choices have to be evaluated as part of the planning process. Similar issues needing evaluation are: what is the appropriate level of "wastage" in respect of each level or type of system, and to what extent "dropout" is the necessary price of widening opportunities for education. The figures of "wastage" for African educational systems as a whole amount to as much as 20 per cent of the enrollment. Figures for Niger show that from the first to sixth year of study 54 per cent of boys and 65 per cent of girls abandon the primary school course. [4]

Care should be taken not to set rigid systems and standards and then to regard short falls in achieving them as failures. Short falls may be of two kinds: those caused by standards being set in excess of the possibilities of the teaching facilities (that is, bad planning), and those which are a legitimate result of the interaction of the educational system and the socio-economic environment. The African "wastage" contains both elements. What may be called "legitimate wastage" relates to children and young people who drop out of education in order to meet the economic and social needs of their environment, family duties, etc. Studies involving both educators and sociologists are needed to analyse the problem of legitimate wastage, a phenomenon best described by a neutral phrase such as "frictional adjustment between the education system and the environment."

The formulation of educational plans must take into account substitution possibilities at two stages: (a) keeping as independent the relationships which flow from given national policies, and working only with the other variables; and (b) testing the implications of changes in these relationships themselves.

The number of variables to be included is usually limited by lack of data, and an important task lies before educational statisticians to improve this situation. In practice, choice is limited by the prevailing constraints and the time taken to overcome them. Suppose a country has an educational policy of making all its adult citizens literate in x years, and of securing compulsory primary education of, say, six years' duration for all its children in y years. A new factor is introduced in the form of a development programme to increase the pace of industrialization, which would call for more secondary and technical education. Under the original hypothesis the planner would examine the resources available and say whether the requirements could be met or what the short fall would be. Under the new hypothesis the problem would be to assess the effect of a shift in the combination required for the industrialization programme. It might lengthen the period during which the original ends have to be achieved. Alternatively, it might shorten the period because of the increased revenue obtained through the industrialization programme.

What are the means available for finding answers to the choices posed, and what are the limitations to them? Decisions on the optimum allocation of national resources to education, as compared with direct investment of production in other social services or physical capital, lie outside the economics of education and are the concern of the economic planner. But both the over-all planner and the educator are interested not only in the size of the educational investment but in its efficiency, since a reduction of unit cost is equivalent to an increase of resources allocated. Many educational systems use their resources below capacity, partly due to the socio-economic environment and to traditional attitudes which consider that education falls outside economic allocation approaches, and partly from the failure to adopt adequate criteria of selection. In one country, out of 100,000 who sat for the matriculation examination in 1959 only 3 per cent passed, and only 30 per cent of students at the universities passed their annual examinations.[5]

The process of integrating the educational plan with the over-all economic development plan presents special difficulties. The strategy of the over-all plan may be one of balanced growth or of moving from one selected imbalance to another. The educator may be asked to adjust his planning to a strategy based on the belief that the country is on the threshold of a development stage which has to be reached by a special push in a particular sector of investment. This will involve careful study as to whether education, as a piece of planned social infrastructure, can or should take part in such "special pushes," except in respect of certain limited parts of the system. At this point substitution processes, such as in-service training, have to be studied and the degree of sacrifice assessed. The first step is to find a common discourse, preferably in quantifiable terms, between educational planners and over-all economic planners to bring about the necessary integration. This involves training programmes in which educators will be co-opted into the processes of economic development planning and economists will be initiated into the problems of educational planning. It involves also the establishment of planning units concerned with these processes, both in the central planning organization and in ministries of education.

In estimating the forward relation of educational planning to economic and social development, the following stages are necessary:

1. Making the projections of the future size and age composition of the population and the movement of the economy in as much detail as possible by sectors. Failing detailed projections, at least a profile of the economy is necessary based on two or three broad hypotheses.

2. Turning the economic data into requirements in respect of different occupations. Alternatively, if there is sufficient data to carry out manpower surveys, an estimate of the future occupational composition of the population can be made from the forecasts of employers of the need for qualified manpower and from the extension of existing trends of employment. Where this is possible, it is also an index of the economic profile required under (1). Many difficulties are involved in manpower surveys of this kind. The number of employers who can

look forward 15 years is limited. There is a tendency for employers to exaggerate their forecasts in periods of labour scarcity and to minimize them when labour is abundant, while professional associations tend to do the opposite.

3. Turning the occupational data so obtained into its educational component. The number of classifiable occupations is of the order of 1,350. Difficulties which arise in this form of projection are that there are no fixed relations between occupations and education, except over broad categories and in a limited number of professions. Classification of skills by educational components can produce 300 items in advanced economies. But for practical planning purposes, the educational classifications of occupations can be reduced to between ten and fifteen. Even smaller groupings are possible, according to the degree of detail which the other factors in the planning process permit in any given case. An addition must be made for non-workers.

4. Forecasting the measures required to produce these educational characteristics in the population through schools, institutions, and on-the-job training.

5. Determining the optimum relation which should exist between the different sectors of the educational system in order to produce the required numbers of students at the different levels.

6. Studying the incentives required to guide pupils into those particular studies and school-leavers into those occupations, including changes in the wage structure and prestige of different occupations. (As we saw above, students' and parents' preferences have to be foreseen and guided.)

7. Forecasting the required flow between the levels, on alternative pedagogical standards and selection criteria.

8. Studying the likely results of alternative technologies of teaching. The number of teachers per class will influence the amount of teacher training required and the size of the investment in secondary and higher education.

9. Establishing what elements have to be maintained or introduced into the educational system to exploit fully the "external economies" flowing from investment in education, such as research, the development of elites and innovators, the formation of stable, responsible middle classes, and the promotion of managerial, entrepreneurial and social skills in the population.

10. Assessing the unit costs of different types of educational technology and means of developing the educational system, and comparing them: for example, large colleges or small; should new universities be placed in dense population areas or spread over the country in small towns?

Clearly the forecasting required goes well beyond that derivable from even the best economic projections or manpower surveys. Such projections and surveys have to be seen against a pattern of norms derived from experience and country studies. Among such norms are the following: (a) the proportion of gross national product devoted to education both globally and (if possible) by sectors; (b) the proportion of public revenue so spent; (c) the proportion of public investment made in education and its different sectors; (d) the proportion of investment in education and its different sectors as compared with over-all investment; (e) the proportion of the population enrolled at the different educational levels; (f) the same proportion corrected in the light of information as to attendance; and (g) the proportion of the student population receiving instruction in different levels and types of education.

Naturally this information has to be interpreted in the light of the special conditions of each country, and should always be cross-checked with the results of manpower assessments and occupation and educational requirements deduced from the economic perspective. But it is possible to establish patterns and trait clusters of educational development by comparisons between countries at various income levels. Economic indices against which to set the demand patterns which emerge are the statistics of growth of gross national product per head (or of *per capita* income), viewed in the light of the facts as regards income distribution. Social indices are more difficult to apply, the best for practical use being those set up by the United Nations Expert Group on Standards and Levels of Living and utilized with the help of ranking techniques. It is necessary to incorporate movement in the analysis, either by tracing patterns for intervening periods of the long-term perspective (say fifteen years) or by recourse to norms. These must be based on what is known as to possible rates of expansion, for example, the number of years it takes to produce different levels of attainment, including not only pedagogic factors and demographic factors but also teacher training (it is known that certain of the advanced countries, France, U.S.S.R., United States, have increased their over-all teaching force by 50 per cent in ten years), the construction of school buildings, etc. On the demand side there are similar norms as to rate of expansion known from experience, which can be applied, corrected for the state of development of different countries. Professor Harbison[6] has estimated that the ratio of annual increase of higher level manpower to the annual increase of national income should usually be of the order of three to one; that scientific and engineering grades should grow numerically three times as fast as the labour force; that the sub-professional grades requiring secondary education should grow six to nine times as fast; and clerical grades and craftsmen twice as fast. Obviously this cannot be true for every type of economy and the estimates themselves need further research. But it is necessary to go through this kind of exercise, combined with the previous types of analysis mentioned above, in order to obtain practical results.

Little has been done so far to construct a series of actual and possible norms of the kind indicated, but progress is being made as statistics come forward and the number of reports of survey missions grows. Inter-country comparisons, like most tools, can be dangerous as well as useful unless they are studied in terms of relative cost and variation of economic and administrative structure, as well as of demographic analysis of the differences in age structure of different countries. For instance, children of five to fourteen years of age make up 25 per cent of the population in Latin America, but only 17 per cent in Western Europe; that is, in Latin America one out of four people should be in school while the proportion for Europe is one out of six; and Professor Arthur Lewis estimates that the cost of giving primary education to every child is 0.8 per cent of national income in the United States and 4 per cent in Nigeria.[7] The collection and use of data of this kind delimits the area within which the precise target is to be found by detailed study or informed judgement, rather on the principle of bracketing techniques developed in naval gunfire. Until further results have been obtained by research into the returns on educational investment, no alternative methodology exists. Since the statistics are varied, the use of rank correlation is recommendable and also the study of clusters of measurable traits which might form patterns.

Two major research attempts have been made so far to show the returns on education. The first (the "third factor" approach, based on the residual in the production function) suffers from the difficulty that no evidence exists of what would have been the effect of alternative combinations of human and physical capital. The second (the "earnings differential" approach) suffers from the difficulty of relating private earnings with social income, and of equating actual with optimum national totals of individual earnings, as well as from the difficulty of holding constant variations in such items as intelligence and family position which, as well as educational attainment, are determinants of earnings. This does not mean such research is not of the highest value. Professor Becker, for instance, has now adjusted his well-known figure of 11 per cent return on secondary and higher education (including public costs) to 9 per cent in the light of data he has collected on the intelligence variable.[8] The problem is how to apply such results to one of the newly developing countries, particularly as the analysis presupposes full employment and detailed census data. This type of analysis is not yet ready to be included in the tool kit of the educational planners of the developing countries, though it is important both as a contribution to economic science and as a measure of the contribution which education makes to economies already achieving high development levels.

Once a pattern of educational development is adumbrated by the methods indicated, the question of finance has to be faced by the planner. Even though the educational plan arrived at may be economic in the sense that it is necessary for development and would not involve an excessive allocation of resources which could be better used elsewhere, it does not follow that the necessary financing can be found. Because education has to be largely financed from current revenue, since teachers' salaries make up three-quarters of the cost, financing possibilities depend on the efficiency of the fiscal system. Here again, reference to norms is helpful. Low-income countries raise on the average about 14 per cent of their national income in revenue, while high-income countries raise about 21 per cent. The part of the financing that requires foreign exchange, which may amount to 5 to 7 per cent of the average over-all educational plan, is dependent on the country's balance of payments position. The educational plan which has been adumbrated may, accordingly, have to be cut back to the extent that the fiscal system cannot be improved or foreign exchange obtained, or means found to reduce the call on revenue or foreign exchange. Means of reducing the demands on the public budget consist of extending the fee-paying sector of educational finance, increasing voluntary teaching, for example, in literacy campaigns, discovering untapped local sources of financial initiative through special contributions from industry, and special local taxes, and by obtaining outside bilateral or multilateral aid.

Apart from cases where governments make direct contributions to the budgets of other countries (for example, metropolitan countries to their ex-colonial territories), international grants and loans are at present envisaged in terms of financing tangible capital such as buildings and teaching equipment. But over-all loans may contain an educational component, and this aspect of international financing has not yet been fully studied or developed. At present the educational planner has to look to internal sources for the overwhelming proportion of finance and to external aid for technical assistance and for physical equipment. Grants or loans for physical equipment from abroad will usually be restricted to the proportion of finance for which foreign aid is required, and to cases where it can be shown that the real resources exist for carrying out the plan envisaged if the fiscal resources can be increased to bring them into action. It does not follow, of course, that the whole of the amount of the foreign exchange involved in such a loan or grant would accrue to the educational system. Any foreign currency beyond the actual foreign exhange component of the educational plan would have to be distributed according to the country's foreign exchange priorities, and the project compensated in internal currency. The educational planning process involves integration of this kind with over-all financial planning.

It will be seen that the final educational plan must be feasible pedagogically, it must attempt to "optimize" the contribution of education to economic and social development, it must show the necessary priorities as between its sectors as well as its priorities in the country's over-all plan. It must also give a timetable for carrying it into effect, and it must contain a sufficient area of manoeuvre so that it can be reviewed periodically and adjusted.

It will have been noted that the planning of education in relation to economic and social development involves many disciplines; education, economics, sociology, statistics, psychology, administration, as well as a closer definition of the political goals of education. The extent to which these disciplines can be called upon in the precise planning of education, as distinct from their exerting a general influence on the judgements of the planners, depends upon their capacity to provide measurable data for planning purposes. Much more research is required in all of the disciplines concerned, as well as a closer definition of educational aims.

It is necessary to extend the link between studies by economists and those in other disciplines, such as sociology and psychology, deeply concerned in the educational process and able to contribute by techniques of social survey, public opinion polling, etc. Development economists are finding themselves increasingly involved in contacts with those disciplines and there has been a great advance in empirical sociology since Professor Hicks pointed out that before the economist can apply his analysis he has to look round for a sociologist and "usually there isn't one." The use of the various disciplines will vary according to the different stages of the planning process. In the quantitative aspects of planning, economic and demographic techniques come to the fore; but at the stage when the ends to be taken as given are discussed, and in evaluating the impact of the plan at the level of the individual and the community, there is a very special role for sociology, political science and psychology.

When economists began to work closely on educational planning, doubts arose in the minds of some educators as to whether this would result in a materialist approach to education. As we saw above, economics is the science of optimum use of scarce resources for given ends, and economists are unlikely to interfere with educational values. It is a science which was invented by professors of moral philosophy in the eighteenth and nineteenth centuries in response to the Industrial Revolution, and chairs of economics are a twentieth-century innovation. Most economists look forward to the time when their science will be reduced to "a position of secondary importance," when the "problem of want and poverty and the economic struggle between nations" will be seen to be "nothing but a frightful muddle, a transitory and unnecessary muddle" (Keynes). The threat to the conservative educator comes in reality not from the economist but from the non-conservative and innovating educator. Research is already on foot in educational circles into such questions as the development of the pupil's intuition as part of the teaching process, and behind the innovating educator the moral philosopher will always be active in this sensitive field. On the subject of intuition Aldous Huxley recently made the following comment in an interview with a French journalist: "Quand je vais voir les étudiants du MIT, je les trouve très préoccupés par le problème de la spécialisation scientifique et nullement fermés à un enseignement spiritualiste. Ils craignent de créer des savants non civilisés. Vingt-cinq pour cent du programme sont consacrés aux humanités, histoire, littérature, sociologie. Je leur dis : Tout ça, c'est très bien, mais où aboutissez-vous ? Vous mitigez une éducation scientifique symbolique, par une autre éducation également symbolique, mais verbale. Il est temps d'inventer les humanités non verbales."[9]

Notes

[1]T. W. Schultz, "Education and Economic Growth," in Nelson B. Henry, ed., *Social Forces Influencing American Education (Sixtieth Yearbook of the National Society for the Study of Education,* Part II) (Chicago: University of Chicago Press, 1961), p. 75.

[2]*Estimates of Worker Trait Requirements for 4,000 Jobs* (Washington: U.S. Department of Labor, Bureau of Employment Security, U.S. Employment Service).

[3]Stanislav Strumilin, "The Economics of Education in the USSR," *International Social Science Journal,* Vol. 14 (1962), pp. 633–646.

[4]R. van Waeyenbergue, *Planification de l'Enseignement; Analyse de la Situation* (Unesco Mission to Republic of Niger, 1961).

[5]Hla Myint, *The Role of Institutions of Higher Education in the Development of the Countries of South-East Asia* (Unesco/I.A.U. Committee of Experts, Kuala Lumpur, February 23–27, 1962).

[6]Frederick Harbison, "High-level Manpower for Nigeria's Future," *Investment in Education* (The Report of the Commission on Post-School Certificate and Higher Education in Nigeria, 1960), pp. 50–73.

[7]W. Arthur Lewis, *The Strategy of Educational Development in Relation to the Economic Growth of Underdeveloped Countries, Priorities for Educational Expansion* (Washington, OECD Policy Conference on Economic Growth and Investment in Education, October 16–20, 1961).

[8]Gary Becker, "Underinvestment in College Education?" *American Economic Review,* Vol. 1, No. 2 (May 1960), p. 340.

[9]Danielle Hunebelle, "L'Univers Spirituel d'Aldous Huxley," *Réalités,* No. 195 (April, 1962), p. 78.

9
Perspectives on Education and Development

At no time since the mercantilists, with their emphasis on the importance of "art and ingenuity," has human resource development occupied so important a place in the main stream of economic thought as it does today. And never, I suspect, have so many battles raged concerning methods and interpretations in both research and planning practice. Meanwhile, we are at a stage when progress in understanding is almost unavoidably accompanied by the multiplication of confusion and of respectable but dangerous fallacy. Much of this multiplication, both positive and negative, emerges at the points at which researcher, policy maker, and planning technician should converge.

I am starting from the research end. What do we know that is so, what do we "know" that is *not* so and how do we know these things? Planning practice starts with one or another set of assumed answers to many of the most critical questions. And what planners do, if it has any impact, in turn conditions the relationships the researcher is studying.

Given the vast scope of my topic and the recent proliferation of writing and talking about it, I shall have to be highly selective and unjustifiably dogmatic. In fact, I shall be deliberately dogmatic on some of the most disputed issues. Incidentally, I shall be particularly summary in disregarding the great diversity of subjects which are sometimes included under the label "manpower planning." My remarks will be organized under three main headings.

Mary Jean Bowman, "Facts and Fallacies in Educational Planning: Perspectives on Education and Development," *International Development Review,* Vol. 6 (September 1964), pp. 3–7.

Education and National Income

I start on this one by making a set of assertions: In cross-country comparisons, both for all countries and for subsets classified by energy resources, Anderson and I found that per capita incomes in the 1930's explained enrollment rates in the 1950's much better than enrollment rates of the 1930's explained income in the 1950's. As of the 1950's, no country with less than a 40 per cent adult literacy rate had a measured per capita income in excess of $200 with one exception, in which oil dominated the picture. Below 40 per cent literacy, there was almost no education-income correlation. This suggests a minimum threshold educational diffusion level at about 40 per cent as a precondition of development.

It is *not* true that the countries that first industrialized took off with literacy confined to a small minority. Anderson has accumulated evidence indicating male literacy rates of over 40 per cent in England and France before the beginning stages of the factory system. In Russia at the end of the nineteenth century, education was lagging. Nevertheless, two thirds or more of the urban males were literates and, taking males and females together, urban literacy exceeded 40 per cent.

It is not true that literacy is of relatively minor importance for agricultural progress. Moreover, progress in agriculture is a *sine qua non* for substantial, sustained growth. On this, I refer you to the new book by T. W. Schultz on *Transforming Traditional Agriculture,* which I consider a remarkable little work, outclassing his book and articles on education.

Though the 40 per cent adult literacy I have reiterated may be a necessary condition for development, it is not a sufficient condition — and neither are higher levels of schooling. Even in the 1950's, there were a few Asian countries with over 40 per cent literacy but incomes under $200. It is probable that in the 1960's and 1970's, there will be such low income countries with adult literacy as high as 60 per cent, for the worldwide education drive is putting schooling out in front of other development efforts and strategies in many countries of the eastern hemisphere.

It is probably true that emergence today requires a higher level of schooling for more people than in earlier periods — even when we correct for the fact that generalizations to this effect typically make tacit assumptions of a much more rapid pace of change. The reasons for the higher schooling requirements are various, but I would note especially the importance of the transformation of communication systems and of the levels of education among the peoples of other countries with which the newly emergent must compete and interact.

The necessary minima are higher, but they are not at 80 or 90 per cent adult literacy. The extreme Addis Ababa and Karachi plans of priorities for universal primary education have no economic justification.

Most readers of this journal are probably familiar, at least to some extent, with the so-called "residual" and the efforts by Schultz and Denison to measure education's contributions to national income growth in the United States. The "residual" in this context is the part of national income growth that remains unexplained in econometric studies of aggregate inputs of labor and of physical capital as conventionally measured. Such work has come up with residuals in several European countries as well as in the United States running to over half of total income growth.

Though Schultz and Denison used quite different methods and were interested in different sets of problems, they converged in approximating what I have termed elsewhere a base-year rental-value measure of contributions of education to growth. This amounts to assuming that the income differential associated with a given differential in education in the base-year (after certain base-year adjustments for ability, parental status, etc.) will measure what the same level of education embodied in a member of the labor force will contribute to national product in other years. More technically, this is a constant marginal returns assumption. On this basis, Denison estimated that for the period 1929–1957 increases in education per worker accounted for 23 per cent of national income growth; this was about two-fifths of the residual.

It is important to remind ourselves, when considering such estimates, that they do not in fact test anything about relations between inputs and outputs. Over the period 1929–1957 in the United States, the estimates have a very reasonable look. National income rose substantially and the estimates credited education with an important part of the increase but still left a plausible amount to be explained by unmeasured improvements in organization and in the quality of physical capital. These changes all worked together. But things do not necessarily come out so neatly.

To take an extreme example, though results are very satisfactory for Russia since 1950, over the period from the middle 1920's to 1940 growth in per capita income is already over-explained by conventional inputs even without counting the substantial increases in per capita education at all. The Schultz-Denison type of treatment of education applied to this period in Russia would "explain" still more of what did *not* happen.

There is plenty of reason to expect equally nonsensical results if we apply such models over the coming decade or so in many developing countries—especially when initial education-related income differentials are large. Indeed, we are already seeing the evidence in the growing problems of urban unemployment in those countries.

Schultz and Denison do not generalize from their empirical findings for the United States. So to generalize is quite irresponsible. Nevertheless, their findings are being misapplied around the world—and sometimes by men of high levels of supposed expertise, certified under the wing of international agencies, as well as in the utterances of small politicos. The fact that what education can do depends upon other, complementary developments (as well as vice versa) is conveniently but unjustifiably ignored.

Generalization of education as a panacea can be dangerous demagoguery. It leads to wastes in the allocation of scarce resources that may impede not only economic development but even, in the longer view, the diffusion of education itself. It leads to faulty diagnoses of reasons for failures and erroneous prescriptions for their cure. Irresponsibility and organized violence among youth is aggravated by frustrations that follow upon exaggerated notions of what schools can do. Paradoxically, perhaps, the over-selling of education as an investment can aggravate the problem of discrepancies between private and social economic returns to schooling, supporting the persistence and even the expansion of socially diseconomic sinecures. Equally serious, in my judgment, is the fact that the other things education can do for individuals and societies tend to recede almost into invisibility, no matter how much we may pay them lip service.

Private Cost-Benefit Comparisons

A great cloud of smoke has been generated by the arguments over one versus another approach to planning and the associated attacks on "marginalism," "opportunity costs" and "the rate-of-return approach." There is a little real fire, to be sure, but it is not at all commensurate with the smoke. Moreover, with all this smoke in our eyes, we no longer see the important potentials in use of private cost-benefit comparisons as instruments of behavioral analysis and hypothesis-testing, quite aside from their potentials as social-accounting first approximations.

The main arguments are not Russian versus American. In fact the earliest application of this family of analytical models was probably Strumilin's 1924 studies in Leningrad—which he revised and republished in 1960. The first comparable approach was that of Ray Walsh in the United States in the early 1930's, and recent refinements of the

method and extensions of its theory and applications have been in-
the United States.

All of these studies, old and new, have in common the use of earned
income differences associated with differences in schooling as a basis
for deriving estimates of both private and societal returns or benefits.
All take into account the entire life-income stream and compare
alternative life-income streams. All include forgone student incomes
as a cost, though in some cases this is made explicit whereas in others
it slips in under other labels.

The most important Russian-American difference is in treatment
of the age-experience component of incomes, and this is where the
"rate-of-return approach" gets its label and its Western coloration.
Strumilin handled age and experience by a statistical standardiza-
tion procedure and then compared age standardized differentials in
life-income totals without discounting. The American work incorpor-
ates the interest concept as the means by which income streams with
different time sequence patterns may be compared. Recent studies
compute the "internal rate of return" that would equate the costs and
returns associated with a given increment (and type) of education.
These rates provide a simple way of comparing alternative investments.

The value of rate-of-return models for behavioral analysis of economic processes depends upon the extent to which markets are the
mechanism through which an economy is coordinated. But their usefulness in such economies does *not* depend upon the existence of pure
competition or upon allocative neutrality in government monetary and
fiscal policies, or upon the extent of participation by government in
direct production, or even on the non-existence of materials and manpower drafting.

So long as large market-coordinated sectors remain, the investment
theory and rate-of-return studies of education and their kin can serve
many purposes. They help explain income distribution patterns, they
contribute to a much sharper analysis of the various economic versus
other elements in demands for schooling and the incidence of drop-
outs, they point to inefficiencies and distortions in the allocations of
resources to schooling and in the functioning of markets for utilization of human skills. And, they open up important routes into the study
of the economics of on-the-job training and learning and the role of
enterprise (both private and public) in human resource development.

In itself any particular empirical rate-of-return estimate is of course
derived from a cross-section of education-income-age associations in a
particular time and place. As such, these are not econometric analyses

of growth. However, multiplication of such studies in time sequence in a particular country and in different countries can begin to give them growth dimensions. Demonstrations of their feasibility and some of what they can reveal for less developed countries have begun – notably for Mexico and India. Others will certainly follow.

One of the most evident and important of the contributions of rate-of-return study in a growth context is in the tracing and interpretation of various sequences in distributions of incomes and of private cost-benefit relationships as these may both condition and reflect self-investments and investments by enterprises in human resource development.

Dropping the precision, real or illusory, of rate-of-return computations and yet retaining the basic investment theory that underlies them, it is possible to extend cost-benefit assessments to incorporate a wide range of past and potential future work on opportunity perceptions and incentives as they shape and are shaped by development. Such work can be of vital importance in the advance of our understanding of the roles of education in growth. With a few important exceptions, the work in this area has suffered from interdisciplinary myopia.

Equally important is the freeing of research from the blinders too often imposed by unquestioned acceptance of particular institutional constraints. A cost-benefit approach to analysis of the history of apprenticeship in England and its metamorphosis, or to the roles of government and private enterprise in human resource development in Meiji (and modern) Japan could provide most illuminating insights. So could an incentive and response analysis of the history of development and utilization of qualified manpower in Soviet Russia, though the structuring and components of the incentive systems are different in many ways.

Complementarities and Substitutabilities

Notions about substitutabilities and complementarities permeate much of the work of both academic researchers and planning practitioners dealing with education and manpower. This is inevitable, for whether the assumptions are explicit or merely implicit they are often of key importance to understanding what and how educational endeavor, of what kinds, may contribute to growth. It is helpful to distinguish two sets of production functions:

Those that define the ranges of substitution and complementarity in the formation of human competencies.

Those that characterize actual and potential combinations of human resources with each other and with other factors in production.

Economists and many upper echelon educators would do well to pay greater heed to sociological research as it is contributing evidence concerning technical substitutabilities and complementarities in human resource development. For example:

1. The products of schools are in fact products of joint inputs of digging sticks or tractors, sanitation or hookworm, radios, advertisers, books and black magic. Strategies developed in disregard of what exists and might be done outside school doors are disregarding important complementarities and are not likely to be the most efficient. This is not just a matter of curriculum adaptation. Our ignorance is great here, but there is also much unused knowledge.

2. Substitutabilities between vocational training on the job and in school are not as extensive as is often assumed. This is the source of many fallacious educational recommendations. Schools are well adapted to prepare men to be able to learn on the job, but these two kinds and loci of learning are more often complements than substitutes.

3. Motivations and opportunity perceptions are important parameters of learning in addition to their significance with respect to school continuation rates and their choices among types of schooling. Moreover, these perceptions are usually more rational than the pronouncements of so-called experts might suggest.

4. Development of innovative behavior is a function of entire systems of opportunity and career patterns and of participation in innovative endeavor. This goes beyond the usual conception of input-output relations to other dimensions of complementarities and to negative as well as positive inputs into human development. Schools that demonstrate innovative behavior are rare indeed.

5. As Kenneth Arrow argued in his "Learning by Doing," human resource development is a function of the stimulus of continuously changing technologies, and these are associated in turn with gross rates of investment in physical capital.

Whereas planners tend to ignore significant complementarities among inputs into human resource development and to see others upside down, the biases in manpower planning all tend toward disregard of potential substitutabilities in the utilization of skills and other factors in production. This can be amply documented from manpower planning experience. It has a number of unfortunate consequences. Briefly:

1. There is circularity in identification of manpower requirements

to start with. John Vaizey developed this theme in one of his papers for an ILO conference of experts last year [1963], and it has been often recognized, but as generally ignored in practice. Empirical evidence amply demonstrates the wide range of alternatives in resource combinations among societies and over a period of time.

2. When manpower assessments are attempted in any detail, and are taken seriously, they are very likely to lead to waste in overtraining and in training that is in fact inappropriate in the light of limited resources and forgone opportunities.

3. Manpower planning creates and aggravates dysfunctional inflexibilities associated with the diploma mentality and certification for entry to various kinds of job and career channels. Here, again, a perverted conception of "standards" is involved. The idea of standards as relative and of standard raising as a process in socio-economic progress dies at birth.

4. Detailed manpower plans, if taken seriously, ramify into detailed controls that discourage innovative and adaptive behavior.

5. The fixed factor proportion approach in manpower planning is part of the rigidifying view of school systems and certifications that blocks experimentation and innovation in institutional arrangements for human resource development and in efforts within existing agencies and institutions. Partly this problem is associated with the preoccupation with schools as *the* agencies for human resource development. But it is a matter also of arrangements that encourage or discourage creative endeavors in which students and faculty participate to overcome obstacles and solve problems. The early history of American land-grant institutions demonstrates some advantages of poverty.

6. These same rigidifying assumptions (if acted upon in practice) will mean a failure to mobilize available human and other resources for education itself. Fortunately, in practice the planning models (and the "standards") break down when pressures are too great; what makes a "teacher," for example, takes on relative dimensions in the dynamics of development through time and the bottlenecks are thereby broken in some degree. But the compromises reached in this way are considerably less than second-best solutions.

7. The large-scale errors that accompany rigidified large-scale planning tend to lead to wasteful cover-up actions to conceal the errors. This is politically almost inevitable.

Some Concluding Remarks

Having aired a number of judgments and prejudices with rather unaccustomed restraint, I shall conclude in the same vein, with two propositions that I would urge upon you. The first is a special, limited one—the case for public encouragement of what I have elsewhere termed "infant-training industries." The second is more general, concerning search processes and the assessment of alternatives in a more analytical and creative approach to human resource development planning.

The most significant truth in the "technological dualism" thesis concerns gaps in development complementarities with respect to skills that are best acquired on-the-job. There can be a vicious circle problem in this. The costs of training an entire group discourage the establishment of the kinds of enterprise that would provide the learning opportunities to develop the labor force to attract the enterprise, and so forth. One alternative has been the international package transfer of entire operations, with their physical capital, directors, engineers, skilled and even semi-skilled operatives. The extent to which this has occurred historically is sometimes forgotten. Even England was helped at an early stage by importation of weavers from Flanders. Entire industries came into the United States with European migrants. Russia imported men along with equipment in the early iron works. Japan's package importations were dramatic and deliberate strategy for investment in the development of native know-how, initially at government expense. The case for one or another public program to protect and encourage training programs in industrial enterprises—and to foster establishment of such enterprises in developing countries—is a strong one provided the subsidized undertakings form the seed-bed for diffusion and multiplication of skills.

If "planning" means anything at all, it must entail some sort of selection among alternatives and logically this means some sort of social cost-benefit assessment. Otherwise what is called "planning" degenerates into mechanistic displays of technical virtuosity, at the one extreme, or of humdrum, automatic and very erroneous bookkeeping, at the other, along with "projections" that are neither accurate predictions nor plans. Attacks by some on rate-of-return estimates and opportunity costing as criteria of use in social decision making are perfectionist, on the one hand—defeatist, on the other. The tests by which these tools are pronounced inadequate could not be met by the methods used instead. Moreover, most of these criticisms take far too narrow a view of the opportunity cost concept and then throw out the whole apparatus of evaluation of alternatives just because simplistic reification is not justified.

Instead of attempting to measure what can be measured and then going on to weigh the other considerations, even the partial measures are discarded. Too often, the strait-jackets of technocratic manpower planning are donned instead. The very inelasticities that were called up to battle marginal analysis as inapplicable are argued as necessitating manpower planning in utter disregard of the fact that inelasticities virtually guarantee that unless the economy is stagnant such planning will promulgate large-scale error.

Rarely are decisions deliberately decentralized to hedge against such error. Neither are flexibility protections built into the planning of education and training to minimize lead times in specialization, to maximize readiness for training, or to locate specialized training close to the job and the employer. Moreover, having both discarded deliberative assessment of alternatives forgone and by-passed the whole problem of the continuous obsolescing of skills, technocratic planners are embarrassed by job mobility. A natural response has been costly cover-up expedients to force fits.

As I see the planner's task, it should be almost the opposite of this. The core of it is in search and comparison — in both the large and the small. The planner must search for strategic and instrumental variables and for openings in the institutional constraints — not only for direct public action but to induce development-supportive behavior over a wide range. Researchers have not yet begun to take on their share of the task and communication is hampered by theologies. Practitioner-technicians have multiplied to fill the gap. The result tends to be increased competence in the avoidance of minor mistakes — and in the repetition of big ones. The result is also bias toward more and more centralization of decisions with a concomitant routinizing of decision processes, which become automatically imitative rather than analytical, deliberate and creative.

10
Education, Politics and Development [1]

Contemporary attention is so concentrated on the role of education in development, that we are inclined to forget its capacity to stunt growth. Yet in most societies for most of recorded time, education has been a reactionary force rather than a progressive one. Education, often closely associated with religion, has tended rather to hallow antiquity than to promote innovation. It has usually been the prerogative of the ruling group, endowing them with the skills to maintain their hegemony and perpetuating the values upon which it rested.

Education, Equality, and the Spirit of Innovation

Even today it may be argued that some aspects of certain educational systems serve rather to retard than to promote growth. One authority[2] attributes much of Britain's failure to match continental economic growth to the traditionalism in which aspects of her system are shrouded.

This is not to be wondered at. The elite of the world have, for the most part, tended to be satisfied with their position of wealth, power and status. They saw no need for radical change and it would have been peculiar indeed if they had espoused a system which threatened to over-turn their world. To the modernisers, education is a means of actualizing more and more of the world's potential brain-capacity, of bringing this great semitapped resource to bear upon the world's problems. But this means disrupting the older, more static habits of mind, and it introduces competition for those who had previously derived security from those very attitudes. This was not the aspect of education that was popular in the past. It is not popular today in some

Adam Curle, "Education, Politics and Development," *Comparative Education Review,* Vol. 7 (February 1964), pp. 226–245.

countries where a ruling minority has much to lose if power—even if only intellectual power—becomes the prerogative of the majority.

But of course all learning, even the most classical scholasticism, carries the germ of growth. In some parts of the desert, seeds which have lain dormant through years of drought begin to sprout after rain. In the same way, new social circumstances can stimulate germination in even the most arid educational systems. Such a change was the emergence of nationalism in nineteenth-century Europe. The drive to establish new types of political entity was closely associated with the founding of national education systems. These systems spread to classes of people who had seldom enjoyed educational opportunities and began to give to education an innovational character. Education began to rival birth as a qualification for positions of prestige. As more people became more educated, so a technological society took shape in which education became more and more important. To some, its importance was as a steppingstone, previously not available, to authority of the traditional type. For the majority, however, education became the tool by which a new class was created which was neither aristocracy nor peasantry and in which skill and knowledge counted far more than inherited status. Thus, in Europe especially, the innovating element in education was closely associated with its social role. Where its function was egalitarian, it stimulated growth; where oligarchical, it buttressed the status quo. It need hardly be said that education's shift from a "maintaining" to a "changing" function was neither steady nor consistent. If in some of the older countries it still serves to preserve privilege, in some of the newer it helps to create a new, exclusive, and even repressive elite.

The rise of nationalism in the European sense was not, of course, the only circumstance to give new force and direction to education. In Japan, for example, the development of education in the Meiji period followed a highly realistic appraisal of the country's economic position *vis-à-vis* the Western world once that country's isolation was ended. This view was formalised in an Imperial (and therefore divine) rescript that was pursued with unquestioning loyalty. Nevertheless, even in this context, the leveling tendencies of an innovating education were not to be resisted indefinitely. For a variety of reasons, among which education must be included, the social structure of Japan is different, specifically more egalitarian, than it was at the dawn of the century.

The United States has not had such rigidities to erode. The mere removal to the New World implied, in many people, a breaking down of traditional social adhesions. However, it was essential that education should have a progressive character. There was no *status quo* to preserve; on the contrary, a new society had to be built and a diversity of peoples welded into one. Above all, perhaps, the ideology which sanctioned this welding was to be promoted and perpetuated.

Except in Japan these processes have all been relatively slow and haphazard. They have resulted from a galaxy of decisions and policies, often contradictory, frequently impractical, but having this much in common: they reflected the changing quality of society. In this respect they may be contrasted with the educational character of many Latin American states. In these countries, so prone to revolution, so dominated by the jockeying for position of dominant cliques rather than evolution, the isolation and ossification of the educational system is inseparable from the stagnation of society.

The official policy of most countries is now to support education, laying stress on its economic and cultural importance. So many clarion pronouncements to this effect have been made that no administration, whatever its inner feelings, dares lag unduly for fear of losing face. Moreover, many nations, as we shall see, have good reason for sincere belief in the role of education in their development.

Relationships Between Education, Politics, and Development

If, as already suggested, there is any relationship between an educational system capable of promoting innovation and a social move in the direction of egalitarianism, then it is reasonable to suppose that there may be various types of connection between education, development and political structure. In order to explore these connections a sample was constructed containing all those countries about which information was available regarding the percentage of national income invested in education and domestic fixed capital formation as a proportion of total expenditure on gross national product. The latter approximates what may be thought of as savings and will subsequently be referred to as such; as we shall shortly see, this was considered as the most reliable single indicator of purposefulness in development (and indeed there is a fairly close correlation in Table I between rank orders for savings and for rates of economic growth[a]). The countries concerned were also rated on a somewhat crude dichotomy of "Competitive" or "Noncompetitive" politically. For those countries for which the information was available, rank orders were given for rates of infant mortality (as possibly reflecting the same type of concern—or unconcern—for human material as does education), post-primary educational enrollment, per capita income, and rate of economic growth. (These will all be found in Table I, together with the correlations, etc. derived from them. Levels of significance will only be referred to in the text in general terms, but letters in the text refer to similarly designated calculations in Table I.)

ECONOMIC AND POLITICAL ASPECTS

TABLE I   Correlations Between Education, Politics, and Development

	Savings as percentage of GNP	Rank order of savings	Investment in education as percentage of national income	Rank order of investment in education	Infant mortality per 1,000 live births	Rank order of infant mortality	Per capita GNP, rank order	Political system	Postprimary enrollment ratio, rank order	Rate of economic growth, about 1954-59 rank order
Algeria	25.5	10.5	3.3	28	117.9	47	43	NC	39	3
Argentina	21.0	23.5	2.5	43	59.1	32	24	C	25	53.5
Australia	27.0	7	2.2	47.5	19.5	5	5	C	6	11
Austria	23.7	14	3.9	17.5	22.9	21	19	C	15	14
Barbados	27.4	6	3.4	26.5	66.4	33	–	C	–	6
Belgium	17.5	36	5.6	4	26.2	13	10	C	8	50.5
Brazil	16.3	41.5	2.6	42	170	52.5	33	C	32	19.5
Br. Guiana	22.5	17	3.7	20	60.9	34	29	NC	45	48
Burma	19.6	29.5	3.6	23.5	130.3	50	52	NC	37	29
Canada	26.5	8	4.5	10	27.3	14	2	C	11	37
Ceylon	12.8	52	4.6	8.5	57.5	31	47	NC	–	37
Chile	8.7	56	2.4	44.5	127.9	49	41	C	28	53.5
Colombia	18.4	32	2.1	49	99.8	43	28	NC	38	37
Congo (L)	18.2	33	5.1	7	143	51	49	C	49	49
Costa Rica	17.9	34	4.0	16	80.3	40	30	C	29	41
Cuba	17.6	35	3.4	26.5	–	–	26	NC	36	52
Cyprus	15.8	45	4.3	12	30.0	17	25	C	16	55.5
Denmark	19.1	31	2.9	38.5	22.5	9	14	C	13	34
Dom. Rep.	15.8	45	1.6	54.5	–	–	36	NC	40	41
Ecuador	14.1	50	1.7	53	105.8	45	37	NC	35	31
Finland	29.9	4	6.3	2	19.8	6	13	C	12	32.5
France	17.4	37	3.0	36	26.1	12	9	C	18	29
Germany (W)	24.0	12	3.6	20	33.7	22	15	C	1	7
Ghana	19.7	28	1.5	56	113.1	46	45	NC	48	8
Greece	25.5	10.5	1.6	54.5	40.1	23.5	35	NC	21	19.5
Guatemala	12.0	53	2.4	44.5	91.7	42	42	NC	41	21.5
Iceland	31.1	3	3.1	33	13.3	1	8	C	4	32.5
Israel	23.4	15	3.0	36	29.8	16	18	C	22	5

Rank order correlations

a. Savings and rate of economic growth: N = 57, Rho = .38, t = 3.00, p = .01.
b. Per capita income and percentage of national income invested in education: N = 52, Rho = .53, t = 4.41, p = .001.
c. Savings and per capita income: N = 52, Rho = .61, t = 3.00, p = .01.
d. Savings and investment in education: N = 57, Rho = .26, t = 2.00, p = .05
e. Savings and investment in education in Latin American and Caribbean countries: N = 18, Rho = .44, t = 1.96, p = .02 .
f. Investment in education and per capita income in Latin American and Caribbean countries: N = 18, Rho = .44, t = 1.96, p = .1
g. Savings and infant mortality: N = 53, Rho = .42, t = 3.29, p = .01 .
h. Per capita income and infant mortality: N= 48, Rho = .75, t = 7.68, p = .001

TABLE I Continued

	Savings as percentage of GNP	Rank order of savings	Investment in education as percentage of national income	Rank order of investment in education	Infant mortality per 1,000 live births	Rank order of infant mortality	Per capita GNP, rank order	Political system	Postprimary enrollment ratio, rank order	Rate of economic growth, about 1954–59 rank order
Italy	22.5	19.5	3.2	30	40.1	23.5	22	C	17	15.5
Jamaica	21.5	22	2.3	46	51.0	29	32	NC	–	9
Japan	31.4	2	5.7	3	28.6	15	34	C	5	2
Korea	11.4	55	4.2	14.5	63.1	36	50	NC	19	29
Luxemburg	23.3	16	1.9	51.5	31.5	20	6	C	27	44
Malta	19.8	27	4.4	11	31.4	19	–	NC	–	15.5
Mauritius	21.0	23.5	3.5	25	69.5	37	–	NC	–	57
Mexico	15.7	47	1.4	57	75.1	39	40	NC	46	24.5
Netherlands	23.9	13	5.2	6	15.4	2	17	C	10	26.5
New Zealand	19.6	29.5	3.7	20	22.8	10	3	C	9	17.5
Nigeria	11.9	54	1.9	51.5	62.9	35	51	C	50	37
Norway	27.8	5	5.5	5	18.5	4	12	C	23	47
Panama	17.0	38	3.9	17.5	57.1	30	27	NC	24	41
Peru	15.8	45	2.9	38.5	103.4	53	44	NC	34	45.5
Philippines	8.5	57	3.2	30	73.1	38	39	C	14	24.5
Portugal	16.9	39	2.0	50	88.5	41	38	NC	33	37
Puerto Rico	20.5	25	7.4	1	43.1	26	20	C	2	21.5
Rhodesia (S & N)	22.4	18	3.6	23.5	–	–	46	NC	–	12
South Africa	20.2	26	3.1	33	126.8	48	23	NC	44	13
Switzerland	21.7	21	3.1	33	20.8	7	4	C	26	26.5
Tanganyika	15.0	49	3.0	36	170	52.5	–	NC	47	36
Thailand	15.4	48	2.7	40.5	41.7	25	48	NC	31	40.5
Trinidad	31.8	1	2.7	40.5	45.4	28	–	NC	–	40.5
Turkey	16.7	40	2.2	47.5	–	–	31	NC	43	47.5
United Kingdom	16.1	43	4.2	13	22.1	8	11	C	7	13
United States	16.3	41.5	4.6	8.5	25.2	11	1	C	3	8.5
Venezuela	26.3	9	4.1	14.5	45.1	27	16	C	42	14.5

i. Savings and post-primary enrollment: $N = 49$, Rho = .59, $t = 4.39$, $p = .001$.
j. Savings and primary enrollment: $N = 57$, Rho = .43, $t = 3.54$, $p = .001$.
k. Investment in education and post-primary enrollment: $N = 49$, Rho = .61, $t = 5.08$, $p = .001$.
l. Investment in education and primary enrollment: $N = 57$, Rho = .40, $t = 3.24$, $p = .01$.
m. Per capita income and post-primary enrollment: $N = 49$, Rho = .64, $t = 5.76$, $p = .001$.
n. Infant mortality and postprimary enrollment: $N = 47$, Rho = .64, $t = 5.58$, $p = .001$.
o. Infant mortality and investment in education: $N = 53$, Rho = .34, $t = 2.34$, $p = .05$.
p. Infant mortality and rate of economic growth: $N = 53$, Rho = .03, $t = .21$, no significance .

X^3 *Distributions*

q. Political system and investment in education: $X^2 = 6.82$, $p = .01$.
r. Political system and infant mortality: $X^2 = 15.0$, $p = .001$.
s. Political system and savings: $X^2 = 2.88$, $p = .1$

The first implication is of some relationship between education and economic development. Indeed, there is a high correlation between per capita income and the percentage of national income invested in education.[b] This, of course, does not of itself demonstrate anything except that rich nations tend to spend proportionately more on education than do poor ones. It was considered that the developmental value of education, if any, might be revealed by relating both investment in education and post-primary enrollment ratios (which are generally considered as having most relevance to development capacity) to rates of economic growth. None of these relationships had any statistical significance, however. It is true that there were some countries, Japan for example, in which high investment in education and rapid economic growth appeared to be connected. But in others, such as Venezuela prior to 1958, very speedy economic expansion was matched with extremely low investment in education; in yet others, such as Norway, high investment in education accompanies negligible economic growth. In fact, the average investment in education of the ten countries which had the lowest rate of economic growth was slightly higher than that of the twelve which had the highest – and both were above the mean.

It would indeed be rash to attempt any precise definition of the role of education and development. Nevertheless, as we shall consider later, it is not inconceivable that with the global absence of relationships there are similarities, often to be defined in terms of political ideology or social structure, between education and economic development in smaller groups of countries.

A further hypothesis relating the possible innovating role of education in European industrialisation is that those countries which are striving to achieve development may be likely to invest most in education. This does not mean that they have yet achieved a high per capita income, nor does it mean that their expenditure in education is necessarily helpful to that end. It simply suggests that those countries that are attempting to innovate and to expand their economies are likely also to be those in which some egalitarian processes are at work, and which believe in the importance of human resource development.

The rate of savings is not, of course, the only means of judging the seriousness of the development intent. Another is the possession of a sound development plan, a criterion which has been employed by certain agencies in determining whether or not to give assistance. Now, however, most countries have a plan, and there is no fully adequate way of discriminating between good and bad plans. In any case it would be virtually impossible on a global scale to do what is more important, to discover whether or not the plans are being consistently followed. Another measure is to determine how much of a nation's expenditure is, from the point of view of development, frivolous. It may be argued that heavy expenditures on armed forces shows a lack of interest in development, but clearly some countries are under much greater political pressure to arm than are others. If, however, one is to take more variable criteria, an elaborate analysis of each economy would be called for, a task which would occupy a substantial volume.

A country's savings proportionate to its wealth are taken as more significant of its drive to develop rather than is its wealth.[c] It is true that it is harder for poor countries to save than for rich ones, and that therefore there is likely to be some correlation between per capita gross national product and savings. It is also true that many countries are all the wealthier simply because they *have* saved. This increases the likelihood that there will be a relationship between the proportion of savings to gross national product and the volume of that product per capita. Nevertheless, it is possible for some countries, such as Japan, to have a very high rate of savings coupled with a relatively low per capita gross national product, while others, such as New Zealand, have, relative to other countries, a much higher per capita gross national product than savings. It has been pointed out that savings will include capital expenditure on education, and thus some relationship between savings and expenditure on education is inevitable. But capital expenditure on education tends to be a small proportion of the whole. Moreover, as we shall shortly see, there are other means of relating the educational effort (for example, through school enrollments) to savings.

It was found that there was some relationship between savings and investment in education.[d] However, a smaller group of Latin American and Caribbean countries showed a higher relationship.[e] It is interesting that in this case there was a much less significant relationship between investment in education and per capita gross national product than for the whole sample.[f] This suggests that in the relatively more homogeneous sample a general principle emerges with greater sharpness.

A further assumption was made that countries which invest in the education of their people will also look after their welfare in other respects. The most obvious of these is health, and the most accurate single measure of effective work in health was taken to be the level of infant mortality. The relationship between savings and infant mortality level was significant.[g] But the relationship between high per capita income and low infant mortality was exceptionally close.[h]

It was also predicated that countries that were seriously pursuing development would have larger school enrollments, particularly at post-primary level. The relationships between both post-primary and primary enrollment and savings were significant.[i,j] The relationships, as might have been expected, were of equal significance between enrollment and investment in education.[k,l] The relationship between per capita gross national product and post-primary enrollment shows a similar situation.[m] There appears to be a slightly greater commitment to post-primary education in the countries both investing most in education and having the largest volumes of savings. Correlations not previously referred to in the text are: infant mortality level with, respectively, post-primary enrollment,[n] investment in education,[o] and rate of economic growth.[p]

The inference that may be drawn is that savings and per capita gross national product (which are clearly apt to be related in the majority of cases) are dominating factors in relation to social development (that is, education and health as understood in various ways). The hypothesis that, on a global scale, educational development is related to savings is not disproved; indeed some correlation is shown; but it is subordinated to economic indicators of a particular country's condition. The fact that educational development (both investment and enrollment) is correlated with economic growth suggests that we should view these relationships as being at least partly within the realm of what is thought to be appropriate, rather than what is more causally related (as low infant mortality and high per capita income). We are, in fact, probably justified in suggesting that countries most concerned to develop pay most attention, *inter alia,* to education.

The next assumptions to be examined were those concerning the relationship between political structure on the one hand with education, savings and health on the other. The same criteria for the latter three variables were employed, but arbitrary distinctions were made between "high" and "low." A high rate of savings was reckoned as over 17 per cent of expenditure on gross national product. A high proportion of national income invested in education was reckoned to be 3 per cent. A low rate of infant mortality was reckoned to be less than 50 per 1,000 live births. The political rating employed was adapted from Almond and Coleman.[3] Their assessments of Competitive, Semi-competitive, and Authoritarian were applied to those countries which were common to their sample and the present one. The author made his own assessment of those which were not in the Almond and Coleman sample. This, however, did not present much difficulty because the majority were European countries of obvious political complexion. In order to give adequate numbers, however, Semi-competitive and Authoritarian were taken together and referred to (as they will be throughout) as noncompetitive. The relationship between high educational investment and competitive politics was significant.[q] Even more significant was the relationship between low infant mortality and competitive politics.[r] The relationship between savings and competitive politics is, however, of borderline significance.[s] There is thus some slight suggestion that the countries which enjoy competitive political systems are also those which save most: the fact that they invest most in their human resources seems to be fairly self-evident.

When Almond and Coleman published their tentative hypothesis that there was some tendency for greater degrees of development to be associated with competitive forms of government, several critics pointed out that the richer countries could "afford" to be democratic, or that democracy was something which "happened" (though obviously not always) when nations reached a certain stage of prosperity. This might come about for all sorts of reasons. One would be, for example, that development depends greatly on the activity of entrepreneurs; that entrepreneurs are frequently persons of a class to whom society denies traditional status, which accounts for their election of entrepreneurial activity as a means of advancement; and that once they have achieved success they wish to consolidate and improve through education the position of their children. The writer suggests, however, that emphasis on education tends to be an integral part of the policy of nations which are striving for development, and that investment in education is not merely a by-product of development already achieved. (As has already been said, it is outside the present frame of reference to attempt to demonstrate the extent to which education actually promotes development.) But it is now apparent that this emphasis on education, and hence on development, is associated with political orientation. There is a relationship among nations' attitudes toward human beings, their rates of development, and the character of their politics.

Sociopolitical Typologies and Their Educational Corollaries

Despite the existence of some fairly close correlations between development effort, political system, and human resource development policy as manifested in educational statistics, a glance at the figures in Table I reveals a number of exceptions. Some of these may at least in part be accounted for by confusions in educational policy. But in others there may be factors not taken into account by the rather crude global measures employed here.

It seems possible that calculations based on Almond and Coleman's typology omit a variable that has considerable bearing upon a nation's development of its human resources. This is the extent to which it is egalitarian in the sense of offering the possibility for anyone, irrespective of class, race, tribe, religion or any other ascribed qualities, to attain the highest positions in the land, so that no one is excluded by the accident of birth from educational opportunities or from the advantages which these opportunities might bring.

A glance at various aspects of national economic and educational performance on a regional basis gives some preliminary grounds for supposing that egalitarianism is a significant feature. Of the 20 independent Latin American states, the seven that may be considered as relatively more competitive and egalitarian than the rest have an average per capita expenditure on education of $15.4 and an average per capita income of $416. The others are not only poorer (per capita income averages $191) but also spend proportionally much less on education per capita ($3.9).

TABLE II   Comparison of Egalitarian and Non-egalitarian African Countries in Terms of Per Capita Income and Educational Expenditure per Person (U.S. dollars)

Egalitarian			Non-egalitarian		
Country	Expenditure per person	Per capita income	Country	Expenditure per person	Per capita income
Egypt	5.0	133	Angola	0.3	70
Ghana	3.5	135	Ethiopia	0.6	54
Guinea	3.0	58	Liberia	1.6	103
Nigeria	1.3	70	S. Africa*	1.7	381
Tunis	6.0	131	S. Rhodesia†	1.0	134
Average	3.8	105	Average	1.0	148

*Non-European only
†Combined for S. and N. Rhodesia and Nyasaland

In Africa the five least egalitarian (and most non-competitive) countries are compared with an equal number which are egalitarian, some being competitive and others non-competitive politically (Table II).

Similar tendencies may be noted in relation to a group of Middle Eastern countries (Table III).

**TABLE III   Comparison of Middle Eastern Countries in Terms of
Per Capita Income and Proportion of the Population in
Post-primary Education**

Egalitarian			Non-egalitarian		
Country	Proportion of population in post-primary education	Per capita income	Country	Proportion of population in post-primary education	Per capita income
Cyprus	3.75	374	Iran	.63	100
Egypt	2.45	133	Iraq	1.05	195
Israel	3.14	540	Jordan	2.50	96
Lebanon	2.35	269	Saudi Arabia	.05	166
			Syria	1.69	111
			Turkey	.77	276
			Yemen‡	.04	50
Average	2.92	290	Average	.96	142

‡The per capita income for Yemen is a very crude estimate. The rather extraordinary case of
Kuwait is exluded from these comparisons. With a per capita income of $2,500 and an expenditure
on education per person of $144 – both the highest figures in the world – only .62 of the total popula-
tion are in secondary education.

It has already been noted that the countries with the highest per
capita incomes tend to have the greatest amount of education. To
that extent the above figures are not unexpected. At the same time it
has been particularly noted by one authority[4] that the economic vigor
of the egalitarian group – though lacking the oil wealth of Iran, Iraq,
and Saudi Arabia – has been closely associated with their commitment
to education.

In Europe it is significant that the three countries that perhaps most
markedly combine non-competitive politics with a non-egalitarian
society have easily the lowest per capita expenditure on education.
With a European average of $34, Greece spends $5, and Portugal
and Spain $4 each.

It is not, of course, enough to evaluate educational systems in terms
of their size and cost. In the ensuing pages an attempt has also been
made to characterize them in terms of quality and function. The
criteria for making such judgments vary so widely from one country to
another,[5] since, apart from the question of establishing standard meas-

urements, information on such vital matters as teacher qualifications is hardly ever comparable. The element of subjectivity in these judgments predominates even after the available evidence has been considered. The main qualitative issues on which the judgments were made include the existence of education planning procedures leading to presumed careful decisions, and the professionalism of the educational system, including measures taken to train and retrain teachers and to revise and evaluate the curriculum. Other factors include the presence of a unitary educational system, as is normally the case in egalitarian societies, or a dual or segregated system as it frequently is in non-egalitarian ones. Three potential roles for education are also considered: *traditional,* which implies an emphasis on maintaining the traditional values of a static society; *economic,* which implies particular emphasis on technical education and various techniques of gearing the output of the educational system to the needs of the economy for skilled personnel; *political,* which implies the use of the school system to implant a political ideology in the young. The extent to which these functions obtrude on what might be termed *general* education, or education for its own sake, depends on the socio-political context.

While most democracies (or competitive systems) espouse egalitarian ideals, many non-competitive societies also practice them. Pre-eminent among these are the Communist countries and the mass party states such as Ghana and Egypt. It is equally true that there are some countries possessing competitive political systems which are socially non-egalitarian. This occurs when elements of the social structure, despite the constitution, create barriers against the progress of certain elements of the population. India with its caste system, the segregated southern states of the United States, and Brazil, especially the northeastern region where the non-egalitarian social system is in marked contrast to the democratic constitution, may all be cited as examples of competitive political associated with non-egalitarian social systems.

There are also, of course, non-competitive political systems having nonegalitarian social structures. These include such traditional oligarchies as Ethiopia and Afghanistan as well as South Africa, Peru, Iran, and Venezuela before the last change of administration.

This suggests the existence of four types of societies: competitive egalitarian; competitive non-egalitarian; non-competitive egalitarian; and non-competitive non-egalitarian.

The first hypothesis to consider is that a country's degree of egalitarianism affects its educational policy regardless of whether or not its political system is competitive. It will not be possible to compare figures on a global basis as was done in the previous grosser calculations, since egalitarianism is a matter of degree. England, for example, is highly egalitarian when compared with many less affluent but still democratic countries. On the other hand, it is much less egalitarian than a similarly prosperous country like France. In addition, although it will be maintained that egalitarian countries spend more on education than non-egalitarian ones, comparisons can be made only among countries of approximately the same per capita income. For this reason it is seldom possible to consider both developed and underdeveloped countries in the same context. Indeed, even within Africa, non-egalitarian (but wealthy) South Africa spends four times as much on education per capita as egalitarian (but much poorer) Ghana. (It must be admitted, however, that the greater part is spent on the education of the white population.) Therefore, except for using the European Communist countries for purposes of illustration, we shall concentrate henceforth on the underdeveloped areas. Most of the sample is drawn from the countries cited in Table I, together with a few others for which it was possible to obtain the requisite information but about which data needed for previous calculations were not available.

The findings may be summarized as follows:

Politically competitive, egalitarian

This category would include the United States, Canada, New Zealand, most countries of Western Europe, Puerto Rico, Trinidad, a few — such as Uruguay — of Latin America, and a handful in Afro-Asia. Most of these nations are long established and wealthy. They have a high rate of economic growth and of post-secondary enrollment. Infant mortality is low. These are, for the greater part, the countries in which the rises of education and of industrialism were associated with nineteenth century nationalism. This is essentially the pattern of the developed nations of the world, embodying not only the values which are dear to the Western world, but the great resources with which they may be realised and maintained.

Omitting the countries of Europe, Australia and North America, it is remarkable how successful economically many of those have been in contrast to the less developed areas which are both less competitive politically and less egalitarian socially. Israel, Japan, Puerto Rico, Jamaica and Trinidad have all registered the most notable economic successes while at the same time investing heavily in education (see

Table I). Nigeria, which, apart from the more feudal Northern Region, is an outstanding example among the new African states of egalitarian democracy, has, despite its great poverty, a surprisingly satisfactory rate of economic growth. Nigeria is also remarkable for the constructive steps being taken to plan and to develop the educational system.

The educational systems of these countries have the following attributes:

1. They are unitary. That is to say, there are not parallel systems, as in South Africa, for white and black, or, as in England, for "upper" and "lower" classes. There are, of course, private schools, but these are not so numerous or so organised as to create a different educational caste.

2. They are carefully planned by specially established agencies either in the Ministry of Education, or a planning organisation, or both. This planning relates not only to the logistics of educational expansion, but also to national man-power needs.

3. Their quality is high. Teachers are adequately trained, or efforts are being made to train them; they receive in-service training; their professional associations are supported and encouraged. Adequate machinery exists for the evaluation and revision of the curriculum.

The function of these systems may be described as both general educational and economic. They promote education both for its own peculiar role of "leading out" the capacities of the individual and for its contribution to the economic needs of the country.

Politically competitive, non-egalitarian

There are perhaps greater divergencies among these countries than in any of the other types, because the extremely varied elements within their social systems give rise to the non-egalitarian elements. In India, it is the caste system which acts counter to the spirit of equality enshrined in all democratic constitutions; in Brazil, pre-revolutionary Pakistan, and several other countries, it is the oligarchy of landlords and aristocrats; in the United States South it is prejudice on the part of a dominant racial group which has also great local political power. It is, of course, extremely hard to estimate the extent to which the non-egalitarian qualities of different countries have affected national performance. It is apparent, however, that countries of this type are characterised neither by the economic progress nor the high investment in education which is common among those in the competitive egalitarian group.

The most important question to ask about any nonegalitarian society is the extent to which governmental power resides in the hands of the non-egalitarian elite. In pre-revolutionary Pakistan the elite were the rulers, and all workings of government, though democratic in constitution, were permeated with their non-egalitarian attitude until in the end democracy withered and died. An entirely different situation exists in the Philippines, where the social elite do not have political power. In the case of Pakistan a non-egalitarian society subverted the constitution, but in the Philippines the democratic constitution is not directly affected by inequalities in the society, although these to some extent impair the effectiveness of government action.

India. The population of India is so vast, and its problems are so complex, that it would be absurd to isolate the socioreligious caste factor as being pre-eminent. Nevertheless, about 40 per cent of her population is denied a large measure of social mobility because of caste, and the effects of denying to the country full use of its reservoir of brainpower cannot but be enormous. Government policy in this respect is enlightened, but in many places the barriers of caste are almost as rigid as ever. The following figures are interesting:

Economic growth rate	3.5
Per capita GNP	$72.0
Infant mortality per 1,000 live births	145.9
Post-secondary enrollment ratio	1.88
Percentage of national income invested in education	1.7
Per capita expenditure on education	$2.0

Philippines. Despite a period as an American colony and subsequent independence, the elite of Spanish descent have retained their economic if not their political supremacy. The Chinese mercantile class, by reason of its wealth, also constitutes something of a social oligarchy. The concentration of so much power in the hands of a racial minority, even on a non-political basis may be related to the educational structure. While the children of the social elite are sent to expensive schools and, in many cases, to universities overseas, the remainder attend national institutions, many of which have extremely low standards. More than 250,000 students are enrolled in higher education, an amazingly large number for a population of 28,000,000 in which there is an illiteracy rate of 30 per cent. But the social barriers mean that qualifications obtained through local education are insufficient in job competition with persons educated abroad who also have the influence of rich connections behind them.

The rate of economic growth has been adequate: 5.6 per cent, but savings have been low, 8.5. Infant mortality is 73.1 per 1,000 live births. Public expenditure on education per head is $6.

Brazil. This country contains many of the contradictions to be expected in a country in which the democratic theory of government is offset by the extreme non-egalitarian character of the social structure in certain areas. Brazil is relatively wealthy and spends a very large amount on education per head, $32 (being second only to Venezuela in Latin America), but her achievement in other respects is very mediocre:

	Brazil	World Mean
Per capital income	$262	$200
Infant mortality	120	84–5
Primary enrollment	34	42
Post-primary enrollment	1.40	2.29

Despite the differences among these countries, certain common features in their educational systems may be noted:

1. They are usually dual, there being one school structure – which is private – for the elite, and another – which is government-supported – for the masses. The quality of the education offered to the elite tends to be superior to that available to the average citizen. (This is even the case in England.)

2. Although in some countries, such as India, a consistent effort is made in planning, there is less homogeneity with regard to planning in this group than in either of the egalitarian groups.

3. These systems also vary considerably in their quality. The effectiveness of state education may be reduced by the loss of good teachers to the more lucrative private schools. In the Philippines state education is excellent but exiguous, and the use of education in job competition with the privately educated elite has led to the proliferation of a vast number of fourth-rate private institutions offering almost worthless qualifications. Thus in a rather unusual sense the non-egalitarian character of the society is associated with a disastrous decline in the standards of education.

To the general and economic functions of education must be added a third, the traditional, by which the private systems of non-egalitarian societies attempt to maintain the status and values of a particular group.

Politically non-competitive, egalitarian

Countries of this character are mostly members of the Soviet bloc and certain of the "uncommitted" Afro-Asian nations, such as Ghana, Egypt, and Indonesia.

Communist countries. Table IV compares in various economic and educational respects a group of European communist countries and an equivalent number of non-communist nations randomly selected, in that they were alphabetically the first eight European nations in a sample. (This table is intended to be suggestive rather than in any sense statistically significant.)

TABLE IV Comparison of European Non-Communist and Communist Countries

Country	Per capita GNP	Rate of economic growth	Investment in education as % of national income	Expenditure per capita on education in dollars	Proportion of total population in post-secondary education
Competitive					
Politically					
Austria	532	6.1	3.9	18	3.81
Belgium	1015	2.3	5.6	46	4.80
Denmark	913	3.8	2.9	34	3.99
Finland	941	4.0	6.3	38	4.10
France	1046	4.3	3.0	32.5	3.39
W. Germany	762	7.4	3.6	27	7.34
Greece	239	5.7	1.6	5	3.17
Iceland	1146	4.0	3.1	50	5.92
Average	824	4.7	3.8	31	4.57
Communist					
Bulgaria	285	9.5	3.9	30	2.90
Czechoslovakia	543	7.5	–	53	1.88
E. Germany	[984]	9.7	5.0	78	1.38
Hungary	387	5.9	2.9	18	1.51
Poland	468	8.8	4.8	19	2.41
Rumania	320	10.3	–	28	1.82
U.S.S.R.	682	10.5	7.1	120	4.35
Yugoslavia	297	10.7	2.8	10	4.58
Average	496	9.1	4.4	45	2.60

The most outstanding inference from Table IV is the exceedingly high growth rate of the communist countries (the average rate, for what this is worth, is approximately double that of the non-communist sample). Next, the communist countries are considerably poorer per capita than the rest. The U.S.S.R., most powerful of the communist countries, is out-ranked in wealth by seven of the other group. Nevertheless, so far as these limited figures can tell us, proportionate investment in education is higher. However, the communist countries, with the exception of Czechoslovakia, East Germany, and U.S.S.R., were extremely "undereducated" until recently, and except in U.S.S.R. and Yugoslavia, post-primary enrollments do not compare with those of the other sample.

In view of the close correlation, on a global scale, between per capita income and expenditure on education it is perhaps more significant to contrast in Table V these communist countries on a basis of paired comparisons with those in the non-communist world which are closest to them in per capita income.

Since, as we have already seen, per capita income correlates highly with these variables, it might have been expected that scores would have been evenly distributed, as they are indeed for health. It is hard not to draw the conclusion that this type of country places great value on education, both as a political and an economic tool. It is hard to say how far this commitment to education is responsible for their high rate of economic growth. It is interesting that only the lowest two in terms of rate of growth are exceeded by their country of comparison. In each case the latter has, for the non-communist world, a high rate of growth; in fact Israel ranks among the first three or four. It is interesting that infant mortality figures do not follow the same pattern and would not appear, in the communist countries, to be subject to the same influences that have affected high expenditure on education.

The case of China is interesting, even though reliable statistics on a number of matters unfortunately are not available. Starting from approximately the same economic base as India, per capita income has increased between 1950 and 1959 by 100 per cent: in India by only 12–15 per cent.[6] (The Chinese rate of growth has, indeed, been one of the fastest in the world: 12.1). Over the same period absolute real investment in China was quintupled, and in India only doubled. These differences can, of course, be explained in many ways. But in no sense can they be said to represent any insuperable superiority of the democratic system, especially if flawed by inequalities. It is noteworthy that the immense economic growth has been accompanied by an

TABLE V   Non-Communist and European Communist Countries: Paired Comparisons*

Country	Per capita income	Rate of economic growth	Expenditure per capita on education (in dollars)	Infant mortality per 1,000 live births
Bulgaria	285	9.5	30	41.5
Turkey	276	5.9	10	(50)
Czechoslovakia	543	7.5	53	22.7
Israel	540	9.0	25	29.8
E. Germany	[984]	9.7	78	38.8
United Kingdom	998	2.6	36	22.1
Hungary	387	5.9	18	43.9
South Africa	381	6.3	10	107.0
Poland	468	8.8	19	54.9
Italy	442	6.0	16	40.1
Rumania	320	10.3	28	71.0
Colombia	330	3.7	12	99.8
U.S.S.R.	682	10.5	120	35.0
Netherlands	708	4.4	32	15.4
Yugoslavia	297	10.7	10	82.2
Malaya	298	2.2	8	68.9

Summary	Highest expenditure on education	Highest rate of economic growth	Lowest infant mortality rate
Communist countries	8	6	4
Non-communist countries	0	2	4

*It must be remembered that the communist system of accounting presents some difficulties in comparison with other non-communist nations. Possibly the similarities in per capita income would not be so great, nor the differences in growth rates so marked, if identical systems of accounting were employed. The per capita income figures for East Germany are highly tentative. The figures for per capita expenditure in the United Kingdom apply only to England and Wales. The infant mortality figures for Turkey are estimated.

equally dramatic educational expansion. School enrollment increased between 1949 and 1959 from 25 to 171 million. Plans are made involving the enrollment of 300,000,000 persons in education institutes (with an increasing emphasis on higher education) and many millions more in literacy classes. [7]

Both Russians and Chinese, but especially the latter, treat education with great seriousness as an economic, and still more as a political, weapon. The Russians spend more per person on education than any other country except Kuwait. Specific political outlook is associated with both rapid economic expansion and a concentration on education. It would appear that the Western nations have something of a lead in size of both their economies and their educational systems, but are fairly rapidly losing it. The problem is whether the non-communist nations, and in particular the underdeveloped ones with which we are concerned, can match the vigor of the communist countries without copying their ideology.

Non-communist countries. Ghana is an egalitarian, non-communist nation. Since this country achieved a measure of self-government in 1952 (it became fully independent five years later), the most strenuous efforts have been made to expand education, as the following figures [8] indicate:

Enrollment in government and assisted:	1951	1960
Primary schools	234,000	477,000
Middle schools	66,175	147,000
Secondary schools (Excluding Achimota)	2,776	15,119

Recurrent expenditure on education increased from £G 1,561,304 in 1951 to £G 6,471,838, while expenditure by local authorities grew from £G 700,691 in 1954 to £G 1,592,143 in 1956. The enrollment in teacher-training colleges grew from 1,437 in 1954 to 4,055 in 1958. In 1961 attendance at primary school was made compulsory and, though enrollment figures are not available, it was anticipated that the first year intake of 124,000 in 1960 would be more than doubled to give a total of around 744,000 in primary education.

Although these figures cannot be correlated with significant changes in rate of economic growth or infant mortality, they indicate a surprisingly vigorous attempt to expand education.

Per capita income, $135, is the highest in Africa, except for South Africa.

The education systems of these countries tend to be:

1. Unitary
2. Carefully planned and closely geared to the country's need for skilled manpower
3. Of high quality

Although general education is not neglected, there is greater stress on the economic function than in any other type, while the political role of education is also given prominence.

Non-competitive politically, non-egalitarian

These cover a wide range, from such "old-fashioned" dictatorships as Paraguay and the Dominican Republic under Trujillo, to the "traditional oligarchies" of Afghanistan and Ethiopia, by way of "colonial and/or racial oligarchies" such as South Africa, Angola, and, to some extent, Peru. They vary greatly in the size of the ruling group (in South Africa, for example, it is 20 per cent of the total population; in the Dominican Republic, it was a single family with its toadies); and the political structure (again in South Africa, there is political competition *within* the ruling white population; in others there is complete autocracy). There are also a number of countries whose status is in some doubt, which are gradually moving in the direction of genuine democracy coupled with a truly open society. A surprisingly large number of the non-competitive, non-egalitarian societies, including many which are not classified by Almond and Coleman as "colonial or racial oligarchies," are divided along lines of race. These include many Latin American countries, Sudan, Afghanistan, Ethiopia, Liberia (in the sense that the ruling group is of an entirely different background and stock, though negro, from the rest), Nepal, Burma, and several others. Most of these countries are extremely poor. This is not surprising: they are countries which have neglected their human resources because they have, for the most part, been completely unconcerned about them. Though this is changing now in places, one can not make up rapidly for such neglect.

The countries in this category as a whole accept, for a variety of reasons ranging from Ethiopian traditionalism to the sophisticated philosophy of Apartheid, the principle of social difference based on race, class, caste, or language. Those in the ruling group are not prepared to accord to those they rule full political rights or social opportunities for educational betterment. Their position is extremely logical, if one assumes the attitude of a group which is prepared to keep another in subjection. Education makes people restless and dissatisfied if they are in a position of inferiority: only the rich and powerful whom it confirms in their authority can receive education unmoved. Moreover, a ruling group can live extremely well on the sweated labor of even completely ignorant workers. The nation as a whole would no doubt profit if the labor force were better equipped, but national considerations are not necessarily the concern of the oligarchy, which is contented with things as they are and fears that a change would diffuse economic benefits and education more widely, thus weakening their position.

South Africa has perhaps grappled with situations with more ingenuity, albeit perverted, than any other nation. It has even recognised the importance of certain levels of education for the Bantu. Per capita gross national product in South Africa ($381) is double that of any other African nation and well above the world mean. South Africa and Venezuela under the . . . Jimenez dictatorship are the only countries in this category to have achieved real prosperity. Both have had considerable mineral resources. South Africa has the additional advantage of long settlement by a vigorous and large white population, and a generally well-endowed terrain. But although South Africa is a prosperous country, as shown by per capita income and the growth rate of 6.3, her wealth is ill-distributed, as might be expected from her political structure. This is dramatically illustrated by contrasting infant mortality rates between the white population (27.6) and the black (126.8). The rates of post-primary enrollment for the population as a whole (0.71) are also well below the world mean. This is especially significant in view of the fact that the white proportion of the population is as intensively educated as almost any other in the world: 1 in every 75 white South Africans is receiving higher education, as compared with 1 in every 250 in Britain.

A few other countries in this category have achieved considerable economic growth, though not yet a high per capita income, through mineral extraction. These include the now disintegrated Central African Federation and the Congo in the days of Belgian colonization. Territories like Angola, which lacked mineral resources, have remained miserably poor and pitiably ignorant in spite of centuries of colonization. The literacy rate in Angola is about 5 per cent and the primary enrollment ratio about 1 per cent — perhaps the lowest in the world. We should distinguish, however, between countries settled permanently by Europeans having a personal interest in promoting prosperity for themselves, and those temporarily colonized by officials and others chiefly concerned to maintain order and to collect taxes. In the former there has often been an almost inevitable diffusion of some prosperity—the South African Bantu are richer than those of neighboring countries.

Venezuela provides an interesting example of the changes related to a dramatic reversal of political power. When in 1958 President Betancourt replaced Jimenez, the policy toward education almost immediately altered radically. Even more interesting is the change in the health picture (Table VI).

TABLE VI   Venezuela: Changes in Educational and Health Expenditure

	1956	1957	1958	1959	1960	1961
GNP	17,930	20,506	22,488	23,176	–	–
Savings	28.89	26.52	28.99	26.30	–	–
Per cent of national income spent on education	–	–	–	1.1	–	4.1
Expenditure per head on education (local currency)	–	–	28	58	117	117
Expenditure per head on education (U.S. dollars)	–	8.4	–	35	70	70
Infant mortality	67.3	65.8	63.9	55.3	45.1	–

Only careful analysis of future trends will suggest possible ways in which the alteration of social policy has affected the economy. It is clear, however, that such alterations are inextricably associated with political changes.

The thesis that these countries spend little on education should be tempered by three observations:

They may indulge in educational "conspicuous consumption." Trujillo, for example erected splendid university buildings, a great museum, and other educational edifices. These, however, contributed little to the educational needs of his people, serving only as show pieces to prove to visiting dignitaries that he was addicted to culture.

Popular pressure, through U. N. conferences and other means, can stimulate some expansion of education. Here we can only try to estimate how sincere and effective this has been.

Statistics may sometimes show high expenditure on education. In some cases these are known to have been falsified.

To sum up, countries of this type cannot be expected to invest much in education. Most are very poor, and the ill-distributed wealth of a few of them comes from some particular national advantage, such as oil or other natural resources.

General features of the educational systems of these societies are:

1. They are dual in the wealthier countries, such as South Africa and Peru. In the poorer nations, such as Afghanistan, there is virtually no education except for the scions of the elite.

2. There is little planning of education as a whole.

3. The quality of education tends to be low, except sometimes for what is given to the elite minority.

The function of education in these countries is mainly traditional, though in some respects and in some cases attempts have been made to introduce an economic function within this general pattern. For example, the Belgian regime in the Congo organized relatively wide-spread education of a simple technical type (but virtually nothing above this level) in the dual attempt to maintain stability and to ex-ploit the country's resources.

The characteristics and functions of educational systems in the four socio-political systems considered in this section are summarised in Table VII.

TABLE VII   Summary of Characteristics and Functions
of Educational Systems

Type of political system	Form of educa-tional system	Planning approach	Quality	Function
Competitive Egalitarian	Unitary	Strong	Good	Economic
Competitive Non-egalitarian	Dual	Fairly strong	Varied, usually good for elite	Economic; Traditional
Non-competitive Egalitarian	Unitary	Strong	Good	Economic; Political
Non-competitive Non-egalitarian	Dual, or Unitary if only for elite	Weak	Poor	Traditional

Education and Development in Egalitarian and Non-egalitarian Societies

Up to this point, both developed and underdeveloped countries have been considered. Now an attempt will be made to see whether the typology developed in the last section has any significance when applied to a sample composed only of underdeveloped countries (that is, one excluding the nations of Western Europe, North America and Australia. The sample is shown in Table VIII: specific calculations are referred to, as previously, by letters in the text).

TABLE VIII   Relation Between Political Systems and Development

Non-egalitarian Countries

Country	Planning organiza-tion	Quality & efficiency	Per capita expenditure in U.S. dollars	Per capita income in U.S. dollars	Percentage of national income in education
Afghanistan	1	1	1	54	0.2
Algeria	3	3	–	–	3.3
Angola	1	1	–	–	–
Brazil	1	2	32	262	2.6
British Guiana	1	1	–	–	3.7
Burma	1	1	1	52	3.6
Ceylon	1	2	5	122	4.6
Chile	1	2	10	180	2.4
Colombia	2	2	14	330	2.1
Dominican Republic	1	1	4	205	1.6
Ecuador	2	2	3	204	1.7
Ethiopia	1	1	0.6	54	–
Greece	1	2	5	239	1.6
Guatemala	2	2	3	179	2.4
India	3	2	1	72	1.7
Iran	1	1	5	100	–
Iraq	1	1	11	195	–
Korea	1	1	2	80	4.1
Laos	1	1	2	–	–
Liberia	1	1	1	103	–
Mauritius	2	2	–	–	3.5
Mexico	2	2	5	178	1.4
Pakistan	2	1	0.6	56	1.2
Panama	2	2	13	350	3.9
Philippines	3	2	6	201	3.2
Portugal	1	2	4	201	2.0
Rhodesia & Nyasaland	1	1	–	–	3.6
Saudi Arabia	1	1	5	166	–

TABLE VIII   Continued

Non-egalitarian Countries

Country	Planning organiza- tion	Quality & efficiency	Per capita expenditure in U.S. dollars	Per capita income in U.S. dollars	Percentage of national income in education
Turkey	1	2	5	276	2.2
Vietnam	1	1	2	133	—
Yemen	1	1	—	—	—
Average	1.45	1.55	5.18	166	2.57

Egalitarian Countries

Country	Planning organiza- tion	Quality & efficiency	Per capita expenditure in U.S. dollars	Per capita income in U.S. dollars	Percentage of national income in education
Argentina	2	2	9	374	2.5
Barbados	3	3	—	—	3.4
Bolivia	1	1	1	66	—
Costa Rica	2	2	14	307	4.0
Cuba	2	2	18	361	3.4
Cyprus	3	3	17	374	4.3
Congo (L)	1	1	4	98	5.1
Egypt	3	2	6	131	—
Ghana	2	2	4	135	1.5
Israel	3	3	28	540	3.0
Jamaica	2	2	—	—	2.3
Japan	3	3	16	240	5.7
Malta	2	3	—	—	4.4
Mexico	2	2	5	178	1.4
Nigeria	3	1	0.7	21	1.9
Puerto Rico	3	2	—	—	7.4
Tanganyika	2	1	0.6	61	3.0
Trinidad	2	3	—	—	2.7
Tunis	2	2	7	133	3.4
Venezuela	2	2	39	762	4.1
Average	2.25	2.10	11.74	255	3.53

X^2 Distributions
t.   Political system and combined rating for planning and educational quality: $X^2 = 15.23$, p $= .001$
u.   Political system and investment in education: $X^2 = 2.18$, p $= > .10$
v.   Political system and per capita expenditure on education: $X^2 = 4.37$, p $=$ between .05 and .02
w.   Political system and per capita income: $X^2 = .41$, p $= > .90$

Working with the relatively limited sample of underdeveloped countries, it has not been possible to explore the four-fold division of systems with extensive statistics. There has been only a handful of competitive countries which were non-egalitarian, and of non-egalitarian
ones which were competitive politically. The calculations which follow
refer, therefore, only to a straight comparison between egalitarian and

non-egalitarian systems. When the politics of the newer African states are consolidated and their social policies have been continuous long enough, however, they may yield a body of statistics that will enlarge evidence about the non-competitive egalitarian group. Such movements as the Alliance for Progress might also introduce egalitarian opportunities to Latin America, without eliminating the old guard, thus enlarging the competitive non-egalitarian group. It may be observed *en passant* that one of the problems of this type of study is the recent spread of decolonisation. Almond and Coleman[9] based some of their calculations on three colonial groups – French West Africa, Central Africa, and Ruanda-Urundi. These three have now become sixteen sovereign states whose political status is entirely different even though their economic situation has scarcely changed. Likewise, Hagen[10] correctly revises one of Coleman and Almond's tables by classing Venezuela as politically competitive rather than authoritarian; but the statistics he employs relate to the period when Venezuela was still under a dictatorship.

The dichotomy of egalitarian and non-egalitarian is frail, especially when an attempt is made to evaluate quality in defining educational variables. For present purposes this has been done by awarding scores on a three point scale (good, average, poor) to each country for planning (that is, capacity for rational decision-making) and quality (that is, teacher training competence and curriculum regulation):

	Planning; average score	Quality; average score
Egalitarian countries (20)	2.20	2.10
Non-egalitarian countries (30)	1.44	1.47

The egalitarian countries' scores are very significantly higher than those of the non-egalitarian groups.

It was clearly necessary, however, that these highly personal ratings should be measured against something more tangible. For this purpose, two measures were employed: the amount spent per capita on education, and the proportion of national income invested in education. Although there may be exceptions, it is in general to be expected that countries spending more on education will have better educational systems. The mean for investment in education in all underdeveloped countries of the world was calculated (3 per cent) and the egalitarian and non-egalitarian groups compared in this respect.

Proportionately more of the egalitarian than of the non-egalitarian countries have investments above the world mean, but the difference is of marginal statistical significance.[u] However, there is a fairly marked difference between the average percentages invested: egalitarian countries, 3.58; non-egalitarian countries, 2.62.

In terms of money spent per capita, the egalitarian group is superior. Taking the world mean for underdeveloped countries ($6) the proportion of egalitarian countries above the mean is significantly higher than in the non-egalitarian group.[v] Average expenditures also show a marked difference: egalitarian countries, $11.62; non-egalitarian countries, $5.70.

The significance of this finding might be largely vitiated however, if the egalitarian countries proved to be much wealthier than the rest, because their expenditure might be a function of wealth rather than of their socio-political structure. For this calculation the world mean of $200 was employed since it provided a relatively even division of the sample. The distribution of per capita income between egalitarian and non-egalitarian countries proved, however, to be random[w] which suggests that egalitarianism, rather than national wealth, is the important corollary of high per capita expenditure on education. It must be recognised that the average per capita income is higher in egalitarian than in non-egalitarian societies, $255 against $173, but this seems not seriously to weaken our contentions concerning the important role of egalitarianism in the promotion of education. Indeed, it is plausible that egalitarian societies also lay more firmly the groundwork for economic growth.

It is not easy to offer any firm evidence for the various orientations of education which are mentioned. Traditionalism can only be assessed through such unquantifiable means as a study of the textbooks, curriculum and similar features.

The political role of education can be judged by a considerable body of literature on the egalitarian and non-competitive societies, but this too is hardly amenable to statistical treatment. It is possible, however, to obtain some support for assessment of the economic role of education. The percentage of the population enrolled in secondary vocational education was taken for all those countries in Table VIII for which it was available (15 egalitarian and 24 non-egalitarian). The non-egalitarian percentage was .14; the egalitarian was .80 — more than five times as much.[11]

Notes

[1] This is good evidence that affluent countries spend more on education than poor ones, but this by no means indicates that they are rich *because* of their investment in education. One might as well argue that rich owe their wealth to the fact that they spend more than poor ones on champagne and fur coats for their wives. In order to demonstrate that education has contributed to national wealth we may either follow the con-

troversial approach of T. W. Schultz, which is acceptable neither to all economists for one set of reasons, nor to all educators for another; or we may correlate educational expansion with subsequent changes in the rate of economic growth over a period of time (assuming, of course, that it will take some years for education to achieve an economic impact). We may be able to trace this relationship in certain countries, and even in groups of countries at specific periods. For example, there is a positive correlation at the .02 level between the size of post-primary enrollment of 36 countries in 1938 and their rate of economic growth during the next decade. This tendency is not reproduced, however, during the post-war period, during which somewhat unreliable statistics are available for a much larger and more economically varied group of nations. This is obviously not to say that education has had no positive impact on the economy, but to suggest that it is very hard to isolate specifically educational factors from political, social, economic and other elements in the growth process. But it must be admitted in addition that some forms of education are far more conducive to development than others.

[2] John Vaizey, *Education for Tomorrow* (London: Penquin Books, 1962), pp. 21–29.

[3] James S. Coleman, "Conclusion: The Political Systems of the Developing Areas," and Appendix; Gabriel A. Almond and James S. Coleman, eds., *The Politics of the Developing Areas* (Princeton, N. J.: Princeton University Press, 1960), pp. 532–582.

[4] A. J. Meyer, *Middle Eastern Capitalism: Nine Essays* (Cambridge: Harvard University Press), pp. 1–17.

[5] For a useful discussion of this difficulty see *Manual of Educational Statistics,* UNESCO, 1961.

[6] These figures are taken from Wilfred Malembaum and Wolfgang Stolper, "Political Ideology and Economic Progress," *World Politics,* Vol. XII, No. 3 (April 1960), pp. 413–421.

[7] These figures are taken from John Wilson Lewis, *Education and the Chinese Polity: Themes in Development* (mimeographed paper prepared for the Lake Arrowhead Conference on Education and Political Development, June 25–29, 1962), pp. 19, 21.

[8] These figures are taken from an unpublished work on the development of the labor force in Ghana by David Williams.

[9] Almond and Coleman, *op. cit.,* p. 542.

[10] Everett E. Hagen, "A Framework for Analysing Economic and Political Change," Robert E. Asher, *et al., Development of the Emerging Countries: An Agenda for Research* (Washington: The Brookings Institution, 1962).

[11] This article is taken from a paper prepared for a seminar conference held at Boston University during the summer of 1963, sponsored by the Comparative Administration Group of the American Society for Public Administration. Save where specific mention is made to the contrary, statistical material is derived from the following sources:

Post-primary school enrollment: *UNESCO, World Survey of Education III, Secondary Education* (New York: International Document Service, 1961).

Primary School enrollment: *UNESCO, World Survey of Education II, Primary Education* (Paris: UNESCO, 1958).

Educational Administration, different system: *UNESCO, World Survey of Education, Handbook of Educational Organisation and Statistics* (Paris: UNESCO, 1955); also *Educational Planning* (International Bureau of Education and UNESCO, publication No. 247, 1962).

Infant mortality: *Demographic Yearbook, 1961* (New York: United Nations, 1962).

Investment in Education (percentage of national income devoted to education): *Basic Facts and Figures, 1961* (Paris: Unesco, 1962).

Savings (the proportion of gross fixed capital formation to expenditure on gross national product, mostly for 1960, but in a few instances for 1959 or 1958): *Yearbook of National Accounts Statistics, 1961* (New York: United Nations, 1962).

Rate of Economic growth: *Yearbook of National Accounts Statistics, 1961, op. cit.* These are mostly given in the yearbook over a period of about 1954–1959. Where not given, they have been calculated for the same period.

Per capita income: Norton Ginsberg, *Atlas of Economic Development* (Chicago and London: University of Chicago Press, 1961).

Per capita expenditure on education: *International Yearbook of Education, Vol. XXII, 1960* (Paris: UNESCO; and Geneva: International Bureau of Education).

Political systems: categories derived from Gabriel A. Almond and James S. Coleman, eds., *The Politics of the Developing Areas* (Princeton, N. J.: Princeton University Press, 1960).

In a few instances, for example, in the case of information regarding Venezuela, data have been obtained from earlier issues of one or other of the periodical United Nations publications.

PART III

Technical Assistance —
The Problem of Transfer

T he process of successfully transmitting the knowledge and the experiences of one culture to another is extremely complex. It requires a deep understanding of the people to be educated. In the first selection in this section, Margaret Mead discusses the kind of cultural insights that must be attained if education is to take place across cultural boundaries. She points out that at one time the Japanese had so sensitized their children to feel that any overt failure was an acute disgrace that teachers had to give every child a prize. This example shows a relatively simple and ultimately manageable aspect of the problem of transfer. The complexity of the problems related to cultural change becomes more evident as we look at another aspect of it. Much of the discussion of cross-cultural contact is based on the assumption that people in the new nations are members of homogeneous, relatively untouched cultures. In reality, more and more people in the world are being drawn away from their traditional cultural roots. Dr. Mead warns that exposing children of rootless parents to modern education before they have been provided with experiences that help them achieve personal integration and group belongingness may seriously damage their personalities.

The impact of Western culture on the traditional cultures of the developing nations is well known. It has disrupted traditional patterns and caused new configurations to take place. In the second selection, P. C. C. Evans defines two cultural patterns that American educators encounter in East Africa — one pattern is distinctly African and tends to obtain more particularly in the lower socio-economic levels, and the other is middle-class and, although still very African, tends to be influenced deeply by British social and institutional norms. Upon encountering both of these unfamiliar patterns, Americans must often come to terms with situations that conflict with their values. The resolution of these conflicts constitutes one of the major problems involved in the transfer of learning across cultural boundaries.

The third selection, written by Arthur Niehoff and J. Charnel Anderson, focuses on the specific factors involved in the dynamics of cultural change. Identifying such factors as flexibility, timeliness, and continuity, the authors formulate a hypothesis of change. The value of their formula is two-fold: it assists in the understanding of cultural change around the world, and it provides technicians with an instrument for plotting the process through which innovations can be successfully incorporated into the local culture.

The first three articles in this section demonstrate the need for securing suitably qualified individuals to work in overseas programs. In the fourth selection, Anne Winslow discusses the numerous problems encountered in recruiting, selecting, and training personnel for overseas duty. Not the least of these problems is an understanding of the personal qualities that instigators of cultural change should have. She says, "The preparation of laundry lists of desirable qualities has become a favorite occupation, but, alas, all that emerges is an ideal man who does not exist." The seriousness of these problems becomes more apparent as it is realized that, in the final analysis, the capacities of the staff determine the success of overseas projects.

The last two articles deal with the re-entry crisis experienced by many technicians upon return to their home country after working overseas. Relatively little is known about this phenomenon that some anthropologists refer to as "cultural shock in reverse." Richard Stolley reports that virtually all Peace Corps returnees experience this difficulty in varying degrees.

Much of the complexity related to the problem of cultural transfer results from the nature of change itself. As one Peace Corps volunteer said, "Rapid change exists only in rhetoric." However, progress is being made toward solving these problems. American universities are extending their area-studies programs to include the new nations of Africa, Asia, and Latin America, and psychologists are conducting extensive research into the learning and the motivational problems that occur in cross-cultural educational situations. Both trends hold great promise for resolving international education's most perplexing challenge—the problem of transfer.

11
Education and the
Problem of Transfer
in Developing Societies

This discussion will be confined to the education of those peoples in dependent countries whose tradition is either non-European, because it stemmed instead from one or more of the other great cultural stocks of the world, or because it is primitive, that is, preliterate, or because the participation of the people in European traditions is of relatively recent date. Thus the people of Indo-China, apart from the French metropolitan residents, would belong to category one, the people of New Guinea to category two, and the inhabitants of the Virgin Islands, of the Philippines, and of the Seychelles to the last category. Problems of education in all of these areas are furthermore inextricably bound up with the problem of education in the ideas and techniques of Western culture, whatever the goal of the education may be. Among the possible goals we can distinguish several: (1) the education of the peoples of dependent countries so that they become world-mobile in one generation, (2) the education of dependent peoples so that over several generations, and by gradual stages of regional participation and growing political responsibility, they finally become world-mobile and able to participate on a world level (It should be noted that the people of countries studied which we now call independent need a corresponding training for resolving their national demands in the interest of world goals.), and (3) the education of such peoples only to the point where they may be successfully exploited by more advanced

Margaret Mead, "Professional Problems of Education in Dependent Countries," *Journal of Negro Education,* Vol. 15 (Summer 1946), pp. 346–357.

economies while they perform relatively simple agricultural or extractive economic functions, subsidiary to the more advanced economy of the countries upon which they are dependent. A fourth possible goal—to leave those groups who have minimal natural resources and which are not of a size or in a position to add to the labor supply of the world, relatively untouched—is so out of the line of the contemporary climate of opinion as not to be worth considering. The third goal defines fairly accurately the past experience and present state of many peoples, the inhabitants of the East Indies, of parts of Africa, of Malaya. It also, however, is incompatible both with world demands and with the demands of the people themselves, enough of whom have been educated in the philosophy of the West so as to be no longer content with such a subsidiary position. The second goal—of gradual change—has much to recommend it to serious students of society who recognize the extreme penalties inherent in too rapid social change, but it recommends itself not at all to the educated leaders of the peoples concerned, and finds little general support in the United States where there is a characteristic desire to hurry the process of maturation—of children, or colonial peoples, or of institutions.[1] In full recognition that the first alternative is the most difficult and poses the most serious problems to the professional educator, it seems nevertheless necessary to consider it as the goal toward which our educational techniques must be aimed, in full recognition of the very poor chance of complete success.

World mobility and world participation in one generation, as an aim for even a section of the peoples whom we are discussing, involves: (1) ability to speak, read, and write some "world language," that is, a language which will make participation in international conferences and free movement about the world possible; (2) a grasp of the framework of Western economy, use of money and credit, and a recognition of the implications of living in a contract rather than a status society; (3) a modicum of cross-cultural sophistication which will enable the individual concerned to work among people with different codes and standards without taking offense or becoming disoriented; (4) a working acceptance of the state of mind roughly summarized in such phrases as "the scientific attitude"[2] with an ability to act within its premises in public interpersonal contexts, political, economic, and technological; (5) some conceptualized view of history which makes it possible to deal with the time perspectives (toward the past and the future)[3] of the great civilizations; (6) a sufficient independence of the living mesh of his own culture to be able to exist outside it without crippling nostalgia. This last requirement is primarily necessary for mobility in space, the others apply to any attempt to deal on a face-to-face basis with members of Western culture, either in the home country or abroad.

In attempting to achieve these objectives, there are two conspicuously divergent methods which have been used. The first and simpler method is to transport individuals from the dependent country to some center where Western-world culture is dominant and expose them, as intimately and intensively as possible, to that culture in its formal and informal educational aspects. History is studded with instances in which individuals from exceedingly primitive settings have been reared among people of another and more complex civilization and have successfully mastered its intricacies. The problem of inducting a juvenile member of any people on earth, with the possible but not certain exception of the pygmies, into English or German, or French, or Russian or Chinese culture, is not a serious one. The real problem lies in so selecting the time for temporary expatriation, and the time of repatriation, that the individuals so educated are able to maintain effective contacts with *both* worlds, to speak the new language without forgetting or despising the old, to subdue both of his possible nostalgias in the periods when they are inappropriate, and to become bicultural rather than de-culturized—the commoner result. This educational method, in which the technical problems lie not in the country of education, but in the timing and choice of pupils and in the provision which is made for their reintegration into their own societies has, however, serious drawbacks. It is primarily appropriate to an aristocratic people, and has been most successfully applied where both the metropolitan power concerned and the people of the dependent country were aristocratic in practice, or at least in theory. Whether one considers the roster of African and Asiatic students who have attended Oxford and Cambridge, or the carefully educated sons of the Javanese aristocrats, the importance of the aristocratic element is obvious. If only one party to the educational plan is aristocratic, it is still possible to make an initial success of such an educational plan, as the aristocrats in the dependent country will accept a scheme which takes their nobility away—as a method of selection—or the aristocracy in the metropolitan country will accept a scheme which selects, for special training, the most able and gifted among a casteless and rankless people. Lacking an aristocratic component, the system becomes unworkable for the very reason which makes it relatively untenable in the world today, that it is incompatible with the tenets of political democracy. Americans are particularly unqualified to appreciate the high education which a few Javanese have received in Holland, or a few West Africans in

England, while the mass of the people remained relatively uneducated and without educational opportunities.[4]

In fact the requirement of preparation for world mobility in one generation is a different one entirely and does not accept the education of a few Burmese gentlemen in the ultimate refinements of English university life as substitute for popular education out of which any individual with ability may receive enough education to make him able to move about and function in the world. We may safely say that the framework within which the article is written, that is an acceptance of the present dominant world opinion with its emphasis upon opportunity for the common people, demands more than the type of selective educational expatriation of the leadership elements in a population, no matter how careful the selection, how adapted the education, and how skillful the reintegration of the privileged individuals so educated. The experience of several centuries in the occidentalization of oriental and primitive peoples is merely valuable data in any controversy which would deny the ability of a people to take on, as individuals, any culture to which they are exposed at a sufficiently impressionable age.

The basic problem of education in dependent countries has become that of devising a system of education which can be applied, on a universal scale, inside the country. While this education may have to rely initially on immigrant teachers, it cannot rely primarily on emigration of students. Within the culture itself—where the very cycle of the seasons and the fluctuations of the weather, the flowers by the wayside, and food that is eaten, all reinforce the existing culture—a system of education must be devised which will give the possibility for every child with normal intelligence within it, finally to arrive, within his single educational lifetime, at the six abilities listed above. The idea of pure number will have to be taught, though the language itself may use piecewords, as in Malay, with different numerical particles depending upon the type of object counted. The potentiality for understanding modern credit systems must be developed while the local valuables are bargained for as desirable, individually, in themselves; and a capacity to discount cultural differences in manners must be developed among the exacting nuances of a caste system. Underestimating the extreme difficulty of this task has led to the travesties of education, under Western auspices, which are found in so many parts of the world.

If, however, this exceedingly difficult task is undertaken, what are some of the major factors which must be taken into account? In the first place the educator will need to consider the character structure of the people, those regularities in their behavior, which can be attributed to their having been reared in a common culture. These regularities can be conveniently described under the headings of motivation, incentives, and values, on the one hand, and ways of thought on the other. Our educational systems are bound up almost inextricably with our own character structure, so that it seems natural to us to build an educational system on such concepts as competition, reward and punishment, graduated success and failure, etc. But in working within other cultural contexts it is necessary to discard these cultural limitations and study first what are the incentives under which an individual will study and learn, and what are the conditions which may make the use of our methods definitely inappropriate. In Samoa, where precocity is deprecated, parents hung their heads when their children were skipped a grade in the American school, and in the missionary schools it was found impossible to use speed of finishing school as an incentive because custom demanded that the first to enter must also be the first to leave.[5] Dr. Klineberg[6] found that the Dakota Indians considered it bad form to give an answer in the presence of someone who did not know the answer. In a Balinese school I once heard a young teacher, discussing the results of an arithmetic test containing twenty examples, say, "One wrong, can be used, two wrong, can be used ..." up to "*Nineteen* wrong, can be used," but he added in a sad low voice, "Twenty wrong out of twenty, cannot be used." In caste societies, the question of who learns a new skill first may be crucial, as the high caste may decide that anything a low caste does, he can do better, or conversely, that nothing that a low caste has done is worth doing, and low castes may decide that they cannot do what the high caste does.

In addition to these obvious differences in motivation and conceptions of achievement, there are deeper ones, as between the people whose moral conceptions of right and wrong, for instance, make it also easier for them to handle cause-and-effect relationships in the material world. Study of the Manus tribe of the Admiralty Islands[7] suggests that a method of up-bringing which sternly fixes individual responsibility for wrong doing, also establishes an attitude of mind to which the ways of engines, telephones, and other apparatus of the modern age, are no longer strange. But in other cultures, character structure may be characterized by a capacity to learn by rote methods, but not by analytical ones.[8] The dichotomies which people use, between work and play, between vocation and avocation, between situations requiring effort and those requiring no effort,[9] etc., all may have a profound bearing upon the willingness and capacity to learn. After the Japanese have sensitized their children to feel any overt failure as an acute disgrace, it is necessary to give every child a prize,[10] but, in certain parts of the Orient, a "failed B.A." is said to be as simple a classificatory statement as the words diploma or some lower degree might be among ourselves. Thus, differences in the values given to success and failure, to moral responsibility, to status, etc., form the background, the conditions for learning, and shade imperceptibly into what might be regarded as more strictly intellectual conditions, such as a premium upon the exact use of words, as contrasted with a love of words for their sound and rhythm rather than their precise meaning, the implications of a native language in which direct quotations are used to describe any situation, whether one has been present or not,[11] so that accuracy of narration is virtually impossible, habits of meticulous repetition of verbal materials without any intellectual comment being permitted. Habits such as those common in China of invoking earlier authorities on a subject may influence and shape any attempt at independent thought. In many cases, when the educator is dealing with previously illiterate people, the problem of attention span is a serious one which has defeated many attempts to measure the intelligence of different races, even when the experimenter rules out the language factor. Only if the experimenter assumes that capacity for an attention span like our own is in itself evidence of intelligence, can tests which involve attention span be regarded as valid.[12] Perhaps one of the most revealing studies of differences in intellectual response to materials is the recall study done by Nadel[13] among two adjacent African peoples which shows the contrast in method and style and secondarily inability to recall a simple story.

It is apparent, therefore, that any system of education should be developed against a very thorough background of a knowledge of the culture of the people to be educated. This may be attained in two ways, by intensive anthropological study supplemented by the use of social psychological techniques, particularly such projective methods as the Rorshach, Vigotsky, "Draw a Man and Woman," simple recall and completion tests, etc., or, when this is impracticable, a great deal could also be learned by a detailed analysis of the methods of education actually being used by native teachers in their attempts to teach alien materials. The gifted native teacher, himself a full representative of his own culture, will both consciously and unconsciously adjust his methods to the emotional and intellectual values and habits which he and his pupils share. Verbatim records of classroom situations, using different materials at different age levels, if subjected to intensive analysis, could provide a background for organizing curriculum and program so that it was much more congruent with the local culture. As anthropologists usually lack practical educational experience and educators have not been trained in analyzing educational practices from a cultural point of view,[14] ideally both methods and both types of personnel should be used in combination.

After an initial reckoning with the basic culture in the construction of a school system, which extends, of course, not only to curriculum and incentives but to the whole interpersonal structure of the school, the next most important problem is probably that of literacy. There is now enough evidence in existence on efforts to teach literacy to illiterate and preliterate peoples to make it possible to say that a basic condition of successful literacy – on any large scale – is that it should be attained in the mother tongue. Literacy achieved in any language other than the mother tongue is likely, except in exceptional cases, to remain superficial and incomparable with the literacy of people who learned to read in the language in which their mothers sang them to sleep. Not only does this fact account for the relatively greater success of the Dutch in bringing native peoples of the East Indies up to college level in one generation, out of village schools, but also for the failure of American efforts to make the American Indian comfortably literate out of the tribal setting. Despite the seeming waste of time involved in teaching children to read and write in languages and dialects in which there is no literature, or at least no contemporary literature, this seems to be the only way in which full literacy can be attained. Once the basic connections are made, the pupils can pass rapidly, as has been repeatedly demonstrated in the East Indies, to literacy in some other language.

Even after this basic requirement of literacy attained in the mother tongue is recognized, serious problems remain in those societies which make special use of other types of script, intermediate forms like Arabic, phonetic syllabic scripts like the Sanskrit, or ideographs like Japanese and Chinese. As each of these types of scripts is the means of perpetuating one or more sacred books, failure to teach the children to read them is exceedingly destructive of continuity in the society, as it breaks the tie between the educated young and their educated elders. Expensive as it may seem to teach young children to use two scripts, it nevertheless would seem worthwhile to proceed by the following steps: a curriculum in which children become literate in mother tongue and local script, even if that script has been restricted in use to scribes and priests, followed by mother tongue in Roman script or whatever more widely used script is to form the basis of their world language skill, then a world language in its appropriate script. In this way the children are never confronted with both strange script and strange language simultaneously, but move by gentle stages from one new skill to another, maintaining their ties with their own culture as they forge ties with other cultures also. Experience has shown that the inferiority which is experienced by westernized young people who cannot read and write their ancestral language is too easily translated into defensive contempt and depreciation of their whole cultural background.

A further problem remains when the people for whom a comprehensive literacy program is planned belong to a linguistic group which is too small to warrant the expense of preparing an orthography and textbooks and training teachers to work in it. Language groups of this sort are found among American Indians, in the South Seas, in Africa and in Asia. Here the principle that true literacy is only achieved through the mother tongue has to be translated into the need for teaching a new alternative mother tongue within which literacy can be established. In fact the literacy of the child must be built upon the ability of the mother to speak a language which is written.

There have been three[15] major methods of solving this problem of the small pre-literate language groups and of the dialect speaking non-literate patches among peoples who are literate in some high language. One method is to teach the children to read and write the high language; this has been pursued at different periods in most European countries and has its Chinese analogue. Here—if the dialect is really a dialect and not a separate language—the child learns in terms of a language which is not too unfamiliar and, while probably not making the bridge as perfectly as does the child in whose home the written language is also spoken, nevertheless does become literate. His literacy, however, is often limited by inability to express emotionally weighted material in the high language. The second solution is through a *lingua franca*. Here also there is usually an already existent bridge as either in grammar or vocabulary the *lingua franca* is likely to resemble the mother tongue of the pupil. There are, however, certain disadvantages[16] inherent in most simplified jargons—the thinness and poverty of the cultural world out of which they spring and the absence of any literature or any tradition to which access may be obtained by learning to read and write the jargon. However, in the case of pre-literate areas of great linguistic diversity, such as that of New Guinea, probably the best step is to encourage the women as well as the men to learn the *lingua franca* so that the children will speak it before entering school, and then to take the initial steps toward literacy in the *lingua franca*, followed as rapidly as possible by induction into the appropriate world language. The other method which has been used with indifferent success is that adopted by certain missions, of selecting one small, unwritten language, for a translation of the Bible and other religious books, and then teaching literacy to the adjacent peoples in this insignificant and often accidentally chosen language. Such education violates the people's relationship to their own cultural background, gives them no capacity for wider participation in the world, and is generally indefensible. The attempts to go directly from a pre-literate background in some small unwritten language and the level of culture which is associated with pre-literate status, to attempted reading and writing in a world language of totally different structure, seems impossible unless the spoken version of the imported language has already become current among both sexes and all ages in the population, as in the case with Spanish in some Indian communities in Latin America. Here the imported world language can be regarded as a supplementary mother tongue. It is most important that this pre-school experience of the language, in which literacy is later to be attained, should be associated with pleasantly toned experiences for the child. Where the official language of school is neither the language of play nor of family affection, but only the language of an often formidable learning situation, this separation between the emotions associated with the two languages may provide a considerable barrier to effective literacy.[17] Failure to enable a people to become literate in the sense that members of Western countries are literate inevitably handicaps them seriously, and its repercussions can be found all through the individual's life. Many intelligent American Indians, for example, fail to attain the status which they deserve because of the difficulties which they experience in writing reports of any degree of complexity.

The next serious problem which confronts the educator is that presented by the accumulated literary, artistic, philosophic, and scientific traditions of the sort which we associate with high civilizations. A certain portion of the population of dependent countries, in fact all of those people whom we describe as primitive or pre-literate, have by definition little such tradition. Their view of the past is only as complex as may be transmitted through oral tradition, and, while the body of tradition sometimes rises to considerable artistic or philosophical heights, it is not comparable in mass, diversity, complexity or potentiality for new developments, with traditions like the Judeo-Christian, the Graeco-Roman, or the traditions of China, Japan, India, or Islam. When these preliterate peoples come in contact with anyone of these higher cultures, the educational problem arises, how to give them rapidly enough a familiarity with this rich past which will make them able to use the language and conceptual framework of their new-world cultural mentor. This problem has sometimes been seen as merely one of teaching the classics — whichever set of classics is being considered — with the same degree of firmness and repetitiousness with which they are taught in the home schools, with the expectation that such teaching will make such symbols as St. Paul, Charlemagne, Plato, Krisna, Lao Tse, David, etc., available to the local population. The slightest experience with the way in which pre-literate peoples handle their contacts with the Bible, the classic to which they are most frequently exposed, proves that this hope is a fallacy. An assimilation of the idea of the Devil to the folklore figure of Coyote does not mean that the American Indian now has access to medieval ideas of good and evil, but usually that he is even more effectively cut off from them. It does not increase the sophistication of a Samoan to teach him to recognize the name Egypt, but leaves him believing that Pharaoh still reigns there. What those who expose pre-literate peoples to our types of traditional education forget is that our great classics are bedded down in a wealth of common speech and imagery. Shorn of this linguistic and cultural background, their effect on the minds of pupils is often sheerly confusing and disorienting. It is much easier to move from an understanding of the classics of one great culture to an understanding of the classics of another, than to begin to absorb any set of classics into a cultural background from which they have been wholly absent.

It is important to point out that very serious snobbery often prompts people, recently emerging from a pre-literate past, to insist upon having a conventional higher education. If Greek and Roman classics have made the gentleman — who too often is a symbol of a height to which the students have been denied access — then Greek and Roman classics they will have. When a local education department contains individuals smarting under the sting of attributed racial or cultural inferiority, this demand is sometimes impossible to resist, even though in yielding to it whole peoples may be condemned to that very inferiority which they are seeking to avoid.

When, however, fortunate historical accidents make it possible to design an educational curriculum for a pre-literate or recently literate people, without the cooperation of members of their own group whose superior education makes it possible for them to make such complicating demands, the whole question can be usefully sidestepped by planning a curriculum which uses the best contemporary methods of thought, applied as often as possible to local content. Instead of learning the history of ancient Greece, the student may learn the methods of stratigraphy well enough to make studies in local archeology which will command the respect of the wider world, and instead of studying Aristotle, he may learn to do studies of local natural history and ecology. For a knowledge of medieval dialectics, he may substitute a mastery of contemporary mathematical techniques or a developed photographic skill. If it is recognized that it is easier to teach an untrained mind good modern science than allusion-studded epics, then a careful search can be made for those areas in which local conditions will provide the content on which high level abstractions and highly developed modern techniques can be exercised. In this way the university graduate who belongs to the first class which has ever been graduated from a new university in a dependent country, stands the chance of facing members of older cultures on a far more equal basis than if he devoted his time to mastering by rote some classic, the basis of which these others learned as children in the casual allusions of mother and schoolmaster.

The problem of education for members of those societies which already possess one high civilization but who now wish to share in another — the well known situation when young people of oriental tradition attempt to become westernized — is a rather different one. Here the demand, both on the part of educators and students, may well be for a break with the cumbersome past, but, as in the matter of script, the loss which this will entail in continuity and cultural integrity is so great that it cannot safely be risked. As the initial hump which any student who is later to be bi- or multilingual must get over, is the realization that there are other languages which are as valid as his own, and not merely translations, imitations, or approximations of his own, so also it is useful in the case of cultural tradition to introduce fairly early into the education of children who are learning the rudiments of some one high culture, the language and some of the literature of another high culture. This applies today mainly to the introduction of Western languages and cultures in countries where children are being taught within an Oriental tradition, but it might equally well be applied in reverse. The children of the Occident will never be fully world-mobile until they have an equal experience of some other high non-European culture. With the present world trend, however, towards an approximation to the skills and ideologies of the West, the more recurrent and pressing problem is the education of young people so that they can participate in Western culture without losing touch with their own people.

All of the foregoing discussion makes one assumption which unfortunately is not universally true. It assumes that the peoples to be educated will be members of homogeneous, relatively untouched cultures, with all the internal consistency and harmony which is characteristic of such cultures. In actual practice, more and more of

the peoples of the world, in dependent countries and among metropolitan and independent nations, have lost their cultural roots. They
exist in a state of deculturation, whether because they have immi-
grated from one country to another, or from country to city, or from
one part of the country to another, or because war, displacement, deso-
lation, and destruction of familiar values and institutions have left them
hopelessly disoriented and impoverished even in the land of their
childhood. The children of such parents—and one may count them
now by the millions, whether one deals with the urban worker in Java
or the sugar cane worker of Puerto Rico, the rural children exploited
in the recently sprung up factories of the Orient, the wandering Mexican casual laborers in the United States, or the mestizo of so many
Latin American cities, the emigrant from the rural Southeastern United
States into large and unfamiliar Northern cities, or the mixed African-
English groups in Liverpool,—can rely upon no homogeneities of
culture, often not even of language. Often the parents have been
reared in different cultures and one speaks poorly the language of the
other. The words used in the home were formed to deal with a different environment, and often there are no words in the parental language
for the material things which surround them. Kin are separated from
kin, and the depth of social perception which comes from listening to
the tales of grandparents and watching one's own parents' relations to
their parents is all lost. The language of the only lullabies a mother
knows employs symbols of which she herself has forgotten the meaning, and the children bring in from the streets words and phrases which
are equally incomprehensible to her. There are deep gulfs between
each individual and his past, between parents and children, and between people and the environment around them which they lack the
equipment to interpret and invest with meaning—and these gulfs are
so deep that they threaten to become internalized and result in split
and disintegrated personalities.

    For such children and young people, the educational problem is not
to take the coherencies of their cultural heritage and graft onto them
whatever new learnings are desired, but rather to devise a curriculum
within which they may somehow attain that minimum of personal
integration and group belongingness which they must have if they are
to learn anything at all. Modern educational trends from Frobel and
Madam Montessori through the whole elaboration of the Progressive
Education movement may be seen primarily as attempts to recreate in
the classroom that closeness to a real world seen through culturally
coherent symbols which members of our deculturated modern society
have lost. The Chinese child who comes from a three-generation

home, firmly placed in a village where his family have lived for a thousand years, can sit all day and recite the alphabet without damage to his personality, and this is equally true of the French school boy or the Syrian or of the child who comes from a relatively intact primitive community. If what he learns is too alien, he will simply forget it, as do American Indians after returning from boarding school, or adult peasants in whose houses there are no books with which to keep up the little reading learned at school. If what he learns is presented incorrectly, it may disorient him. But in any case, he is a whole personality before he comes to school and only very drastic educational errors can rob him completely of his integration. But the child of rootless parents has no such strengths to fall back upon. Set down in a schoolroom to learn by rote matters which also have no meaning to him, he is likely to be seriously maimed. The schools for these children need to emphasize expression rather than assimilation, for the child is not ready to assimilate anything into the confused, incoherent mental background with which he enters school. A liberal use of the arts, intensive use of the methods by which all skills are integrated about daily life, and the illumination of the processes of food getting, market, exchange, manufacture, etc., are very important here. If such children are given, first, some basis for meeting the world, they may then become more easily world-mobile than those who spring from a more stable cultural background. But there remains a continuous danger that their world mobility will lack depth, that they will move from town to town, or country to country, never making any contact with the people and things they see, because the initial poverty of their childhood robbed them of the means of making a contact with themselves. The lack of introspection, the emphasis on action rather than thought, or facts rather than theory, so characteristic of American culture is itself a product of just such a huge process of deculturation. Without traditional symbols, the individual has no ready means to express himself and so turns away from himself out to the world, which at least in a material form can be dealt with by his five senses if not by his imagination. Modern methods of education do provide ways for repairing this damage, and, whereas the introduction to literacy is perhaps the crucial learning situation for children from homogeneous cultures, the introduction to a sense of the self, is equally crucial for rootless deculturized people. Any educator before making a plan should be very sure with which group he is dealing.

Notes

[1] "The Role of Small South Sea Cultures in the Post War World," *American Anthropologist*, Vol. 45 (April 1943), pp. 193–196.

[2]C. H. Waddington, *The Scientific Attitude* (London: Penguin Books, 1941).

[3]Lawrence K. Frank, "Time Perspective," *Jour. of Social Phil.,* Vol. 4 (1939), pp. 293–312.

[4]J. F. H. A. de la Court, "Some Proposals for Postwar Education in Indonesia," *Far East Quarterly,* Netherlands Indies Issue, 1946.

[5]Margaret Mead, *Coming of Age in Samoa* (William Morrow & Co., 1928); *Cooperation and Competition Among Primitive Peoples,* Edited by Margaret Mead (New York: McGraw-Hill, 1937).

[6]Otto Klineberg, *Race Differences* (New York: Harper & Row, 1935).

[7]Margaret Mead, "An Investigation of the Thought of Primitive Children with Special Reference to Animism," *Jour. of the Royal Anthropological Inst.,* Vol. 62 (January 1932), pp. 173–190.

[8]G. Bateson and M. Mead, *Balinese Character: A Photographic Analysis,* Special Publication (New York Academy of Sciences, 1942).

[9]G. Bateson, "Social Planning and the Concept of 'Deutero-Learning,'" in *Science, Philosophy and Religion* (New York, 1942).

[10]Ruth Benedict, *The Chrysanthemum and the Sword; Patterns of Japanese Culture* (New York: Houghton Mifflin & Co., 1946), pp. 177–194.

[11]E.g., in Iatmul, our phrase, *the man went to get his canoe,* would have to be translated, "He wènt saying, 'I'll get my canoe.'"

[12]Beatrice Blackwood, *A Study of Mental Testing in Relation to Anthropology,* Mental Measurements Monographs, Vol. 4 (Baltimore: Williams and Wilkins, 1927), p. 117.

[13]Nadel, "A Field Experiment in Racial Psychology," *British Jour. of Psychology,* Vol. 28 (1937, c.), pp. 195–211.

[14]Willard Waller, *Sociology of Teaching* (New York: John Wiley & Sons, 1932).

[15]All such statements are subject to the provision that we have no adequate information about the methods pursued by the Soviet Union in educating their non-Russian-speaking peoples.

[16]G. Bateson, "Pidgin English and Cross-Cultural Communication," *Transactions,* New York Academy of Sciences, II, 6, Vol. 4 (February 1944), pp. 137–141.

[17]D. J. Saer, "The Effect of Bilingualism on Intelligence," *British Journal of Psychology,* Vol. 14 (1923), pp. 35–38.

12
American Teachers in East Africa: The Problem of Cultural Adaptation

All developing countries, but more especially perhaps those of Tropical Africa, tend to suffer severe shortages in a number of fields of national development. This applies particularly to the field of education and is the consequence, in many cases, of sudden expansion, the move toward political independence, and the general conditions of the post-war world. Faced with acute shortages, development planners for a long time were inclined to regard lack of funds as the major obstacle to progress, and undoubtedly the availability of funds is often the trigger which sets off development in almost any sphere. In recent years, however, it has become evident that lack of skills, and more particularly of skilled personnel, may on occasion be of even greater importance than the availability of funds. This applies particularly to secondary education in East Africa, where up to the present a dire shortage of secondary school teachers has crippled educational and other expansion.

There are a number of reasons for this. With the approach of political independence many expatriate staff (mostly British in these countries) tend to leave the educational services. Since they are costly and specialized imported staff, they are usually found in the strategically more important posts such as those of teaching in secondary schools. It is these schools, therefore, which tend to suffer most when expatriate staff begin to leave. Second, in any expanding economy or developing country there is a constant and insatiable demand for educated and

P. C. C. Evans, "American Teachers for East Africa," *Comparative Education Review*, Vol. 6 (June 1962), pp. 69–77.

qualified local people to fill new positions in politics, government, the civil service, the professions, and commerce. Again, it is the secondary schools which usually suffer, for their teachers provide an obvious source of recruitment. Third, the popular demand in developing countries in Africa to establish widespread facilities for primary education—sometimes universal primary education—as a major priority in a new educational policy often deprives secondary education of the necessary finance and facilities for reasonable expansion.

Since World War II there has been a growing demand in many parts of the world for East African products such as tea, coffee, sisal, and pyrethrum. This has had a healthy effect on the economy of the countries concerned, and there has been more money to spend on education than ever before. Consequently, in the decade of the fifties a quite startling expansion (of the order of 350 per cent in the field of secondary education) has occurred throughout the territories of Kenya, Uganda, Tanganyika, and Zanzibar, as shown in the accompanying table. But this has only served to aggravate the already acute shortage of secondary school teachers, more particularly since the expansion of secondary education has not led to a corresponding increase in the number of recruits for teaching in secondary schools. Lastly, even if finance and the necessary students for teacher training were available, it is doubtful whether local training facilities in East Africa could have been expanded to the point where they could have dealt adequately with the demands of what is now essentially an emergency situation. In short, a situation had grown up in East Africa where the problem of providing an adequate number of secondary school teachers was incapable of any on-the-spot solution. The only answer to the problem lay in the provision of massive international assistance from outside and this, in fact, has recently been supplied by the United States in an exercise commonly known as the Teachers for East Africa program, T.E.A. for short.

Secondary School Enrollment, East Africa, 1952 and 1960

	1952			1960		
	Boys	**Girls**	**Total**	**Boys**	**Girls**	**Total**
Kenya	1,160	64	1,224	4,623	786	5,409
Uganda	4,410	645	5,055	21,113	4,311	25,424
Tanganyika	2,726	91	2,817	4,163	482	4,645
Zanzibar	672	148	820	944	410	1,354
Totals	8,968	948	9,916	30,843	5,989	36,832

Note: Figures for Kenya, Uganda, and Tanganyika are for African Education only.
Source: Department of Technical Co-operation Statistics.

In December 1960, a conference was held at Princeton, New Jersey, to consider the educational problems of East Africa – Kenya, Uganda, Tanganyika, and Zanzibar. The conference was sponsored by the Africa Liaison Committee of the American Council on Education and the participants included representatives of the governments of East Africa, of the voluntary agencies concerned with education in those territories, of the United States, and of the United Kingdom. Those speaking on behalf of the East African governments stressed that their most pressing problem was the expansion of secondary education, but that the dire shortage of secondary school teachers was making this impossible. It was proposed that the United States should undertake to meet this shortage, not eventually but immediately. The idea was fully endorsed and became a leading recommendation in the conference report. Thus was the T.E.A. program born.

After the conference great activity ensued in many quarters: in the International Cooperation Administration in Washington; in the ministries and departments of education of the territories concerned; in the Colonial Office, London; at the University College of East Africa, Makerere, Uganda; and in the offices of the Afro-Anglo-American Program for Teacher Education, Teachers College, Columbia University, which has close links with the University of London Institute of Education. Eventually, it was decided that Teachers College should take major professional responsibility for the American end of the plan, but it was also hoped that a number of British university graduates would participate in the scheme. Between December 1960 and June 1961, 150 American teachers were recruited from all over the United States for short-term service in East African schools – two years in the first instance – and they were later joined by nine British teachers.

In view of the general international interest likely to be created by this considerable American operation to assist East African educational development it may be well to analyze some of the problems and human factors involved in a project of this nature. There is some likelihood that this experiment may be the forerunner of others, and President Kennedy's Peace Corps is said to be watching it with great interest. The latter already has a considerable number of teachers in Ghana and Nigeria, and others are to be sent to Sierra Leone. Although these educational experiments are operating on opposite sides of the African continent there can be little doubt that experience gained in one part of Africa may have valuable lessons for work in others.

East African secondary schools are not so numerous that the impact of 150 American teachers entering them in one year is going to be negligible. If the experiment is repeated again next year and another batch of roughly the same number of teachers is recruited, then undoubtedly the total impact on East African education will be very great indeed. However, we do not know precisely in what particular directions this impact will be most evident, but it seems reasonable to assume that it will lie largely in three main areas: in the field of culture-contact, with special reference to the educational context and the teachers themselves; in the field of general aims and philosophy of secondary education; and in the general pedagogy and teaching methods of the secondary school.

As a preliminary comment to this discussion, it must be made clear that many people with an intimate knowledge of Africa are convinced that American teachers have a unique contribution to make to education in that continent. Because of this, some Britishers support their action with even greater enthusiasm than that sometimes shown by the teachers themselves. This is not to suggest for one moment that the latter are not enthusiastic and dedicated — they are, many of them pre-eminently so — but they have probably appraised the situation more carefully and realistically, both in respect to themselves and to the image they are likely to create in Africa as a result of their American heritage. Many of them realize, for example, that their advent in Africa represents a new departure in American foreign policy. There is, therefore, not much experience or tradition to go on, and what there is is not always appropriate, inasmuch as American policy in places like Hawaii and Puerto Rico tended for a long time to be strongly assimilationist in character. It therefore does not provide relevant guides for action in present-day Africa. In this matter of experience or tradition American teachers are probably at a disadvantage, compared with their British counterparts. For the latter, service in Africa in the past has been conditioned strongly by two factors: first, that there is a long tradition of such service in Britain which, certainly until World War II and even to some extent today, carried high status and social prestige; second, partly because of this tradition but more especially because African society has been influenced deeply by British institutions and values, Britishers do not, on the whole, tend to suffer the same degree of "culture-shock" on going to Africa as other nationalities. They move into situations there which, paradoxically, can sometimes be described as "more British than the British." In short, Americans in Africa have a double adjustment to make: they have to adjust virtually to two culture patterns, one of which is distinctly African and tends to obtain more particularly in the lower socioeconomic levels, and the other which is middle-class and, although still very African, tends to be

influenced deeply by British social and institutional norms. There can
hardly be doubt that for Britishers, on the whole, this double adjustment is less arduous than for their American colleagues.

This raises the whole problem of culture-shock. In orientation programs for American teachers going to Africa the concept of culture-
shock has played an important role. It is also a commonplace in the
parlance of social anthropology in America. It is less well known in
Britain and because of this there is a tendency to discount its validity.
Many Britishers, for example, declare that they cannot recall (on first
going to Africa) situations in which they themselves experienced
culture-shock. Naturally, there is a tendency in most people to forget
unpleasant things – and culture-shock is usually unpleasant – but even
allowing for this, in the main they are probably right, for they went, as
we have seen, into situations which contained at least some elements
of their own culture. They were also supported by the presence of
many of their compatriots and a social context which was not entirely
strange. Because of this, it would be unwise, perhaps, for Britishers
to discount altogether the importance which Americans attach to this
concept. Indeed, the recent unfortunate incident in Nigeria, concerning the reactions of a young Peace Corps woman teacher to the conditions she found there, illustrates only too well that culture-shock can
be a vivid reality. If, then, this concept is a realistic one for Americans,
in what educational situations in Africa are they most likely to suffer
from it?

One of the most important, obviously, concerns the whole question
of American values, or what is generally known as "the American way
of life." It is part of the historical background of the United States
that the school system was, and still is, used to inculcate common core
values such as those of democracy, individual freedom, educational
opportunity, and so on; in fact, all those values generally described as
American values, though, of course, they may exist elsewhere. The
daily oath and salute to the flag which every American school still
practices bear testimony to this. But its equivalent cannot be found in
Britain. The parallel with Britain is drawn here simply to make the
point that in the United States national values tend, on the whole, to
be emphasized strongly at the conscious level, whereas in Britain they
are often ingrained at a more subconscious or even unconscious level.
This is important in relation to culture-shock, for it is reasonable to
assume that core values held largely at an unconscious level tend on
the whole to survive culture-shock better than others held more
consciously or overtly. This, of course, may be debatable, but great
care has obviously been taken to see that, in fact, these teachers do

not flaunt their American values or be dogmatic about them, and it is reasonable to assume that this is so because a fear exists that were they to do so, they would damage the American image abroad. The influence of *The Ugly American* has apparently spread far and wide and, quite apart from having been a bestseller in the United States, it has probably received far more attention than it deserves in quarters which should have known better. It certainly seems to have exerted an influence on policy making out of all proportion to its size.

American teachers in Africa, therefore, may sometimes find themselves in something of a dilemma. They may not assert their American values, above all they may not do so dogmatically. On occasions, undoubtedly, they may even find that their students do not share these values, or are even able to sympathize with them. How, then, would it be possible currently to deal with the concept of democracy in a Ghanaian secondary school? Or will it always be possible to deal adequately in East Africa with the concept of personal liberty irrespective of race or color? Perhaps in anticipation of such difficulties American teachers are sometimes told that it is not an American way of life which Africa is seeking, nor a British way of life, but an African way of life. To the extent that any emerging culture, or the result of any process of social change, is a synthesis of many elements, there is a lot of truth in this, but implicit in it also may be the denial of fundamental American values previously held strongly and consciously by these teachers. Will such a denial help them adjust more adequately or teach more successfully? Or would it be truer to say that to be apologetic about one's basic values is not generally conducive to either of these? This is in no sense an argument intended to suggest that American teachers should preach their American values from the housetops in Africa, nor is it one suggesting that they abandon them altogether; it is simply to say that most people can only act sincerely or teach successfully in terms of their basic values, and that the unique contribution these teachers have to make in Africa may well be in terms of those values. Their real problem, therefore, is likely to be that of coming to terms with teaching situations which sometimes conflict with their basic values. In dealing with such situations it is clear that a bellicose affirmation of their American beliefs will not be the appropriate answer; neither will a supine acceptance of the trends they may see around them. But somehow, by their beliefs and their living example, they have to be the exemplars of a way of life which must demonstrate visibly its superiority over local models. The writer feels strongly that, in the case at least of some of the teachers destined for East Africa, the process of "deculturization" in orientation programs had proceeded to the point when, in fact, basic beliefs and values were threatened, and all this in the name of easier adjustment to conditions in Africa and the creation of a more favorable American image abroad. The British have a graphic phrase to describe such a process — they call it "throwing out the baby with the bath water."

We have discussed the question of American values so far in general terms. It might now be more profitable to turn to more concrete educational situations, particularly in relation to the second of the areas mentioned earlier, namely, the general aims and philosophy of secondary education in East Africa. These have been influenced strongly by English models, chiefly the English grammar and public schools, and they are therefore biased heavily in favor of English educational values and objectives. These are fully shared by most Africans, even though they may not always be prepared to admit it. Like people all over the world, including ourselves, Africans can be very good at rationalization, and although they sometimes dislike the British or react strongly against colonialism, they will nevertheless tend to defend fiercely the social institutions and their inherent values which they have inherited from the British. Nowhere is this more true than in the case of the secondary school, though in its rationalized form it may well take on the guise of a defense of high academic standards, etc. In point of fact, the East African secondary school is more firmly based on British models than any other educational institution in tropical Africa, and it is bound to strike American teachers as very British indeed. They will find its atmosphere and distinctive ethos strange after American high schools, but the strangeness will be more marked in some ways than in others.

In the first place, they are bound to be puzzled, and not a little worried, by the meager availability of secondary grammar school education in East Africa. In the United States, and in Britain since 1944, secondary education has been the undisputed right and privilege of all students who leave the primary school. In the circumstances of economically underdeveloped countries such as those of East Africa, however, there is not enough money available to make this possible. In these countries approximately only 1.3 per cent of those students who leave the primary school will, in fact, go on to secondary education of the grammar school type, leading to the Cambridge School Certificate or the General Certificate of Education. Such education, therefore, is highly selective and extremely competitive. It is only the intellectual cream which can look forward to secondary grammar education. These students, therefore, are very much an intellectual elite. This would not disturb a Britisher unduly, for he is accustomed, even in conditions where secondary education is available for all, as in his own country, to isolate an intellectual elite at a student age of approximately eleven years. These chosen few then proceed to the British grammar school, which is the model for the East African secondary school, and for the most part are destined later to occupy the principal roles of leadership and responsibility in the national life. This may prove difficult for American teachers to accept, for the tradition of educating an elite runs counter to the whole American conception of the common school and to their belief in the equality of educational opportunity for all, irrespective of individual ability and socioeconomic background. Most Americans also reject, rightly or wrongly, the whole notion of a closed society run by an elite such as the British now seem anxious to get rid of, but which now seems to be the emerging pattern in East Africa. Yet, in the circumstances of an underdeveloped country, what is the alternative when funds are so strictly limited? And if there must be elimination on financial grounds (more euphemistically called "selection") should there be any other criterion than intellectual ability? In this connection an interesting experiment is being set up currently in Nigeria, where a joint Nigerian-American project is on foot to establish a comprehensive school after the American pattern. But one of the basic tenets of this project is that *all* the children of secondary school age in the vicinity of this school shall be admitted to it. This may be feasible for a small area, but would it succeed if extended to a wider scene? Can Nigeria, in other words, afford secondary education for all?

The secondary schools of East Africa, again, have strong religious affiliations. Historically, they follow the pattern of the development of education in Britain, where popular education was initiated and in its early stages supported by the churches. Only later did the state come into the educational picture, but after it did so the idea of partnership in education between church and state has remained one of the funda-mental bases of English educational theory and practice. There was a similar development in East Africa, where education in the early stages was initiated by, and became the sole responsibility of, the Christian missions. Practically all the secondary schools now existing there were founded by the missions, and to this day they maintain and jealously guard their strong religious affiliations. Indeed, they would go even further and say that they recognize not only a religious affilia-tion but also a denominational one. Will American teachers, bred in a tradition where the public schools have turned their faces firmly against a religious influence in education, understand or even sym-pathize with a viewpoint which not only recognizes the place of religion in schools, but asserts that dogma and belief are essential parts of schooling, that religion can be the only basis for a sound education?

Yet another important difference between the American and British systems of secondary education is the importance each attaches to the place and value of external examinations. Secondary schools in East Africa all work toward the school certificate and the higher school certificate examinations of the University of Cambridge Local Examinations Syndicate, which conducts such examinations all over the world in countries which have had, or still have, a close relationship with Britain. Students normally take five years of secondary education to prepare for the former examination and a further two or three years to prepare for the latter. The case for and against external examinations at the secondary school level is a complex one which cannot be entered into here, but some schools and many teachers are of the opinion that such examinations tend to have a cramping and restrictive influence on the work and curriculum of the secondary school. Also, the students themselves tend to believe that only that which is examinable for the Cambridge examinations is truly educational; all else is merely frills and of little educational account. In addition, these examinations unfortunately tend to test only attainment, theoretical knowledge, and to some degree reasoning ability; hence, they are partly responsible for the charge that secondary education in Africa is bookish and largely divorced from the problems of life outside the classroom. Indeed, some would say that it is even unrelated to life in the continent of Africa. Nevertheless, the prized school certificate is the open sesame to good posts in the outside world, so parents and students are usually unanimous about what they expect from the secondary school. Even the teachers tend to measure their worth by the successes their students score in these examinations. Those American teachers going to East Africa who had the opportunity of seeing English grammar schools at work formed many impressions, some of them good and some of them bad, but one on which nearly all were agreed was that, compared with American high schools, English grammar schools tend to lay great emphasis on formal learning, sometimes even rote learning, and rely on strict discipline as the chief means of achieving their purpose. They would almost certainly have said the same thing if they had seen French *lycées* or German *gymnasien* at work, for the common element in both these and the English schools is that all work toward an external examination, and for all the basis of the curriculum is knowledge-centered through the medium of books and teacher, while in their own system (if one *can* generalize about

American education) the curriculum is knowledge-centered through the medium of student participation and experience. This great difference in approach may call for considerable adjustment on the part of teachers not steeped in the British tradition.

A unique feature of the English grammar school likely to be introduced far more widely into East African secondary schools in future because of the eased teaching situation brought about by the advent of the 150 American teachers is that of the sixth form (or class). Some schools already have such senior classes but others will undoubtedly now follow suit. The sixth form is essentially a phenomenon peculiar to the English grammar school, and it represents two or three years of further study after the school certificate, usually for the purpose of obtaining the higher school certificate, or the advanced level of the general certificate of education, as entrance qualifications to a university. In England sixth-form study is growing steadily in popularity as a cultural benefit for those students who receive it, and as such is no longer associated exclusively with the taking of an external examination. But with the utilitarian view of education which obtains in East Africa, however, a similar development there seems unlikely for some years to come. In England, one cause at least for continuing school in order to do sixth-form work unassociated with the taking of an external examination is the saturation of the labor market for secondary school graduates. This is unlikely to occur in East Africa for a considerable time to come, for an enormous demand exists for all the graduates which the secondary schools can turn out.

To appreciate fully the professional problems of American teachers who will teach such advanced study classes in East Africa, some account of the nature of the sixth form is necessary. Historically, such classes grew up in England mainly to occupy a halt period between the achievement by the student of university matriculation (necessary for university entrance) usually through the medium of a certain level of performance in the school certificate examination, and his actual entrance into the university. Usually, this represented a period of about two years. It was natural, therefore, that universities should grant credit for such work, which was properly of a postsecondary and university nature. Successful completion of the sixth form, therefore, usually earned one year's credit at a university toward a degree course. Until recently, in the absence of sixth-form work in all schools in East Africa, such preliminary university work had to be done at Makerere College itself, but recently, in certain faculties, it has been possible to devolve such work to the sixth forms of certain secondary schools. As sixth forms increase in number in the secondary schools of East Africa, so will it become possible for Makerere University College to devolve the initial degree work of other faculties also.

This close relationship between sixth-form work, university studies, and university entrance has affected fundamentally the nature of sixth-form work, both in curriculum content and in teaching methodology. In respect of the former, such studies are definitely of a very high standard and properly pertain in America to the college level and in Britain to the initial stages of the university. The students themselves may represent anything from one-tenth to one-third of those who complete successfully the school certificate course. Intellectually speaking, therefore, they represent "the cream of the cream" and are capable of deep and sustained intellectual performance. In Britain, only the best and most highly qualified teachers can teach such students successfully and even so, they have to admit (as some do with frank humility) that they are often working with their intellectual equals or superiors. It is this realization that also affects the nature of sixth-form teaching. In sixth-form work the teacher is *primus inter pares* but nothing more, and the teacher-student relationship often undergoes a significant change from that which pertains before the sixth form. Teaching methods now approximate to those of a university; mutual and joint explorations are made by teacher and students in the realm of thought and the intellect; the discussion group becomes important as a teaching medium and the seminar is introduced usually for the first time; thought and its stimulation now take precedence over curriculum content, though the latter is never devalued; private research is of more importance than having information supplied. Papers are written; debates are frequent; private study and personal responsibility and maturity are always emphasized; intellectual and emotional independence by the end of the sixth form is the main goal. For those teachers who can teach such students successfully there results a great feeling of satisfaction and stimulation, a real joy in teaching such as may not always be given to those who teach other age groups in the secondary school. Although American teachers teaching such classes in East Africa will undoubtedly find themselves extended greatly, both intellectually and pedagogically, they may find, in fact, that the sixth form approximates more to their own American conceptions of high school teaching than other parts of the secondary school. Those who do have this experience will undoubtedly appreciate it.

One final point about the general philosophy of secondary education in East Africa concerns the role which community and parents play in the secondary education process there. The American tradition recognizes very explicitly that both these agencies have definite responsibilities and rights in education which the professional educators must take into account, both in determining the curriculum content of the school and in planning its general organization. The assumption is made that education is not a matter for professional educators alone but is the joint concern of school, students, parents and community. Again, this differs sharply from the British tradition which, though usually welcoming parental and community interest and cooperation in what the school sets out to do, nevertheless is quite definite that school education is a professional affair, to be decided entirely by professional educators, who alone have rights in framing curricula, deciding school policies, and so on. Parent-teacher associations certainly exist and relationships with their schools are often extremely cordial, but this is so only on the understanding that they have no *rights,* as such, to determine the direction in which a school sets out to do its work. When some parents appear to overstep the mark, headmasters or principals of schools reserve the right to discontinue the association.

As in so many other things, this English tradition tends to harden significantly when taken overseas, particularly to a country like East Africa. In such a community the school, and particularly, perhaps, the secondary school, is an exotic institution which bears little relationship to community desires or wishes, other than to fulfill the main wish that almost all parents have for their children who attend it, namely, economic preferment and a white-collar job. Moreover, most parents in any case are illiterate and tend to feel that they are unqualified to express opinions about education in educated secondary circles and also that secondary school teachers are a race apart, far above them in social status and likely to greet any views they may express with a certain degree of contempt. There is, therefore, very little interaction in East Africa between secondary schools, parents, and community, and this will undoubtedly appear somewhat strange to American teachers who are used to a very different tradition.

This brings us to the last area where American teachers in Africa may find some need for adjustment, namely, that of teaching method. We have already seen that many of those T.E.A. teachers who saw English grammar schools at work in England were impressed with what they considered to be the formality of the teaching situation, and the teacher-centeredness of secondary education generally. In most English secondary schools, teachers are treated with deference and respect and to some extent remain aloof and distant from their students. In boys' schools students are referred to by their surnames and rarely by their Christian names; this is part of the tradition and tends to reinforce the social distance between teacher and taught. There is a great deal of emphasis on the use of the blackboard and the textbook as teaching instruments and teaching assignments are usually in terms of factual knowledge to be learned, often by rote, rather than of experiences to be gained. There is, on the whole, little relation of curriculum or lesson content to conditions in the environment outside the classroom. Similarly, there is little or no emphasis on learning about, or discussing, British values. There is no oath, and there is no flag ceremony. There is often considerable interaction between teacher and taught through question and answer, but always in terms of correct or incorrect answers to special questions or topics. Rarely is great weight given to student opinions, or to original thought (at least, below sixth-form level) for it is assumed that greater minds have already thought out these matters and there is little that adolescents can contribute to the discussion. And always the specter of the examination looms ahead, with its demands that this shall be known, or that understood, in precise terms which suffer no alternatives. The teacher tends to dominate the scene; he leads, the students follow; he suggests, the students take note; he assigns the work, the students do it or are punished for failure to do it. And yet, there are many brilliant and democratic teachers, who develop the closest and most estimable relationships with their students, who are loved and truly respected rather than feared, and who are remembered later for the great good and formative influence they had on young growing minds and characters. This must be true in any educational system.

It certainly is true of the secondary schools of East Africa, except that there the students, too, are convinced that formal methods of teaching are the only ones worth while. A few years ago the writer had the privilege of preparing a young Englishman for teaching service in an East African secondary school. This young man was convinced of the efficacy and rightness of modern, progressive methods of education. He went to teach in his East African school, but after two semesters he wrote a despairing letter. He had, he told the writer, practiced his progressive methods with, as he thought, great success. His classes had enjoyed their work and they said they had benefitted greatly from their association with him. But then they had sent him a deputation saying it was now time they stopped playing and began to work, for the examinations were not far away. If he was not prepared to cooperate and teach as the other teachers taught, they threatened they would strike, for he was endangering their whole careers. After long remonstration, he was forced to accede to their demands and to adopt the teaching methods he had previously despised.

And so, American teachers in Africa will not find their assignment an easy one. But all who have known them have been greatly impressed with their quality and know that for the most part they will succeed in their mission. They are young, enthusiastic, and deeply conscious of the importance of the work they have volunteered to do. They are not sentimentalists but have realistically appraised the situation into which they are going, as well as their attitudes toward teaching in Africa. They are motivated, almost all of them, by a sense of service, tinged with a sense of adventure, which augur well for the schools they are going to serve. Those Britishers who have worked with them are confident they will be a credit to the United States of America.

13
The Process of
Cross-Cultural Innovation

In human behavioral studies the area of the dynamics of culture change
has been largely neglected. Social scientists in the past, particularly
anthropologists, have tended to study human groups from a static
point of view. Researchers have gone to given areas, studied the behavior of the people there, and described it as they found it. Even
where studies took cognizance of the phenomena of change, these
have been primarily tasks of reconstruction. That is, specific changes
were identified and described but the process by which they had taken
place was not known to the researchers.

Since World War II a new source of data has appeared which holds
enormous promise for the study of culture change. We refer to the
guided technical change projects that are taking place all over the
world. For the first time the actual process of change within a delimited
social environment is in the spotlight, and the circumstances are such
that the details of the cultural interaction process can be observed.

Books appearing in the last ten years have utilized some of this data
but still leave much work to be done. Some, such as *Human Problems
in Technological Change,* by Edward K. Spicer (ed.), and *Health,
Culture and Community,* by Benjamin D. Paul (ed.), have assembled
excellent case study material for teaching purposes, but have not
sought to develop a general theory of change. Others, such as *The
Traditional Culture and the Impact of Technological Change,* by
George Foster, *Man Takes Control,* by Charles Erasmus, and *Technical Change and Cultural Reality,* by Arensberg and Niehoff, while

Arthur H. Niehoff and J. Charnel
Anderson. "Positive Negative and
Neutral Factors — The Process of
Cross-Cultural Innovation," *Interna-
tional Development Review,* Vol. 6
(June 1964), pp. 5–11.

contributing to theory, are limited by the fact that they overemphasize certain culture areas and are basically intuitive.

What we feel is lacking is a clear, overall treatment of technical change as a process in which an innovation is introduced into another culture by an innovator and during which there is reaction by the members of the recipient culture and ultimate rejection or acceptance of the new idea of technique.

Toward A General Theory of Change

It is our contention that if enough data, based on actual field studies, can be collected and analyzed, then specific characteristics of this process can be isolated and evaluated. Even more important, a recurring pattern of the most important characteristics should emerge and a general theory of the change process could be formulated. We have made a preliminary attempt to describe the process by using the following method:

Published case histories describing specific efforts to introduce innovations into other cultures were collected. There were several criteria for case selection, the primary one being that the characteristics of the innovator and the recipient groups be described. These cases were evaluated according to quantity and quality. The country was listed, the specific type of innovation proposed (community development, road building, well drilling, etc.), and the specific description of the change effort. The cases were then evaluated in terms of success and failure, and the final categorization was to list the factors considered to be most important in influencing the outcome.

After assembling, organizing, and relating the factors responsible for acceptance or rejection, a pattern emerged of the total process. Its characteristics are as follows:

There is a *goal,* the introduction of some new idea or technique into another society by a change agent. This we call the plan and in terms of process this is the action initiated.

Then throughout the process, until the innovation is either rejected or integrated into the local society, there are a number of *techniques used by the innovating agent.* These are the positive actions used by the innovator to implement his plan. The process can be viewed solely from the innovator's point of view, and a legitimate analysis can be made concerning those characteristics alone. If this alone were done, one would then be prepared to make statements as to which techniques tend to produce acceptance and which end in rejection.

There is another side of the process, however, which is the *behavior of the recipients of the innovation.* This can be characterized as the reaction produced by the agent's action. It can be divided into two subcategories: the *motivation* for accepting the new idea, or its obverse, and the *characteristics of the traditional culture* in producing sanctions or conflicts toward the projected innovation.

In terms of process, any projected innovation will be subject to the categories of these three influences: behavior of the innovator, motivation of recipients, and behavior stemming from the nature of the traditional culture. The innovation can fulfill the requirements of these categories and be ultimately integrated, or it can be rejected somewhere along the line because it conflicts with some of them. The process can perhaps be clarified by a schematic outline such as that shown on page 161.

Within this process most of the listed factors, or multiples of them, can serve as either barriers or stimulants to acceptance or rejection of an innovation, or else have no bearing on the outcome. These can be regarded as positive, negative, or neutral influences. For instance, a *positive* influence of "participation" would be when the individuals of a local community, the recipients of an innovation, were brought in to participate throughout the planning and implementation of the project. An example of a *negative* influence would be one in which the innovating agent made no effort to get the local population to take part in either planning or implementation. A *neutral* instance would be when participation by the local people was irrelevant in terms of the outcome of the project.

Some factors will appear only as negative influences and never as positive ones, or vice versa. The significance of this is that either that factor can by definition only appear as having a negative or positive effect, or else the reverse possibility has been ignored by research workers. Category XI-C, prestige emulation, is an example of the first type. That is, it will appear only when individuals are attempting to improve their status positions. Since presumably no one is interested in making his status position inferior, this never appears as a negative factor. Category XII-A-1, role of the individual, appears only as a negative influence, because the researcher normally recognizes a conflict between the traditional role of the individual and how it has to be changed if the innovation is to be accepted. Positive instances would not be so readily apparent, because there would be no conflict.

In general, there seems to be a tendency for more examples of negative instances, evidently because social scientists do not usually become aware of influencing factors except when they are acting as barriers to acceptance. Also, the most frequent role of social scientists is that of problem-solvers, and they consequently look for the significant barriers.

Plan (of innovation)

Behavior of Innovator	Behavior of Recipients
——————→ **Action**	←—————— **Reaction**

I Communication (established)	XI Motivation
II Role (image created)	A. Felt Need
III Demonstration (of innovation)	B. Practical Benefit
IV Participation (obtained)	C. Prestige Emulation
V Traditional Culture (utilization of)	D. Competition
VI Environment (utilization of)	E. Reward
VII Timing (utilization of)	F. Novelty
VIII Flexibility (of implementation)	XII Traditional Culture
IX Continuity (of implementation)	A. Social structure
X Maintenance (established)	1. Role (individual)
	2. Status (individual)
	3. Kinship
	4. Caste-class
	5. Ethnic
	6. Political
	7. Central authority
	8. Vested interest
	9. Leadership
	10. Religious fraternity
	B. Economic Pattern
	C. Beliefs
	1. Theological
	2. Magical
	3. Medical
	4. Realistic fatalism
	5. Project negativism
	D. Recreation Pattern
	E. Consumption Pattern
	F. Value System

Integration

There are undoubtedly other influencing factors in the change process and some of these listed may need to be subdivided or consolidated. But on the basis of 106 cases analyzed, these seem to be the most significant. In the following we will attempt to define these components and give illustrative examples of each, taken from published case histories.

Behavior of Innovator

I. Communication

The interchange of ideas between the innovator and the innovation recipient for planning and implementing the innovation. *Positive*

Influence: A community development advisor in Egypt advertised his project and overcame village prejudice through community meetings, contests, informal health lectures, and demonstrations.[19] *Negative Influence:* A public health innovator in Ecuador did not educate the local people in the germ theory of disease, so they saw no connection between a pure water supply and health, nor did he give them any other reason to keep well areas clean.[6]

II. Role of Change Agent

The image of the agent as perceived by the innovation recipients, due to his ability in language, cultural understanding, technical competence, and official affiliations. *Positive Influence:* A community development agent in Iran, a young Iranian woman, was highly motivated and well equipped for community development work. She gained the respect and cooperation of the villagers.[13] *Negative Influence:* Innovators in community development in Philippine villages were local teachers, who, though generally respected, were not looked upon by the local farmers as agricultural experts, so the entire agricultural phase of community development failed to be accepted.[20]

III. Demonstration

Showing the new idea or technique to the innovation recipients as a method of convincing them to accept it. *Positive Influence:* In a pilot project in North India, animals were inoculated right before an epidemic reached the particular area. Not a single inoculated animal contracted the epidemic disease, though in the same village region several non-inoculated animals died as a result of it.[1] *Negative Influence:* In an animal husbandry project in Laos, although improved varieties were introduced into villages, they died from a lack of nourishment or disease, or failed to breed with the local varieties (Niehoff: personal observation).

IV. Participation

The voluntary participation obtained from the innovation recipients in planning and implementing a project. *Positive Influence:* In a public health project in Lebanon, the innovators insisted that, in order to get assistance, the villages must contribute labor, money or kind as much as possible. The villagers did contribute small sums of money, much farm produce, and all manual labor.[24] *Negative Influence:* In an effort to establish rural cooperatives in India, the innovators assumed the difficult task of developing markets, and the local recipients had few responsibilities and few chances for involvement in the administrative aspects of the cooperative.[7]

V. Role of the Traditional Culture

The change agent's efforts to adapt the innovation to local cultural patterns or a lack of such efforts. *Positive Influence:* In an effort to introduce "green manuring" in North India the innovators delegated authority according to local leadership patterns. The innovation was accepted.[21] *Negative Influence:* In a charity hospital in Ecuador the innovators usually broke all traditional rules for post-partum mothers. But because they were willing to relent if a mother was adamant and because treatment was free, the program was not a failure.[6]

VI. Role of environment

Positive or negative utilization of the local environment when relevant to innovation's acceptance. *Positive Influence:* In a soil erosion project in southern Chile, the agent worked only in areas that were slightly eroded in order to be able to bring about changes that would not be too difficult and where chances of failure were minimized. His project was successful.[6] *Negative Influence:* In an animal husbandry project in Laos, it was discovered that the highly bred chickens and pigs that were introduced into the local villages were unable to survive or breed in the village environment and in competition with the village varieties (Niehoff: personal observation).

VII. Timeliness

The introduction of an innovation at an advantageous or a disadvantageous time in relation to the local culture or a local occurrence. *Positive Influence:* In a road improvement project in North India, the work was planned to coincide with seasonal unemployment so village laborers would be free.[11] *Negative Influence:* In an animal improvement project in the Philippines new breeds of swine were introduced just at the time a hog epidemic was occurring. Most of the new animals died as well as the local varieties. The villagers blamed the innovators for their losses.[5]

VIII. Flexibility

The willingness of the change agent to alter his project in order to meet conditions which were not foreseen in the original plans. *Positive Influence:* In the Ceylon program to introduce mass hookworm treatment, the doctors found they could win popularity by treating illnesses other than hookworm, even though previously they had been warned against doing this by the home office.[16] *Negative Influence:* In an irrigation project in South Laos, the innovator came to realize that the local people were not using the canals for irrigation, but instead were washing their clothes in them and getting water from them. He made no alterations in his plan, however, and the project was abandoned (Niehoff: personal observation).

IX. Continuity

The consistent follow-through of a plan within a given social unit even though sometimes revised. *Positive Influence:* In a community development project in Iran, the government and private agencies were regular in furnishing supplies and advising people as soon as they were called upon.[13] *Negative Influence:* In a community development program in Laos, promises made to villagers for construction materials were made periodically but were broken just as often because of administrative difficulties with the AID organization. The villagers became apathetic about community development projects (Niehoff: personal observation).

X. Maintenance

The means of maintaining the innovation within the abilities and cultural facilities of the recipients. *Positive Influence:* In a program in the Cook Islands of the South Pacific for establishing adult education recreational centers, the innovators managed to get the local people to maintain and control their own centers, though the government continued giving advice and aid when asked for and also audited the books.[10] *Negative Influence:* In a program to introduce better varieties of poultry in Jordan, the stock degenerated because supervision in the villages was not maintained. Also, necessary complementary programs of housing and feeding the new fowl were not introduced.[2]

Behavior of Recipients

XI. Motivation

A. Felt need. A need for change recognized by the recipients prior to influence by the change agent. *Positive Influence:* In an agricultural extension program in India, where an effort was being made to introduce new agricultural implements and tools into a village complex, the villagers had already shown an inclination to adopt improved implements of their own.[11] *Negative Influence:* In an effort to introduce sanitary latrines to a rural complex of sixty-seven villages in India, the villagers had no desire for latrines at all. It was the innovator's idea and failed to be accepted.[7]

B. Practical benefit. A benefit which produces an obvious advantage to individual recipients in this life. *Positive Influence:* An effort to introduce disease-resistant varieties of Arabica coffee in Laos was based on the knowledge that better prices would be paid for them in the local market (Niehoff: personal observation). *Negative Influence:* In a public health project in India, latrines were a decided inconvenience. The women would have to carry extra water for flushing them, and the men would have to return from the fields to use them.[7]

C. Prestige emulation. Individual acceptance of an innovation in imitation of individuals or groups of higher status in order to improve one's own status position. *Positive Influence:* In a public health program in Peru, some people who accepted the idea of boiling their drinking water were influenced by city relatives and the idea that they were being progressive. They were also influenced by the talks and pronouncements of the doctor on the project, primarily because of his prestige position in the community.[26] *Negative Influence:* None.

D. Competition. Competitive efforts on the parts of social groups to maintain or improve their status position vis-à-vis other groups. *Positive Influence:* In a community development project in the South Pacific, group rivalries of clubs, teams, districts, and families were used for constructive competition.[3] *Negative Influence:* None.

E. Reward. Immediate reward provided by innovator or authorities to induce recipients to accept a new idea or technique. *Positive Influence:* In a maternal education project in Indonesia mothers who reported to the prenatal clinic were given various gift articles — soap, delivery kits, and wads of cotton.[25] *Negative Influence:* None.

F. Novelty. Acceptance or rejection of an innovation because it is either impressive or suspicious and fearsome. *Positive Influence:* Acceptance of Rhode Island Red chickens in a poultry improvement project in Lao villages because they were so much larger than local chickens (Niehoff: personal observation). *Negative Influence:* Fear of a pump and iron pipe in a well-drilling program in Lebanon — fear of the pump because it had never been seen before and wariness of the iron pipe because it was thought to spoil the taste of the water.[24]

XII. Traditional culture

A. Social Structure.

1. *Role (of the individual).* Conflict or sanction produced by the innovation due to traditional role of the individual in the society. *Positive Influence:* None. *Negative Influence:* A cooperative in an Egyptian village was organized without including the women because of their traditional lack of participation in village institutions. The women felt their interests were being ignored and tried to organize a

separate cooperative, thus causing conflict in the village. They were finally admitted to the innovator's cooperative.[19]

2. *Status.* The position of the individual, normally in a hierarchical relationship. *Positive Influence:* None. *Negative Influence:* In community development projects in Philippine villages, the organizers were usually young, unmarried, elected officials. Such people ignored the traditional respect for age, and the elders felt insulted. They did not cooperate.[20]

3. *Kinship group.* Any formalized group of individuals with a common ancestry, whether the ancestry can actually be traced or whether it is merely believed to exist. The largest such group would be a clan. *Positive Influence:* In a tractor cooperative project in Pakistan, villagers were reluctant to organize themselves into cooperative groups because of their mutual distrust. Finally, a village leader convinced his relatives to join him in a coop and their success set an example for the others.[9] *Negative Influence:* In an agricultural and public health project in South Africa, milk consumption was tied in with elaborate kinship customs so that a family could not supplement its milk supply if they could not get milk from their own cows.[4]

4. *Caste and class.* Groups with status positions, normally in a hierarchical relationship to other such groups, and sometimes with separate racial identity. *Positive Influence:* In an effort to establish cooperatives among leather workers in India, the activities in the cooperatives corresponded with traditional occupations of caste members. A profound sense of caste solidarity made the cooperative function smoothly.[7] *Negative Influence:* In the same project, an effort to establish a cooperative among cloth weavers failed because the weavers were of different castes, which produced differences in decision-making, paralyzed activity, and in general discouraged cooperation.[7]

5. *Ethnic group.* Any group with a distinctive, independent cultural or subcultural pattern. It need not be, but can be, racially distinctive also. *Positive Influence:* None. *Negative Influence:* In a community development program in Israel, three out of fourteen settlements were not affiliated with a religious movement. They could not be integrated as well into the total program.[22]

6. *Political group.* Locally organized sections of central political groups, functioning as units within a village, district, or town context. *Positive Influence:* None. *Negative Influence:* In a community development project in Brazil, the village community was accustomed to personal authoritarian rule by the members of the party in power. The change agents sought to create and work through a nonpolitical com-

munity council whose members were chosen regardless of political leanings. The inclusion of those out of power, and normally disenfranchised, disrupted the political equilibrium. The party in power, seeing its authority undercut, fought the whole project.[14]

7. *Central authority.* The attitude and reaction of the local population toward the centralized control of their own national government. *Positive Influence:* As a whole, lower-class Puerto Ricans have confidence that programs undertaken by their government will benefit them and deserve their support. Thus a government-sponsored urban renewal project in San Juan had the voluntary cooperation of the local people from the very start.[12] *Negative Influence:* In an agricultural extension project in Jordan, when the agents tried to record the plot and parcel numbers of land for introducing improved grape plants, the villagers became suspicious that the government was ready to take over their land and failed to cooperate.[2]

8. *Vested interest.* The reaction of individuals or groups to an innovation that will affect their entrenched interests positively or negatively. *Positive Influence:* In a joint land reform-community development program in Bolivia, landowners gave an estate to the project for agricultural experimentation purposes and cooperated with project personnel. They were motivated by the fear that government expropriation was forthcoming and hoped that under some sort of arrangement with the project they might retain part of the estate.[18] *Negative Influence:* An effort to establish cooperatives in a complex of sixty-seven villages in India threatened the middlemen who were making a profit off their leather workers. The cooperative would eliminate their profit and they resisted its establishment.[7]

9. *Leadership.* The traditional system of leaders and arbiters of social control. *Positive Influence:* In a community development project in Egypt, the change agent sought out the local leaders and organized them into a formal village council. The project was a success.[19] *Negative Influence:* In a community development program in the Philippines, not one of the six chief leaders in a village supported the project due to a conflict with the change agent. The project ended in failure.[20]

10. *Religious fraternity.* Organized groups of a priesthood, or formal religious leaders. *Positive Influence:* In a mass hookworm treatment program in Ceylon, the Buddhist priests and Muslim religious leaders, as well as the important secular leaders, were enlisted to assist in spreading information about how to rid the villagers of hookworm.[16] *Negative Influence:* In a water supply program in a Peruvian village community, the priests and the conservative element

told the people that the shortage of water was due to secularization and modernization and that drilling wells would actually have a negative effect on the water supply. No effort had been made to enlist the priests to assist in the project. It failed.[8]

B. Economic pattern. The local system of economic relationships. *Positive Influence:* In a project to establish a cooperative brick industry in a rural village complex of India, it was discovered that the brick-molding season came during the off season in agriculture. It was an ideal subsidiary industry. Also, almost all of the raw materials were easily available locally at cheap prices, and there was a steady demand for brick in the immediate area.[11] *Negative Influence:* In a poultry improvement project in South Africa, it was found that the local tribesmen believed it was uneconomical to eat eggs, because the eggs would later hatch and become chickens. To them eating eggs was a sign of greed.[4]

C. Beliefs.

1. *Theological.* Beliefs stemming from the dominant formal religious beliefs of the local people. *Positive Influence:* None. *Negative Influence:* In an effort to improve animal husbandry techniques in North India, it was discovered that the veneration of cattle interfered with the breeding program and prohibited the slaughter of useless cattle who were competing for the benefits of the feeding program.[11]

2. *Magical.* Beliefs stemming from supernatural ideas outside the dominant, formal religious beliefs of the local people. *Positive Influence:* None. *Negative Influence:* In a program in Angola to relocate villagers from their worn-out highland patches to virgin bottomland, it was discovered that the local tribesmen believed that their wives would die if they worked in the valleys. The valleys were used as burial grounds for the children and could not be disturbed.[17]

3. *Medical.* Beliefs concerning the nature of the human body and physical ailments, not stemming from supernatural preconceptions. *Positive Influence:* None. *Negative Influence:* In an effort to establish a charity maternity hospital for lower-class mothers in Quito, Ecuador, it was discovered that women believed the afterbirth should be buried, the mother should stay in bed for two weeks, and a forty-day period should be observed during which time she should not bathe, cut her fingernails, or be exposed to fresh air. According to hospital practice, the mother was sent home in five days and all other local medical beliefs were violated, which caused resistance.[6]

4. *Realistic fatalism.* An attitude of apathy produced by prior or present conditions, which prohibit or inhibit the possibility of self-

improvement. *Positive Influence:* None. *Negative Influence:* In an effort to relocate a number of families in Sardinia, it was discovered that the refugees, who had lived in camps for many years, had lost faith in themselves and their will to work. They were apathetic about promises from the government and the change agents. [15]

5. *Project negativism.* Apathy toward innovations induced by previous project failures. *Positive Influence:* None. *Negative Influence:* In an effort to introduce tractor cooperatives in East Pakistan, the villagers' initial reaction was negative because they had seen a number of similar projects fail before, during which money had been squandered and misused. [9]

D. Recreation pattern. Patterns of recreation or pleasure-giving behavior. *Positive Influence:* None. *Negative Influence:* It was found that women resented an effort to introduce sanitary latrines to a rural complex in India because they were accustomed to go to the village reservoirs and their peripheries, where they could meet other women for gossip, relaxation, etc. With latrines, this interaction would have been difficult or impossible. [7]

E. Consumption pattern. The traditional goods consumed, particularly foods and drinks. *Positive Influence:* In an effort to improve the diet of South African Zulus the innovators introduced powdered milk, which was accepted because local people were accustomed to milk in their diets. [4] *Negative Influence:* An attempt to intensify the cultivation of home vegetable gardens in rural Costa Rica failed because vegetables were not traditionally regarded as an essential food. Villagers were satisfied with their existing low level of vegetable consumption. [1]

F. Value system. Systems of beliefs of what is right and proper and what is wrong and improper. *Positive Influence:* None. *Negative Influence:* In the family-planning program in Puerto Rico, it was discovered that men objected to the use of contraceptives because they subtracted from their pleasure. Men believed that sexual satisfaction was their right. They also felt that contraceptives were bad or dirty since they were commonly used in relations with prostitutes. Also, they were afraid that the use of contraceptives would encourage infidelity with their wives. [23]

Two Case Histories

To give an indication of the manner in which this process operates in individual cases we will describe two efforts at producing change in Laos by American technical aid advisors, one accepted, the other rejected. In this way the relevance of the separate variables can be assessed and the total process viewed. Only those components which affected the outcome in a positive or negative way will be listed. Those not listed had no bearing on the outcome.

Case No. 1

Plan: To promote through community self-help action the construction of several hundred schools, markets, roads, and bridges, from June 1960 to June 1961.

I. Communication *Positive*. Though not intensive, a two-way system was inaugurated in which the government officers and American advisors informed villagers of assistance available and allowed villagers to choose and implement their own projects, with a few limitations.

IV. Participation *Positive*. Villagers only undertook projects they wanted, and organized their own work groups and schedules.

V. Utilization of Traditional Culture *Negative*. Since villagers chose their own projects, they picked those which did fit into their culture. Innovators took little notice of such problems, allowing the villagers to work them out themselves.

VI. Utilization of Environment *Negative,* and VII. Timeliness *Negative*. The government and American advisors provided nails, roofing, cement, and other supplies to complete the projects. Due to administrative difficulties, many of these supplies were not provided until after the rice-growing season had started. However, the felt need was great enough that many projects were continued right into the work season.

IX. Continuity *Negative*. The project had been started and stopped several times in the previous years due to administrative problems within the American aid mission. It was interrupted also for six months due to a military crisis. During the last six months it was continuous.

XI. Motivation. A. Felt Need, B. Practical Benefit, *Positive*. In all cases these two factors were present, since villagers chose their own projects and since only those which did have a practical benefit (schools, roads, bridges) were approved.

XII. Traditional Culture. B. Economic Pattern *Negative*. There was a conflict due to the necessity of working through the rice-growing season. But the desire for the projects was great enough that the villagers developed new work patterns. Women and children were organized in many instances to work on schools while the men worked in the rice fields. Also, work was done at night to get projects finished.

Integration *Probable*. Since all projects were decided on and carried out by the villagers themselves, they probably maintained them as well as any other village constructions or institutions.

We believe the analysis of this case is the following. There were four positive factors: communication, participation, felt need, and practical benefit. Of these, the last three are the critical ones, since communication was not intensive. There were five negative factors: lack of utilization of local cultural patterns, faulty utilization of the environment, lack of good timing, lack of continuity, and lack of fitting the project into the local economic pattern—their work schedule. It is our belief that the presence of a felt need and a strong practical benefit, along with full participation in implementing and planning the projects, counterbalanced the barriers that existed. The great freedom of choice given to the villagers is probably the main ingredient in the success of the project.

Case No. 2

Plan: To introduce improved varieties of chickens and pigs in Lao villages from 1957–1960.

I. Communication *Negative*. Villagers never had the opportunity to openly discuss their problems and objections in keeping the new varieties with the government officials or American innovators.

III. Demonstration *Negative*. Although improved varieties were introduced into villages, they died from lack of proper feed or diseases, or failed to breed with local varieties.

IV. Participation *Negative*. Although villagers took the new animals, they made little effort to follow instructions in caring for them.

V. Utilization of Traditional Culture *Negative*. New animals were introduced along with new methods of caring for them, with no effort being made to adapt to traditional animal-keeping practices.

VI. Utilization of Environment *Negative*. Little effort was made to introduce breeds that could survive in village flocks or herds. American varieties had been bred to exist in a completely different environment.

VIII. Flexibility *Positive*. The innovators tried several expedients, though none worked. For instance, when local roosters drove off roosters of improved varieties, one American innovator tried requiring the villagers to eliminate their local roosters before receiving new ones.

IX. Continuity *Negative*. The innovators visited the villages only occasionally when they happened to be in the area.

XI. Motivation. A. Felt Need *Negative*. Ideas of improvement all came from American innovators; E. Reward *Positive*. Animals were given to villagers if they would promise to follow handling instructions; F. Novelty *Positive*. The villagers accepted the new varieties largely because they were so big and handsome.

XII. Traditional Culture. B. Economic Pattern *Negative*. The normal village practice was to let animals fend for themselves. Villagers were uninterested in growing the necessary special foods or following the special handling instructions.

Integration *negative*. The project was completely abandoned without the establishment of any flocks of birds or herds of swine in any villages.

Our analysis of this project is not very difficult, since the innovators violated most of even the most basic techniques for introducing new ideas. They failed to provide for two-way communication, good demonstration, voluntary participation, continuity, and did not take into much consideration either local culture patterns or the environment. The two reasons for accepting the innovation in the first place, novelty and reward, are not very solid ones for permanent acceptance. The only positive factor left, then, is the flexibility of the innovators in trying new methods. However, such minor changes in plan were not enough to make up for all the negative factors. One ventures to suppose that correction of one negative factor alone might have made a difference; this would have been the establishment of effective two-way communication. If the villagers had had some way to voice their objections and discuss their problems, the innovators might have learned some of the characteristics of the local culture and environment which were preventing integration.

A Hypothesis of Change

Case No. 1 can be compared with Case No. 2 in terms of process, even though one deals with community development and the other with animal husbandry. A hypothesis can be drawn up as follows: when a felt need and a strong practical benefit exist, along with the willing cooperation of the recipients for planning and implementation, other negative factors such as lack of awareness of the local cultural patterns on the part of the innovator, lack of continuity, and non-utilization of the local economic patterns will be effectively counter-balanced. On the other hand, when no strong practical benefit or felt need exists, along with a lack of real voluntary participation, the project cannot succeed, even if initially accepted through novelty and reward motivations and even if the innovator is willing to alter his project in order to meet unforeseen conditions.

Obviously this hypothesis is only illustrative. But by using a consistent scheme such as this one to evaluate large numbers of cases it might be feasible to establish the relative importance of the different process components. For example, it might then be possible to state in just what instances voluntary participation or demonstration must be a part of the process and when they are unnecessary. The other process components could be similarly evaluated.

The final question should be, "What is the utility of such an approach?" Our reply is that it is two-fold. In the first place, this process should assist in understanding culture change in general, and apart from direct change. Some similar complex of factors must have been met every time any innovation was successfully introduced into another society, as, for instance, when tobacco was being carried around the world from one society to another.

Secondly, in terms of applied social science, it should enable the technician to understand the process through which his innovation must pass if it is to be integrated into the local society. The proportional relevance of the different factors responsible for acceptance or rejection could be delineated. Although the technician is now usually exhorted to learn about the local culture, it may be that certain aspects of that culture are much more relevant than others.

Notes

[1] M. Alers-Montalvo, "Culture Change in a Costa Rican Village," *Human Organization,* Winter 1957, pp. 4–5.

[2] American Friends Service Committee, *A Village Development Project in Jordan 1953–1956* (Philadelphia, 1958).

[3] H. G. Barnett, *Anthropology in Administration* (Evanston: Harper & Row, 1956), pp. 143–150.

[4] John Cassel, "A Comprehensive Health Program Among South African Zulus," *Health, Culture and Community,* Benjamin D. Paul, ed. (New York: Russell Sage Foundation, 1955), pp. 22–29.

[5] Luz A. Einsiedel, *Success and Failure in Selected Community Development Projects in Batangas* (Quezon City: University of the Philippines, 1960), pp. 34–38.

[6] Charles J. Erasmus, *Man Takes Control* (Minneapolis: University of Minnesota Press, 1961), pp. 17–21, 29–31.

[7] Thomas M. Fraser, Jr., "Sociocultural Parameters in Directed Change," *Human Organization,* Spring 1963, pp. 96–98, 100–102.

[8] Allan R. Holmberg, "The Wells That Failed," *Human Problems in Technological Change,* Edward H. Spicer, ed. (New York: Russell Sage Foundation, 1952), pp. 113–124.

[9] Anwaruzzaman Khan, *Introduction of Tractors in a Subsistence Farm Economy* (Comilla, East Pakistan: Nazeria Press, 1963), pp. 1–63.

[10] Clarence King, *Working with People in Small Communities* (New York: Harper & Row, 1958), pp. 93–102.

[11] Albert Mayer and Associates, *Pilot Project India* (Berkeley and Los Angeles: University of California Press, 1959), pp. 166–169, 248–259, 272–277.

[12] Gitta Meier, "El Embalse: The Creation of a Community through Community

174   THE PROBLEM OF TRANSFER

Organization and Urban Renewal," *Community Development Review*, Washington, D.C., June 1960, pp. 18–47.

[13] Najmeh Najafi, *Reveille for a Persian Village* (New York: Harper & Row, 1958).

[14] Kalvero Oberg and Jose Arthur Rios, "A Community Improvement Project in Brazil," *Health, Culture and Community*, Benjamin D. Paul, ed. (New York: Russell Sage Foundation, 1955), pp. 349–375.

[15] Belden Paulsen, "Citizens of No Countries," *University of Chicago Magazine*, February 1960, pp. 19–22.

[16] Jane Philips, "The Hookworm Campaign in Ceylon," *Hands Across Frontiers*, Howard M. Leaf, Jr. and Peter G. Franck, eds. (Ithaca: Cornell University Press, 1955), pp. 267–302.

[17] A. Richardson, "Everyone Who's Hungry Can Belong to My Church," *Human Organization*, June 1943, pp. 44–48.

[18] L. D. Schweng, "An Indian Community Development Project in Bolivia," *Community Development Review*, Washington, D.C., March 1963, pp. 13–19.

[19] Mohammed M. Shalaby, *Rural Reconstruction in Egypt* (Cairo: Egyptian Association for Social Studies, 1950), pp. 16–38.

[20] Willis E. Sibley, "Social Structure and Planned Change," *Human Organization*, Winter 1960–1961, pp. 209–214.

[21] Rudra Datt Singh, "An Introduction of Green Manuring in Rural India," *Human Problems in Technological Change*, Edward H. Spicer, ed. (New York: Russell Sage Foundation, 1952), pp. 55–67.

[22] State of Israel, Ministry of Social Welfare, Department of Research and Planning, "Community Organization in Israel," (Jerusalem, 1955), pp. 9–14, mimeographed.

[23] Mayone J. Stycos, "Birth Control Clinics in Crowded Puerto Rico," *Health, Culture and Community*, Benjamin D. Paul, ed. (New York: Russell Sage Foundation, 1955), pp. 189–210.

[24] Afif Tannous, "Extension Work Among the Arab Fellahin," *Applied Anthropology*, 1944, pp. 1–12.

[25] Robert B. Textor, *Notes on Indonesian Villagers' Participation in Programs to Modernize Rural Life*, (Indonesia, 1954), pp. 110–123, mimeographed.

[26] Edward Wellin, "Water Boiling in a Peruvian Town," *Health, Culture and Community*, Benjamin D. Paul, ed. (New York: Russell Sage Foundation, 1955), pp. 71–102.

14
The Technical Assistance Expert

Where Are We?

The practice of technical assistance is strangely reminiscent of Gertrude Stein. A well is a well is a well. An expert is an expert is an expert. Only recently has there begun to dawn the painful realization that a well is not a well, and that an expert is not an expert, in any meaningful sense. The intricate process of effecting social change, of translating into workable terms knowledge and experience from one culture to another, of communicating across boundaries, is not an occupation for amateurs. Yet the empirical research needed to lay the foundations for professional activity has not been carried out.

We do not even know the number of experts that may be needed in five years' time, although we can make a guess by projecting the rate of past increases into the future. We can assume, judging by present trends, a growing need for high-level, broad-gauge economic planners, institution builders, engineers, teachers of teachers, and highly specialized specialists, but again this is only an assumption. The number and type of foreign experts needed in the underdeveloped countries cannot be determined unless development plans have been formulated and local manpower resources assessed. This is no easy task in a fluid situation, where the very success of one program may affect demands in another area: if infant mortality is lowered, the need for schools increases. Knowledge regarding the availability of experts is dependent upon reliable forecasts in the industrialized countries of their own needs and, hence, of their ability to provide personnel. Again, this poses problems.

The nature and number of technicians needed depend on a variety of economic factors not easily ascertained and upon "often unfore-

Anne Winslow, "The Technical Assistance Expert," *International Development Review,* Vol. 4 (September 1962), pp. 17–24.

seeable political decisions (economic development plans, creation of an atomic energy administration, European common markets, etc.)."[1] But a serious, concerted effort must be made by host countries, technical assistance agencies, and recruitment bodies to arrive at some reasonably valid and realistic estimates — both short-term and long-term — if suitable training programs are to be developed.

Our ignorance regarding the personal qualities needed by instigators of social change is even greater. The preparation of laundry lists of desirable qualities has become a favorite occupation, but, alas, all that emerges is an ideal man who does not exist. We do not know how to create him, and we might not recognize him if we saw him. "He must be cultured and cross-cultured. He must be disciplined and inter-disciplined. He must be well stocked with empathy and antifreeze. He should be a model himself, and he should know about model-building, institution-building, stadium-building, and body-building."[2]

Here we need research in the field. We need some effective criteria for evaluating success and failure, and some method of distinguishing the personal failure of an expert from the failure of a project for reasons beyond the expert's control. We need to know whether certain types of individuals do better in one culture or another and to what extent experience in one culture is transferable to others. How can desirable tests be devised that are not culture-bound? What modifications is it possible to make in an adult's outlook and approach? How can latent qualities be brought out?

"No sane person would attempt to put a space ship in orbit without elaborate supporting educational and research activities. Yet this is precisely what we have attempted in the more subtle and complex areas of overseas operations."[3]

Recruitment and Selection

"The problem of scarcity of human skills and of highly qualified specialists is as important as the scarcity of physical capital formation which has been the focus of more attention in many developing areas."[4] Yet the reservoir of available technical assistance experts is shrinking rapidly. At the same time, needs for experts are multiplying and are changing in character. As development proceeds and as training programs build up a stratum of technicians, the demand for high-level and specially qualified personnel grows. Many of the industralized countries are undergoing a period of economic expansion that is creating new demands for precisely this type of manpower. Terms and conditions of service at home are far more appealing than abroad. A recent survey of some agencies in the United Kingdom revealed the fact that two-thirds of the available posts for overseas personnel remained unfilled for upwards of a year and some technical posts for five years.[5]

The best opportunities for recruitment now lie in the two extremes — those persons who have already reached retirement and those not yet embarked upon a career. With the growing realization that technical assistance is here to stay — at least for the foreseeable future — serious attention is being turned to the "junior" or "associate" expert. The Netherlands and a few other countries have made junior experts available — at the government's expense — to the United Nations Expanded Program of Technical Assistance, and similar action is under consideration by other countries. The United States has embarked upon a major "associate" expert program in its Peace Corps.

The possibilities of a career service in technical assistance are also being explored. The United Nations Expanded Program and the International Bank for Reconstruction and Development are now both developing modest career services of this type. The advantages of such a service are manifest, but there are also limitations: some types of expertise are needed only intermittently and some require frequent contact with evolving professional knowledge. However, the potential further availability of even the expert seconded for a single mission can be enhanced by keeping him informed of the evolution of a project he was involved in or of projects growing out of his particular task, through the medium of a newsletter, for example, or by correspondence between the expert and his counterparts.

Another approach to recruitment problems which is receiving increasing attention is the use of consultant and other business firms. The firms have available their own teams of seasoned experts and are in a position to provide planning and backstopping services. Although such firms are not suitable for all types of projects or where there is a potential conflict of interest, they have a useful place and one that is likely to grow.

In addition to increasing the total supply of experts, it is important to use them with maximum efficiency. At the Rome conference, it was suggested that greater use be made of regional experts, that is, one expert serving three or four countries in rotation. After several months in country A, the expert would move on to country B, and so on. At the end of perhaps a year, he would return to country A and complete the circuit again. During his absence from any given country, the work would be carried on by technicians or possibly by junior experts. This scheme has the advantage of permitting periodic check-ups of work in progress. It poses real problems, however, for experts who are accompanied by their families. A second suggestion emanating from the Rome conference, applying to the United Nations, is the use of regional economic commission personnel to help in defining the job and in filling the post while the expert is being recruited.

The most efficient allocation of currently available experts is clearly of prime significance. Competitive anarchy is finding fewer and fewer adherents. National committees have been established in a number of European countries to channel requests and locate, screen, and propose candidates. In many cases these serve both bilateral and multilateral agencies. In Sweden, for example, there is a "central body for information, planning, cooperation, execution and control of all matters related to Swedish assistance to the underdeveloped countries."[6] A central roster of presumptive experts will be maintained and kept up to date. A public information officer provides information about expert assignments.

At the Rome conference the hope was expressed that such committees might be developed in other countries since they appeared to produce better and more consistent results than any other existing method of locating, screening, and proposing candidates for overseas assignments. Such committees should have at their disposal adequately trained and experienced staff, and an effective recruitment network organized on a functional basis. They should generate, through the use of all national and regional media, a climate favorable to recruitment and promote the adoption of national legislation and formal agreements designed to facilitate the release of personnel for assignments abroad, the protection of their promotion, pension, and social security entitlements during the period of their absence, and their reinstatement, on their return, in positions not less favorable than they could have reasonably expected if they had remained at home. The committees should maintain a roster of candidates whose suitability has been carefully determined. Finally, they should promote the further training of technically qualified younger personnel and facilitate arrangements for foreign language tuition for candidates otherwise considered suitable for foreign assignments.

The employing agencies for their part should provide a job description clearly setting out the nature, level, and duration of the assignment, and the final date for the receipt of candidatures; the actual tasks to be performed; environmental factors; the availability of technical services and equipment on the spot; information on terms and conditions of service; the criteria to be applied in recruitment; and such background information as a serious and busy candidate is believed to need to be persuaded of the worthwhileness of the assignment. In addition, they should make available full information on the status of each post for which recruitment had been requested, including notice of postponements, modifications, or cancellations, and estimates of future requirements.[7] It was also urged at the Rome conference that employing agencies make known their reasons for rejecting proposed candidates so that the committees could establish meaningful selection criteria. Even where an agency uses other recruitment channels, it should at least keep the national committees informed of its activities.

The existence of good channels of recruitment, however, does not automatically imply a flow of candidates. The charm of overseas service often lessens in the face of practical considerations. International organizations, particularly, are at a disadvantage in providing attractive offers. Salaries tend to be under the market price in some countries, equivalent salaries are not always paid for equivalent posts even in the same country, and hardship post allowances are extremely difficult to establish on any meaningful basis for international personnel. What may be a hardship post for a national of country A may not be for one from Country B and vice versa. Furthermore, "the U. N. agencies are generally so worried about their administrative costs that they can seldom give the expert the necessary supporting services,"[8]

Another handicap is the restraint placed upon them by the nature of their relationships with host countries. Many business concerns seal off their employees in compounds with all the conveniences to which they are accustomed and more, but special privileges granted to an international official such as duty-free imports are immediately resented. Even the salary differential between expert and counterpart can be a source of friction.

Moreover, many employers, particularly business and academic institutions, are reluctant to submit to the administrative inconvenience incurred in seconding personnel. To some extent this attitude can be modified by educational campaigns; here chambers of commerce can be particularly helpful. The experience gained from a field mission may give an individual new insights and contacts that will redound to the advantage of the employer. This has been increasingly recognized by governments and has been an added factor in predisposing them to look favorably on technical assistance missions. The French government, for example, now guarantees the expert an equivalent post upon return and the retention of all seniority and promotion rights; similar provisions are incorporated in a draft law under discussion in the Italian parliament. Even in some of the less developed countries, where there is a desperate shortage of personnel, the short-run sacrifice is seen as a long-term gain on condition that the return of the expert within a reasonable period of time is guaranteed. There is an urgent need for a similar attitude in business and academic circles. An inquiry conducted among some 200 persons in England elicited the fact that the main reason for refusing technical assistance missions was the fear of prejudicing career prospects at home.

One important factor influencing both prospective candidates and employers is the time lag between the first interview and the dispatch of the expert, which may be a year or more. If the expert doesn't withdraw in disgust, both he and his employer are subjected to considerable inconvenience. A royal committee, charged with studying administrative arrangements in Sweden relating to technical assistance, proposed that a candidate should receive a definite reply regarding his eventual appointment within one month from the date of his application. If the day is to come "when technicians and specialists as well as administrators will take absences of a few years on technical assistance missions during their professional careers as a matter of course," [9] both host governments and employment agencies will have to tighten up their administrative procedures.

The availability of candidates is obviously a prerequisite for recruitment, but this is only the beginning of the story. The recruiter must know what he is looking for. The international official, at least, does not. He is presented with a job description that sometimes conceals more than it reveals and may be quite irrelevant.

All too rarely are requests for technical assistance designed as implementation of a coherent development plan. As a result the job description has been known to refer to an idea that has vanished by the time the expert arrives, to a plan conceived by a donor without reference to local needs and desires, or to a project that cannot be carried out because it was poorly conceived. Frequently, it is not even clear whether the expert is to design a project, set it in motion, or diagnose problems in an already functioning operation. Each of these calls for a different type of experience, different qualities of mind and personality. Still less information is available on the responsibilities of the expert and the milieu within which he is expected to operate. Is he to execute, to advise, or to train? With what level of officials will he be working? What is their background and training? Will his contacts be wide or narrow? What facilities and material resources are available? What are the expectations of the host government, as regards both the expert himself and the objective of the project? The recruiter needs this information to find his man, and the candidate needs it to decide whether in fact he himself thinks he is fit for the job in question. At the Rome conference it was also pointed out that the "qualifications" listed by international organizations are frequently couched in terms relevant only to particular countries, and it was urged that a list be established of equivalent degrees or diplomas in the various educational systems.

But the job description is only a tool. How it is used depends on the nature of the recruiting and selection process. Unfortunately the effort to develop a rational system is continually diverted by a deep-seated belief inherent in most human beings, although not in well-trained recruiters. "I can tell at a glance whether he is a good man or not" is the mark of this sixth sense. Compounding the problem is the technician's insistence that he be the final arbiter in total disregard of the basic tenet that no man can be accepted as a technician without being accepted as a man. The recruiting services are low man on the totem pole, used for intractable or uninteresting problems.

Many large businesses long ago realized that recruitment and selection require highly specialized skills, that such skills must be adequately compensated and that services carrying out these functions must be located high in the hierarchy so that they can command authority and know in advance the needs they will be called upon to fill. Businesses have learned that a fairly high investment in recruitment and selection is far less costly than the failures and fumblings that otherwise are bound to result.

One of the recurrent themes of the Rome conference was the necessity of strengthening the recruiting services and giving them adequate funds to do the job, including travel allowances to interview candidates and their families, ascertain needs, and perhaps assist in developing the job descriptions. The role of the technician should be advisory, not decisive, it was maintained, and the host government should be involved, in some appropriate fashion, in the selection process so that its interests and wishes may be accurately reflected.

"There is a growing tendency to favour methods which involve extensive checking of personal and professional references, detailed confidential inquiries and the building up of comprehensive documentation on the antecedents of individual candidates prior to the arrangement of a series of interviews, each of which is intended to ascertain a particular aspect of the candidate's personal or professional suitability."[10] The more that is known about a candidate, the greater is the probability that his future behavior can be predicted with reasonable accuracy. As in the case of the French Training Center for International Technical Cooperation Experts, the knowledge available to the selector is significantly increased. One of the interviewing techniques that has found favor is the numerical weighting of the selection criteria attaching to a particular post. Each interviewer rates the individual item and totals his score. The individual scores are consolidated and any glaring discrepancies discussed before making a decision. The perfection of such techniques, however, must wait on further research and, as far as international agencies are concerned, on the translation of tested methods into forms suitable for multinational selection.

The Rome conference did not attempt to follow the well-trodden path and describe the qualities of the ideal man.   Certain needs, however, were stressed and certain questions raised. A representative of a less developed country remarked pungently, "We do not need a book but someone who understands our local problems." Emphasis was laid on the importance of the expert's conviction of the validity of the project and his acceptance of both host government objectives and employing agency. The expert cannot change the philosophy of either, and if he is not in sympathy he will merely frustrate himself, his employer, and the host government. The expert must be able to express himself clearly and simply, and work himself out of a job by developing a cadre of enthusiastic and trained counterparts. Questions were raised about the facile assumption that because an expert had done well in one country, he would, *ipso facto,* do so in another. Questions were also raised about too close identification with host country nationals lest the expert lose his objectivity and his ability to achieve results. Questions were raised about the importance of language qualifications and the types of situation where these are a crucial factor. Another question that needs further investigation is the influence of different milieus upon the success of an expert. There seems to be some evidence that people from small towns who may never have seen a foreigner do better than the more cosmopolitan urbanite. Finally, on a more philosophical level, there is a question that pervades the whole operation of technical assistance. How can one avoid "turning a good Chinese into a bad Westerner?"

Training

There is general acceptance of the fact that a technical assistance expert serving overseas needs more in his luggage than his professional training. Although the objective has been described as the task of making the individual "more creative in a world of different values," there is no clear definition of who should be trained, where, and how.

Obviously, any expert needs to know about the agency employing him. He needs to know its principles and objectives, its character and personality. He has to know how it works administratively: what authority will be delegated to him, what support he can expect, what channels of communication and reporting he will be expected to use. It should go without saying that, before he is hired, he should know in full detail all the conditions of service and should be given a sober, realistic picture of his mission.

How much does the expert need to know about the particular country in which he will be working, and about its language? What does he need to know about the process of fostering change and about the human relations aspect of his mission, and what *can* he be taught? These are all questions that have stimulated much debate and ·discussion and that are still in a highly unscientific stage of conclusion.

It seems clear that all experts need some training. Even a "sheep expert deals not only with sheep but also with the owner and the shepherd." And the mission chief—that exalted being—is not born to his role. He is the keystone of the project; his knowledge and leadership can tip the scale toward success or failure. He too must be trained although special training devices may be required. This has been recognized, at least in principle, in the United States, where an intensive nine-month training program has recently been recommended for senior AID personnel.

While it seems clear that all experts need some training, they are not the only ones involved. The expert may have a wife and children. The failure of the family to understand and adjust has probably induced more failures than any other single factor. This is why businesses increasingly include the wives in the training program.

The third element in the picture is the counterpart, who shares equally with the expert responsibility for the achievement of the objective. It was suggested at the Rome conference that appropriate aspects of training be conducted jointly for experts and counterparts.

In most agencies, governmental and intergovernmental, there is a curious blind spot. What the eye of headquarters does not see, does not exist. It does see—with pain—the time and money spent on training an expert before departure. The guilty conscience of the bureaucrat does not see the far greater expenditure of time and money spent in undirected on-the-job learning in the field.

It has been suggested that all personnel would probably benefit from six months to a year of training, but this is clearly utopian, particularly for experts going out for a year or less. For technicians, the feasible range lies somewhere between two weeks and two months. In this period they are supposed to learn about their new employer; familiarize themselves with technical assistance in general, understand why it exists, how it operates, and what a technical assistance program really is; learn how their project originated, what results it is expected to yield, and what program it fits into; glean the essentials regarding the culture and economy and the political, administrative, and value systems of the host country; acquire a knowledge of the typical situations and conditions they will face and an understanding of their role as instruments of social change operating in an advisory capacity. Even these basic ingredients tend to get squeezed out in the press of departure. The following description of a United States expert could be duplicated in many other capitals.

The recruit who probably has spent many months waiting for security clearance, not knowing whether to sublease his home, ask for a leave, prepare his family for an overseas move, or otherwise do or not do the thousand and one things of normal living while he is being investigated and before getting the firm appointment which, at the last minute, could fail to come because of program changes, suddenly finds himself rushed to Washington with or without his family, a recruited technical assistant. Once there and on the federal payroll, Washington is most anxious and somewhat impatient to send him to the country of his assignment, which, of course, has been awaiting his arrival for six to fifteen months. At best, therefore, he is offered a brief noncompulsory "training" period lasting two to four weeks, during which time he is also expected to familiarize himself with his new project and agency, learn about and visit other related Washington agencies, finish taking his shots, arrange for his and the family's transportation, acquire passports and otherwise manage himself and his family. . . .[11]

In the international agencies, the training period ranges from zero, except for administrative details, to a few days. The World Health Organization is the only United Nations agency that has developed some systematic training. As a first step toward a more satisfactory situation, the General Conference of UNESCO decided in 1960 to establish a briefing center for international experts near Paris. Courses last for two and one-half days and cover the following points:

The United Nations: its political aspects, economic and social activities, autonomous services, regional commissions, the specialized agencies.

Technical assistance: historical background, principles, modalities of action, organization, procedure, evaluation.

The role of the expert in the United Nations and in technical assistance.

The phenomenon of underdevelopment: its characteristics by countries or groups of countries, its economic and social implications.

The expert's adjustment to the country in which he is to work, most common problems, requisite personal qualifications.

The expert's professional problems, possible weaknesses in the project, counterparts, study grants, teamwork, delays.

On the national level there are, here and there, a few examples of similar post-entry training courses. Oversea Service in England, a private institution, runs a three-to-five-day post-entry course for experts recruited by various public and private agencies. In addition to background information on the area or areas to which the experts are going and the problems of adjustment, considerable attention is devoted to such practical questions as clothing, living conditions, and health precautions.

The training requirements for a high-level administrator or policy advisor are obviously more exacting than for a technician, and the gap between need and fulfillment is even greater. For such individuals, the necessary training period has been estimated at three months, and the range of subject matter to be included covers such questions as processes of induced change and the rate of change requisite for political acceptance; effects of such factors as natural resources, traditions, values, and moral systems on development tasks; the balance between planning and execution within the limits of available resources; principles and practices of capital formation; institution building; cross-cultural understanding and communication; and political systems, social philosophies, and ideologies.

One of the unresolved questions is that of language training. There is a general belief that the expert is more successful and more readily acceptable if he knows the local language. Yet it is manifestly impossible in pre-entry training to teach all the languages that may be required. Africa alone has some 1,200 languages. For practical reasons, it is equally impossible, as a general rule, to devote adequate time to language training in a post-entry course. Obviously in many cases a knowledge of the four vehicular languages — English, French, Spanish, and Arabic — would be sufficient and would certainly facilitate the learning of additional languages, but there are still too many exceptions for this to be a solution, even it it were feasible. There is a "language laboratory" in Paris working on this problem, and experiments on accelerated training have been conducted in Leiden and Hamburg, but so far there are no established techniques that can be relied upon.

Another and very difficult aspect of training is that relating to attitudinal change and psychological preparedness. To what extent are attitudes susceptible of modification by training and how can this be achieved? Two studies conducted in the United States in recent years concluded that it is not possible to change an individual's value system; it is possible, however, to develop more empathy for the environment and to create new insights.[12]

This can be achieved most successfully in small groups, the interaction of the members being itself an important aspect of the educational process. There are also advantages to a multidisciplinary group so that specialists have an opportunity to transcend their own field of specialization and understand something of the multifaceted complexity of the task on which they are engaged. In other aspects, however, some degree of homogeneity is probably desirable. From the UNESCO experience, it would appear that too great disparity is a disadvantage and that "as soon as two languages have to be used, any discussion is more or less inhibited."[13] Some people believe that groups should be composed of nationals of one country and participants selected according to the nature of the employing agency — industry, government, and so forth. It is argued that under such conditions much freer discussion is possible. Whether this advantage outweighs the broadening and stimulating effects of an interdisciplinary group is something that needs further research.

There is much that we do not know about the optimum composition of a group, the possibilities of profitable interaction, and the use of returned experts or other experienced personnel. What purposes can be achieved by informational brochures and bibliographies? What should they include? When should they be given to the expert? What is the role of films and other visual materials as an adjunct to training? It was suggested at the Rome conference that there was need for clearing-house services to permit a better exchange of training material. There should also be developed, it was believed, "field laboratories" and pilot projects in which research would be carried on and in which apprentices and newly arrived employees could take part as an aspect of field training.

Responsibility for training should not devolve upon one pair of shoulders. It should be shared. The home country has a responsibility for seeing that its potential experts receive the basic general training upon which specialized orientation can be built in a relatively brief period of time. There are two aspects to this foundation work. The first involves a general understanding of other societies and cultures in both their historical and dynamic aspects and of the processes of social change. This is a function of the formal academic institutions. In Sweden, a royal committee has suggested that the various university authorities be asked to consider the special problem of the under-developed countries in the planning of curricula; the study of the public administration systems of other countries will be included in the program of a proposed administrative staff college. In the United States, there is an important developing relationship between professional schools and foreign area programs in some universities. The Cornell College of Agriculture is specializing in research and training on agricultural development in Latin America and the Philippines, in which it is assisted by the foreign area programs. There is graduate training for both American and foreign students requiring research in the field under direction of Cornell professors. The attempt is to study not only the technical aspects of agriculture but also the psychology and cultural motivations of peasant farmers, in order to discover how to introduce changes more successfully. The universities must also bear a primary responsibility for "developing theories to explain these far-reaching phenomena, research programs to test theory against relevant experience, and a body of professional knowledge and practice which can form the nucleus of educational programs to prepare those who will participate in overseas operations."[14]

The second aspect of home-country training is more directly concerned with the processes of economic development and the kind of knowledge regarding technical assistance that the expert will need. One of the best examples of this type of training is that provided by the French Training Centre for International Technical Cooperation Experts, established in 1957 by the Ministry of Foreign Affairs. Since it is designed to train those capable of becoming technical assistance experts, candidates are rigorously screened and only those with the requisite experience and competence are accepted. The average age is 40. Two courses are held yearly; there are 100 to 150 candidates of whom about a quarter are selected. One annual session is geared to those active in professional occupations in the Paris region, with most lectures and seminars held out of working hours. The course of some 13 hours a week lasts three months. The second session is an intensive one-month course of about 40 hours a week. Both courses include information about the various regions of the world with emphasis on traditional and cultural patterns in certain countries; problems of economic and social growth; the mobilization of human resources; the structures, procedures, and machinery of technical assistance, both bilateral and multilateral; and problems of financing economic development. Courses are structured to bring out the relationships that exist in developing countries between the expert's field of specialization and other areas, and to throw light on the psychological and material difficulties involved in the adaptation of the expert to a developing country and to the human and material requirements for economic development.

The experience of this center, of a special course recently inaugurated in the Netherlands for future experts, of courses under the auspices of the Società Italiana per l'Organizzazione Internazionale in Italy, and of the Deutsche Stiftung für Entwicklungsländer in Germany, indicates a surprisingly enthusiastic response to such training facilities. They inevitably tend, however, to attract certain categories of experts — civil servants, economists, industrialists, teachers, and only rarely the extra-specialized expert or the practitioner, since these become experts fortuitously rather than by intent.

Responsibility for an understanding of and knowledge about the employing agency must rest with the headquarters of that agency. It and the recruiting service must brief the expert fully in the nature of his tasks, the history and background of the project. Such briefing should be factual and congruent, not "glossing over the project's weak points and hinting at desired, rather than actual prospects." At the Rome conference, emphasis was laid on the importance of a briefing officer who can direct and supervise the expert's activities, thereby sparing him "many useless visits and long waits in corridors, and a thousand other sources of irritation and confusion." Such training presumably can and should be supplemented in the field, in the case of United Nations organizations by the regional economic commissions or regional offices, and by the resident representatives.

It is also the responsibility of the employing agency to see that the expert knows about the processes, functions, and purposes of technical assistance and has some understanding of social change and of the attitudinal and behavioral requirements that will be made upon him. It is not necessarily the function of the employing agency to conduct such training. In fact, a good case could be made for centralizing this aspect under appropriate auspices. Operating agencies are seldom materially equipped to become teaching institutions, and, in the case of the international organizations, the flow of experts is too small and erratic to warrant individual training facilities.

Another aspect of training for which the employing agency should assume responsibility is retraining and refresher courses for long-term experts. In many fields of specialization, expertise diminishes fairly rapidly if the technician is cut off from his professional contacts. Thus provision must be made for periods of study in which the expert can catch up on new professional knowledge and on the improved application and adaptation of existing knowledge to conditions in developing countries. The generalist needs to broaden his horizons from time to time, compare notes with others in similar positions, and gain new insights. The reluctance of governments to make funds available for such training has already taken its toll, and loss of expertise among many specialists has become a matter of serious concern.

As far as education regarding the particular country of assignment is concerned, it would seem appropriate that a large share of responsibility should fall upon the host country. In the first place, the country has a manifest self-interest in creating an understanding of its mores and problems and is certainly in the best position to do so. In the second place, the host country may be less impatient at the expert's wasting his time if it is providing the education. In the third place, the expert is more psychologically receptive when he is actually in the field with the evidence under his eyes. Although no studies have been made, it is generally felt that the best period for field indoctrination is after the second month. By this time the expert has begun to realize what he doesn't know, what he wants to know, and what he needs to know.

Iran now has its own training program for United Nations experts to introduce them to the cultural and social aspects of an Islamic country. Nigeria is hoping to establish a similar program. The pilot project in this area and the most ambitious to date is that of the Delhi Training and Orientation Centre, established in 1954 with a grant from the Ford Foundation. Six to seven sessions of two weeks' duration are held every nine months, and wives and adult children are included. There is a library of 10,000 volumes dealing exclusively with India. Courses cover geography, history, culture, Islam, urbanization, Hindu way of life, social structure, administrative structures, agricultural problems, handicrafts, community development, the role of foreign experts in India, the Indian constitution, economic planning, education, culture, political parties, and so forth. In addition to lectures and discussion periods, participants are shown films, visit an Indian village, and are served an Indian meal with Indian etiquette.

Presumably such centers could be established only in the large countries, but small countries might band together and establish a regional center. A university would appear to provide the most acceptable auspices, with its resources supplemented possibly by lecturers from United Nations regional economic commissions.

All over the world, in countries exporting technical assistance and in those importing it, efforts are being made to find some answer to the problem of training, but information is still lacking upon which sound foundations can be laid. Some of the existing confusion arises from the effort to make up in the relatively brief period after recruitment for inadequacies in the previous educational background. The result is a grandiose curriculum calling for years of study. To fit the Procrustean time bed, subjects have to be covered in such generalities as to be relatively meaningless.

Until a generation of experts can be given in their formal education the requisite basic orientation and knowledge, the employing agency should, however reluctantly, accept the fact that its experts are going to fall below the ideal and concentrate on those aspects of training that can be meaningfully instilled within the allotted time. This will require field research in cooperation with experts and with host governments — preferably by some independent authority — on the types of knowledge and attitudes that make for success. It will require research units in donor agencies to capture their experience and make it available to the researcher. Upon the findings of such investigation, it should be possible to determine what can and must be taught and the minimum periods that must be devoted to such training. It should also be possible to indicate areas of emphasis appropriate for academic institutions and and the respective educational roles that might be played by employing agencies, host governments, and others.

Notes

[1]André Chafanel, Report prepared for the Conference on Recruitment, Selection, and Training of Technical Assistance Personnel, French, Mimeographed (Rome, 1962), p. 2.

[2]Robert E. Asher, "In Conclusion," *Development of the Emerging Countries: An Agenda for Research* (Washington: The Brookings Institution, February 1962), p. 215.

[3]Milton J. Esman, *Needed: An Education and Research Base to Support America's Expanded Commitments Overseas* (Pittsburgh: University of Pittsburgh Press, 1961), p. 8.

[4]M. A. El-Shafie, *General Observations and Comments Pertaining to the Problem of Recruitment and Selection,* Report prepared for the Conference on Recruitment, Selection, and Training of Technical Assistance Personnel, Handwritten, p. 3.

[5]Oversea Service, *An Enquiry into the Recruitment in the United Kingdom of Personnel for Posts in the Developing Countries* (London: Oversea Service, January 1962), p. 2.

[6]*Den Svenska Utvecklingshjälpen Expertrekrytering och stipendiamottagning* (with a review in English: *Swedish Technical Assistance Expert and Fellowship Problems*), Statens Offentliga Utredningar 1961:50 (Stockholm: Emil Kihlströms Tryckeri Aktiebolag, June 1961), p. 69.

[7]See Gordon Menzies, *The Recruitment and Selection of Personnel for Overseas Assignments,* Working Paper No. 2, prepared for the Conference on Recruitment, Selection, and Training of Technical Assistance Personnel, Mimeographed, pp. 7–10.

[8]*Den Svenska Utvecklingshjälpen, op. cit.,* p. 72.

[9]Sylvain Lourié, *Note d'Information sur certains problèmes du recrutement des experts, pour des missions de coopération technique internationale,* prepared for the Conference on Recruitment, Selection, and Training of Technical Assistance Personnel, French, mimeographed, p. 6.

[10]Menzies, *op. cit.,* p. 2.

[11]Frank N. and Helen G. Trager, "Exporting and Training Experts," *The Review of Politics,* Vol. 24, No. 1 (January 1962), p. 95.

[12]See Philip E. Jacob, *Changing Values in College* (New York: Harper & Row, 1957) and Edward D. Eddy, Jr., *The College Influence on Student Character* (Washington: American Council on Education, 1958).

[13]Henri Laurentie, *Post-Entry Expert Briefing (a) as Undertaken by UNESCO and (b) as Considered as a Basic Problem of Technical Assistance,* Working Paper No. 1, prepared for the Conference on Recruitment, Selection, and Training of Technical Assistance Personnel, p. 5.

[14]Esman, *op. cit.,* p. 8.

15
The Re-entry Crisis

One night last March, an attractive young Peace Corps volunteer named Janet Hanneman got off a plane at Washington National Airport, took an airline bus into the city and checked into a downtown motel. She was wearing a shalwar, the striking national dress of Pakistan, where she had served for the last two and a half years. She had brought home with her no Western dresses at all. Next morning, eye-catching in another orange-and-red silk shalwar, she went off to work at Peace Corps headquarters. In the elevator a man recognized her as a heroine of a Peace Corps recruiting film and said, "Oh, you're the girl in the movies."

Everyone in the car turned to look at her. Embarrassed, Janet became dizzy and nearly fainted. "I was mortified," she recalls. "A woman does not get that kind of attention in Pakistan. Then suddenly I realized that I was reacting not like an American but exactly as a Pakistani woman would in the same circumstances." A long ordeal for Janet Hanneman had begun.

Janet Hanneman was, in fact, experiencing the first pangs of what Peace Corps officials have come to call "the re-entry crisis." There are, at the moment, some 3,500 returned veterans of the corps in the United States. . . . As thick files of pain-touched letters in Peace Corps headquarters testify, virtually all the returnees suffered when they came back: "The first month was hell." "I was depressed for six weeks." "I don't feel at home anymore." What had been a great experience overseas was turning sour at home.

The volunteers feel unwanted, uncomfortable, apologetic, or defensive — sometimes all of these. As the corps begins its fifth highly successful year, the question of what to do about re-entry is at the top

Richard B. Stolley, "The Re-entry Crisis," *Life,* March 19, 1965, pp. 98ff. © 1965 Time Inc. All Rights Reserved.

of the corps' comparatively small list of problems. A three-day conference in Washington last week [March 1965] was devoted to it. In long workshop sessions, ways of "opening up opportunities for further service in public life" were hashed over by more than 1,000 volunteers and national leaders. The aim was not only to put the unique talents of the returning volunteers to work but also to ease their readjustment problems.

Typically, these difficulties begin as the homecoming welcome congeals rapidly into disillusion. For the volunteer, the United States has changed mysteriously and uncomfortably while he has been away. He sees now only a crowded, car-jammed, commercialized mess — surfeit and superabundance everywhere. His friends and relatives seem not to be too clear on where he had been or what he did there or why it was important. They don't appear to be much interested in the rest of the world. And the volunteer in turn cannot get excited about the things that stir them: new cars, color TV sets.

Once the joyous spasms of reunion are over, his family sees that their son has changed in disturbing ways. He seems moody, preoccupied, irritated by their well-meant questions. Talk peters out. The young man just home from Sarawak (or Ghana or Colombia or any of 46 countries) is not the same person who left home two years before. Nor will he ever be.

In considering the matter of re-entry, Peace Corps psychiatrists, led by Dr. Joseph English, have come to two conclusions. One is that, in one form or another, major readjustment shocks are inevitable. The initial and most severe phase lasts an average of about four months, although the duration varies with the individual. Later, after about a year, the volunteer will go through another crisis, the psychiatrists say, in which he will begin to doubt the value of whatever he happens to be doing. A student may start to question the whole philosophy of education. A businessman may wonder what kind of real contribution he is now making to society.

The second conclusion Dr. English and his associates have reached is that the spark — the discontent — that produces these crises is vital and should on no account be allowed to dissipate. "It is healthy and it is reassuring," says Dr. English. "It has great catalytic energy. If volunteers let this restlessness and dissatisfaction die away, then we have lost a great resource."

This special seed of discontent with the world is precisely what impelled many volunteers to join the Peace Corps in the first place and what later made them so effective abroad. By training and instinct they moved into situations and, by their own hands, changed them.

Often they found themselves performing jobs, giving advice and accepting responsibility far beyond anticipated limits. And, paradoxically, perhaps the truest measure of their accomplishments is the pain they endure when they return to the United States.

"We were the big shots of the village," says Robert Morgan, now a teacher in Walla Walla, Washington, speaking of his small group of teachers in the mountains of Ecuador. "People would bring us all their problems. When we helped a mechanic figure out instructions printed in German for a new piece of equipment, the story spread all over town. It was a little thing, but we became local celebrities."

When volunteer Frank Guido of Philadelphia left the Ghanaian village where he taught science, the local chief presented him with a gift of rare value—a piece of tribal land so that Frank would always have a place to come back to. In Peru, 28-year-old Leon Haller, holding only a master's degree in economics from Stanford, worked on equal terms with the country's top bankers to set up a network of savings and loan associations—a level of responsibility hopelessly out of the reach of such a young man in the United States.

These volunteers came back to this country loaded with self-confidence. "We got things done," says Kathryn Hannan, who taught English and science in the rural Philippines and now does social work in a Chicago hospital. "We wouldn't take no for an answer."

For most Peace Corps volunteers the two years abroad passed swiftly and were deeply felt—"the most intense period of emotional involvement we ever had," one of them has said. Then—suddenly—they are home. Sometimes after a few weeks of travel, sometimes by overnight jet, they are dropped back onto the American scene—excited, filled with a sense of accomplishment, often unashamedly patriotic ("When President Kennedy asked what we could do for our country, I was in the chorus that answered him").

But when they step through customs, the adventure is done and their special status has disappeared. They have been out of touch with America during deeply impressionable years, and comparisons they now make between it and the country they have just left are almost inevitably disturbing. Unerringly, their eyes fasten on the less appealing aspects of American life: the noise and frantic pace, the fuss over ZIP and telephone area codes ("Those three silly little digits," says one girl, "are they really so important?"). "We're called an affluent society," says another volunteer, "and now I know what that really means. We have everything. But so much of it seems like only cheap veneer."

Janet Hanneman, the woman who wore her Pakistani dress when she came home to the United States, is the classic case of re-entry crisis. She is 28 now, a registered nurse, and a graduate of the University of Kansas. In 1961 she volunteered for the corps and was assigned to a huge mental hospital in Lahore, West Pakistan. There she "took charge of everything." For two and a half years in Pakistan she almost singlehandedly pushed through an astonishing number of improvements – a bed for every patient, the hospital's first psychiatric research, even a cheerier shade of paint on the walls. Her devotion and effectiveness became a legend through the Peace Corps. She was featured in recruiting films and brochures. To her patients and the staff she was known as "Miss Janet," a term of special affection and respect, since in Urdu, the language of West Pakistan, the word *jannat* means paradise.

As the months went by, Janet adopted more and more Pakistani habits and gradually shed her American ones. She lived with a Pakistani family, learned Urdu, ate Pakistani food, and eventually discarded her traditional white nurse's uniform for native dress – the flowing sari or the shalwar, baggy slacks worn with a chemise and a dopatta, a neck scarf. "I thought and acted and lived like a Pakistani," she says. She was even courted by a local businessman – romance with foreigners is almost unheard of in Pakistan, but Janet was not regarded as an "outsider."

After she had extended her tour for six months, a job she wanted opened up in Peace Corps headquarters in Washington and she decided to come home.

Everywhere she went, her Pakistani clothes created a sensation. But it irritated her to hear anyone call them a "costume." "Costumes are what you wear in a play," she says. "This was what I ought to wear, what was right." Yet she was painfully conscious of people staring at her.

In Pakistan an orthodox woman does not look into the eyes of a man when she speaks to him unless she is his wife. For weeks Janet kept her eyes cast down. Unconsciously she moved about with the graceful gliding walk of the Pakistani women, and she was outspokenly scornful of the form-fitting dresses and short skirts fashionable in this country.

When she went home to Junction City, Kansas, to visit her family, her mother waited until the two of them were alone in the kitchen and then asked simply, "What are you doing to do when those clothes wear out?" Janet said, "Go back to Pakistan, I suppose." Sadly Mrs. Hanneman replied, "That's what I was afraid you'd say."

In the first weeks after her return to the United States, Janet was often ill – psychosomatically, she now thinks. "It was a difficult task to get through a whole day," she recalls. "There was so much to get used to again." At a private showing of a film that includes some scenes of her hospital in Pakistan, she wept openly. "It was an awful mistake to come back," she thought. "And for what?"

Other Peace Corps volunteers quickly recognized Janet Hanneman's odd behavior as an extraordinary effort to keep her overseas experience alive. "For two-and-a-half years I didn't want to let go," she says. "I was trying to hold on to tangible things. I wanted to see and feel them every day."

In June 1964 she was moved up to a staff job with greater responsibility. Gradually she began to settle down. "I began to understand that I couldn't keep on living in the past," she says. "I told myself the important thing is what I'm contributing *now,* not what I did in Pakistan."

Shortly after changing jobs Janet received a confidential letter from a high-ranking Peace Corps administrator whom she greatly admired. He told her that she had been wonderful overseas but that her insistence on wearing the Pakistani clothes at home – and the disillusionment with America that this behavior implied – was damaging her reputation and her value to the Peace Corps.

"I knew he meant it for my benefit," Janet says. "The letter was written in late April, but a secretary had lost it and I didn't see it until June. Thank goodness. In April my only reaction to advice like this would have been resentment."

Next day she went to a smart dress shop on Connecticut Avenue and bought a gold raw-silk suit for $110. As she slipped on the first Western clothing she had worn in two years, she had a very simple, very feminine and very American reaction. "My gosh, think how much less this would have cost me if I'd had it made in Pakistan."

From that moment Janet Hanneman committed herself to her six-day-a-week job as recruiting administrator. She still shows the marks of her overseas Peace Corps experience in ways that are less obvious but familiar enough to the other volunteers – dedication to the civil rights movement, study for self-improvement, formulating plans for her future. She is learning to paint and is reading university graduate school catalogs, having decided to go after her Ph.D.

Not every re-entry case follows Janet's pattern. Among other things, she came back to the United States to work for a sympathetic organization. But nearly all the individual crises have the same basic cause. "The Peace Corps experience," says Dr. English, "stretches the volunteers far more than other young people their age and makes it impossible for them to fit back into their old surroundings with any kind of comfort."

Their distress is always quite open and occasionally is demonstrated in bizarre form—like the young man back from Ethiopia who ate himself into obesity while trying to adjust. Sometimes a returnee lands a very good job and then quits it without explanation after perhaps 48 hours. Only a few, recognizing that they need professional help with their emotional problems, have asked Peace Corps headquarters to recommend a psychiatrist. But until now there has been no official cognizance of the re-entry problem, and the vast majority of returnees have been left to bump around, alone and unhappy, as they sweated through their adjustment.

"Almost nobody understands or cares to understand what I went through," a girl volunteer says. This estrangement—the feeling that "nobody cares"—is a bitter experience for many volunteers. Returning joyfully to old friends, they discover that they have nothing much to talk about. "I came back more serious, I suppose, much more concerned about things like peace and civil rights," says Joseph Mullins of Griffin, Georgia, "but my friends seem to think mostly about their own pleasures." In Philadelphia, Frank Guido looked up the companions he had known, "but all we had in common was the past."

Almost nothing appalls volunteers more than the misinformation about foreign countries that Americans possess and cheerfully pass on. "I talked with people who had never been farther south than San Francisco, but they had all the answers to the problems of the people of Latin America," says Robert Morgan, who returned from Ecuador. "They wouldn't listen to me."

Although they are all bright and in their eligible mid-20's, these returnees often think of themselves as social disasters. "I can't talk to people anymore," says John Bond, who served in Ethiopia. "I think they're boring, and I'm sure they think I'm the same." At cocktail parties Kathryn Hannan finds herself tongue-tied. "I'm not in tune with all the conversational status symbols anymore—where you went to school, whether you ski, how you spend your weekends," she says. "It's ritual, and I haven't learned it again." A California girl stopped going to welcome-home parties because she finally couldn't stand any more superficial questions about her experience—or people's impatience with her effort to answer the questions in depth.

Though the Peace Corps always rates high in American affection, volunteers report that face-to-face encounters with citizens can be dismaying. "People are instantly suspicious of me," says Miss Hannan. "They think I must be very idealistic, very concerned about helping my fellow man, very serious about everything, very liberal and just a little bohemian." When a poised and well-dressed girl from the Middle West introduced herself to a businessman on an airliner as a former Peace Corps volunteer, he raised his eyebrows. "You're the first one I've ever met," he said. "I never would have guessed a volunteer would be like you."

This sort of nonsense leads many returnees to adopt a lofty — even irritating — attitude about their experience. Judy Conway saw some of her Peace Corps friends become so overwhelmingly condescending that she wrote to headquarters: "I sometimes wonder if we give our own countrymen the understanding we so readily gave foreigners."

The most popular place for escape is the campus. Nearly 60 per cent of the volunteers who got out last year are now either back in college or at universities studying for advanced graduate degrees. There they feel a familiar, basically unchanging world, the one most of them left when they joined the corps. "A buffer," one calls it, "a good place to readjust."

In addition to its relative tranquillity, there are other reasons favoring the campus. Liberal scholarships, grants and fellowships earmarked specifically for the volunteers make it financially easy for many to re-engage in academic life. Furthermore, while they are overseas many volunteers decide to pursue careers in teaching or social work after their enlistment is up. This frequently involves a switch in academic training or the need for additional courses, undergraduate or graduate. About half the volunteers change their career plans while in the corps — engineers decide to become psychologists, business majors become history teachers, anthropologists turn to international politics.

Schools generally welcome the serious-minded volunteers as students. Spot checks by the corps indicate that returnees tend to earn far better grades than they did before they volunteered, although their scores on graduate school entrance exams — usually taken near the end of their two years overseas — are only average.

Somewhat to the surprise and dismay of Peace Corps officials, only a minute 8 per cent of volunteers ultimately enter the business world when they get out. This may be partly because that sort of life seems somehow tame and unsatisfying after a tour of duty in a remote part of the world. But it is also true that a good number of volunteers *do* originally come home itching to get into business and start making up for lost time. When they discover that business is not itching to hire them, they see themselves as victims of a huge doublecross. The Peace Corps itself is largely responsible for this reaction.

From campus to campus, recruiters called upon students to sacrifice two years of their lives to make a better world and broadly hinted that the pay-off would come when they returned. Recruiting pamphlets made the same point: "Many new opportunities will open to men and women with actual experience abroad," one of them promised. "... Careers in government, industry, labor and education." Also, at the request of the Peace Corps, scores of firms pledged their interest in the volunteers in a "Career Opportunities" column appearing in the monthly newsletter distributed to corpsmen all around the world. From big businessmen came encouraging words: "It seems clear to me that members of the Peace Corps," wrote the president of one large United States corporation, "will be particularly employable when they complete their tours of duty. . . . There are never enough people of this kind available for any enterprise."

These were cheering remarks to read in a Philippine thatched hut or a jungle school in Africa. But volunteers have not found the actual reception especially warm. If they are "particularly employable," they say, businessmen don't seem to realize it. "The corporation president may want Peace Corpsmen," says one corps official, "but evidently the word hasn't filtered down to the people in personnel who actually do the hiring."

In recent months, the Peace Corps has made a conscious effort to throttle down the hopes of volunteers. "You should not lose sight of the fact that a highly competitive employment situation still exists in the United States," a bulletin now warns them. ". . . Overseas service is not viewed as being applicable to the needs of many employing organizations."

The discovery that his Peace Corps experience is not considered priceless is understandably shattering to a returnee. Leon Haller came back from two years of working in Peru's top financial circles only to have a New York banker practically laugh in his face when he told him that he had been in the corps. "I used to put 'Peace Corps' at the top of my résumé," Haller says, "but I soon stopped that. I described the work I did in Peru, and at the end I noted that it was done as a volunteer. It was the only way to keep their interest." Unable to crack the New York investment banking front, Haller took a job in Washington with the State Department at the Agency for International Development.

Employers often appear puzzled when they find themselves facing a real live volunteer across the desk. How do these employers react? "Not impressed," says one volunteer. "'Peace Corps' was no good as a job recommendation," another found. A New York girl, Susan

Feller, says, "They thought my experience interesting, but that it didn't mean much in terms of professional competence or ability."

"It's good public relations for firms to show interest in volunteers," says Donald Richardson, who now works for a New York bank. ;'I think they do it mostly for publicity."

On the other hand it is true that a Peace Corpsman undergoing re-entry and in search of a job can be a rather difficult applicant. Despite some careful advice from the Peace Corps Career Information Service on how to go about landing a job, volunteers often fumble the whole business.

"Companies tell us the volunteers don't come off well in interviews," says Dr. Robert Calvert, director of CIS. "They should remember that these young men and women have been out of touch with our culture for a long time. They don't always look or sound good. They may be very independent, very picky. They are bright and creative, but they need elbow room."

Another handicap volunteers often carry into the job hunt is an extravagant self-confidence. One Peace Corps official calls it "the old Sarge Shriver line – that, for them, anything and everything is possible." Volunteers often think they are better qualified and more valuable than interviewers do. Calvert has found that executives are generally unimpressed by a volunteer's proffered credentials: working 60 hours a week, his self-confidence, his ability to deal with other people. "The average businessman," says Calvert, "wants to know specifically how the volunteer is going to help his company."

Tony Picariello, a 27-year-old volunteer from Medford, Massachusetts, thought he had the right answer to that question time after time during six painful weeks of job-hunting.

He had served in Chile and was considered one of the better volunteers in his group. An outgoing young man and a fine baseball player, he had been popular with the Chileans, especially the kids. Six months before his term was up, he diligently sent off letters to fifty major United States firms, saying in effect: Here comes Tony Picariello! He planned to marry a Chilean girl and wanted to work either in the United States or Latin America. From most of the companies he got an answer. (Volunteers report that certain major companies don't even bother to answer their inquiries.) In a matter of hours after Tony reached New York last June, he was on the phone, calling personnel offices.

Things went badly from the start. It was midsummer and many executives were on vacation. One by one, Tony visited the companies he had written to. Their reactions varied, but all added up to no job.

One said it hired mostly nationals for its overseas branches. Another was looking for someone to travel all over the world, but Spanish was the only foreign language Tony knew.

Several companies told him they would be interested in him if he were an engineer. He got the same answer at three international employment agencies. Firms which had advertised that they were interested in Peace Corps volunteers now told him he was not qualified for positions they had open.

He went to Boston to look for work, then returned to New York, living at the "Y," walking the streets all day. When he appealed to the Peace Corps for assistance, they gave him the names of two more corporations which had advertised for volunteers. One of them turned him down flatly; his application is still languishing at the other.

Sometimes Tony would try a company cold, without calling or writing ahead. He always got an interview — as much for his language fluency, he feels, as for his Peace Corps background. Certainly not all the companies were impressed with his experience as a volunteer. One young interviewer told him frankly that it certainly was not so valuable as an advanced degree. "I told him I thought he was wrong," says Tony, "and I walked out."

Tony could have had government jobs — the State Department offered to send him to South Vietnam, the Secret Service wanted him as an agent — but he had his heart set on private industry. He finally landed a job as salesman in Maine and New Hampshire for Hallmark Cards, is doing very well and hopes to move into the company's international division someday.

"The Peace Corps isn't much help unless you want to go on to graduate school, or teach or go back and live in the jungle the rest of your life," Tony says. But he's quick to add, "Even so, I'd sign up again."

Tony Picariello, for example, may be a young man long on aspirations and short on temper. By nature he is honest and direct, and a poor dissembler — qualities which the Peace Corps experience seems to bring out in its volunteers. In comparison with the gray-flannel smoothness of some college graduates, volunteers like Tony may often come off a poor second.

One of the tasks of the Peace Corps Career Information Service is to educate the American businessman against making hasty judgments about volunteers, however abrasive they may appear. CIS Director Calvert has respectfully suggested to the business community that it recognize what one volunteer has described as "the intangible long-term value of the Peace Corps experience."

But Calvert has not been spectacularly successful in preaching that line. Just a year ago he sent out letters to 2,000 companies asking them to keep volunteers in mind. Only 25 of them bothered to write back. "My letter was too soft-sell," he now says.

Congress has shown no eagerness at all to move in on the problem. It reluctantly authorized a program of career counseling only after Corps Director Sargent Shriver promised economy-minded legislators to keep it modest. He has. The Career Information Service is only about one-twelfth the size of the University of California at Berkeley placement center, which Calvert managed before coming to the Peace Corps on a leave of absence. By law the CIS may work with a volunteer for only a year after he leaves the Peace Corps—thus making it relatively useless for volunteers who return immediately to school. And CIS can only counsel, not find jobs.

But other avenues are being explored. At a Peace Corps request, President Johnson already has instructed all federal agencies to give special consideration to hiring volunteers and has asked for a report by June 30 [1965] on how many are employed. Johnson particularly hopes to enlist Peace Corpsmen in his war on poverty. And Shriver recently wrote a letter to all state governors, many of whom he knows personally, requesting them to canvass their state agencies as the President did in Washington.

But no career counseling program, however imaginative, will ever eliminate the readjustment pains of volunteers. Nor, perhaps, should it try. In the long haul, the dissatisfaction of returnees with things as they are, or as they find them, one volunteer believes, "may be the best thing to come out of the Peace Corps."

They are a rare group, if only because they go overseas largely out of an innocent idealism and they come back with that idealism bruised from use but generally intact.

"You can't convince us anymore that it's no use fighting city hall, or ignorance, or backwardness," one of them says. "We've done it." How to preserve that kind of calloused idealism and put it to work was one of the purposes of the recent Peace Corps conference.

There have been some dramatic examples of how this dissatisfaction can be harnessed at home. . . .

A young Negro volunteer, Tom Williams, had returned from Ethiopia to a job on the Peace Corps headquarters staff. When he answered an advertisement for an apartment on upper Connecticut Avenue and the rental agent stalled him, Williams discovered that the neighborhood was White Only. To make certain he was being discriminated against, the wife of a white Peace Corps official went to the rental agent and asked to look at the apartment for her "mother." She was told she could have it at once, if she would be willing to predate the rental contract—a device that would have enabled the agent to tell Williams the apartment was already gone.

Not this time. While an official complaint was filed with Washington's Council on Human Relations, 40 of Tom's friends from Peace Corps headquarters—many of them returned volunteers—took several hours of annual leave and went out to picket the real estate firm. They carried hastily drawn signs—"Apartheid Apartment" and "Peace Corps Volunteers Return to Bigotry"—and the protest caused quite a stir in Washington. After only a few days, the company backed down, and Tom Williams and his new wife moved in, the first Negroes ever to live in the apartment building.

The pickets had only one anxious moment. As they were leaving Peace Corps headquarters for the real estate company, they ran into Corps Director Sargent Shriver on the sidewalk. Shriver took a look at the signs and asked, "What's up?" The young people hadn't counted on meeting the boss. Would he veto the plan for fear of alienating supporters of the Peace Corps in Congress? They told him the whole story. Shriver listened carefully, and then said, "Great! This is what the Peace Corps is all about, what we *should* stand for. Go to it!"

PART IV

*Cultural Relations
and Education*

T he primary purpose of most cultural-relations programs is to promote a favorable image abroad of the donor nation or the sponsoring body. Charles Thomson and Walter Laves describe the cultural-relations activities of the United States between 1953 and 1962 in an effort to explain and interpret for foreign people those characteristics of American life and culture that might encourage them to be more sympathetic to United States policies.

Over the years, the most hotly debated issue regarding these programs has been the proper balance between short-term maximum impact activities of a propaganda character and long-term impact activities of an academic or an artistic nature. Recently, there has been a declining emphasis on information in the old form of propaganda and news dissemination. This trend is represented in the enlistment of the arts in United States cultural programs. Music and dramatic presentations abroad are being used increasingly in the hope that other peoples will develop a more balanced impression of American life.

The United States Information Agency and the Bureau of Educational and Cultural Affairs within the State Department share major responsibility for American cultural-relations activities. In addition to the exchange of persons, cultural-relations activities include the exchange of books and periodicals, the maintenance of overseas libraries and bi-national cultural centers, exhibitions, the loan of music and recordings for concerts, and the production and circulation of educational and documentary films.

Philip Coombs, in a selection taken from *The Fourth Dimension of Foreign Policy: Educational and Cultural Affairs,* describes the cultural-relations activities of France, the United Kingdom, Germany, and Russia. He notes that in the programs of all these nations there is a heavier emphasis than ever before on genuine intellectual, technical, and cultural exchange without immediate ideological connotations. Coombs discusses technical assistance and cultural relations jointly. His rationale is that all technical-assistance activities are exercises in cultural relations. Of necessity, two cultures come into contact in all overseas technical-assistance programs, and the participants form impressions of each other's culture. However, the fact that the two activities are similar in some ways does not mean that they are not without significant differences. The primary purposes are quite distinct. The purpose of technical assistance is to promote human knowledge and competence. It is related to nation-building. Cultural-relations activities, on the other hand, fall into two broad and frequently quite separate categories: to promote a favorable image of the donor nation or the sponsoring body and to promote international understanding and world peace.

The selection written by Harold Isaacs describes a nongovernmental cultural-relations program—Operation Crossroads Africa. Crossroads is basically a project to promote international understanding among youth. As conceived by its founder, the Reverend James Robinson, the principal aim is to expose young Americans and Africans to each other and to bring them together in settings where they can learn the most about each other.

Unesco is the major organization devoted to promoting international understanding and world peace. This objective is pursued through such activities as the publication of the *Index Translationum,* which contains notations on works translated from one language to another throughout the world, and through the compilation of the first history written by international consensus, *The History of the Scientific and Cultural Development of Mankind.*

These aims are ambitious, and the separate projects are impressive. However, as George Shuster points out in the last selection in this section, the achievements of Unesco have been limited because of modest funding and the impact of the cold war upon institutions of international cooperation. When Unesco was founded, the French tried to promote the view that the organization should be composed of cultural leaders of prominence who would attend meetings and decide policy as individuals acting on their own rather than as representatives of individual nations. What has happened, however, is that Unesco has become an organization of member states. As a result, the political conflicts of the member states enter into every decision and determine what Unesco can or cannot do.

16
United States Cultural
Relations Activities

United States cultural relations have experienced increasing recognition and significant growth since 1953. A number of interlocking developments have contributed to this expansion. (The developments described in this chapter are limited generally to those occurring before the end of 1961.)

One development involved an intensified emphasis on general cultural activities in information programs. Not long after USIA [United States Information Agency] had been set up outside the Department of State, Theodore Streibert, its director, initiated efforts to emphasize and expand cultural activities. Its program already included interchanges of books and periodicals, overseas libraries and binational cultural centers, exhibitions, the loan of music and recordings for concerts, broadcasts of American music and other cultural material, and production and circulation of educational and documentary films. In July 1954, Mr. Streibert dispatched an instruction to all posts abroad, recommending the strengthening of such activities. Specifically, he recalled the mandate to USIA from President Eisenhower to delineate "important aspects of the life and culture of the people of the United States," and adopted a sweeping definition of culture, viewing it as encompassing "not only scholarly and artistic fields but all significant manifestations and aspirations of the spirit of America, from athletics to political oratory."

These activities were to be emphasized because of their "fundamental importance and lasting quality" and also because they could in

Charles A. Thomson and Walter H. C. Laves, *Cultural Relations and U.S. Foreign Policy* (Bloomington: Indiana University Press, 1963), pp. 109–129, 133–137.

his belief influence political attitudes and actions. He referred to what he termed the Soviet "cultural offensive" and to Soviet propaganda picturing the United States as a nation of materialists, who for that reason could not be trusted with political leadership. As one step in the new activity, he had named a Cultural Affairs Adviser and planned to appoint "cultural representatives" to be sent to foreign countries.[1]

The Department of State looked askance at this initiative, considering that some of the proposed activities would invade its field of responsibility for educational exchanges. It held that it should be responsible for cultural relations, while USIA should limit itself to so-called cultural information.[2]

Following a joint meeting of the Advisory Commissions on Educational Exchange and on Information, a "task force" representing the two agencies was appointed to clarify the problem of their respective fields of responsibility. Its report, presented in April 1955, recommended a compromise. It did not accept the distinction between cultural relations and cultural information suggested by the Department of State. Instead it recognized that cultural activities might form a part of the program of USIA as well as of the Department of State. It presented a detailed listing of the cultural activities each agency should properly carry on, but left it open to both of them, depending on their respective resources, to participate in such enterprises abroad as the development in universities of American studies, the teaching of English, and the conduct of seminars, colloquia, and workshops, together with efforts within the United States to elicit the cooperation of universities and colleges.[3] These findings were more practical than logical, but they had the virtue of recognizing the complexities of the *de facto* situation, and they seem to have provided the basis for a reasonably satisfactory working relationship, which apparently functioned with less friction in the field than in Washington.

The USIA concern with cultural activities was not short-lived. In contrast with the "Campaign of Truth," in which short-term information and propaganda objectives had tended to dominate cultural activities, USIA programs in radio, press, and film, as well as in other fields, were increasingly directed as time went on toward cultural goals. International understanding was declared to be the fundamental objective. In 1959, the Advisory Commission on Information urged that the information program embody characteristics which traditionally had been claimed for cultural activities. It not only turned away from a propaganda emphasis, recommending that USIA function as a "reliable, honest, non-slanted, authentic reporter of the news"; it stressed the importance of long-range objectives, noting that beliefs and opinions could not be changed overnight. It remarked on the greater interest among other peoples in nonpolitical matters relating to the United States—in American literature, music, and graphic art; in science, education, and economic and social organization. It emphasized reciprocity, pointing out the importance of "a two-way exchange of information and ideas and people," which would correct misconceptions in the United States about other peoples as well as their misconceptions of the American way of life.[4]

Ranking officials of USIA, especially its director, George V. Allen, stressed the increasingly educational character of its program as a contribution to international understanding. In contrast to a declining emphasis on "information in the old sense, the 'propaganda' business and the business of disseminating news," the cultural content of all material was strengthened and expanded. Greater support was given to libraries, university reading rooms, bi-national cultural centers, art exhibits, and English teaching. Much of the radio and press wireless material had been converted "from the argumentative to the educational and cultural," featuring educational forums and reviews of serious books. The educational approach was termed more effective and more acceptable to foreign peoples. The shift to it from the former "propagandistic" emphasis had resulted not from whim but from a careful evaluation of means and results.[5] As one move to underline the significance of the cultural program, USIA established the policy of assigning an officer experienced in cultural affairs to one of the two top positions in each of its missions abroad.

In his report to the U.S. Advisory Commission on Educational Exchanges in 1961, one of the authors of this . . . [chapter] urged broadening the content of information services through the development of more integrated cultural activities and through more central direction of them under the guidance of the Department of State.

This orientation of information activities has continued under the new administration of Edward R. Murrow. He has been an enthusiastic supporter of the libraries and English language programs. Under his direction there has been increasing emphasis upon quality and cultural sophistication, in all the activities of the Agency.

Relating educational exchanges and technical assistance

Another development grew out of increasing recognition of the importance of education and science to economic development. This drew attention to the relationship between technical assistance and educational exchanges, which had developed within the government as separate programs, though the origin of both was found in the Interdepartmental Committee and the Division of Cultural Relations.

With the advent of the Eisenhower administration in 1953, the Foreign Operations Administration (FOA) had absorbed the Mutual Security Agency and the Technical Cooperation Administration (the Department of Defense operating military assistance). In 1955, FOA was replaced by the International Cooperation Administration (ICA), which functioned as a semi-independent unit in the Department of State.

The ICA program, with its emphasis on training for so-called technical occupations relating to economic development, had far outdistanced, in financial support and number of persons involved, the International Educational Exchange Service (IES) of the Department of State. During fiscal year 1956, ICA under its technical cooperation and defense support programs was spending $136 million (including about $16 million for supplies and equipment) for training activities and the exchange of specialized personnel which involved approximately 8,900 persons. The International Educational Exchange Service of the Department of State received for the same year something more than $18 million for exchanges involving close to 5,500 persons.

The expansion of the two programs accentuated concern about their relationship. As early as 1953, Congressional committees had begun to express apprehension about the possibility of duplication and overlapping. In 1955, the Department of State was requested by the Senate and House Appropriations Committees to make a study looking toward the coordination and possible integration of the exchange activities of the two agencies.[6] Dr. J. L. Morrill, President of the University of Minnesota and formerly chairman of the Advisory Commission on Educational Exchanges, was asked to prepare a report on the question, which he presented on May 1, 1956.[7]

The programs of both agencies had to do with the movement of specialized personnel from one country to another, were active in many of the same countries, and were concerned in numerous cases with the same subject matter. But the objectives were defined differently. The purpose of the educational exchange activities of the Department of State, as defined by the Smith-Mundt Act, was to foster better understanding of the United States in other countries and to increase mutual understanding. The purpose of technical cooperation was to help the peoples of the less developed countries, through the sharing of technical knowledge and skills, to expand their resources and to forward their economic development.[8] It was related to the larger context of economic aid.

The two objectives overlapped to a considerable degree, forming what the Morrill Report called a large "grey" area. For example, both agencies were active in the field of education, which plays an important role in the promotion of international understanding and at the same time is an essential factor in economic development. One of ICA's most significant efforts had been the series of contracts made with universities in the United States to aid foreign peoples in specific phases of their economic development. Similarly, overlapping was evident in exchanges relating to public administration, labor, atomic energy, and other fields.

The report noted that ICA in the course of its history had expanded and broadened the meaning of the term "economic development." It stated: "In effect, ICA has so operated . . . as to be concerned with nearly the whole of the body politic of those countries in which it operates programs." Thus, its activities impinged on the educational exchange activities of IES and exerted marked influence on the principal objective of IES, the development of international understanding. The presence abroad of some 3,000 American technicians and the introduction into the United States from foreign countries of 6,000 learners, or "participants" as they were called, inevitably increased in those countries knowledge of the United States and of its social and political structure.

IES on its side was charged under the Smith-Mundt Act with the responsibility for rendering technical and other services to foreign peoples, as well as for the interchange of persons. In addition to the academic type of exchange, IES carried on activities designed to meet the technical needs of other countries. According to one estimate, 80 per cent of the foreign students coming to the United States under the IES program could be classified as taking technical training. Thus, according to the report, the two programs "have reached a common point in their growth where the needs they seek to meet cannot be fully met save through an acceptance of their essential unity of purpose and effect."[9]

The report did not, however, consider it wise or feasible to merge the two programs. (The proponents of educational exchange in the Senate and elsewhere feared that such a merger might mean the swallowing up of the broader educational activities sponsored by the Fulbright and Smith-Mundt Acts by the more "practical" and "technical" activities of the larger technical-cooperation program.) Each program had its own purpose and function. The report did not favor as a solution the wholesale transfer of undertakings from one agency to the other, or an attempt to redefine in detail their respective spheres of activity. Instead it presented two basic recommendations. First, it urged an "authoritative coordination" of the two programs, to solve the problem of the "grey" area. Second, it called for "an upgrading of United States exchange activity in governmental, Congressional, American public and foreign consciousness," thus assuring governmental leadership "in elevating cultural and technical exchange to the level of a major instrument of American influence and assistance in international affairs."[10]

The approach recommended, it was suggested, would combine effectively the resources of the two programs, while maintaining the values and integrity of each. Scholars, students, and others under the educational exchange program travel abroad as private individuals. ICA technicians go overseas as government employees. IES exchanges often involve some degree of reciprocity. ICA activities imply "no contribution in return." ICA represents largely the material side of American life. The IES program brings into play more prominently human and spiritual values.

The report cited on this point a "Joint Statement on United States Government Participation in Cultural Exchanges" by the National Planning Association which declared:

While American material achievements thus have a positive and creative significance for the whole free world, there are non-material qualities of American culture which are even of greater importance to human progress and which indeed, *are in large measure responsible for our material accomplishments.* These are mainly in the cultural and human relations fields. Our ability to translate into practice our regard for freedom of thought, our belief in the equality of all before the law and in social and economic opportunities, our receptivity to new ideas, and our sense of friendliness and mutual help, are perhaps our most important non-material assets. Today, these qualities yield the social cohesion and voluntary cooperation which make possible the largest functioning democracy in history. These qualities—and their fruits in artistic and intellectual achievements—are not too well recognized abroad, and we can and should make them much more apparent to the peoples of other countries through effective cultural exchange programs and in other ways.[11]

The Department of State accepted the general principles of the Morrill Report, and took some steps toward the more effective coordination recommended. The procedure of "upgrading" the cultural activities program was initiated in December 1958 by the appointment as Special Assistant to the Secretary of State for Educational and Cultural Relations of Robert H. Thayer, who took over the general direction of the Department's program from Andrew Berding, Assistant Secretary for Public Affairs. The latter has commented on the shift as follows: "But cultural relations are without any doubt sufficiently important unto themselves to warrant their being placed in a separate bureau under the full-time direction of an Assistant Secretary of State."[12] Early in 1960 the U.S. Advisory Commission on Educational Exchanges requested Walter H. C. Laves of Indiana University to review the cultural activities of the United States government with a view to increasing their effectiveness. The integration in both policy and operations of educational exchanges and technical assistance was one of the major recommendations in the Laves Report.[13]

Thayer was succeeded in 1961 by Philip H. Coombs and in 1962 by Lucius Battle with the title of Assistant Secretary of State for Educational and Cultural Affairs. Both Coombs and Battle served as head of the Bureau of Educational and Cultural Affairs, which brought together the principal elements in the Department concerned with cultural activities.[14]

Congressional action on educational exchanges

The expansion of cultural activities has also been encouraged by Congressional approval of new legislation on educational and cultural exchanges to supplement the Fulbright and Smith-Mundt Acts and to pull together various existing pieces of legislation into an integrated whole. A considerable amount of financial support for such exchanges already derived, in fact, from a series of separate legislative acts dating back to the end of World War II. Under the "G.I. Bills," 19,000 veterans of World War II and (by 1960) more than 6,000 veterans of the Korean conflict were given opportunity to study abroad.[15] While this legislation concerned only American citizens, other laws were designed for the benefit of individual foreign countries. The Philippine Rehabilitation Act of 1946 (P.L. 370, 79th Cong., 2d sess., 60 Stat. 128 [1946] as amended) provided for training in the United States of some 850 Philippine citizens in scientific, technical, and public-service fields. In 1949, the Finnish Educational Exchange Act sponsored by Senator H. Alexander Smith allocated part of the annual payments by Finland on its post-World War I reconstruction loan to the interchange of students, teachers, and technicians, and the exchange of books and educational equipment with that country (P.L. 265, 81st Cong.). In 1950, the Iranian Trust Fund (an indemnity of $110,000 paid by Iran in 1924 and 1925) was assigned to the education of Iranian students in the United States (P.L. 861, 81st Cong.).

The conquest of the Chinese mainland by the Communists cut off cultural interchange between the United States and that area. This led to the setting up of a Chinese Emergency Aid Program for students and scholars, administered by the Department of State. It was financed by the Economic Cooperation Administration by funds authorized by the Foreign Appropriations Act of 1950 (P.L. 327, 81st Cong.) and by the China Area Aid Act of 1950 (Title II of P.L. 535, 81st Cong.). These sources made it possible to assist some 3,500 Chinese students and about 100 scholars stranded in the United States to finish their educational programs and to bring to the United States for short periods of study two score Chinese students and scholars from various areas of the Far East. Following the aggression against the Republic of Korea in 1950, similar aid was authorized for a small number of Korean students stranded in the United States (P.L. 165, 82d Cong.). (The program for assistance to China and Korea came to an end in 1955.) In 1951, a provision of the India Emergency Food Aid Act, sponsored by Senator Karl E. Mundt, authorized use of the interest payments (not to exceed $5 million) for educational exchanges similar to those with Finland (P.L. 48, 82d Cong.). In 1954, an agreement with Ireland provided for the use of approximately 500,000 Irish pounds for scholarship exchange with that country (P.L. 665, 83d Cong.).[16]

Legislation of a somewhat different character in 1948 (P.L. 402, 80th Cong., as amended) authorized the Information Media Guaranty Program. This program made possible the commercial sale of American books, periodicals, and motion pictures to citizens of foreign countries that were short on dollar exchange. The program guaranteed the exporting publisher payment in dollars in return for the foreign currencies he had received from his foreign customers. During the period 1948–1959, this legislation made possible the sale abroad of $40 million worth of these materials in eighteen foreign countries at a net cost of approximately $13 million, this latter figure representing the loss incurred when the foreign currencies were resold to replenish the supply of dollars.[17]

After 1953, new legislation of prime importance was approved along two lines. One concerned the dwindling supply of authorized foreign currencies, which threatened to terminate the Fulbright program in certain countries. The sources of foreign currency were broadened under the Mutual Security Acts of 1954 and 1956, notably by the Agricultural Trade Development and Assistance Act of 1954 (P.L. 480, 83d Cong., as amended), which authorized the use of proceeds from the sale of surplus agricultural commodities for educational exchanges, and later also for the translation, publication, and distribution of books and periodicals abroad, for assistance to American-sponsored schools, libraries, and community centers, and for promotion of "American studies" in foreign countries.

By 1962, these various pieces of legislation enabled 44 countries to participate in the Fulbright program—countries situated in all major areas of the world outside the Communist bloc.

The second major legislative measure was the International Cultural Exchange and Trade Fair Participation Act of 1956 (P.L. 860, 84th Cong.). This act authorized on a continuing basis appropriations for a program originally initiated in 1954 as the result of a special request by President Eisenhower. In the field of cultural interchange, it facilitated the appearance abroad of American musicians, dramatic companies, and sport groups which will be discussed below.

The question of appropriations for educational exchanges during the period under review brought forth expressions of widespread public support, and, in the Congress, sharply contrasting attitudes in the Senate and the House of Representatives.[18] When the 1955 appropriation for such exchanges was slashed by the House from $15 million to $9 million, full restoration of the cut was urged before the Senate Appropriations Committee by Vice-President Nixon, Senators Homer E. Capehart, J. William Fulbright, Karl E. Mundt, and Edward J. Thye, as well as by Congressman Walter Judd. Favorable testimony and communications were presented by a broad battery of national organizations, including the American Association of University Women, American Council on Education, American Federation of Teachers, National Education Association, and National Student Association, as well as by the American Federation of Labor, American Veterans Committee, General Federation of Women's Clubs, National Catholic Welfare Council, National Council of Jewish Women, National Council of Negro Women, National Farmers Union, and the American Chambers of Commerce of Brazil.[19] The entire cut was restored. Similarly, when the House cut the appropriation for 1956 from $22 million to $12 million, widespread protest was raised.[20]

The negative actions taken by the House were in large part a reflection of the attitude of Congressman John J. Rooney, chairman of the appropriations subcommittee for the Department of State, and certain of his colleagues. The subcommittee's crippling slash of the 1956 appropriation was defended on the floor by only one Representative—outside of its own membership—while 16 Congressmen of both parties spoke out against the cut and in support of the program. A motion for restoration, however, failed to muster the necessary majority.[21]

When the Department of State reduced its request for educational exchange in the 1957 appropriation from $22 million for the previous year to $20 million, it was challenged by Senator Fulbright. In answer to its defense that the administration had imposed a budget ceiling, the Senator pointed out that USIA had been permitted to ask for a $50 million increase. Further, the Advisory Commission on Educational Exchange had recommended a figure of $31 million.[22] Senator Fulbright declared: ". . . the administration is completely wrong in decreasing this very modest exchange program, because it has a special influence, I think, in many countries which have long felt that this country has no appreciation of the intellectual activities of mankind or their cultural achievements." He concluded, "I am not satisfied with the evaluation of this program by the Department of State, and I do not intend to be satisfied with it." The Department had recommended a decrease in "the only program that is related to the cultural activities of civilized human beings."[23]

As one move to redress the situation, the Committee on Foreign Relations, noting that "there is a serious question whether a proper balance is being maintained" between the information and educational exchange programs, recommended as one amendment to the Smith-Mundt Act permission to the President to transfer 10 per cent of the funds for information to educational exchange.[24]

For the 1959 appropriation for educational exchanges, the Senate Appropriations Committee, largely on the initiative of Senators J. William Fulbright and Lyndon B. Johnson, recommended an increase of $10 million over the amount of $20.8 million requested by the Department of State and approved by the House Appropriations Committee.[25] However, the final amount agreed on by both House and Senate was $22.8 million.

The legislation dealing with cultural activities approved by the Congress had been impressive in its range and variety. But it had added up to a mass of often unrelated acts. It had been a patchwork of pieces that did not fit together to make a unified picture. Serious gaps existed—for instance, the limitation of support for the Fulbright program and certain other activities to countries where counterpart funds from surplus war stocks or surplus agricultural products became available. There was urgent need to codify and amplify the existing mass of legislation. On March 2, 1961, Senator Fulbright introduced a comprehensive bill (S. 1154) designed to achieve these ends for a wide range of cultural activities, not including, however, educational programs involved in technical assistance. As a participant in planning the new legislation, in testimony before the Senate and House Committees as well as in his report to the Advisory Commission on Educational Exchanges, Laves urged that a much closer relationship be assured between these two aspects of United States cultural activities abroad. A companion bill (H.R. 8666) was introduced by Representative Hays on August 14. The final Fulbright-Hays Act was passed by Congress on September 16 and signed by President Kennedy on September 21. The size of the Congressional vote (Senate 79–53; House 378–32) is eloquent testimony of the support which this part of the United States cultural relations program now enjoys.

A detailed commentary by the Executive Secretary of the Conference Board of Associated Research Councils, Francis A. Young, provides excellent summaries of the most significant changes brought about by the Act.[26]

The statement of purpose in the Act succeeds much better than does previous legislation in harmonizing educational and political objectives. It makes clear that the ultimate purpose of the Act is political in the broadest and best sense, namely "to assist in the development of friendly, sympathetic and peaceful relations between the United States and the other countries of the world." But this basically political objective is closely linked with the educational and humanitarian ideal by specification in the statement of purpose that the legislation seeks "to promote international cooperation for educational and cultural advancement" and by a clear stress upon the mutuality of the programs. The Act itself is to be known as the Mutual Educational and Cultural Exchange Act, and the old phrase "to promote a better understanding of the United States in other countries" becomes in the new Act "to increase mutual understanding between the people of the United States and the people of other countries."

To the kinds of cultural activities previously authorized by various pieces of legislation are added United States and foreign representation at international nongovernmental educational and scientific meetings held under American auspices in or outside the United States and independent research into problems of educational and cultural exchange.

Financial support is made much more flexible by permitting use of funds made available under the Act for any of the programs authorized and permits exchanges to be arranged on the basis of grants, contracts, or otherwise through institutions as well as on an individual basis. More than this,

. . . not only may the President enter into multilateral as well as bilateral agreements, but these agreements may cover all aspects of educational and cultural relations, and not merely the kind of exchanges included in the limited Fulbright agreements of the past. There is a similar broadening of the potential role of the binational foundations or commissions which have heretofore administered the Fulbright program abroad. These agencies may now be used for the overseas administration for any of the programs conducted under the Act. The way is also open for cooperating foreign countries to share in the cost of the programs, especially in the use of their own currencies and in the support of their own grantees. The result is not only to increase and strengthen the elements of mutuality in the program but also to widen the area of activity in which the educational community shares responsibility with the government.

[Furthermore] . . . the fiscal provisions of the Act contain some important new authority. Appropriations remain available until expended, thus permitting the assured financing of particular projects over a period of years. There are also no legal limits, other than those imposed by appropriations, on the annual size of country programs, thus removing the old ceiling of $1,000,000 contained in the earlier Fulbright Act. This is a matter of some practical consequence in the case of a country like India, for which very large reserves of foreign currencies are available. Another interesting provision is that the President may transfer from one government department to another funds appropriated in furthering the purposes of the Act. This provides a financial mechanism for closer interdepartmental coordination of related programs; it would be a miracle of the bureaucracy however if it should become extensively used.[27]

Of particular importance is authorization for importing foreign cultural presentations on a nonprofit basis as well as the exportation of American cultural presentations.

The Act gives the President wider discretion in assigning administrative responsibility for the various kinds of activities included under the Act.

The Act provides many administrative improvements relating to the operation of exchange programs. There are also some modifications in the functions of the three advisory boards and there are major modifications in immigration regulations affecting exchangees.

New emphasis on the arts

Another development contributing to the expansion of cultural activities was the enlistment of the arts in the United States cultural program. Aside from certain war-time projects in Latin America supported by the Coordinator of Inter-American Affairs, the arts had been treated as a stepchild. Had it not been for the challenge of Soviet cultural competition, the value of the arts as an expression of the American spirit might have continued to go largely unrecognized.

An incident in 1946 had a decisive effect in relegating them to the sidelines. In that year the Department of State sponsored two exhibitions of contemporary American painting to tour Europe and Latin America. The pictures had won praise from the critics at a showing in the Metropolitan Museum of New York City. But their "advanced" character was attacked by Congressmen and by conservatives outside government circles. In consequence the exhibitions were called back, and Secretary Marshall announced that the Department would buy no more examples of American painting.

The hostile attitude in the Congress led to disregard and neglect of the fine arts in general and to a specific injunction against government-financed exhibitions of paintings that had not received individual, prior approval from the legislative body. [28]

The situation in Germany was an exception to the general rule. When in 1949 the cultural program in West Germany was transferred to the Department of State from the army, the request for appropriations included the term "art." The Department dispatched several exhibitions to Germany and, in addition, government funds were used to send American musical and dramatic productions to the Berlin Festivals of 1951, 1952, and 1953, including *Oklahoma, Porgy and Bess, Medea* with Judith Anderson, the Juilliard String Quartet, and two ballet companies. [29] Support by public-spirited private citizens made it possible to present to other European countries a number of productions in the field of music and drama.

But private efforts were at best fragmentary and sporadic and by the mid-fifties opinion was growing that the government should assume a larger share of the financial burden. The Soviet cultural offensive continued with increasing momentum. Too many of the leaders of thought and opinion in other countries still cherished the conviction that "Americans live in a cultural wasteland, peopled only with gadgets and frankfurters and atom bombs." [30]

In consequence, President Eisenhower sought and was given in 1954 an Emergency Fund of $5 million annually for musical and dramatic presentations abroad and for United States participation in international trade fairs. [31] Two years later the program was made permanent by Congressional enactment of the International Cultural Exchange and Trade Fair Participation Act of 1956 referred to . . . [previously]. Under this legislation, government funds were to supplement the fullest possible private support—income derived from private contributions in the United States as well as that from box-office receipts for performances overseas. An Advisory Committee on the Arts was established to advise the Secretary of State regarding programs.

By June 1962, 24 dance projects, 21 theater projects, 63 sports projects, and over 100 musical projects had been carried out in more than a hundred countries. The program made possible the appearances abroad of almost a dozen leading American symphony orchestras; numerous choral groups and ballet troupes; dramatic companies presenting such plays as Eugene O'Neill's *Long Day's Journey into Night* and Thornton Wilder's *Skin of our Teeth;* and such individual performers as Marian Anderson, William Warfield, Rudolph Serkin, and Isaac Stern.

American jazz, which on its own momentum had won its way to

worldwide recognition, entered the program in 1956 as a result of many field requests and was welcomed by immense audiences, in which students and other young people were prominent. Jazz groups sent on tour included those of Louis Armstrong, Dave Brubeck, Benny Goodman, Sauter-Finegan, and Jack Teagarden.[32]

The effects of the cultural presentations program went far beyond the persons attending the performances. Television and radio broadcasts reached vast audiences exceeding the capacity of the largest theater or concert hall. Showings of motion pictures of the performances expanded and continued the impact of the tours. Reviews of the events in the local press were seen by millions of readers.

While the program emphasized primarily professional performers of the highest caliber, a small number of amateur and student groups were also included, such as the Westminster and Howard University choirs and theater groups from several universities. Groups of this character made a special appeal to university audiences and served to build a youth-to-youth relationship.

Sports figured in the President's Special International Program from the start, calling forth an interest that cut across all economic and social levels and almost all age groups. Outstanding individual athletes and baseball, soccer, tennis, and swimming teams put on exhibitions. Athletic competition with the Soviet Union rose sharply as a result of the bilateral agreement signed in 1958.

These presentations, both artistic and athletic, reflected varied aspects of American life. In a number of groups, Negroes and whites lived and traveled together and performed side by side. Off stage as well as on, the American performers showed themselves approachable, friendly, and helpful. They offered special performances for students and for children. They sought contact with their colleagues in the host countries, sharing knowledge and ideas.

In the field of the visual arts, private agencies in the United States have played a more prominent and decisive role than government bodies. Among the latter, the United States Information Agency, which at its establishment was given the responsibility for exhibitions, has been most active in showing American art abroad. It has circulated exhibitions, not only of paintings, but of prints and drawings, American architecture, Indian arts and crafts, and the widely shown "Family of Man," a collection of photographs by Edward Steichen, depicting the basic human qualities and practices of mankind in all parts of the world. USIA has frequently enlisted private individuals or organizations on a contract basis to prepare exhibitions for showing in foreign countries.

While USIA has regarded domestic exhibition of foreign art as beyond the bounds of its responsibility, the Smithsonian Institution has been active in sponsoring such showings. Among these exhibitions have been showings of Austrian drawings and prints, Chinese landscape paintings, and collections of abstract paintings by contemporary artists from both Canada and Japan. Shows in the applied arts have presented Burmese embroideries, Danish silver, contemporary Indian crafts, Italian industrial design, Swedish textiles, and collections of photographs on postwar Brazilian, Finnish, and German architecture.[33]

The program in music, ballet, and theater, so far as government participation is concerned, has been a one-way street. Official funds have gone to "exporting" American attractions abroad, none to "importing" foreign artists into the United States. But private impresarios have redressed the balance to a degree, by bringing French and British theater groups and dance companies from Bali, India, Japan, and the Soviet Union — to mention only a few — to this country. In addition, the American performers going abroad have frequently shown active interest in learning about and learning from the national arts of the people they are visiting.

The official objectives of activities in the arts have been to counteract Soviet influence and propaganda and to correct and humanize the image of the American people held by other peoples, thus to develop a more rounded understanding of the United States and greater confidence in its leadership in world affairs. According to this view, the United States is well known abroad for its technological skills, its fabulous capacity for mass production and consumption, its extension to a large majority of its people of well-being and what passes for luxury in other societies. But other peoples have been disposed to look down on the United States as a nation concerned only with the creation of material wealth and with the satisfactions provided by creature comforts and ingenious gadgets. If they were to look upon Americans as capable of understanding and sharing the finest achievements and values mankind has created, it was necessary to correct the distorted image so widely held.

Private activities have tended to emphasize rather the reciprocal values of artistic interchange, which may stimulate the development of the arts themselves and broaden and deepen the appreciation of the arts by the general public. Presentations of music and drama as well as of the visual arts have been cordially received. The visits of artists of the first rank have often been interpreted as a mark of respect and esteem. One newspaper editor remarked, "If this is cultural imperialism, let us have more of it."

A companion activity to the cultural and athletic exchanges under the President's Special International Program has been United States participation in international trade fairs. In this field, also, the Soviet Union has been, expanding its activities. Together with the other countries of the Communist bloc, it increased its participation from 15 fairs in 1950–1951 combined to 93 in 1956. While the trade fairs have the expansion of commerce as their primary objective, the American exhibits necessarily present a vivid and variegated picture of certain aspects of American life. They are purveyors of information, knowledge, and perhaps the beginnings of understanding. Among the exhibits shown have been a one-room air-conditioned school, an American-type children's playground, a well-stocked American bookstore, and a medium-priced, one-floor suburban residence, fully equipped and furnished.

The challenge of Soviet competition

Another development that had an important bearing upon the expansion of cultural activities was the changing attitude of the Soviet Union toward cultural exchanges with the West. The policy of coolness toward cultural interchange which had prevailed substantially since the latter half of the 1930's and which warmed up during World War II only to freeze again by 1947, had been definitely modified by 1953, and even to some extent before that time. By 1950, the Soviet Union began to admit some students from non-Communist countries and a little later to dispatch some of its most prominent musical and ballet performers as well as certain motion pictures to participate in international festivals and competitions.

But it was not until the death of Stalin in 1953 that the U.S.S.R. initiated a widespread endeavor to use cultural activities as a significant element in its relations with non-Communist countries. From 1953 to 1955 the number of delegations entering and leaving the country (the U.S.S.R. computes this movement by delegations rather than by individuals) increased threefold. In the latter year, two-thirds of the total was with countries outside the Communist orbit. [34]

Scientists lecturing to scholarly audiences, musicians playing in concert halls, and football and other athletic teams performing in stadia were all parts of the same offensive to impress foreign peoples with a favorable picture of life in the Soviet Union and with the cultural fruits of Communist society. Soviet books were actively flooding into many of the countries of Asia. Often handsomely produced but subsidized to sell at low prices, they ranged from literary classics and elegantly illustrated books on art to children's story books, from volumes by Marx, Engels, and Lenin for intellectuals to low-cost propaganda pamphlets for the general public. The Soviet Union began a foreign aid program in 1954. Linked with this was a growing program of technical assistance for the less developed countries. By 1959 some 4,700 Communist-bloc technicians were providing aid to non-Communist countries (the United States had 6,000 technicians abroad at this time), and approximately the same number of students from these countries had gone for training to the Iron Curtain countries. [35]

The Soviet Union was disposed not only to press cultural rivalry with the United States in the industrialized countries of Europe and the less developed countries of other continents, but also to embark on cultural interchange with the United States itself, if such interchange could redound to its benefit. At the same time, the United States was eager to pierce the Iron Curtain and to establish direct contacts with the Soviet people.

This was one of the principal proposals at the summit conference in 1955. However, nothing came of discussions on the matter at the succeeding meeting of the foreign ministers later the same year. Some specific exchange projects were nonetheless carried out at that time, and negotiations that began in the fall of 1957 resulted in the approval of a bilateral U.S.-U.S.S.R. cultural agreement in January 1958 to run for two years. It provided for a wide range of exchanges: industrial and agricultural delegations; scientists, artists, and writers; symphony orchestras and ballet companies; athletic groups; and a small number of students and professors—all of which eventually totaled about 2,000 individuals on each side—as well as motion pictures, exhibits, and a varied array of publications. In the summer of 1959, an exhibition of American life with emphasis on science and art was presented in Moscow's Sokolniki Park and a similar Soviet exhibition in New York City's Coliseum. The results of the agreement were sufficiently satisfactory to both parties to be continued for a second two-year period during 1960–1961 and again for the two-year period 1962–1963.

Substantial use has been made of the opportunities under the modified Soviet policy and the three cultural exchange agreements of 1958, 1959, and 1962. During the period January 1, 1958, to December 31, 1961,[36] some 303 projects known to the State Department were undertaken by the United States, taking 3,797 Americans to the Soviet Union. This does not include American tourists going to the U.S.S.R., estimated at about 3,500 during the four-year period. Some 318 Soviet projects brought 3,105 Soviet citizens to the United States and, in addition, there were an estimated 1,200 Soviet tourists in this country.

Most of the scientific, educational, and other scholarly exchanges were arranged under the three governmental agreements or the supplementary agreement involving the National Academy of Sciences of the United States, the American Council of Learned Societies, and the Inter-University Committee on Travel Grants. These exchanges included students, professors, and research workers. In the field of the natural sciences were included projects for specialists in various fields to attend conferences and to visit research institutions.

During 1961, industrial delegations were exchanged in fields such as petroleum, railroads, cement, highways, and civil air transport. Agricultural exchanges involved delegations in food processing, agricultural information, soil research, chemical fertilizer, and livestock production. Medical exchanges included delegations for conferences on topics such as cancer and heart disease and for individual research. A number of performing arts exchanges have been included over these three years.

There have been exchanges of motion pictures, radio and television programs, of the two governmental publications, *Amerika* and *USSR,* and of exhibits such as those on plastics, transportation, and medicine sent by the United States and some on children's books, medicine, and children's arts sent by the U.S.S.R.

There has been an increasing number of exchanges arranged directly by universities and other institutions. These have been generally in the areas of science and scholarly research, but there have also been some for youth groups, track, tennis, and other athletic teams, and for music and ballet.

One of the most interesting United States cultural activities has developed in the setting of the U.S.–U.S.S.R. agreements. The Inter-University Committee on Travel Grants was founded by a group of universities (now totaling 35) to increase knowledge in the United States about the Soviet Union. Their initiative came from a conviction that upon the universities rested a major responsibility in our kind of society to increase the educational efforts toward this end. Within the terms of the intergovernmental cultural exchange agreements, and financially supported by foundation, government, and university funds, the Inter-University Committee deals directly with the Soviet Ministry of Higher Education. It arranges with the ministry for the annual program of exchanges of students and scholars and is responsible for the selection of Americans and approval of Soviet names proposed for exchanges. It assists in the placement of exchangees at universities in the two countries. It negotiates directly with the ministry over basic issues such as access to libraries and archives. In spite of the inherent

difficulties due to different educational systems, to immensely complicated placement problems, to the position of an inter-university committee vis-à-vis a powerful governmental bureaucracy, and to the
inevitably different objectives of the American universities and the
Soviet Ministry of Education, this method of handling the exchanges
has been highly useful. It has permitted on the American side the development of a system of selection and administration consistent with
highest academic standards and the greatest possible separation of the
exchange system from the day-to-day political tensions between the
two governments. It has permitted flexibility and experimentation
in developing relations with the Soviet government, relatively free
from preoccupation with the prestige position of the United States
or other immediate political objectives. It has placed the American
exchangees outside the immediate official family of the United States
Embassy in Moscow, emphasizing thereby the primarily scholarly
interests of the American universities. Finally, and perhaps most
importantly, it permits Soviet visitors sponsored by the Committee
under the program to observe the vitality, quality, and nonpolitical
character of the American academic community.

East-West Center in Honolulu

A unique effort to combine many kinds of cultural activities in the
context of a program designed to develop and strengthen relations between Western and non-Western countries was authorized in the establishment by Congress of a Center for Cultural and Technical Interchange between East and West at the University of Hawaii. The
Center came into being on October 25, 1960, with the help of a grant-
in-aid made by the Department of State to the university. Congress
is to continue annual appropriations for support of the Center.

The significance of this action lies not merely in the commitment of
direct governmental support[37] for this kind of academic institution,
but also in the focus of the Center, which combines the promotion
of understanding through educational exchanges, teaching, study, and
research; the deliberate effort to reach not only established persons
but promising potential leaders; and insistence that the educational
experiences and research at the Center shall be designed to advance
the human welfare of the developing countries. In many respects,
the Center reflects in an academic setting the convergence of most of
the different elements in United States transnational cultural activities.

The United Nations and its specialized agencies

The United Nations and its specialized agencies from their creation in 1945 had been working to develop worldwide cultural cooperation along several different lines: to advance knowledge by fostering the educational, scientific, and artistic resources of mankind; to promote human welfare through a cooperative approach to major world problems of poverty, disease, illiteracy, malnutrition, and world communication; to advance international understanding among the peoples of the world. Their achievements were in many respects modest, in part because of limited funds provided by member states and in part because of the impact of the cold war upon the institutions of international cooperation. Nevertheless, the U.N. agencies made significant progress in promoting important research on such subjects as desalinizing sea water and increasing arability of desert lands; control of epidemics that endanger human and animal health; outer space; and improving agricultural seeds. They have helped to develop worldwide attacks upon illiteracy, disease, and malnutrition; they have achieved reductions in barriers to international trade in educational, scientific, and artistic materials; they have promoted accessibility to people everywhere of more objective knowledge about the history of nations and peoples and the differences among their cultures. A major role has been played by these U.N. agencies in mobilizing technical assistance to be available on a wholly nonpolitical, non-national basis to the vast underdeveloped areas of the world.

A thoroughly effective relationship between the work of the U.N. agencies and bilateral activities of the United States has not yet been achieved and remains an issue of major importance to the fashioning of the United States governmental cultural program.

As the United Nations embarks upon its "Decade of Development," the United States as the principal contributor is faced by the need to appraise with care the advantages and disadvantages of increasing the share of its own educational and technical assistance effort that should be channeled through the multilateral agencies.

Again, in the area of information activities there is great need for strengthening the role of the U.N. and its specialized agencies, and correspondingly adjusting the activities of the United States. In this area, the U.N. could play a unique role in establishing direct communication to the peoples of the world community on matters of U.N. policy, program, and action. The absence of channels for such communication is a major barrier to understanding of the U.N. itself, and therefore to the strengthening of the world community. The achievement of the overriding objective of American foreign policy—a genuinely effective United Nations community—requires that the United States further the development of direct information services by the U.N. A challenging opportunity to make available channels for such

U.N. services is provided by the development of communication satellites such as Telstar—a medium peculiarly appropriate for use as a channel through which the U.N. could regularly report directly to the people of the world community.

The United States government has become progressively involved in a wide variety of cultural activities throughout the world — including such diverse elements as exchanges of students and professional people, information broadcasts, libraries, cultural centers, . . . and overseas presentations in the arts. Most of these activities were initiated under pressure of world events or in direct response to challenges or threats from without: . . . the urgent postwar need for re-education of the occupied countries; the barrage of anti-American propaganda from the U.S.S.R.; the rising demand of the underdeveloped countries for educational and technical help. Other activities represented government efforts to support or supplement programs primarily undertaken by private agencies — for example, the promotion of scholarly interchange or support of American schools abroad. Still others were cooperative ventures with other governments, growing out of our commitments to the U.N. and other international bodies, especially UNESCO, WHO, FAO, ILO, the World Bank, the International Atomic Energy Organization, and the Organization of American States.

In the course of these developments, many questions of policy arose and were debated, intermittently and with more or less ardor, both within the government and among interested groups in the general public.

One of the most hotly debated issues, as we have seen, was that of the proper balance between short-term, "maximum impact" activities of a propaganda character and the longer-term programs such as educational exchanges and joint scientific and cultural undertakings. . . . In time of war or great international tension, the former tended to dominate the scene. Relaxation of tension brought a swing of the pendulum toward greater emphasis on the long-range measures.

Another persistent question concerned the proper relationship between governmental and private agencies in the various types of cultural activity involved. Should the role of government be limited generally to stimulating, encouraging, assisting, and supplementing private effort? Or should the government actively initiate programs required by the exigencies of foreign policy, enlist the cooperation of the private sector, and direct the activities undertaken?

What administrative pattern, both in Washington and in the field, can best facilitate the government's performance of its role? Should all cultural activities be directed by one agency, or should they be dispersed among various agencies, and, if the latter, how can they be effectively coordinated? And how should the administration of cultural activities be coordinated with that of related activities such as economic development assistance or trade?

To what extent should the transnational cultural programs of the United States be deliberately related to those of other countries, and should this be done primarily through multilateral means or through bilateral, reciprocal means? For that matter, to what extent *can* cultural relations be made genuinely reciprocal?

What should be the magnitude of an adequate total cultural relations program, and what should be the relative magnitude of each of its component parts?

These questions, and many others like them, have been the subjects of discussion in innumerable studies, reports, conference sessions, Congressional hearings, etc., as a conscious search for over-all policy has developed and become increasingly insistent.

Underlying all these questions, and in a sense conditioning the answers to all of them, are the fundamental questions: *What are the overriding objectives of United States foreign policy? Can cultural programs contribute to their advancement?* If so, how?

Notes

[1] *U.S. Information Agency Instruction No. CA-8 of July 6, 1954* (Washington, 1954). USIA in 1956 set up a Cultural Operations Division and broadened the title of its Advisory Committee on Books Abroad to that of Advisory Committee on Cultural Information.

[2] Department of State, memorandum of January 4, 1955, "Principles to be Observed in Administering the Educational Exchange Program and the Overseas Information Program" (Washington, 1955), from Undersecretary of State Robert Murphy to Assistant Secretary of State Carl W. McCardle. It carried among several attachments a memorandum on "Clarification of Distinction Between Cultural Activities of USIA and Educational Exchange Activities of the Department."

[3] *Report of the State-USIA Task Force on International Cultural Activities* (Washington, April 22, 1955).

[4] *Fourteenth Report of the United States Advisory Commission on Information,* House Doc. No. 106, 86th Cong., 1st sess. (1959), pp. 8–11.

[5] Statements of George V. Allen, Director of the United States Information Agency, and Saxton Bradford, Deputy Director, in, respectively, *Tenth Review of Operations,* January 1–June 30, 1958, p. 3; and *The Annapolis Conference on International Education,* April 4–5, 1959 (Washington: Department of State, Bureau of International Cultural Relations, July 27, 1959), pp. 13–15.

[6] *Conference Report on Departments of State and Justice, the Judiciary, and Related Agencies Appropriations Bill, 1956,* House Report No. 1043, 84th Cong., 1st sess. (1956); and J. L. Morrill, *A Proposal for the Coordination of the Exchange of Persons Programs of the International Educational Exchange Service and of the International Cooperation Administration,* Part II (Washington: Department of State, May 1, 1956, mimeographed), pp. 1–5. Hereafter this source will be cited as *Morrill Report.*

⁷*Morrill Report*, Part II, cited, p. 5. The ICA figures did not include administrative costs or costs of foreign nationals employed on technical cooperation projects.

⁸Section 302 of the Mutual Security Act of 1954 defined technical cooperation as follows: ". . . the term 'technical cooperation programs' means programs for the international exchange of technical knowledge and skills designed to contribute to the balanced and integrated development of the economic resources and productive capacities of economically under-developed areas." *Morrill Report*, cited, Part V, p. 35.

⁹*Ibid.*, Part V, pp. 36–38, 40.

¹⁰*Ibid.*, Part I, p. 1.

¹¹*Ibid.*, Part IV, p. 22, and Part V, p. 42 (italics added). For the complete text of the statement, see "U.S. Government Participation in Cultural Exchange Programs," *Looking Ahead*, Vol. 4, No. 3 (Washington: National Planning Association, April 1956), pp. 5–8.

¹²Andrew Berding, *Foreign Affairs and You* (New York: Doubleday, 1962), p. 212.

¹³*Toward a National Effort in International Educational and Cultural Affairs, Twenty-Sixth Semi-Annual Report on Educational Exchange Activities*, 87th Cong., 1st sess., House Doc. No. 199, Committee on Foreign Affairs (Washington: Government Printing Office, 1961). Also available as Department of State Publication No. 7238 (July 1961).

¹⁴The Bureau, established July 2, 1959, comprises the Office of Educational Exchange (OEE), formerly the International Educational Exchange Service; and the Office of Cultural Exchange (OCE), which includes what was formerly the Cultural Presentations Staff for the President's Program in the Arts, the Program Development Staff, and the UNESCO Relations Staff.

¹⁵The program for World War II veterans under the Servicemen's Readjustment Act of 1944 (P.L. 346, 78th Cong., 2d sess., 58 Stat. 284 [1944]), terminated substantially in 1956. That for Korean veterans under the Veterans Readjustment Assistance Act of 1952 (P.L. 550, 82d Cong., 2d sess., 66 Stat. 663 [1952]) was scheduled to end in 1965.

¹⁶For a special review of the Finnish program, see Department of State, *An Investment in Understanding: Educational Exchange Program between the United States and Finland, 1950–54* (Washington, 1956). On aid to Chinese students see *Federal Activity in the Field of Education*, House hearings, Committee on Education and Labor, 83rd Cong., 1st sess. (1954), pp. 198–199; Department of State, *The Program of Emergency Aid to Chinese Students, 1949–1955* (Washington, 1956); and Committee on Educational Interchange Policy, *Chinese Students in the United States, 1948–55: A Study in Government Policy* (New York: Institute of International Education, 1956).

¹⁷*Departments of State and Justice, the Judiciary, and Related Agencies Appropriations for 1961: United States Information Agency, President's Special International Program, Commission on Civil Rights*, House hearings, 86th Cong., 2d sess., pp. 813–821. Books constitute 54 per cent of the material exported under the program, periodicals 20 per cent, and motion pictures 23 per cent. *Ibid.*, p. 889.

¹⁸*Report on the Operations of the Department of State* (under P.L. 584), 86th Cong., 2d sess. (June 3, 1960), House Doc. No. 410, p. 1. For a general summary of the Fulbright program to 1960 and accomplishments of grantees, see Francis J. Colligan, "The Fulbright Act and Grants," *Dictionary of American History*, Vol. VI (New York: Charles Scribner's Sons, 1961), p. 126.

¹⁹*Departments of State, Justice, and Commerce, and the United States Information Agency Appropriations, 1955*, Senate hearings, 83d Cong., 1st sess., Part 2, pp. 1172–1201, 1769–1845.

²⁰*Departments of State, Justice, the Judiciary, and Related Agencies Appropriations, 1956*, Senate hearings, cited, pp. 165–254.

²¹*Congressional Record*, Vol. 101 (April 14, 1955), pp. 4460–4499.

²²*Fifteenth Semiannual Report on Educational Exchange Activities*, House Doc. No. 335, 84th Cong., 2d sess. (1956), pp. 1–3.

²³*United States Information and Educational Exchange Act Amendments of 1956*, Senate hearings, pp. 104–105; and *Departments of State, Justice, the Judiciary, and Re-*

lated Agencies Appropriations, 1957, Senate hearings, 84th Cong., 2d sess., pp. 441–442.

[24] *1956 Amendments to the United States Information and Educational Exchange Act of 1948,* Senate Report No. 1959, 84th Cong., 2d sess. (1956), p. 7.

[25] *Departments of State, Justice, the Judiciary, and Related Agencies Appropriations, 1959,* Senate hearings, 86th Cong., 1st sess., pp. 16, 24.

[26] Francis A. Young, "Educational and Cultural Exchange, the Fulbright-Hays Act of 1961," *American Council of Learned Societies Newsletter,* Vol. XII, No. 9 (November 1961), pp. 3–7.

[27] *Ibid.*

[28] Ralph Purcell, *Government and Art* (Washington: Public Affairs Press, 1956), pp. 84, 85.

[29] *Federal Grants for Fine Arts Programs and Projects,* House, Report of a Special Subcommittee to the Committee on Education and Labor, Committee Print, 83d Cong., 2d sess. (1954), p. 7.

[30] Quoted from a newspaper in Djakarta, Indonesia, in House hearings, . . . *for cultural and athletic exchanges and participation in international fairs and festivals,* Committee on Foreign Affairs, 84th Cong., 2d sess. (March 6, 7, 13, and 15, 1956), p. 5.

[31] *The President's Emergency Fund for Participation in International Affairs, Supplemental Appropriations Act, 1955,* P.L. 663, 83d Cong., 2d sess., 68 Stat. 800, 824 (1954); $2.25 million was allotted to the Department of State for cultural presentations, $2.25 million to the Department of Commerce for trade fairs, and $500,000 to the United States Information Agency for coordination, promotion, and publicity.

[32] The sources for the above and the following material are, for the period from December 1954 to June 30, 1956, the mimeographed *Quarterly Reports* issued by the United States Information Agency under the title "President's Emergency Fund for Participation in International Affairs"; and from July 1, 1956, onward, the successive *Semiannual Reports* issued by USIA entitled "President's Special International Program."

[33] *The International Cultural Relations of the United States, Policies and Programs, 1955–1958* (Washington: Department of State, n.d.), pp. 31–33, which summarizes material presented in the Smithsonian Institution; *Report on the National Collection of Fine Arts including the Freer Gallery of Art* (Washington: Government Printing Office, annual). This is an interesting example of international cultural activities of other agencies of the federal government independent of the principal agencies in this field. There are others whose implications for our international relations vary with their terms of reference. Most are listed in Francis J. Colligan, *Programs of International Cultural Cooperation and Technical Exchange of Agencies of the U. S. Government and Related International Organizations* (Washington, 1957, mimeographed).

[34] *Departments of State and Justice, the Judiciary, and Related Agencies Appropriations, 1956,* Senate hearings, cited, pp. 246–247; and *ibid.,* 1957, Senate hearings, cited, p. 643.

[35] Columbia-Harvard Research Group under the administration of Columbia University, *United States Foreign Policy, U.S.S.R. and Eastern Europe,* Senate, Committee on Foreign Relations, Committee Print, Study No. 11 (February 14, 1960), p. 32.

[36] Department of State, *Report on Exchanges with the Soviet Union and Eastern Europe,* Report No. 18 (January 1, 1962).

[37] Peace Corps, *First Annual Report to Congress* (Washington, 1962).

17
The Cultural Relations Activities of France, the United Kingdom, Germany, and the Soviet Union

A survey by UNESCO in 1959 revealed that well over half of the 81 member states queried, including virtually all the larger ones, had official cultural-relations programs. The number of countries and the scale of their activities are undoubtedly even larger today. Since limitations of space and evidence rule out a more comprehensive review, this chapter provides a tiny sketch of the cultural-relations background and current policies and programs of four major European powers: France, the United Kingdom, Germany, and the Soviet Union.[1]

France: Conquest by Spirit

France has made cultural relations a serious element of its foreign policy ever since Napoleon's Egyptian campaign and has had no equal in the field. Today, more than half the Foreign Ministry's budget is devoted to cultural activities, and the overseas aid program puts its heaviest emphasis on education. "France believes," a recent official report states, "that the human factor is paramount in the accelerated economic development of these overseas countries. For the individual represents both the end and the means."[2]

A few facts bear testimony to the seriousness of the French effort in this field:

The French government spent more than $100 million in 1962 on education in developing countries, primarily in Africa and Southeast Asia.

Philip H. Coombs, *The Fourth Dimension of Foreign Policy, Educational and Cultural Affairs* (New York: Harper & Row, 1964), pp. 77–95.

Over 30,000 French teachers, regular members of the national educational establishment, were serving abroad in 1963 – the great majority in former French territories of Africa and Southeast Asia, but over 250 in Latin America. At least an equal number of other French citizens, many of them members of religious orders, were also teaching abroad. This vastly exceeds the total of American and British teachers overseas.

About 10,000 French technical assistance experts were stationed overseas under government auspices in 1961, engaged chiefly in "on-the-spot training of middle management, skilled labor, and other qualified personnel." (The nearest comparable figure for AID was 1,190.)

Some 30,000 foreign students were studying in French universities in 1963, more than 20,000 of them from developing countries. Over 10,000 Africans were attending French universities, engineering schools, and business schools in 1961 – several times the number of Africans studying in the United States that year. In addition to special scholarships for some, the French government provides all foreign students free tuition, subsidized meals, social security services, and other advantages enjoyed by French students. (This assistance, incidentally, makes it financially possible for many American students to spend a year of study in France.)

Approximately 3,000 foreign technicians come to France under government auspices each year for specialized training in French government offices or businesses and in special schools – about half from Africa, one-quarter from Latin America, and over 10 per cent from Asia.

The Ministry of Foreign Affairs supports about one hundred French libraries overseas. Twice this number are run by the Alliance Fran-çaise, a private cultural organization encouraged by the government. In addition, about one hundred overseas phonograph record centers and a similar number of film libraries are supported by the government. Book gifts totaling $200,000 were made in 1961.

In a recent year, the Foreign Ministry supported 60 tours of theater groups to 38 different countries; 77 tours by musicians (symphonies, chamber music ensembles and individual virtuosos); and about 20 art exhibits.

The Alliance Française runs about 800 cultural centers outside France for teaching the French language and civilization. (In the United States, however, the Alliances Françaises are independent American groups, not administratively connected with Paris, and are usually more social than instructional.)

These substantial current efforts are in keeping with a policy of long standing, about which the French have never minced words and in whose efficacy they have great confidence. The theme was sounded by Napoleon in his twilight reflections at St. Helena: "I have been forced to conquer Europe by the sword; he who comes after will conquer it by the spirit. For the spirit is always more powerful than the sword." For Napoleon, and for French leaders after him, this was not a matter of nostalgia or sentiment but of hard realism. "Intellectual and moral expansion," as the French called it, was aimed at the elites of other societies and became a major instrument in building and assimilating the second great French colonial empire of the late nineteenth century. Wherever possible, cultural penetration was substituted for force. "What political operation or armed invasion," a French deputy candidly asked his colleagues in 1900, "was ever able, with less expense, to produce such important and lasting results?"

French universities and French overseas schools were called "true centers of propaganda in favor of France" by an official report in 1920 which asserted that "the Ministry of Foreign Affairs and its agents abroad must direct and control efforts, inspire and encourage at any price French intellectual penetration, in the conviction that it is one of the surest and most effective of our activities abroad—one of our foreign policies that is richest in resources and least debatable." Although French cultural-relations programs have been administered separately from economic and information programs, their commercial and political advantages have not been ignored. The view expressed by a French deputy in 1912 is still alive today: "If commerce follows the flag, it follows for even stronger reasons the national language."

With the liquidation of the colonial empire after World War II, France has redoubled its cultural effort, shifting the strategy from the promotion of what was earlier called "assimilation" to what is now called "contractual cooperation" with the former colonies and territories. This, again, is much more than a sentimental affair, though the sentiments run deep on both sides. It is part of a strategic effort to consolidate a large, close-knit, French-speaking cultural and economic community—somewhat comparable to the British Commonwealth— that will fortify the political and economic position of France and sustain its international power and prestige.

It is plain that these old French cultural ties are made of strong fiber—rugged enough, for example, to have survived the angry Bizerte incident in Tunisia in 1961. Though political relations at that time reached the breaking point, educational and cultural cooperation remained in full force.

Building on past accomplishments, France seems well on the way to

consolidating a "culture empire" — based now on voluntary membership — which may well prove more viable and profitable than its two
lost political empires. It could prove an asset also to the whole democratic world by helping to ensure the independence, prosperity, and
stability of the twenty or so new nations of Africa and Asia that have
now emerged where the second French Empire once stood. But all this,
one suspects, will hinge partly on whether the French have the foresight to permit and indeed to encourage these new nations to build
supplemental cultural ties with other advanced democratic nations too,
for without that they can scarcely feel fully independent.

There is also the question whether France's cultural effort will become more broadly international both geographically and psychologically. The impressively large educational aid effort, for example,
is largely confined to the former French territories in Africa, whereas
aid to Latin American countries, which would undoubtedly welcome
more, is very modest. In part, this concentration reflects a conspicuous
need to make up for lost time in building indigenous educational systems staffed by Africans. But it also reflects — on the part of some
French officials, though by no means all — the survival of a narrow
nationalistic approach to cultural relations. Others argue that this high
concentration represents a failure to grasp the opportunity and obligation to bring France's great cultural and economic strengths to bear on
the larger, cooperative task of harmonizing the entire community of
independent nations, old and new alike. The future course of French
cultural relations will be strongly affected by the outcome of this
current debate within France between defenders of a narrow nationalism and proponents of a broader international view.

The United Kingdom: National Interpretation

British experience is especially rich in possible lessons for the
United States. The approaches of both nations are philosophically
close and, being relatively new in the field, both are less inhibited by
tradition from striking out in fresh directions. The British, like the
Americans, were initially pushed into an official cultural-relations program by the hostile maneuvers of Nazism and Fascism, but once in,
they rather liked it. They approached the matter in a uniquely English
fashion, mainly through the British Council — one of those private arms
of government which non-Britishers find hard to fathom.

Working for years on a shoestring, the Council did an impressive
job, and its activities have grown far beyond the original vision. For
its size, the British cultural-relations program is perhaps unequaled in
quality and effectiveness, though some critics consider it too stuffy and

unimaginative. To judge from the greater budgetary support now provided, Her Majesty's Government is convinced, even if tardily as history goes, that educational and cultural affairs deserve an important role in foreign policy.

The British Council's central mission from the start was described as "national interpretation," which was regarded as "a happier phrase than cultural propaganda." To avoid any suspicion of propaganda, even in wartime, the Council's management has been kept in distinguished private hands and sharply divorced from the British Information Service. While substantially autonomous and semiprivate in character, the Council receives most of its funds from Parliamentary grants and cooperates closely with the Foreign Office. Its budget rose from about £3 million in 1953 to £8 million in 1963, not counting substantial technical assistance funds which the Council administers for other national and international bodies.

The British program (like the American) is notably broader geographically than either the French or German, despite a heavy concern for former colonies and the Commonwealth. Well over half the Council's 1963 "Regional Services" budget was earmarked for countries outside the Commonwealth. Its overseas offices serve some 75 countries and territories. While the Council's earlier emphasis on teaching English and disseminating British books and other publications still continues, important new activities have now been added, including extensive work with foreign students and other visitors, sending British lecturers and performing artists on foreign tours, increased attention to science and technology, and the development of a substantial exchange with the Soviet Union.

Despite its far fewer institutions for higher education, Britain had about the same number of foreign students and trainees in 1962 as the United States (60,000), three-quarters of them from less-developed nations. (Not all were university students; many were attending technical-training institutes or learning on the job.) Whereas foreign students accounted for less than 2 per cent of total higher educational enrollments in the United States, in Great Britain they represented 8 per cent of university enrollments, 9 per cent in technical colleges and 3 per cent in teacher-training institutions.

Though only a small fraction of foreign students receive direct scholarship aid from the British government, virtually all are indirectly subsidized. The "hidden" costs of their education defrayed by tax funds flowing into British higher education have been estimated by the Overseas Development Institute at nearly £10 million annually. A large proportion benefit also from the advisory and hospitality services of the Council, which maintains 20 offices within the United Kingdom primarily to serve foreign students. The Council also administers a recent £3 million government grant to expand foreign-student hostel and housing accommodations. No comparable services for foreign students are supported by the United States government.

The Council is the government's main instrument for handling other foreign guests and for sending distinguished lecturers, artists, writers, scientists, and other leading British figures on overseas tours. In the performing arts, the Council in 1961–1962 financed 23 tours to 35 countries by some of the nation's finest musical and dramatic organizations.

The British support their overseas schools more generously than the United States, but less generously than the French and Germans (partly, perhaps, because over the years the British have placed more emphasis on training indigenous teachers for British-type schools). The Council now provides assistance to some 60 British-sponsored schools in 27 countries, mostly outside the Commonwealth.

British financial aid to educational development in the new nations (largely through agencies other than the Council) has concentrated — in contrast to French and American practice — on capital grants for new higher education facilities, mainly in the former British colonies of Africa. Since the war more than $30 million has been allocated for new higher technical colleges and university colleges, designed to become full-fledged universities eventually, as part of a calculated effort to prepare the colonies for independence.

That overseas demand for British teachers far exceeds the supply is due partly to the recruitment handicap imposed by the decentralized pattern of British education. "In this context," a recent British Council Report observed, "one cannot help but envy the French system under which teaching overseas is so much less of a career hazard than it has seemed in the past to teachers in Britain." The Council, with the aid of other official and professional organizations, is now making a major effort to expand the flow of teachers overseas. Faced with similar problems, the United States may find useful clues in this British experience.

Over-all, except for receiving foreign students and trainees, British educational aid to developing countries has been surprisingly small, both in absolute terms and as a percentage of total aid, considering the importance which the British generally attach to education. The Overseas Development Institute estimated that in 1962, through both bilateral and multilateral programs, the United Kingdom put only 6 per cent of its total aid effort (or about $30 million) into education and training projects. France has given education a decidedly higher priority in its aid program and, as nearly as one can judge from the inadequate facts available, so has the United States. In fairness it should be noted, however, that when British colonies achieved independence, most were better endowed with educational institutions (many built earlier with *private* British funds) and with well-educated local people, including teachers and administrators, than were most other European colonies.

Germany: New Aims and Old Methods

Germany's cultural-relations policies have undergone a succession of striking changes over the past 80 years, reflecting major shifts in Germany's domestic politics and in its international posture and objectives. Some knowledge of this earlier experience is important to understanding the present situation.

In the first phase, from the 1880's to World War I, German cultural-relations policy was focused almost entirely on Germans abroad and what came to be known as Germanism (*Deutschtum*). It was more concerned with nationalism and the quest for international influence and power than with cultural contacts with other peoples. The second phase began after World War I, in the bitter wake of the Treaty of Versailles. For the first time, with a small cultural section established in the Foreign Office, the German government adopted the policy of using German education and culture to influence not only overseas Germans but non-Germans as well. It was essentially an effort to substitute cultural strength for the economic and military strength lost by the war. But the Weimar Republic did not have much time, and with Hitler came a new phase. He turned all the mechanisms of Germanism and of cultural relations—the overseas schools, churches and clubs, foreign-student programs—to the service of Nazi propaganda, penetration, and subversion. That story is too familiar to need retelling.

In the fourth phase, under the postwar German Federal Republic, cultural relations at first languished, but within a few years the Bonn government was rapidly building a program. Between 1952 and 1960 the cultural budget of the foreign ministry rocketed from 2.8 million DM. to 95.8 million DM. (about $24 million). The prime aims were to build confidence among the nations of the West in the new government's peaceful intentions and democratic character; to show the world at large that Germany had been the land not merely of a Hitler but of Bach and Beethoven, of Kant and Goethe; and to restore the good will of those overseas Germans who were rudely disillusioned and disaffected by the Hitler era. In short, the aim was to recover Germany's lost world position and prestige, to begin the hard task of rebuilding good relations and good markets.

The recent phase, beginning about 1960, has been marked by an impressive further rise in the budget to 163 million DM. in 1962, but more importantly by a broadened international outlook as shown, for example, by a heightened interest in aiding developing countries and by a more serious participation in UNESCO, involving many of Germany's leading cultural and scholarly groups. This new aim of moderating narrow nationalism among all nations—something quite new for Germany—was added to the old and continuing objectives of keeping strong ties with overseas Germans, building friends among foreigners, and enhancing Germany's prestige and economic position. In mood the new endeavors are in striking contrast to the frustration and bitterness which followed World War I and to the aggressive arrogance of the Hitler era. Yet Germany seems still to be in the process of clarifying its aims and adjusting actions to match them.

The actual pattern of the Federal Republic's cultural-relations program does not seem to have caught up yet with the new objectives. For one thing, it is still narrow, both geographically and in the pattern of activities. German-sponsored schools abroad, for example, receive nearly one-third of the total cultural budget, and the bulk goes to a few countries (such as Brazil, Argentina, and Chile) where past German immigration was heaviest. It is a striking fact that in 1962 the Federal Republic gave fifteen times as much support to German-sponsored schools in Latin America as the United States government gave to American-sponsored schools there (about $3.8 million versus $250,000). The United States contribution was clearly inadequate, but one wonders if some of the German aid might not have been applied more usefully to the development of indigenous Latin American schools, to which the United States contributed vastly more.

The German cultural program puts strong emphasis on educational exchange. The Goethe Institute, which is private but supported by government, supplies German teachers and professors for service abroad, trains foreign teachers of German, and carries cultural programs overseas. University exchanges, financed by the Foreign Office, are handled by an inter-university exchange organization which has a high degree of autonomy. The interest of the German government in student exchanges is demonstrated by its recent commitment to bear half the future costs of the Fulbright exchange program. Germany is attracting more foreign students than ever before, despite serious problems for overcrowded German universities. The 24,000 foreign students studying in Germany in 1962 — financed largely by nongovernment resources — constituted 10 per cent of total higher educational enrollments.

The German program of technical and educational assistance to developing countries, operated largely by several separate agencies outside the Foreign Office, has been considerably smaller than the French, British, and United States programs, but it is now showing signs of expansion. Private efforts have considerably supplemented the modest government program. The language obstacle and the very limited colonial heritage of Germany have undoubtedly been important factors in holding down overseas educational and technical assistance aid, but it seems evident that Germany has a considerably greater potential for rendering such aid than has thus far been exercised. Lately there have been mounting pressures from both within and without to use this potential more fully.

The Soviet Union: The Great Risk

Soviet cultural relations are in a class by themselves because they express Russia's unique political system, traditions, nationalism, and international aims. No nation, not even France, has made cultural affairs a more vital and integral part of its foreign policy or invested more generously in them. In so doing, the Soviet Union is perhaps taking a great political risk. In the decade since Stalin's death, the Soviet cultural program has grown rapidly in scale, sophistication, and liberality. These recent trends, if continued, are likely to produce important changes not only in the U.S.S.R.'s external relations but within the Soviet society itself.

Historically, Soviet cultural relations have had sharp ups and downs. During the initial period of civil war — which coincided with Lenin's rule — the Soviet Union was culturally isolated from the outside world; but in 1925, with the revolution fairly well consolidated, a concerted effort was launched to tell the "new society's" story abroad, to win friends, and to advance communism's international aims. The All-Union Society for Cultural Relations with Foreign Countries (known as VOKS) was established to promote Soviet "friendship societies" abroad and interchanges of various professional, artistic, and labor groups. Since the fledgling Soviet government enjoyed only limited diplomatic relations at the time and was generally considered a pariah by the older powers, cultural channels provided a means of bypassing governments and appealing directly to their peoples. One aim was to foster popular restraints upon such governments against hostile policies and acts toward the Soviet Union. Another was to strengthen the "progressive elements," and, most of all, the Communist organizations within these other nations. By 1930, VOKS had developed cultural relations with private groups in 77 nations, only 46 of which had formal diplomatic relations with the Soviet Union.

These early efforts – a blend of genuine cultural interchange, politics, and propaganda – were often crudely ideological and, by Western standards, mutually contradictory. While advocating "cultural co-operation" on the one hand, Soviet officials also espoused the Marxist-Leninist view that "socialist culture" and "imperialist culture" were irreconcilably in conflict. The worldwide socialist revolution, they argued, must include a cultural revolution which would establish a "truly unified and universal human culture."

In the official Soviet view, then as now, scholarship, science, and the arts were inseparable from politics. Artists and scientists were expected to play their part in the movements for peace and for the popular front, and in other campaigns intended to promote the political aims of the U.S.S.R. Cultural societies abroad, as the Vice-President of VOKS told a group of visiting Czech students in 1931, were to organize their work to attract such representatives of the working intelligentsia who, in times of great trial, could stand in defense of the U.S.S.R. "These societies must create a ring of trust, sympathy and friendship around the U.S.S.R., through which all plans of intervention will be unable to penetrate."[3]

The rise of fascism in the 1930's and the political purges within the Soviet Union itself led to a contraction of external cultural contacts, and the outbreak of World War II forced a still greater shrinkage. Late in the war, however, and immediately after, a fresh cultural effort was launched in support of the Soviet Union's postwar aims. It focused especially upon Latin America (where, for example, an ambitious new Russo-Mexican Cultural Institute was established in 1944 to promote Soviet cultural activities in the whole region) and upon neighboring small countries of Europe and the Near East where the Soviet Union's policies – viewed from the West as expansionist – were soon to precipitate a cold war with its wartime allies. Cultural activities of many sorts were stepped up. Over 500 scholarships for study in the Soviet Union were given in 1946 to students from Albania, Yugoslavia, Hungary, and other Eastern European countries; Soviet book èxports reached impressive levels; Soviet friendship societies, pan-Slavic organizations, and a constellation of anti-fascist committees were created or rejuvenated; and the flow of distinguished foreign visitors to Russia rose sharply. Cultural interchange remained, as earlier, the handmaiden of Soviet political aims. "Hitlerism has been smashed," a high Soviet official told a group of visiting Western scientists right after the war, "but the struggle against the remnants of reaction is continuing and no scientist who holds progress dear can remain aloof from this struggle."

The expanded cultural dialogue between East and West which immediately followed the defeat of Germany and gave great encouragement to many on both sides, proved, however, to be short-lived. With the hardening of the Stalinist line and the intensified cold war after 1948, the Soviet cultural curtain was once more drawn tight. Following Stalin's death in 1953 and the adoption of Khrushchev's "peaceful coexistence" line, however, the curtain began to lift again, this time higher than ever before. And despite recurrent political-military crises, which seemed to belie the proclaimed policy of "peaceful coexistence," Soviet cultural interchanges with the West continued to expand. In the decade from 1953 to 1963, the Soviet government made a special effort to accumulate cultural treaties with the developing nations of Asia, Africa, and Latin America. For the first time, moreover, formal cultural-exchange agreements were established with such Western powers as the United Kingdom and the United States.

With Soviet cultural relations thus becoming "normalized" through intergovernmental agreements, the old VOKS machinery was scrapped, and a new State Committee for Cultural Relations with Foreign Countries was created as the central clearing house to coordinate all external exhange activities. Reflecting the importance attached by the Kremlin to these matters, this new State Committee is tied directly to the Council of Ministers; its head enjoys ministerial status and is empowered to secure the full cooperation of all ministries, academies, institutes, and nongovernmental organizations concerned with educational, scientific, and cultural affairs. (It is as if, in the United States, the Bureau of Educational and Cultural Affairs were lifted out of the State Department, attached directly to the President's cabinet, endowed with full departmental status and given a clear mandate to establish policies and coordinate all international exchange activities, both governmental and private.)

Under these arrangements, the Soviet cultural-relations program has expanded rapidly and can be expected to continue growing as long as Khrushchev's policy of "peaceful coexistence" endures. The scale and diversity of this effort are suggested by the following examples:

In the fall of 1963, according to a high Soviet educational official, some 25,000 foreign students were enrolled in Soviet higher education, many from neighboring Communist nations but a sharply growing proportion from Africa, Asia, and Latin America. The typical foreign student is given full scholarship for four or five years. Many spend an initial year at the Patrice Lumumba Friendship University, learning Russian, remedying academic deficiencies, and otherwise being prepared for admission to the regular Soviet academic institutions.

Tourism to the Soviet Union has also grown by leaps and bounds in the past five years, and most Western visitors have apparently encountered fewer restraints on their freedom of movement than anticipated, despite some dramatic exceptions, which did incalculable harm to the Soviet cultural-relations effort.

Even more significant, perhaps, has been the new phenomenon of Soviet citizens going abroad as tourists. Some 10,000, for example, were permitted to attend the Brussels Fair in 1958. It seems likely that the United States will receive a good number of nonofficial Soviet tourists in the next few years, provided the present severe stringency of Soviet foreign currency supply is relieved.

The Soviet overseas book program has also expanded rapidly. According to official figures, exports rose from about 27 million books (698 separate titles) in 1958 to over 40 million (1,068 titles in 34 foreign languages) in 1961. A much larger number of books was produced abroad with Soviet financial assistance, for sale usually at below-cost prices. All told, USIA analysts believe it to be "a reasonable assumption that some 150 million books in free-world languages were produced by the Soviet Union (directly and indirectly) for distribution abroad in 1961." Not all of these books are of Communist origin, though they are obviously selected with an eye to advancing the Soviet cause.

The Soviet Union has been pre-eminent in sending its best artistic talent abroad for cultural presentations. (I suspect that the Bolshoi and Moiseyev ballet companies and the Leningrad Symphony Orchestra, for example, have lately built more goodwill for the Soviet Union in Europe, the United States, and Latin America than all the VOKS bulletins and other earlier propaganda activities combined.) In the less developed countries, especially in Asia, the Soviet Union has cultivated the goodwill of local audiences (and spread political ideas) with its traveling circuses, trained bear acts, puppet shows, and other folksy entertainment groups.

The Soviet cultural-relations effort also emphasizes appreciation for the artistic and literary accomplishments of other nations. The enthusiastic and sometimes almost unrestrained reception by Soviet audiences, of American singers, musicians, and art exhibits have been matched by the flattering attention paid them by high Soviet officials. Chairman Khrushchev's occasionally picturesque criticisms of American modern art and jazz have served mainly to emphasize that he took the trouble to attend a United States concert or exhibit. The Soviet Union also makes much of the artists and writers of developing countries. Many performing groups of folk dancers, singers, and the like are invited to the Soviet Union and are well received. Many Latin

American writers, who have felt ignored and unappreciated by the United States, are naturally pleased and impressed to have their works translated in the Soviet Union and elsewhere in Eastern Europe – and to receive generous royalty payments.

The Soviet cultural-relations effort places great emphasis at home on the learning of foreign languages by the Soviet people, not merely by specialists but by "the masses" as well. The younger Soviet experts one encounters around the world today have significantly better foreign language skills than their elders and are accordingly more effective in their work and personal relationships (though this applies mainly to those trained for diplomacy rather than for technical specialties). The Soviet Union is now developing a few hundred special schools in which Soviet children will receive virtually their entire education, from the first grade on, in a foreign language. Such schools already exist for the more widely used languages, such as English, French, Chinese, Spanish, Arabic, and Hindi; but others will soon embrace less familiar languages of Asia and Africa, some of which are known in the United States only by a mere handful of specialized scholars and are taught, if at all, only in the graduate schools of universities. One can well imagine the advantages that this investment in foreign language schools will have some years hence for Soviet cultural, commercial, and political relations all over the world.

Since Stalin's death the Soviet Union has joined UNESCO and is taking the work of this organization seriously. It has provided a number of first-rate experts to serve in the UNESCO secretariat and on UNESCO missions. The Soviet Union has also expanded considerably its educational aid and technical assistance to developing countries. Recently, for example, it has built and staffed an advanced technical training institute in India and is operating important educational projects in Afghanistan and Mali. Many foreign trainees are brought to the Soviet Union for specialized training, usually in how to operate or maintain Soviet-type industrial facilities or products in their home countries.

This impressive array of cultural, scientific, and educational activities, similar in form to many American activities, is aimed at several Soviet objectives, only some of them associated with the cold war. The most fundamental aim, of course, is to strengthen Soviet world power and prestige, to advance Soviet aims and influence in selected countries, and to augment Communist strength wherever possible. It is noteworthy that the Soviet cultural effort, in contrast to that of the United States, tends to concentrate on selected countries, presumably those of greatest importance to Soviet foreign policy objectives. Mexico,

Cuba, and Venezuela, for example, have long received more attention than most other Latin American countries, and several former French colonies in Africa today receive more attention than most former British colonies. Within these selected countries, again in some contrast to American practice, there is a heavy concentration of attention upon selected key groups and individuals, such as youth leaders, labor leaders, writers and other intellectuals. Although the Soviet Union has an impressive foreign broadcasting program and is expanding its film program (especially in Africa), less of its total effort is spent on trying to influence mass opinion directly. Relatively more is directed at strategic local people who are shapers of popular attitudes and political developments.

It is noteworthy also that today the Soviet cultural program, at least with respect to exchanges with advanced Western countries, is less obviously preoccupied with propaganda and immediate political matters than during the prewar period. There is heavier emphasis now on genuine intellectual, technical, and artistic exchange without immediate ideological connotations, though certainly considerations of ideology and national interest are always present. There may be several reasons for this change. One is that the Soviet Union, still much concerned with its own economic development, is anxious to acquire useful scientific and technical knowledge from other countries; another is that it clearly suits the current policy of "peaceful coexistence." Present Soviet leadership appears to have concluded that communizing the Western nations is not a practical goal for the foreseeable future and is therefore pursuing a strategy of accommodation. How long this policy will last is still an open question, but the improved mutual understanding that is gradually being brought about by these interchanges is certainly helping to create conditions that will make any other policy increasingly difficult.

From all appearances, Soviet leaders are finding it more important to justify their policies and actions to their own people; and the better educated and informed the people become, the greater this necessity is likely to be. Indeed, it appears that one other objective of the present Soviet cultural program is to demonstrate to the Soviet people themselves that their government is on good terms with others and is pursuing a peaceful course.

The Soviet cultural effort is not without its difficulties, some being similar to those encountered by the United States and other Western nations. Soviet technical assistance officials, for example, have by now discovered that rendering aid is often a very difficult, frustrating, and thankless business, regardless of one's ideology. But the Soviet

Union also has its unique problems. With respect to foreign students, for example, it not only has a serious language barrier to overcome but frequently is obliged to accept less well qualified students who have been unsuccessful in securing an opportunity to study in Western Europe or the United States. And ironically, the Soviet Union, which officially denies the existence of race prejudice, seems to be having much greater difficulty on this score with African students than the United States, which freely admits to having a race relations problem and is trying to do something about it.

Another special problem of the Soviet Union is posed by the bureaucratic complexities, rigidities, and delays which inevitably result from trying to handle all external cultural relations through government channels. Some of the difficulties encountered in the U.S.–U.S.S.R. exchange program which are popularly attributed to political motives are, I am convinced, more bureaucratic than political in origin.

The most fundamental problem for the Soviet Union, however, is how fast and how far to move toward relaxing restrictions upon a full and free interchange of people, ideas, and knowledge with other nations. By previous standards there has been a marked liberalization in recent years. Yet Soviet officials are still far from ready to permit the kind of uninhibited flow of books, films, magazines, broadcasts, and people that has long been taken for granted among the nations of Western Europe and North America, and among many developing nations as well. It is exceedingly difficult, as Adlai Stevenson has pointed out, to keep a closed society closed. Even more difficult is to open it part way, as has now been done, and to continue to control the situation thereafter. Beyond a certain point the process of opening up becomes irreversible and then uncontrollable. Thus, despite the evident short-run values which increased cultural exchanges have for the Soviet Union, the long-run inevitably involves a risk. By its very nature cultural interchange is the natural enemy of ideological rigidities and of closed societies. Soviet leaders must surely realize this. Their very willingness to take the gamble is itself cause for encouragement.

A particularly fascinating question right now, of course, is whether the serious deterioration of Soviet-Chinese relations will accelerate or retard the liberalization of Soviet cultural relations with the West. Thus far, this struggle within the Communist family appears to be favoring rather than discouraging a greater cultural rapprochement with the so-called capitalist nations.

Conclusions

It is difficult and risky to attempt a detailed comparison of different national efforts in international educational and cultural affairs, but a few general conclusions seem warranted. As to absolute size, the over-all American effort, including private activities, is undoubtedly larger than that of any other nation; but relative to national resources and foreign commitments and obligations, our public activity in this field is smaller than that of the Soviet Union or France and perhaps smaller even than that of Germany and the United Kingdom.

The European nations, especially the Soviet Union and France, obviously take cultural affairs more seriously as a dimension of their foreign policy than does the United States. They do so, quite evidently, not out of woolly-headed sentiment or starry-eyed idealism, but because they are convinced that a large investment in cultural relations pays off in very practical terms. It is ironic that those Americans who fancy themselves hard-headed realists have been slow to reach this same conclusion. The practical men of Congress who more than a century ago created the land-grant college system as a means to develop America's internal strengths would probably be the first to recognize the importance today of using educational means to develop America's external strengths.

One other contrast is worth noting, namely, that in this field the Americans and British are relatively less nationalistic and more international and universal in their approach than the French, Germans, and Russians, and in this respect are perhaps more realistic than the others, in view of the broad thrust of world history. Given the vast changes in the world since the last war, the narrowly nationalistic strategy of cultural relations that was followed in the nation-state system of the nineteenth century is no longer appropriate, especially for great powers whose interests lie in building a strong and harmonious international community.

Notes

[1] I am indebted to several officials of the first three of these nations for supplying me with current information and for making valuable comments on an earlier draft of this chapter. For data on recent Soviet activities, I have relied mainly upon unclassified United States government reports and on Frederick Barghoorn's *The Soviet Cultural Offensive* (Princeton: Princeton University Press, 1960). The historical references have been drawn primarily from Ruth McMurry and Muna Lee, *The Cultural Approach— Another Way in International Relations* (Chapel Hill: University of North Carolina Press, 1947).

[2] *France—Aid and Cooperation* (Washington, D.C.: Service de Presse et d'Information of the French Embassy, 1963), p. 3.

[3] McMurry and Lee, *op. cit.*, p. 117.

18
Operation Crossroads Africa – A Non-governmental Exercise in Cultural Relations

In the last week of June 1960 several planeloads of American college students put down at points along the West African coast: Dakar, Monrovia, Accra, Lagos. Their total number was 183, and divided into 14 groups of 12 to 15 each, they fanned out to various places in 10 West African countries: Senegal, Sierra Leone, Guinea, Liberia, Ivory Coast, Ghana, Togo, Dahomey, Nigeria, and Cameroon. After travel, delays, some adventures and minor vicissitudes, each of these groups made their way to towns and villages, usually from 30 to 300 miles from the capital cities, joined up with cooperating teams of Africans and went to work on a variety of local community projects. They built schoolhouses, clinics, parts of training centers and improved market places. They cleared bush for roads and dug drainage ditches. After some five or six weeks of this toil, they traveled about either to other parts of their host country or briefly into some neighboring country. In the last week of August they regained their assembly points and took off again in their chartered planes for Europe and for home. This was Operations Crossroads Africa, organized and led by Rev. James H. Robinson of New York City.

As conceived by its organizer, Crossroads is not a project in eco-

Harold R. Isaacs, *Emergent Americans: A Report on Crossroads Africa* (New York: John Day Co., 1961), pp. 23–25, 29–34, 107–117. Copyright © 1961 by Massachusetts Institute of Technology, Reprinted by permission of The John Day Company, Inc., publisher.

nomic aid or technical assistance but primarily an undertaking in *communications.* To be sure, the labor of 183 young Americans was not intended to be exclusively symbolic or merely a device. It was certainly part of the Crossroads purpose to make a practical demonstration of Americans' readiness to help Africans help themselves in places where much needs to be done. The results were to be visible in the new schoolhouses and other physical improvements in the villages and towns where they worked. But it would completely misread the primary purpose of Crossroads to try to assess its results by measuring the dollar value of its contributed labor or its product. The principal aim was to expose young Americans to Africa and to bring them together with young Africans in settings where they could learn the most about each other. . . .

Let it be said here at once in a large summary of a great host of particulars that Crossroads was a major experience for all of its participants and for many it was life-changing.

For the American Crossroaders it was adventure: a sudden and great leap across the oceans and continents to a drastically different world. It was participation in history: they moved right into the arena of great world-changing events, and some of them had grandstand seats for the spectacle of African states acquiring their independence. It was a major learning experience: they replaced their scanty stock of early notions about Africa — mostly the jungle, animals, safaris, wild savages, and Tarzan — with a great new mass of actualities about places, people, and events. It was an incalculably revealing intercultural experience: they learned in the most direct and most taxing physical way what it means to be "underdeveloped" and something of the complexity of the process of social and economic change. But most crucially of all, for a great many it was a life-changing experience: some made major career decisions. Almost all made major discoveries about the problems of "race" relations. And some learned a great deal about themselves.

For the Africans who came most intimately into contact with Crossroads — and they were primarily the students who joined the projects as fellow work-campers — the experience was equally one of fresh discovery. Very few of them had ever actually met an American before or had close contact with any. Virtually all of them had the same small stock of odd notions and stereotypes about America and Americans from sources that were either quite scanty or highly prejudiced or both. Very little of this could survive the actuality of contact with individuals and the weeks of almost constant question-asking and question-answering. Even where prejudice was so strong that it sought only its own reinforcement – and this was the case here and there on the basis of strong political or racialist biases – it had to adapt itself somehow to new information and at the very least it had to exclude present company.

.   .   .   .

The selection process

James Robinson is not a very parochial man; he sees his Crossroads project usually through the large windows of world affairs, politics, and race relations. But he is also a Christian minister who manages to convey to his listeners that he is also working for more love and brotherhood among men. He appealed to young people on both counts, and it was precisely in both contexts that the major self-selection for Crossroads took place. Crossroads tapped a widely felt urge among many young Americans to do something important, something useful, and even, without apology, something good. Much the same urge moves many of the recruits coming forward for the Peace Corps. It is an impulse with a venerable history among Americans. It is subject to distortion and vulnerable to cynicism; and it is easy to underestimate and dissipate, along with so many other valuable national resources. But it was this impulse that brought out most of the self-selectees for Crossroads. This means that they were largely *service-oriented,* the broadest term I can find to distinguish them from the missionary types of an older generation and from the more privatistically motivated members of their own generation.

For a large number, perhaps more than half the entire Crossroads group, the source of this impulse was to a large extent religious. Given the position and character of James Robinson and the environments in which Crossroads recruiting was so largely done, it follows unsurprisingly that a great many Crossroaders were serious religionists; that is to say they were not merely churchgoers but also concentrated a great deal of their activity in church-connected enterprises. Although Dr. Robinson did what he could do to modify it, the project did give the impression that it was primarily seeking just such persons. This came out of the fact that the organizer himself was a minister, that the meetings he addressed were so often called by campus religious groups, that the sponsors of Crossroads included quite a sprinkling of church-connected figures, that the application form specifically asked for recommendations from ministers or chaplains and asked for evidence of church-connected activity. Indeed, it may be assumed that at least some applicants gave a slightly overstated version of their church-connected activities in order to satisfy the apparent stress on these matters in the application. On the other hand, it is rather unlikely that this slight impulse to exaggeration also extended to the statement of motive for coming with Crossroads. Most of those who were moved by distinctly nonreligious interests generally felt quite free to indicate this, and several, as we have already indicated, made it clear that they had no religious affiliations of any kind. When the group first got together (at Union Theological Seminary in New York) all found they could meet their similars all the way along the range from active religionists to practicing atheists.

. . . .

Our times are in fact not very hospitable to the old-style missionary impulse. Rather large events have conspired to make it seem quite "unrealistic" now. To its own misfortune, much mission work was associated in some measure with colonial power and with all the premises of Western domination over much of the world. Neither the power nor the premises are surviving the current changes. Most of the great missionary bodies have been revising their philosophies and programs in order to survive and in order to attract young people like these Crossroaders who want to do good in the world but who also are thoroughly in sympathy with the new self-assertion of Asians and Africans and the rebirth of their own cultural identities. Hence the new accent is on *service*. It was in search of opportunities to be of service that these young men and women found their way to Crossroads, and some of them will doubtless find their way to larger opportunities either within or outside their churches. Indeed, this impulse to help, to do good, to make the world over, can now find outlets entirely outside the religious sphere. It merges readily enough nowadays with the larger and more secular shape of things in the nation and in the world. American involvement in world affairs in the last twenty years has more and more had to take the shape of *giving,* of *aid,* of *assistance.* It is, in an ironic kind of way, something new under the sun: a form of power based on benevolence instead of rapacity. The old "colonialist-imperialists" (to say nothing of "Wall Street") would not have known what to make of it. Starting with Marshall aid to Europe in 1947, the United States has given away without hope of direct monetary return three times more than the total value of American private investments abroad as of 1945. I am certainly not suggesting that this is not a self-interested benevolence, but I *am* suggesting that this new form of wielding power offers obvious opportunities to indulge the old American missionary impulse in new ways and in new settings. As a small but dramatic illustration of this in our present group, there is one Crossroader whose summer in Africa led him to question the usefulness of the direct religious approach to service abroad. He came back and entered the theological seminary as he had planned, but left after one term to enter government service and will go abroad instead with an aid mission.

But this heaving world offers challenge enough to many young people who are not moved primarily or at all by religious or missionary impulses. This is a time of great and chilling events, of the making of history in the large. The American involvement in this history is filled with dangers and promises that plainly affect every individual's future. Most people just live with it. But a great many, especially young people, feel curiosity and concern and, most of all, a need to participate in some meaningful way in all that is going on. They want a role, they want to make some personal impact on these great and impersonal events. Crossroads offered them a way of making contact with these events in the African setting, to bring them close to the great process of emergence from colonialism and backwardness and to the emergence of new problems and new demands on Americans in world affairs. This also drew a great many self-selectees to Crossroads, even as it is drawing many more now to the Peace Corps. One index to this kind of interest is shown by the distribution among the Crossroaders of their major subject interests at school. Among the 183, the greatest clustering by far took place in history (30), political science and international relations (26), sociology (15), with a significant drop to only three in economics. These interests are of course shared by both religionists and nonreligionists, but the spread is shown in my own group of 44 interviewees, where, alongside the 17 already mentioned as aiming for church-connected careers, there were also 7 who said they would seek careers in the United States foreign service and 14 who said they were hoping to go into graduate work in order to teach in related fields and perhaps also go into government service.

The self-selection, then, produced a great majority of Crossroads recruits moved by an urge to "service," whether in a religious or a secular framework, or by the urge to learn and participate in significant affairs affecting the nation and the world, or in varying combinations of all these elements. Even though it may not have seemed to some of them the thing to stress on the Crossroads application, let it be said that there was also a fair share of the simpler urge to have an exciting and adventurous summer of travel and new experience, to take in new impressions, to see new places and people, to do things they had never done before, and to test themselves against a variety of new demands. Not every Crossroader who went to Africa was intent upon taking the world upon his or her shoulders, at least not right away. Whether they looked inward or outward, some of them had other things on their minds, and this too was as it should be. No one, least of all a young American discovering the world in 1960, could be of one piece in mind, spirit, or outlook.

This process of selection and self-selection did not produce a group of uniformly crackerjack work-campers, supersuccessful adjusters-to-Africa or relaters-to-Africans. But it did provide Crossroads 1960 with a body of 183 young men and women who worked hard at trying and were, on the whole, remarkably successful.

They sustained with many minor but few major casualties the shock of the sudden transplant from American to African conditions. They learned a great deal about living way out of their accustomed norms of privacy, sanitation, and familiar food. They suffered a scatter of cases of malaria and a variety of gastro-intestinal maladies but came through, as far as I know, without any serious or lasting effects.

They put up with a considerable array of adversities, including a great deal of administrative bumbling and a number of leaders who were not always marvels of sensitivity or competence. They also put up with each other—in itself often no small accomplishment.

They learned quite a bit from the Africans who joined them in the work camps and whom they met along the way, and they taught some Africans quite a good deal in return.

They worked hard and they put a number of small but visible new marks on several African landscapes.

.   .   .   .

The impact

Very little has been said so far, and with good reason, about the impact of Crossroads on the Africans who came into contact with it. The good reason is that I have only certain rather superficial impressions of what that impact was. This does not refer to the impact of the actual work projects, for I simply do not know whether the completed jobs have proved useful, or how many of the unfinished jobs were later carried to completion. These are important matters, and it would be good to know more about them, but as I stated at the outset, the primary objective of Crossroads did not have to do with bricks and mortar but with communication between Americans and Africans. The effects of this communication now dwell in the minds of the Africans and the Americans who had the experience. The effect on the Americans is the main burden of this report. Of the effect on Africans I know rather little. I shall be able to report first on what the Crossroaders themselves thought of the impact they made, and secondly, on the impressions of a group of African secondary school students. . . .

As seen by Crossroaders. The majority of Crossroaders felt they had made a considerable impact on Africans, that they had made quite a scratch on some African minds about America and Americans. Examples:

> From the letters I've gotten I think they found it quite wonderful and feel quite strongly about it. We got to know each other as people, with different cultures, but knowing each other as friends, personal friends . . . I think there will be a lasting memory of Crossroads.

> One of the students wrote me that the villagers became more conscious of what they could do to improve their village. I've received over 40 letters so far, and I'm sure they will remember us for years and years. I think we did a lot of good and a lot of them hope to come to the U.S.

> I am convinced that Crossroads had a very positive and even tremendous effect on them. There were things they had never imagined possible, working on an equal level this way. It was difficult too for them to understand at first and they were suspicious of our motives, but after a time they realized we were sincere.

Overcoming suspicion was a recurring problem of the impact:

> I think some of them came to know Americans better, getting to know us as individuals, seeing so many different types. I think they keep on wondering if Americans are like the people in the movies they've seen. They seemed to think we were pretending all the time. They were friendly, but always suspicious, thinking maybe we were hiding the "real truth" from them. D_____ would ask me some questions, then he would ask the same question of others, and still others, to see what answers he would get. These would be questions like: "What do you think of Africa?" or "Would you really come back to Africa to live?" I think with some we finally overcame this mistrust and that they learned that all kinds of people make up a country or a culture, many different points of view.

Hardest of all was to persuade Africans not only that the Crossroaders had not been paid to perform all this toil but also that they had actually paid themselves for the privilege:

> They were surprised that students would work this way, and as volunteers. It kept being said that we were being paid, and I don't know if we really persuaded them of the truth. Some students were still very dubious.

There was a battle fought out along this line all summer, often without feeling of positive result. Said one girl:

> I spent a lot of time trying to convince them that we had paid our own way on the project. They just wouldn't believe it. And you know, when I stopped to think about it, it *did* sound like an unlikely story!

Some had the feeling that they had made a strong individual and personal impact:

I've gotten some 25 letters, some of them very emotional. It meant a lot to them. But I do think I changed M_____'s mind. He raked me over the coals about our capitalist system. I took a pragmatic, not a moral approach and tried to prove how it did more for more people, not out of exploitation, or love, but simply as a better way of doing things. I don't suppose I quite changed his mind, but he had more respect for the American point of view as I gave it—he listened to me. But I think I was effective as a human being, not as an American.

Some were hopeful that the credit they won as individuals might rub off on Americans in general:

I think the impression we made on the students was very lasting and deep and can't be measured. I think we opened a lot of eyes. On the villager, I am not too sure. Perhaps the next American to come along will be held in esteem because of what we did, but this could be easily changed or blotted out by other Americans if they acted differently. I think we made a few close contacts in each village we were in and I think—or I hope—that the Africans will credit all Americans with what we did.

But most of the time, alas, this did not happen. For their virtues, the Crossroaders were marked out as exceptions to the American rule, as in this remark, from Ghana:

B_____ said we were just *too* good, *too* willing to work, *too* smart. "You can't make me believe," he would say, "that everything in America is like that, that everyone is like you."

Or again in Guinea:

As individuals, they accepted us and were glad to see us, but we didn't change their picture of the United States. They saw us as exceptions. I am sure that if we had made a negative impression in any way, this would have been applied in general to the whole United States.

I think some people may have a better opinion of Americans, the high school kids we were with. But not the powers that be. In town, I don't know. Our communication with people in the town was not much.

In the realm of ideas there was this modest judgment from a boy who went to Senegal:

I think they became a little more tolerant of the democratic process. In our long discussions we went into the whole process of democracy, the good points and the bad points.

The spectacle of American university students working with their hands was seen almost everywhere as a major item in the Crossroads impact. A girl from the South who had race problems very much on her mind came up with this vignette:

> I think they felt we shouldn't be working that way because we were white. As soon as one of us would stop to rest, one of the villagers would take the shovel, and it would be hard to get it back. I think this is what was in their minds because of one women who would take a pail of water away from me and say: "You shouldn't do this!"

Or this observation on the same subject from a Crossroader in Senegal:

> I think some students did change their attitudes about work. They feel they are the elite and that the elite does not actually work. But I think some of them found some good in actually getting out working with us. They were reluctant, at first, but toward the end a few stayed with it and liked it very much.

As seen at the Remo Secondary School. This matter of American students engaged in manual labor was an arrestingly new sight in West Africa and apparently made more of an impact on Africans than anything else. This was true even in Guinea, which had entertained visiting youth groups from all parts of the Communist empire, European and Asian, but never one that had come, like the Americans, to work. In times past or present neither white men nor educated Africans had set a precedent for anything like this. By the mores of colonialism and equally by the standards of the emergent African, manual labor was inconsistent with power and status. So the descent of these Americans — from a land of great power and with the status of university students — boys and girls, full of a vivid and open spirit and readiness to do lowly toil for some common good, was in some places disconcerting, in a few exhilarating, and in all quite unforgettable.

It happens that I have a small firsthand record of some African reaction to this American performance. It comes from a large group of African youngsters to whom nothing had as yet happened to make them tired, defensive, suspicious, or prickly. A band of our young Americans descended upon their school in the wonderful vigor and euphoric enthusiasm of the first weeks. These African youngsters took the Americans at face value, which was considerable. I am sure there were many others in other places just like them, but these happened to be the pupils at the Remo Secondary School, just outside the village of Shagamu, halfway between Lagos and Ibadan in Western Nigeria. The principal, Mr. E. O. Dada, responded readily to my suggestion of a way to get a view of his students' response to this American invasion. In the second week the entire school body was assigned, as its regular English composition assignment, to write on the topic: "What I Have Learned About the Americans This Week." Their papers proved to be quite a revelation. It was almost impossible at the time even to imagine what these remarkably decorous African boys and girls were taking in about their American visitors. We now discovered that they had taken in a great deal. In one paper even my wife and I appeared, and we were described as "old." Perhaps some Crossroaders will recognize themselves better in this striking passage:

> Fifteen American students arrived on the twenty-eighth day of June, 1960, to our school. There are seven men and eight women. They have greyish hair and very long legs. They have a yellowish colour. Their faces are round. Their eyes are very sharp.

Another paper begins to mark important facts:

> They come from different universities and of different tribes, but still they move together as they are born of the same blood. They dine together, both ladies and men. They sleep together, except in the case of the ladies.

From more of these papers, impeccably legible, remarkably grammatical, and often highly expressive, let me now simply quote — and I urge the reader not to run his eye over them too swiftly but to follow them with care, because they may contain the truest picture of the impact of Crossroads to be found anywhere in these pages:

> My class joined the group at work on their road project, which is about a hundred yards behind the laboratory and terminated at the Ikenne road. I was exceedingly startled to find the great work that had been done by these young students within five and a half hours. More astonished was I when I saw the ladies amongst them handle the cutlass in such a way as I have never seen a girl do in this part of the world. With music from the bush radio set that was hung somewhere in the woods, things went on smoothly. While some were resting, the others continued to work without complaint about that fellow sitting down or the other playing, as one would find here. Some were detailed to remain behind at home, to prepare a meal for the group. This they did without complaint. I observed that some left the road work for the compound, either for water or for any other purpose any time they felt like doing so. They never reported to anyone that they were going away. But they soon returned to carry on their work harder than before. The fact of it all was that there was the spirit of responsibility in them that we can never expect to find here. . . . I was forced to think about the shame we youths are likely to [inflict on] Nigeria even after attaining independence. With only school certificates, we feel that manual work should be despised and relegated [out of] our lives. But here we are with University students who have travelled over 9000 miles doing such work as we call base and mean here in Nigeria. We have got much to learn from our American friends if we want our independence to be a reality and not a flop.

I learnt from their habit that they call each other his or her [first] name. Moreover when any one of them talk to you or you talk to them, they say yah and not yes. I could see that they are not too big to do anything. They work with all energy, play with all their strength, dance with joy. . . . Imagine the road they are constructing, if it were us students, at least two or more students must have been suspended or caned several times or driven here and there before we could work. . . .

.   .   .   .

From these American students we Nigerians can learn a great lesson. Whatever our position may be, we must not think too high to do dirty work like road-making. Nigerian students will say that such work is below their dignity. But these American students have shown us that there is no work that students in secondary school or university cannot do. The ladies proved to us that what a man can do a woman can also do it. The boys should learn from the men cooking. If it is our men, they will say that the girls must do the cooking because it is their work. But they do not say so, they do everything together.

When these people first arrived, I was much surprised to see them. This was due to the fact that I never knew that Americans were white in colour. And frankly, I have never seen a white American before. So I stood gazing at them for more than five minutes.

.   .   .   .

The American students neither wait for anybody to prepare food for them nor remain elegant at work to hear praise from people. They work beyond expectation. . . . At leisure hours they seize every opportunity to improve on their knowledge of nature. Apart from reading, they take note of little-important creatures. For example, many snapshots of a column of driver ants were taken by everyone of the American students when they were in the compound yesterday. . . .

The American students joke with our scholars without regarding for their dignity which is far greater than that of our scholars in all aspects. . . . This week I have learned about the American students that faithful services, free-will dealings, obedience, and loyalty are the causes of the great progress they have in their works. . . .

.   .   .   .

The way in which they play among themselves would make one think they come from the same school or even from a family, whereas they come from different universities. They are never annoyed or tired whenever some of us ask them to tell us something about America. And so if we students in Nigeria adopt such a spirit of service, we shall live to enjoy and be proud of our country, Nigeria.

On July 4th, the day of their celebration of the American independence, they gave me a picture of the love they have for their mother country. They told us the history of the cause of the American Declaration of Independence and about the states which were represented by stars. They told us of some of their great leaders who fought very bravely for them to see that America became an independent state. . . .

I rather suspect that wherever Crossroaders went there were at least some Africans on whom they made some part of this kind of impression. Who can say that this wide-eyed discovery by youthful Africans of American ways of working, playing, being open, polite, and mutually respectful was not the most significant and enduring of all the Crossroads impacts on Africans that were made all summer long?

19
Cultural Relations Activities of UNESCO

It may seem strange that a definition of UNESCO should be needed today, when, after all, it has been carrying on its manifold activities during seventeen years. But quite apart from a probably unavoidable public ignorance intensified by widespread and often misinformed criticism, one must bear in mind that although there was a precursor, no precedent existed for an organization of this kind; and that as a matter of fact all international agencies must necessarily be experimental, even problematical, so long as the idea of national sovereignty is cherished as deeply as it now is in almost every part of the world.

The Changing Character of UNESCO

UNESCO is an organization which has seemed to breed uncertainty about its very nature. It has altered its basic plan and orientation almost continually as time passed and is indeed now in the grip of profound change. This is to some extent attributable to an expanding membership. The original cadre of 1946 consisted of twenty-eight member states — seven were European; six were in the British Commonwealth; five were Middle Eastern; eight were in the Americas, North and South; and only two, China and the Philippines, were Far Eastern. The initial outlook was therefore strongly formed by the Western cultural tradition. By the time the Soviet Union joined in 1954, along with its associated "states," Byelorussia and the Ukraine,

George Shuster, *UNESCO: Assessment and Promise* (New York: Harper & Row, for the Council on Foreign Relations, 1963), pp. 10–26, 29–40.

the roster included 72 states. This action also dampened the ardor for secession voiced in the early 1950's by Czechoslovakia, Hungary, and Poland—three states which still maintained significant ties with the West in the first years of UNESCO but had been forced to capitulate to communism. As of 1963, the membership numbers 113 and may well grow somewhat larger. Moreover, a tendency to form blocs, to some extent noticeable from the beginning of UNESCO history, has been considerably intensified. Finally, polarization at the antithesis between the United States and the Soviet Union had its effect on UNESCO, as it has on all other international agencies in which the Soviet Union has membership.

As a result, the key factor in the organization has become the member state. At first the French, cherishing the doctrine which had formed the Institute of Intellectual Co-operation, strove to promote the view that the delegations to the General Conference, then meeting annually to determine UNESCO policy, would consist primarily of cultural leaders of eminence, attending as individual delegates from the countries represented. These leaders would function much as does the faculty of a university or the membership of the Académie Française. While they would bear in mind the political climate favored or indeed fostered by their governments, they might, in advising or instructing the Director-General, exercise a good deal of autonomous individual judgment. This view did not prevail insofar as the constitutional provisions governing the General Conference are concerned, but is on occasion still advocated as a matter of principle, with evident nostalgia. On the other hand, there was also created an Executive Board, akin to a university senate, which was given powers deemed appropriate to it and instructed to function during periods between sessions of the General Conference. Its principal task was defined as supervising the execution of the program. The Board was at the outset formed as a group of distinguished spokesmen for the arts and the sciences, responsible to the General Conference but not in the first instance to their governments (although to be eligible for the Board, they had to be members of the delegations chosen by their governments).

It became increasingly apparent in practice that the Board could not function as a group of independent intellectuals; like the delegates to the General Conference, they in fact represented their governments as part of an international organization of states. The reasons were several. First, the political implications of what UNESCO was doing became more and more obvious and, of course, later took on a dramatic character once the Russians and their satellites had joined. It was necessary on all sides to coordinate national positions in

UNESCO affairs with over-all national directives on foreign policy. Furthermore, the earlier conception had been in part based on the assumption that the National Commissions would function as quasi-autonomous bodies. They did not do so. . . . Elsewhere, as in Great Britain, the Commissions became to all intents and purposes organs of the ministries of education and thus acquired at least a semi-official status.

Another factor was perhaps still more important. This was the budget. Since the U.N. scale of contributions by member states was adopted, the fact soon became evident—and would naturally be steadily more so—that the wealthier countries were purveyors of assistance and the poorer ones were recipients. The latter were understandably persistent in recommending projects designed to advance their educational and cultural progress, while the former were placed in the difficult position of asking for appropriations from legislative bodies not always prone to be generous. There were times when a cynical observer from a well-to-do country might have been tempted to liken the organization, from this point of view, to a considerately financed and properly adjusted slot machine into which a country could deposit without risk a small membership fee and get a handsome return. Criticism on this count from France, Great Britain, and the Soviet Union made things difficult on more than one occasion. Spokesmen for UNESCO in these and other countries (including the United States) were obliged on the one hand to act as critics of the budget at Headquarters in Paris and on the other hand to function as counsels for UNESCO's needs before their ministries, legislatures, or dictators. It was often a quite bizarre assignment which could and did create international diplomatic embarrassments. Sometimes it produced a crisis threatening the very stability of UNESCO.

Representatives named to the Executive Board, as well as delegates to the General Conference, therefore assumed diplomatic functions in increasing measure. The older hope for a role of autonomy was not, however, completely abandoned. The Board was expected to continue to be a group of individuals who enjoyed some reputation as exponents of cultural activity; and nominees were supposedly scrutinized for their measure of achievement in this respect. Thus the United States has been represented by a Librarian of Congress, three college presidents, and the dean of a graduate school. But upon occasion the credentials of persons from certain member states, whose relationship to cultural activity was tenuous indeed, were duly accepted. Delegations to the General Conferences included scholars, men of letters, and educators, but their roles were subordinated to over-all political management. In short, their performance of their functions was coordinated with the foreign policies of their home countries.

Nevertheless, curiously enough, there have been times when the liaison between some Board members and their governments has been tenuous, with the result that agreements carefully negotiated between governments behind the scenes were unexpectedly upset because this or that spokesman proved ruggedly individualistic. In general, the reason was that the government in question had not bothered to give instructions, or that the spokesman for it at home had possessed even less authority than the Board member. But sometimes it was also the result of a Board member taking the bit in his teeth. Not infrequently the Director-General in particular would be sorely tried by these manifestations of eccentricity. In preparing his position, it was always necessary for him to take into consideration the views of member states, conveyed orally or in writing. Then to have these views somewhat impertinently disavowed in Board or Conference discussion could be as disconcerting as it was surprising.

In many ways the discussions of the deliberative bodies which in some measure determine the policy of UNESCO began to reflect the tensions manifest generally in the U.N. system. Soviet proposals have normally included demands for the admission to the organization of the People's Republic of China, the ouster of the "iniquitous regime of the unspeakable Chiang Kai-shek," recognition of the German Democratic Republic, and acceptance into the roster of cooperating nongovernmental organizations of the various "front" groups for youth, "democratic women," and so forth. Soviet delegates made unflagging efforts to press for resolutions favoring disarmament, peaceful coexistence, and similar causes currently serving their propaganda campaigns. The anniversary of the October Revolution was commemorated with long and rousing allocutions, and the "crimes" of NATO were not ignored. More recently, it has been the Peace Corps which has formed a special target for denunciation. The Executive Board could take these things in stride, but the more cumbersome procedures of the General Conference were often badly clogged by what was less discussion and debate than a torrent of abrasive and repetitive eloquence. Of late some improvement is noticeable. The Soviet Union seems to be using two kinds of orator. One is an academician who may indeed read a fiery piece about the October Revolution but who normally outlines a position with restraint and manifests a desire to cooperate. The other is a diplomatic functionary who lays down blistering barrages. The representatives of other member states view this as a salutary arrangement; they can usually suspend business until the functionary has finished.

That these things have been so accounts for most of UNESCO's difficulties in operating effectively during the first dozen years of its existence. Could it have functioned as an international society of scholars dedicated to tasks in which scholars are interested, it would probably have managed, not without a great deal of effort to be sure, to enlist the support of major universities and educational organizations throughout the world. But being an agency of member states, it was necessarily meshed with the policies of those states, either in a general or a pedagogical sense. This was at first almost a condemnation to futility because, once the wartime alliances had broken down and the cold war was in progress, the UNESCO program seemed of minor significance, if indeed it was not held to be utopian and given to beclouding the major issues. What, for example, could a Secretary of State, when confronted with ominous situations in Korea or West Berlin, do with an organization which declared that wars begin in the minds of men? This declaration, one of the glories of the preamble to the UNESCO constitution, could not but seem an unrealistic and pacifist utterance at a time when the grim chances of survival haunted the chanceries of the free world, and so it gave rise to more or less fanatical campaigns of counterattack by extremists.

In the circumstances, the character of the Director-General's duties was drastically changed. He would no longer be a quasi-chancellor who would wrestle with his colleagues to bring about an effective meeting of minds about an over-all international educational and cultural program. Henceforth, he would perforce be the advocate of a policy based on compromises between the views of member states, and that was another matter entirely. Two illustrations may serve to clarify what has been said. The first is the gradual fading of the idea of an international university, to be conducted under UNESCO auspices, which Sir Alfred Zimmern and others advocated with great zeal and persistence during the first two years of the organization's history. Any number of people continue to press for the establishment of such a university, but they do so now in a different context. Had UNESCO been an association of intellectuals, and had adequate support been forthcoming, such a university might today be a reality. But it is no longer conceivable as an institution professionally operated from the modern building on Paris's Place de Fontenoy. The second illustration is the resignation of Señor Torres Bodet from the Director-Generalship in 1950. He had visualized the office in terms which were no longer in accordance with reality. And he remains, until the present time, the last man of genuine eminence in the field of education and scholarship to be considered for the post.

Many things conspire to make the position of the Director-General difficult. Probably in no other way can his situation be better illuminated than by the process of making appointments to the Secretariat. Although from the outset the constitutional provisions directed him to select competent personnel while respecting the rights of member states to be represented, he enjoyed during the earlier years a measure of freedom of action. Some unsatisfactory or mediocre persons were appointed during the period of haste to get the organization going, but a certain amount of homogeneity was achieved, and so the formation of an international civil service in UNESCO seemed not unlikely.

Today the principle of geographical distribution is dominant. Member states are entitled to representation in proportion to their respective contributions to the budget. In practice, this means, for example, that virtually no candidates can now be presented by West European countries other than the Federal Republic of Germany (which obtained membership in the organization at the relatively late date of 1951), because the number appointed earlier exceeds the quotas of those states. In contrast, the Russians and their satellites have the right to make a goodly number of nominations. And as the roster of member states increases, it becomes necessary to consider candidates put forward by each of them in turn. It has therefore become increasingly difficult to recruit an efficient and harmonious staff. Admittedly no country or region has a monopoly in well-qualified persons, and obviously, too, excellent people can be found everywhere. There is also much to be said in favor of representation on as broad a basis as possible. The real difficulties lie in selection and in continuity. And they are augmented by the seeming inability of the United States to present qualified candidates in sufficient number or to press for their appointment. . . .

The Program

It is against this organizational background that the further part of the question, "What is UNESCO?" must be considered. What is its program? Since UNESCO is an international agency concerned with the exchange of cultural goods, it must of course work side by side with, and in an effective way complement, a great variety of national agencies serving the same purpose while also seeking to advance the interests of their respective countries. Learning to know what can be done with more success through *multilateral* than through *bilateral* efforts has been and continues to be a very difficult task. For a number of years the far-flung assistance and exchange programs of the United States, for example, have dwarfed UNESCO efforts by comparison. In addition, it is not possible to strain political implications out of multilateral activities altogether, try though one may. These and other obstacles have not, however, prevented the organization from obtaining a measure of success no one could have anticipated. The achievement is due to the persistent efforts of men, for the most part wholly unknown to the general public, who worked in the shadow of almost constant criticism and under stringent budgetary limitations.

.   .   .   .

The "fragmentation" of the UNESCO program has become a grim refrain to almost any discussion of that program. Probably no other issue so differentiates official from unofficial comment in the United States. If one looks at international cultural relations from the standpoint of the struggle between communism and freedom or of the relations between the advanced and the underdeveloped countries, it may well seem that the only task which really matters is bringing the resources of education to bear on meeting the needs of peoples struggling to throw off the shackles of poverty and ignorance. Since finding money to do this job is so difficult, why waste it on undertakings of marginal utility? But if one then proceeds to ask what education is, apart from literacy and machine-shop skills, the answer given by the arts and the sciences is sure to range over the gamut of the human mind. Consequently, professors of the humanities as well as natural scientists are sure to oppose making the training of man's mind a purely technical process; and so the members of the U.S. National Commission have steadfastly demanded a strengthening of the "basic" or "continuing" program. Still there can be no doubt that, particularly during the earlier years, the Secretariat was literally shoved into some pleasant blind alleys by enthusiastic General Conferences, and that by now life in some is so agreeable that those who benefit from that life resist moving out into more turbulant roads. Some tasks UNESCO has assumed ought unquestionably to be lopped off. But they are not as numerous as is sometimes supposed, nor do they affect either the budget or management in any very appreciable sense.

The Provision of Services

The first and second parts—the service activities and the indirect educational action—constitute what is called the "basic" or "continuing" program of UNESCO. They cannot properly be isolated from the other parts though attempts have sometimes been made to do so. UNESCO's provision of services carries on and has significantly enlarged the work of the International Institute of Intellectual Co-operation. It is a multiform endeavor, which employs in the main these methods: the gathering, analysis, and reporting of information in the fields of UNESCO's interests; other publications; and conferences. Although in the category of other publications the Department of Mass Communication accounts for many journals, books, and pamphlets, all departments or divisions are involved – Education (which is the largest), Natural Sciences, Social Sciences, Cultural Activities, and International Exchange Service. In addition, there is a sort of "Department *ad interim*" (destined eventually to lose its separate status), concerned with a "Major Project" designed to promote cultural understanding between Orient and Occident. The administrative services required to support these activities are considerable and complex. Since UNESCO is a multilanguage organization, using English, French, Russian, and Spanish as official tongues, the arts of translation, far from easy to master, are also a major responsibility.

The statistical documentation being provided seems gradually to be acquiring the quality and status that will make UNESCO a great center for this kind of service, which may lack glamour but is very badly needed. Indeed, if fully developed it would constitute a good reason, were there no other, why the organization should exist. At present, statistics are provided in a number of fields – among them, education (enrollments, teacher-training data, opportunities for study abroad, etc.), the social sciences, library services, and mass communication. In view of the almost unsurmountable difficulties which attend the gathering of statistical data in many parts of the world, the results obtained reflect credit on the UNESCO staff. But a great deal would have to be done in terms of modernization of the equipment and of additions to personnel if UNESCO were to attempt to achieve its manifest destiny in this important area. To a marked extent, the ground is being prepared by sending experts to member states to help them develop or refine their statistical methods.

Other informational and exploratory services are in many ways more problematical in character and may be described as a blend of some activities which have become traditional with others which have largely been improvised. Sometimes, as in the case of the *Index Translationum,* an heirloom from the past that records as correctly as possible whatever has been translated from one language into another throughout the world, the result is a bibliographical product which, however often applauded by librarians, probably costs more in time and effort than it is worth. At the other end of the spectrum are film strips now available in a wide range of subjects from arid-zone research to practical education in such matters as building a stove. Sometimes the dimensions of a task contemplated may be titanic. Thus, at the request of another U.N. agency, UNESCO undertook to collate reports of scientific work being done all over the world. The information was found to be so broad in scope, and the task of arriving at precise descriptions and definitions proved so baffling, that it seemed unwise to seek an immediate solution of the problem. Nevertheless, the assignment was manifestly important; the fact that entrusting it to UNESCO was thought eminently natural affords a good indication of the reputation its reporting services have earned over the years.

At the close of 1962 recommendations were being formulated for effecting further progress in scientific documentation. For it is clear that the peoples who must achieve a measure of success in coping with modern technology cannot succeed unless some way is provided for gaining insight into both the philosophy and the ever-continuing progress of the natural sciences. It is now proposed that the whole of the present bewildering area of publication, abstracting, translating, and coding be subjected to careful scrutiny; that less advanced regions be assisted by setting up centers designed to deal with the very difficult problem of keeping abreast of scientific advance; and that new technical means – notably machine translation – be developed in order to speed up improvement. If the matter is pursued with adequate vigor (which will to a large extent depend on the amount of financial support made available), there is little doubt that within a relatively short time science and technology will have taken another hurdle in stride.

The sheer bulk of what UNESCO publishes, under the rubric of "documentation" and otherwise, is almost overwhelming. *A General Catalogue of UNESCO and UNESCO Sponsored Publications* (Paris, 1962) lists 2,681 titles as having appeared by the close of 1959; and even if some entries are duplicated by reason of publication in various languages, the number is still impressive. Anyone who goes on to consider what is issued by the several departments might begin to feel that nothing is done except to see publications through the press – a quite erroneous assumption, since perhaps department heads should have more time to read and criticize manuscripts before they see the light of day in print. Just to scan publications in the field of social sciences, for example, one would discover that what was originally the *International Social Science Bulletin* was expanded tremendously and became in 1959 the *International Social Science Journal*. Nearly everything else has developed comparably; *Basic Facts and Figures,* a yearbook reporting events in fields of interest to

UNESCO, has now become the *UNESCO Statistical Yearbook.* There is an *International Bibliography of Political Science,* and comparable attention is given to sociology. One would also have to consider—the enumeration here is much briefer than the subject warrants—*Reports and Papers in the Social Sciences* as well as a veritable host of major and minor publications of a comparable kind. UNESCO pioneered, for instance, in publishing a series of books on the question of race. These were perhaps more hortatory than scientific, it is true. Not all the other departments assail the reading public with equally formidable barrages, but each does have its program, which is usually diverse and broad in scope.

Then there are more general journals of information, designed for a wider reading public even when the subject matter is somewhat specialized. First there is the UNESCO *Courier,* a lively illustrated magazine which now has a paid circulation of about 300,000 copies and a vastly larger free circulation. It discusses appropriate themes and certain organizational concerns such as observing the anniversaries of distinguished men and women. The UNESCO *Bulletin,* on the other hand, provides a running commentary on the organization's activities— is, in short, a kind of house organ. Published directly or through contract are such periodicals as *Diogenes* in the field of the humanities, *Impact,* which is a scientific journal, and *Museum,* which as its title indicates has to do with an institution important in the annals of the organization. The circulation of most of these publications is small, the quality normally good. There is a persistent temptation to increase the number of UNESCO-sponsored periodicals.

These informational and exploratory services seem on the surface devoid of political content. Yet how baffling they may sometimes be is suggested by a review of several recent incidents involving the Soviet Union. Human rights have concerned UNESCO since 1946, and particular attention has been given to the rights of racial and other minorities. By reason of its constitution and its character, UNESCO is to all intents and purposes precluded from using sources of information about what is going on within a member state when the sources are not indigenous to that state. Now the literature about the treatment accorded the Negro in the United States is quite uninhibited. Indeed, much of the best part of it is produced and disseminated by an agency of the federal government—the Commission on Civil Rights. An issue of the *Courier* presented some of this material. It may have been somewhat luridly written and illustrated, but it was in the main quite faithful to the account we Americans have ourselves given of our conduct. In contrast, it is not possible to discuss anti-Semitism in the Soviet

Union on any such basis, because no one desirous of living in peace and comfort in that member state could deal with the topic except by denying that Jews are discriminated against. Therefore, no issue of the *Courier* can deal with human rights in the Soviet Union. From the point of view of the United States this is a most undesirable dichotomy. For UNESCO publications, unfortunately, can be used unctuously and sometimes effectively in the cold war.

Probably spurred on to do a noble deed by the flurry thus caused, someone in the Secretariat arranged to have a Russian author prepare a brochure setting forth the "enlightened" and "democratic" attitudes toward race relations prevailing in the Soviet Union. Unfortunately, the editor did not bother to embroider his brief preface with the customary disclaimer of responsibility for the views expressed in the brochure, which, judged by any standards, was a stupid and biased performance. When this "masterpiece" appeared early in 1962, the United States lodged a formal protest; and indeed the thing seemed destined for speedy oblivion. But a year later it came to the attention of members of the United States Senate, who thereupon proceeded to castigate both UNESCO and the Department of State with vigor and abandon. It is probably fortunate that the great New York newspapers were strikebound and not publishing at the time, because if what appeared in some of their more provincial competitors is any criterion, the uproar might have been substantial.

Another incident had to do with a UNESCO pamphlet dealing with education in the Soviet Union. What the editor had done, quite injudiciously, was to publish in translation three addresses delivered by Soviet spokesmen at a meeting designed to advertise the achievements of "socialism." Not only were these speeches sadly lacking in objectivity, but they abounded in blatant and erroneous comments on schools in the so-called capitalist countries. No doubt in this instance the legitimate purpose of UNESCO, namely to provide an evaluation of Soviet education within the framework of comparative education, would have been better served by a wise selection from available statements by Soviet educators. But what happened helps to make evident some of the difficulties which the organization must confront every day. The Secretariat may often consider it wiser to publish nothing about a controversial issue than to risk criticism as frank as was received on this occasion from many countries in the free world.[1]

These and other incidents, most of them growing out of real or alleged faults in UNESCO publications, led the Director-General to request early in 1962 that the Executive Board assume responsibility for formulating a publication policy. The Board has accordingly taken the matter under advisement but has not manifested undue haste to get its fingers pricked by the sharp thorns of the problem. Again it is evident that if UNESCO were an organization of scholars, they could agree upon standards of erudition and weather the storms. But for better or for worse it is a confraternity of member states; and the conflicts between them are bound to be reflected in publications which are not merely factual or statistical. If one leaves the United States — Soviet Union antithesis aside, who is to "censor" what is said by Portugal and Morocco about Angola, or a presentation of educational issues involved in relations between Indonesia and Malaya? Perhaps the most helpful step the organization could consider would be the appointment of an over-all editor, responsible for maintaining policy at a high level. No Director-General can find time to resolve issues such as publication creates, and when he does intervene it is likely that he will act in haste and certainly without exhausting the possibilities of discussion and compromise.

Exploring a field for educational effort is often most effectively begun by holding a conference. The Specialized Agencies of the United Nations, and indeed that body itself, have all used the device with diligence and determination. The number of UNESCO conferences is nothing short of awesome. No typology of these meetings will be offered here, though the matter is of some significance. The variety of conferences is especially great in the field of pedagogy. There can hardly be a professor of education alive who has not participated in some gathering under UNESCO auspices, unless he has deliberately gone into hiding. But other parts of the program also rely heavily on conferences. To cite just one example, the program and budget proposals for 1963–1964 envisaged four international conferences in the field of youth activities alone, one on a "world" scale. Whether all this convening succeeds in accomplishing what it is supposed to is debatable, but assuredly it prevents the Secretariat from crawling into its shell or taking up quarters in an ivory tower. And it is equally certain that the Paris office has become a Mecca for intellectuals and other people interested in conferring — which most of them seem to be. During recent years, many of the most important of these gatherings have, however, been held in the Orient, Africa, and in the Middle East — a practice consonant with the growing worldwide character of the organization's activities.

Educational exchange

Discussion of this part of the UNESCO program may close with a brief mention of the Exchange Service. Originally very few fellowships were made available, but the number has since substantially increased. Yet by comparison with what is done by governments or by private organizations in this field, the UNESCO effort is still not impressive insofar as size is concerned. *Open Doors,* the 1962 report of the Institute of International Education, cites activities in the United States alone which dwarf what is being done by all international organizations. Still, the UNESCO effort is not negligible and is steadily being extended because of the demands of other international agencies for this kind of service. It often presupposes, however, cooperation with governments or other organizations. One reads, under the rubric "Study tours for women adult education leaders":

Travel grants will be offered to women adult education leaders. The grantee will undertake study abroad for a period of three months or more. . . . Sponsoring bodies will be required to plan the study project and to ensure maintenance costs, while UNESCO will defray travel expenses.

The program for promoting cultural relations between the Orient and the West has placed particular stress on exchanges. Under this program, grants are given for cultural research; young workers in the pertinent areas of study may apply for fellowships; teachers who wish to specialize in teaching about East-West relationships are given travel grants; and help is provided for training translators of masterpieces of Eastern literature into Western languages. In particular, there is a travel grant arrangement for Latin American students who seek to specialize in Oriental studies. Although much more could be said about the UNESCO Exchange Service, these remarks will suffice to indicate that the organization has at least in some measure kept pace with the remarkable expansion of exchange opportunities which has taken place since 1945. When one remembers that the cultural-relations program of the United States began with a handful of exchange fellowships awarded during the 1930's under the Good Neighbor Policy, one can see clearly from what a small seed the great exchange tree of today has sprung.

For good or for evil, the present intense activity is competitive from several points of view. Exchange offerings have become instrumentalities of the cold war, so that Moscow lures young people into its domain while the United States counters with fellowships for students from the wide world. The resources of France and Great Britain are greatly taxed, the French in particular striving, and with a measure of success, to retain their cultural influence in parts of Africa and the Near East. But virtually all the countries of Western Europe are heavily engaged, none more so than the Federal Republic of Germany. UNESCO has striven to emphasize the total situation in terms

of its own program and conciliatory aspirations, but the measure of
success which can be achieved is necessarily very small.

. . . .

The History of Mankind

Perhaps the most venturesome and controversial of the affiliated
organizations so far established by UNESCO has been the International Commission entrusted with the preparation of a *History of
the Scientific and Cultural Development of Mankind.* This was the
brainchild of the French historian, Lucien Febvre, who later (1953)
began to edit for UNESCO a *Journal of World History.* The majority
of American historians consulted took a dim view of both enterprises,
an attitude that was shared by many of their European colleagues.
Nevertheless, in 1950, the General Conference had in a moment of
enthusiasm authorized the International Commission to proceed on its
own responsibility, with the assurance that substantial UNESCO sub-
sidies would be forthcoming. The persons appointed to the Commission were a brilliant if somewhat heterogeneous and unruly company, who at a subsequent time welcomed representatives of Communist countries to their midst. An over-all editor was named and a
staff assembled. Authors for the six volumes contemplated were secured after a kind of talent hunt. The underlying idea was that each of
them — few could have known at the outset what was in store for them —
would profit on the topic assigned to him from memoranda written by a
bevy of writers the world round and would then present a text for comment to all member states, which in turn would pick their best historical
brains in the hope of thus advancing the cause of criticism. Later on,
member states grew anxious and introduced a proviso that the manuscripts were to be submitted also to the various National Commissions.
That this served any useful purpose is doubtful.

The work proceeded during twelve years, making manifest one by
one the truly staggering difficulties attendant upon an enterprise of
this kind. The first volume deals with prehistory. It survived international scrutiny reasonably well, though not without some curious
by-products, and was actually in galley proof by midsummer of 1962.
But as the less fortunate authors approached the contemporary scene,
the history they put to pasture encountered a bewildering variety of
thistles, wasps, and stray dogs. It remains to be seen what the final
outcome will be. But though doubtless the serenity of the finished
product will not recall the work of Theodore Mommsen or Douglas
Freeman, the effort will have been made, and for the first time a sort
of history written by international consensus will have come into

being. It is safe to say that if the year 1950 could be recaptured, the enterprise would not be begun. Yet perhaps the effort will prove worthwhile, though some parts of the narrative will in all probability be adjudged dull, colorless, and replete with meaningless compromises.

Lucien Febvre had continued a French tradition in the realm of international cultural affairs begun with the Institute of Intellectual Co-operation. For the Gallic daughter of the Muses and the Marshals has found joy in presiding over a special kind of cradle – that in which mankind can be nursed into awareness of a common human dedication to culture. We Americans have probably not managed to create a comparable assignment for ourselves, though we have done reasonably well in sponsoring concern for peoples struggling to throw off the shackles of poverty and illiteracy. Perhaps we should have manifested more fully our deep interest in the preservation and development of culture, for this interest *is* deep. No doubt we have been handicapped by the inevitable difficulties, embarrassments, and glories which have grown up round the task of serving as almoner to the world. An American historian accepted responsibility for seeing the *History* through to its conclusions. The fact that he was unable to complete the task may symbolize some of the problems we confront in the area of cultural affairs.

The East-West project

Another project, in some respects equally ambitious, came into being during 1956, when the General Conference convened in New Delhi. At the time, the term "Major Project" was in vogue, because it was felt that applying it to important tasks would gradually divert UNESCO from firing at every target under the sun. Yet in all sober truth, this project, envisaged as extending over a period of ten years, was about as rich in diversities and challenges as anything could well be. The Director-General shivered as he contemplated the future. The idea of the project, to bring about "the Mutual Appreciation of Eastern and Western Cultural Values," no doubt owed its inception to the belief that the great cultures of the Orient were not understood in the Occident. Perhaps this manifesto was a little forgetful of the efforts made by generations of great Western scholars to bridge the gulf; and it would be discovered later that the Eastern countries were themselves somewhat unaware of the import of their own cultures or their interrelations. But Kipling was in the minds of many, and the glories of Delhi and the Taj Mahal could not easily be resisted. A considerable portion of UNESCO's resources were committed to this project, and the attack was made on a broad front – colloquies, publications, exchange of personnel, reading materials designed for the lower schools, art presentations, and much more besides. A summary statement, couched in unadorned bureaucratic language and describing the program as it developed at a later stage, reads in part as follows:

Efforts will be made, in co-operation with Member States and the competent organizations, to concentrate the basic studies on certain crucial problems emerging from the execution of the Project. These include a definition of the values peculiar to each cultural group, as perceived both by the people who participate in them and those belonging to other cultures; on positive and negative factors of communication, mutual understanding and co-operation; on intercultural problems connected with the development of newly independent countries . . . these studies will be conducted in such a way as to present the cultural implications of the great historical and contemporary changes in broad perspective.

With regard to the great and permanent needs to which the Project makes a practical response, the two fundamental objectives will continue to be the training of personnel able to interpret it to the public, and the dissemination of material on cultural values and their relationships. Efforts will be made, however, to combine these two objectives within the framework of a given activity. This principle will be followed in awarding study and travel grants. In addition, exchanges of radio and television producers arranged in close collaboration with the broadcasting authorities will be supplemented by exchanges between topical writers for whom the newspapers will provide an outlet.[2]

It is evident from this statement that one goal of the project has been to promote mutual understanding where it had not existed before. Manifestly the achievement of this purpose must henceforth largely depend on what is done to implement and popularize the program within the member states themselves. This was of course understood at the outset, though realization of the purpose was often not possible. And it is encouraging to note that for a time effective cooperation could be secured in the United States. Recently, popular interest in this country has turned in considerable measure to Africa, as is no doubt understandable in view of the dramatic shift there from colonialism to independence. Rightly or wrongly, moreover, the political trends in India caused some disillusionment. This great and culturally illustrious country, whose independence we welcomed, professed to stand aloof from the raging ideological struggles of the day and to view with pacific neutralism both the Communist countries and the West. It was not always easy for American public opinion to accept this position with benevolent nonchalance; and although the Chinese threat to India has to some extent induced a change in Indian thinking and in our own, the quasi-romantic interest of yore has not been reawakened. The conclusion which suggests itself is that in practice cultural exchange cannot be wholly divorced from the existing political climate, nor can it be conceived of as taking place in a static society.

The directors of the East-West Major Project in the Secretariat have wisely worked for some measure of permanence by fostering the establishment of "associated institutions" for "the study and preservation of cultures." This is a memorable development because it was one of the few early modifications of the policy, clung to for some time with tenacity, that UNESCO was to "stimulate" educational activity rather than "operate" anything outside the framework of the basic program. Accordingly, three institutions were established — a Center for Asian Cultural Studies in Tokyo, a Research Council for Regional Cultural Studies in New Delhi, and a sort of twin Center for Middle Eastern Cultural Studies in both Beirut and Damascus. Two others are contemplated, one in Teheran and the other in Southeast Asia. While the major responsibility rests on the states in which the centers are erected, UNESCO provides some financial support and fosters international awareness of the work being undertaken. To date the Tokyo Center is the only one which has been placed on a sound basis; but if the plan as a whole can be realized, it should be possible in due time greatly to enrich awareness of the principal Asian cultures and to bring about some genuine expansion of interest on the part of Asians themselves in their respective heritages and in the meaning of these for one another.

Liaison

. . . It should be noted here that in many of the more sensitive areas of education as it is concerned with cultural values UNESCO has opportunities which are not open to countries operating bilaterally. Few people attribute to it any propagandistic intent; and since those whom it sends as experts or counselors must be approved by the host country, its mission is accepted as disinterested. Nevertheless, one must immediately add, many states in need of help prefer bilateral assistance because of the greater volume of support likely to be forthcoming. National attitudes are as always complex and far from predictable.

The most significant of UNESCO's liaison services in the area of education, science, and culture are no doubt those which have been developed in the Department of the Natural Sciences. Soon after the close of the Second World War, it became apparent to thoughtful scientists that a large measure of international cooperation would be required if genuine progress was to be brought about in certain important fields, both of inquiry and application. This cooperation would ensure the exchange of knowledge and endeavor across national boundaries otherwise virtually closed to traffic, and it might also make possible in some instances the pooling of resources. As was to be expected, UNESCO would be considered the international agency potentially best qualified to effect the collaboration needed; and in 1950 a formal request was addressed by the U.N. Economic and Social Council to the organization, as an associated member of the U.N. family, for leadership in determining the need for international scientific research institutes and in evaluating ways and means of establishing them. During the same year, the General Conference, meeting in Florence, instructed the Director-General to proceed with the request for liaison services.

The first such center was an international laboratory erected in Geneva by a Council of European Member States to provide for collaboration "in nuclear research of a pure scientific and fundamental character." CERN (the name derives indirectly from the French equivalent for European Organization for Nuclear Research) arose from an intergovernmental preparatory conference convened by the Director-General of UNESCO at the close of 1951, but almost immediately thereafter it began to lead an autonomous existence. Nor was the situation different insofar as other studies associated with nuclear energy — for example, the effects of radioactivity on living organisms and the use of radioisotopes for medicinal and other purposes — were concerned. Although UNESCO might take this initiative and stimulate efforts, it did not yet possess the strength, nor perhaps did it inspire sufficient confidence, to take the lead in scientific research of such obviously vital importance.

Still another venture in international scientific organization dates from the early 1950's. This is the Major Project on Scientific Research on Arid Lands. In this case UNESCO's participation and leadership have been more direct and persistent. During 1951 it created an Advisory Committee on Arid Zone Research, which has since then convened annually to consider studies conducted throughout the world on some aspect of aridity control. The reports prepared by the Committee are then published by UNESCO. This program is still being carried on. Continuing efforts are made by the Secretariat to enlist the interest of competent scientists and also to ensure consideration for problems faced by those member states which are particularly affected by soil aridity.

But is was doubtless the effectiveness of UNESCO as an instrumentality of international liaison during the period of preparation for the International Geophysical Year (1957–1958) which first earned for it the respect of scientists. It could open doors which otherwise would have remained closed, and in particular it made possible Soviet participation on a scale which seemed the precursor of an era less afflicted with international tensions. The value of UNESCO was again demonstrated when international cooperation in oceanography was being planned during the late 1950's. But something new had now been added. Scientists placed a high estimate on UNESCO's ability to sponsor educational action designed to conjoin research and teaching, particularly insofar as countries likely to benefit from oceanographic inquiry were concerned. The financial share in the costs of the enterprise borne by UNESCO has been a modest one. As a result of the experience gained, the area of interest has been expanded to include other sciences, notably hydrology and seismology. The latter took on special human interest because of the plea for help made by Morocco after the catastrophic effects of earthquakes suffered there. Once again a country not yet in command of modern scientific knowledge turned to UNESCO for assistance, which in turn was able to tap the resources of the U.N. Technical Assistance Program.

Other departments likewise exercise a liaison function. Of particular moment during recent years has been the study of the problems arising from social and economic development, particularly in Asia, Latin America, and Africa. We may allude here to one problem, that of coordinating progress in education with economic development. If the higher schools of a given country or region educate young men and women in relatively large numbers without any regard for what they are to do later on, the result will be an "academic proletariat" which may highlight the fate of the unemployed with notable venom. Cuba has had too many lawyers. The slums of Calcutta are doubtless teeming with philosophers having nothing to do except learn to revel in dialectical materialism. Meanwhile the real manpower needs for teachers, engineers, doctors, nurses, and technicians may not have been met. Practical international work in this field depends to a considerable extent on the proper coordination of the various interested agencies of the United Nations. Faithful to what is now one of its traditions, UNESCO has established two centers, one at Calcutta to deal with conditions in South Asia, and another at Rio de Janeiro which it is hoped will minister to Latin America. Such success as these may have must depend on the ability of the Director-General to enlist the interest and support of the member states involved, and of course also upon how well the appropriate agencies of the United Nations can work together in developing experience in this complex field.

The free flow of information

One area in which UNESCO's liaison efforts have been persistent, but unfortunately only in part successful, is that of the free flow of information. In the early years great stress was laid on this task because international understanding can develop organically only when it is possible to create an uninhibited traffic in information, considering the barriers of ignorance, fear, prejudice, and sheer surfeit of materials. But the nature of the time in which we live has not been favorable for the application of this principle. In several respects the situation has undoubtedly deteriorated. Armed conflict in parts of the world, the cold war, intensified nationalist sentiment in some areas, animosities between peoples, and sometimes a failure of technical organization have all led to censorship and, more regrettably still, to waves of propaganda designed for the most part to obscure the truth. It was quite impossible for any international body, no matter how widely supported, to remove all these deleterious factors from the scene.

UNESCO has therefore worked, and upon occasion effectively, to improve the mechanics of exchange. As early as 1950, the General Conference approved an international agreement designed to eliminate import duties on books, periodicals, and certain educational materials. The Director-General likewise urged the GATT [General Agreement on Tariffs and Trade] Conference in 1956 to propose a reduction of duties in the same categories. In both cases a measure of success was achieved. Help of a different kind was effectively provided through the UNESCO Book Coupon Scheme, authorized in 1948 when the purchase of books needed by scholars in war-devastated countries was a matter of vital necessity. Since UNESCO was operating in Paris and to some extent at least in "soft currency" areas, it could manage to pay publishers in the United States, for example, in hard currencies and accept the equivalent in other kinds. By 1956, when the scheme was modified, coupons in the amount of nearly $9 million had been redeemed. The service was not abandoned, but a reorganization of the procedures eliminated the drain on UNESCO's budgetary resources. In retrospect, the Book Coupon Scheme can surely be characterized as an effective means of aiding in educational reconstruction.

Efforts to remove financial obstacles to the free flow of information continue. The GATT agreement is to be reviewed presently, and UNESCO has taken steps to help safeguard the gains so far made, as well as to seek the cooperation of states not yet involved. More recently three conventions, proposed by UNESCO and the Customs Co-operation Council to facilitate the import of mass communication equipment and material designed for exhibitions, have been drawn up and wide acceptance of the provisions is anticipated. Another convention dealing with scientific instruments and equipment is under consideration. These constitute additional useful instrumentalities for removing barriers in the interest of education. While these achievements do not come near accomplishing what is desirable, they are nevertheless very much worth while.

The Nubian Monuments

An unusual venture in liaison was begun in 1960 when the Director-General of UNESCO, responding to a request from the governments of the United Arab Republic and the Sudan, launched an appeal for contributions to rescue the monuments of Pharaonic culture in the Nubian Valley from inundation as a result of the building of the Aswan High Dam. For decades British officials stationed in Egypt had known how to use the three months of the year when Nubia is almost as close to being paradise, insofar as climate is concerned, as it is possible to come on this woeful earth. Nor had they lacked skill to advertise it. But that art works of priceless value were to be submerged under the pent-up waters of the Nile was news for most people. (If the United States had chosen to build the High Dam, the major temples would doubtless have been preserved as a matter of course, but it did not so elect.) The appeal which the Director-General thereupon addressed to the world was in accord with one of the responsibilities which has been entrusted to UNESCO, namely the preservation of cultural monuments as parts of the precious legacy of mankind. But what was to be done? The language used in the Director-General's Report of 1960 says in part:

An organizational structure has been set up, commensurate with the importance of this project. It comprises: a Committee of Patrons, under the chairmanship of His Majesty, Gustav VI Adolf of Sweden, bringing together some forty persons of world-wide renown; an International Action Committee, consisting of 15 leading figures in the world of culture; a special consultant to the Director-General, Prince Sadruddin Aga Khan; advisory panels of experts attached to the two governments directly concerned; National committees in more than 20 Member States. . . .

In short, all the secular icons had been aligned, and it remained only to be seen whether the response would be adequate to make available the huge sum required, estimated as high as $100 million. The project was divisible into four parts: first, archaeological research on sites which would be inaccessible once the waters of the Nile had been artificially raised — research which was in fact rather widely undertaken as a result of the appeal; second, the removal of several smaller temples, stone by stone, and their transfer to new sites—a task which several European countries undertook and which the United States has in part subsidized; third, the building of a protecting wall round the Temple of Philae, gem of the Nubian Valley, which the United States agreed to sponsor; and finally the rescue of the Temple of Abu Simbel from the waters, an enterprise which has not yet been underwritten. In order to save Abu Simbel it was thought necessary to cut sections into the rock out of which the twin temples of Rameses and Nefertari have been carved, two vertical sections and one horizontal one, and then to raise the huge severed mass two hundred feet. Doubtless the Pharaonic builders would have considered this a feat worthy of their best tradition.

The Director-General tried in vain to induce the General Conference which convened during 1963 to accept responsibility for salvaging Abu Simbel and to allocate funds for the purpose. Orators indicated that there were monuments elsewhere that badly needed rescuing, and so the unfolding vista was one to rouse fear in even the staunchest fiscal officers. All eyes have therefore naturally turned again to the United States. Could sufficient money from the funds accruing in Egyptian currency as a result of shipments of surplus wheat and other commodities be diverted to saving the great temple? A number of practical problems arose. Did the Egyptian government itself attach sufficient priority to Abu Simbel? Was the method proposed for lifting it above the anticipated water level the only possible one, or were there other less costly possibilities? And, more generally, could the expenditure be justified?

It might be argued, and sometimes was, that since the Russians had undertaken to build the dam, it was properly their affair. For were they not vehemently contending that their engineering skills would serve the masses? As a matter of fact, there was no lack of feeling that a sum so large should rather be expended on education or some similarly beneficent purpose. After all, is there not a surfeit of Pharaonic memorials, at Luxor and elsewhere? But when all has been said and done, every lover of mankind's cultural heritage must deeply regret the possibility that Abu Simbel, jewel of the Nubian Valley, may disappear from view. Even from a strictly utilitarian standpoint, it might add sufficiently to the charm of the landscape to make the Valley, assuming a normal amount of tourist energy, a magnet which would bring a measure of life during several months of the year into the desert world through which the Nile flows like a lost ribbon of silver.

In any event, this is the story of what no doubt can be characterized as UNESCO's most romantic enterprise. Whether it was wise to undertake it, in view of the bewildering complexity of the tasks assigned to the organization, is a moot question. But beyond any doubt it stirred the admiration of many throughout the world and proved that an international organization need not be merely a bureaucracy. The plan required daring, imagination, and a large measure of optimism.[3]

Notes

[1] When the pamphlet referred to was criticized in the Executive Board by the representative of a European member state, the Soviet delegate retorted furiously by declaring that his country has as much right to present its point of view as did any other in UNESCO publications. In my intervention I said that we had welcomed to the United States a number of qualified spokesmen for Soviet education and had published their views in our journals. It seemed to me, I said, regrettable that the addresses contained in the UNESCO pamphlet were of lesser value. Whereupon the Soviet representative responded by saying that if I had in mind better essays than those which UNESCO had published, he would be quite ready to accept my suggestions. Of such mysteries are American-Soviet relations compounded!

[2] *Proposed Programme and Budget for 1963–1964,* p. 143.

[3] On June 13, 1963, the Department of State announced that a plan for preserving the temples of Abu Simbel drawn up by a firm of Swedish engineers had been approved by an advisory committee to the Department, by the government of the United Arab Republic, and by the UNESCO Executive Committee for the Nubian Monuments. This plan calls for the dismantling of the temples and their reconstruction on the surrounding heights. The cost is expected not to exceed $38 million. Subject to the approval of Congress, the United States will contribute approximately one-third of this amount, to be paid in Egyptian pounds accruing from the sale of surplus agricultural commodities, provided that the balance required is contributed by other countries. As of the date indicated, about $7.7 million has already been pledged, and there is considerable hope that the great temple can be preserved.

PART V

Exchange of Persons —
The Promise and the Reality

*C*laire Selltiz and Stuart Cook have found that the generally assumed view that exchange-of-persons activities increase international understanding is oversimplified and overly optimistic. In fact, there is evidence that being in another country even for an extended period of study may have very little effect on the attitudes of the visitor toward the country visited. Dr. Selltiz found in a study she made in 1956 that the impressions of a group of Frenchmen who had been in the United States on a training mission were not significantly different from the opinions held by a group who had never been to the United States.

It is exceedingly difficult to generalize about the value of exchange-of-persons activities because the participants differ so greatly. They vary in personality, life history, preconceptions, experiences en route to and within the host country, and anticipation of return to their home country. If they are students, they also differ in the type of institution they attend, participation in orientation programs before the start of the first academic year, and social relations with classmates and people beyond the campus.

Many studies of foreign students are made in terms of national background, a factor that seems to be a major source of differences in perception of a host country. William Sewell found that Scandinavians studying in the United States are not usually detected as being natives of a foreign country. As a result, when compared to other foreign students, Scandinavians are found to adjust to the American scene with remarkable ease.

In the study, "Indian Students and the United States: Cross-cultural Images," Lambert and Bressler conclude with the observation that "visitors from low-status nations develop their attitudes toward the United States not so much on the basis of their reactions to American life, but rather as an end product of a 'looking-glass' process based on their perception of the American image of their home countries." If this is true, mere contact can have a negative effect especially if protracted contact serves only to accumulate a series of assaults on the self-esteem of the nationals from low-status countries.

There is evidence to suggest that foreign students go through a typical cycle in their feelings toward their host country. Selltiz and Cook note: "Starting with highly enthusiastic reactions, they are likely to become more critical after a few months; a period of relatively negative feelings is likely to be followed by a return to more favorable evaluations, though the initial rosy view may not be recaptured." William Sewell found a relationship between a student's reactions to his experiences in the United States and the length of time he spent here. He found that students whose sojourn extended beyond 18 to 24 months had a much more relaxed attitude in matters pertaining to social relationships and that their judgment of the new culture was more favorable and differentiated.

Donald Shank reviews the variety of programs that take Americans abroad for study. He also identifies the five objectives for which Americans go abroad. These are: to see other countries, to learn about other peoples and cultures, to learn a foreign language, to pursue some specific field, and to teach or to help abroad. Unfortunately, there are few empirical studies of foreign students in countries other than the United States. Thus, it is impossible to make any generalizations about these programs outside the limits of the American setting.

20
Factors Influencing Attitudes
of Foreign Students
toward the Host Country

"Well, what do you think of our country?" This is perhaps the single question most frequently put to the foreign student by ordinary citizens of the country in which he is studying. With elaborations and specifications, it seems also to be one of the questions most frequently asked by investigators of the process of cross-cultural education.

This paper presents a brief summary of what the most common answers seem to be when the host country is the United States, and then examines evidence about factors that make for differences among students in their views of the host country. It draws heavily on two studies carried out by the Research Center for Human Relations of New York University, but it takes account also of the findings of other studies. The focus on students who have studied in the United States reflects the distribution of studies of cross-cultural education; to date there have been so few systematic studies of foreign students in other countries that it is not possible to draw even tentative generalizations beyond the American setting.

Data for the two Research Center studies were gathered in 1954–1955 and in 1955–1956, respectively. Both studies utilized a before-and-after interview plan, with an initial interview within the first few weeks of the student's stay in this country and another toward the end of his first academic year. The subjects were all men. In the first

Claire Selltiz and Stuart Cook, "Factors Influencing Attitudes of Foreign Students Toward the Host Country," *Journal of Social Issues,* Vol. 18 (February 1962), pp. 7–24.

study, students comparable in nationality but studying in three types of American college-community settings were compared. There were in this study 348 students from 59 countries, attending 34 colleges and universities in the northern and western United States. The second study included 184 students; 97 men attending a summer orientation program were matched with an equal number comparable in age and in academic and professional achievement as well as in nationality who did not attend the orientation program. They came from 26 countries and attended 34 schools and universities throughout the United States. The findings of these two studies are reported in detail in Selltiz, Christ, Havel, and Cook (published in 1963; University of Minnesota Press).[1]

Space does not permit description of the subjects and procedures in the other studies on which we have drawn for this summary. Such information is, of course, available in the reports of those studies. Wherever a statement rests on evidence from one or two studies, specific references are given; statements for which there is support in a number of studies have not been given specific documentation.

It should be emphasized that this overview leans heavily upon exploratory research, suggestive findings, tentative conclusions, plausible interpretations. We have attempted to piece together what seems to be the most probable account of influences on attitudes[2] toward the host country. However, there are many questions to which the answers are still unclear, and many others where what is known with some certainty points to further questions.

Foreign Students' Image of the United States

From a number of studies it appears that certain views about Americans are held quite generally by people of many other countries—both those who have been to the United States and those who have not. Americans are widely believed to be friendly and informal, practical, efficient, materialistic, ambitious, optimistic, egalitarian, and lacking in individuality. These views are not new. De Tocqueville noted many of these characteristics in Americans of the 1840's, and a stream of foreign observers have commented on them since.

From many accounts—both anecdotes and research reports—one gets the impression that foreign students are highly critical in their evaluation of Americans. But in both of our studies, when students were asked to select from a list of some twenty-five traits five that they considered especially characteristic of Americans and then were asked whether they considered each of those traits desirable or undesirable, the average student attributed more desirable than undesirable traits to Americans. A study by Morris (1960), using a slightly different approach, gives a similar impression, though there the preponderance of desirable traits seems less than in our studies. Lysgaard (1954), too, found that a group of returned Norwegian students described "the typical American" in somewhat more favorable than unfavorable terms.

Many foreign students see personal relationships in the United States as shallow. They describe friendships in this country as quickly formed and of short duration. They believe that there is less sharing of thoughts and feelings, and less sense of mutual obligation, among friends in the United States than in their home countries. Nevertheless, in the Research Center studies, evaluations of friendship patterns in the United States ranged from "dislike somewhat" to "like very much," with the average student expressing moderate liking. Other studies, however (for example, Morris, 1960), have found considerably less favorable evaluations.

To many foreign students, the difference between family relationships in the United States and in their home countries is striking. The great majority see both emotional ties and sense of obligation among family members as less strong in the United States than in their countries. There is considerable agreement that in the United States the wishes of the individual take precedence over family obligations, whereas the reverse is frequently said to be the case in the home country. Foreign visitors are frequently struck by the high status of women in the United States and by the amount of freedom children enjoy. Reactions to family patterns are mixed. Disapproval of some aspects seems to be balanced by a feeling that less strong family ties may mean greater freedom and happiness for the individual.

Turning to the broader social scene, there is, of course, general agreement that the standard of living in the United States is very high. There is considerable agreement, too, that there is a rather high degree of democracy. Americans are seen as active in community affairs, and this meets with approval. But foreign visitors are also aware of discrimination against minority groups in the United States; this is the aspect of American life that elicits the strongest expressions of disapproval. But the disapproval is tempered by a general recognition that the position of Negroes in this country is improving, albeit slowly.

With respect to views about freedom of speech, the findings of different studies are contradictory. At least two studies based on repeated intensive interviews with small numbers of foreign students in the United States in 1952–1953 (Lambert and Bressler, 1956; Sewell *et al.,* 1954) noted considerable criticism of restrictions on freedom of speech in the United States. On the other hand, in both of our studies and in the Morris study (all of which were carried out in 1954–1955 or 1955–1956), substantial majorities expressed the opinion that there is little or no restriction on freedom of speech in the United States. It is possible that the earlier studies, in which students talked repeatedly with interviewers whom they knew, elicited franker statements. It seems equally likely, however, that the difference in findings reflects a genuine difference in views, based on a real change in the political atmosphere of the United States between the times of the two sets of studies. Students in the earlier studies expressed considerable disapproval of this aspect of American life, in line with their perception of considerable restriction; those in our studies and that by Morris, most of whom believed there was little or no restriction, expressed more approval than disapproval.

It is difficult to arrive at a clear picture of "typical" views of foreign students about American foreign policy – perhaps because there are such great variations in opinion that no view can be considered "typical." One has the impression that foreign visitors are sometimes reluctant to express themselves freely on this issue; one or two of the students in our studies told the interviewers that they had been cautioned not to discuss American foreign policy. Anecdotal reports suggest considerable criticism. In both of the Research Center studies, however, the dominant evaluation was one of moderate approval with definite reservations. The majority of students in these two studies saw the major goal of United States foreign policy as being to stop the spread of communism; whether they considered this desirable or undesirable depended on their own political leanings. Altruistic goals such as preserving peace, promoting international cooperation, guaranteeing freedom and improving living conditions throughout the world were attributed to the United States by considerably more students than were exploitative goals such as getting rid of surplus American goods, protecting the colonial system, or imposing the capitalist system on other countries.

The General Impact of the Cross-Cultural Experience

It is a common assumption that getting to know the people of another country will lead to liking them; this assumption underlies the expectation that exchange-of-persons programs will increase international good will. In its simplest form, this hypothesis would lead one to expect that, on the whole, visitors to a country will leave with more favorable views than they held before their arrival, and that their views after the trip will be more favorable than those of their compatriots

who have not visited the country in question. The entire body of research on cross-cultural education, however, suggests that this expectation is oversimplified and overly optimistic. There is considerable evidence that the sheer fact of having been in another country,
even for an extended period of study, has quite limited effects on attitudes toward that country. For example, Riegel (1953) reports that,
although Belgians who had been in the United States on grants were
more favorable in their feelings toward the American *people* than
comparable Belgians who had never been to the United States, they
did not differ in their views about other aspects of American life.
Selltiz (1956) found that the impressions of a group of Frenchmen
who had been in the United States on a training mission were quite
similar to the opinions held by a comparable group who had never
been to the United States; such differences as appeared were on specific points, rather than in general favorableness or unfavorableness.
Nevertheless, when the group who had been to the United States were
asked directly whether their ideas about America and Americans had
changed as a result of the trip, roughly a quarter of the group said
their ideas had changed "for the better"; this was the most common
single answer. Lysgaard (1954), interviewing Norwegians who had
been in the United States on grants, distinguished between "Americans" and "American democracy," and asked with respect to each of
these, "Was the impression you got generally in accordance with the
ideas you had before you left?" With respect to both aspects, approximately half of his respondents said they had found things in general as
they expected. Among those who reported that what they found in
America differed from their preconceptions, the preponderant direction of the changes was favorable in the case of Americans as people,
unfavorable with respect to American democracy. Their estimates of
the areas of American life about which most Norwegians have a false
picture corresponded with their reports of their own changes in impressions; most of those who mentioned false conceptions about the American *people* felt that most Norwegians held unjustifiably derogatory
views about Americans, while most of those who mentioned aspects
of American *society* (notably the scientific and technological level,
the standard of living, and the extent of social mobility) felt that most
Norwegians overrate these aspects of the United States.

Thus it seems clear that it is an oversimplification to expect that a
period of study in a foreign country will uniformly result in more
favorable attitudes toward that country. In order to assess more realistically what effects the cross-cultural experience is likely to have on
attitudes toward the host country, we need to think about the ques-

tion more analytically: to take into account the fact that there is no such thing as *"the* foreign student," but a large number of individuals who differ among themselves in many ways; that the experiences they have in the host country may vary widely; that a country presents many different aspects about which a visitor may gain impressions or make evaluations, and that his views about some aspects may be especially likely to be influenced by certain kinds of experiences, his views about other aspects may be influenced by different kinds of experiences, and those about still other aspects may be untouched by any experiences he may have.

Factors Associated with Differences in Attitudes

Despite the trend toward consensus on many questions about the United States, there is considerable variation among foreign students in what they believe the "facts" to be, and, even with similar descriptions of the "facts," in approval or disapproval of them. As suggested in the preceding paragraph, there are undoubtedly many factors that contribute to such variation, but only a few of them have been investigated.

First of all, the visitor to a country does not come with a blank — or perhaps even an open — mind. He brings with him a set of preconceptions, or expectations, built up through the years. His preconceptions may be quite definite or they may be rather vague. They may be realistic or unrealistic. It seems likely that the more realistic they are, the less they will be changed by his stay in the country. Since few studies of foreign students have been able to ascertain their preconceptions of the host country before their arrival in it, we do not know whether people who arrive with certain kinds of preconceptions are more likely to undergo changes than others.

The problem is complicated by the fact that visitors bring with them not only preconceptions about the host country but a variety of motivations that may influence the extent to which experiences in the host country lead to changes in their beliefs and feelings about the country. For example, both Lysgaard (1954) and Scott (1956) suggest that, at least among Scandinavians, established scholars who go to the United States for specific research purposes are likely to be less sensitive to other aspects of the life of the country, and therefore less likely to make observations or undergo experiences that might change their views, than are students whose goals include, in addition to getting training, becoming familiar with a different way of life.

Differences in national background seem to be a major source of differences in perception of the host country. Within the general agreement that family ties in the United States are weak, for example, students from non-European countries are likely to see them as even weaker than do those from European countries. Scandinavian students are likely to think of Americans as irresponsible in public affairs, while students from most other countries are likely to be struck by the extent to which Americans feel a sense of civic responsibility and participate in the affairs of their community. Students from countries as diverse as India and Scandinavia are struck by the hurry and movement of American life; a group of French visitors reported that one of their major surprises was the calm and orderliness, the *lack* of rush and commotion.[3]

Students from different countries probably start with preconceptions that differ to some extent. One source of these preconceptions is the nature of the relations that obtain between the home-country government and the host-country government. Buchanan and Cantril (1953), summarizing the findings of public-opinion surveys carried out in nine countries under the auspices of UNESCO, note that feelings of friendliness or unfriendliness toward the people of another country correspond closely to international political alignments. They suggest that most people do not distinguish clearly between the *people* of a country and the *country as an actor on the international scene* (that is, the official actions of its government), and advance the hypothesis that the stereotypes held by people of one country about the people of another country tend to follow from their feelings about the official position of that country vis-á-vis their own country. A number of investigations which have compared characteristics attributed by members of one country to the people of another country before and after events that have changed the relationships of the two governments have found shifts in stereotypes corresponding to the change in relations between the two countries. However, the international events reflected in these changes of opinions involved conflicts severe enough to limit, if not entirely stop, exchange of persons between those countries. In general, students who go abroad to study are not likely to go to a country with which their own country is in open conflict. Although there are differences in the degree of cordiality and cooperation in the official relations between the United States and the various countries from which foreign students come, they are all officially friendly; the differences in official relationships are probably not great enough to lead to marked differences in preconceptions about the characteristics of Americans.

Students from different parts of the world have somewhat different experiences in the United States; it has frequently been found that European students are likely to interact more extensively with Americans and to experience less difficulty in adjusting to certain aspects of life in this country. Such differences in experiences may contribute to differences in views about the United States, but many of the differences in views between Europeans and non-Europeans remain even when differences in experiences in the United States are taken account of.

It appears that an important basis for the difference between students from different world areas in their perceptions of the United States is the fact that one tends to judge the situation one is currently observing in relation to one's accumulated background of experience with similar situations. Thus, for example, even if European and non-European students observe the same American families, the non-Europeans, comparing what they observe with the very close family ties that are likely to prevail in their countries, tend to see ties among American family members as very weak; European students, comparing with the moderately strong ties that are typical in their countries, tend to see American family ties as weak but not so weak as they seem to non-Europeans. However, such "contrast effects" do not always appear. Especially on characteristics where the position of the host country is clear and extreme, students from countries that differ in terms of those characteristics may not differ in their perceptions of the United States. For example, most students, wherever they are from, describe the standard of living in the United States as extremely high and describe Americans as friendly; such variations as occur seem to spring from *individual* differences in standards or experiences, or from some other source, rather than from differences in the average situations in their homelands. [4]

Home-country practices may provide a basis not only for comparative placement of the host country with respect to various characteristics but for evaluation of the desirability of host-country practices. Comparison of the discrepancy between students' ratings of their home country and of the United States on a variety of characteristics with the extent of their expressed liking or disliking of these same aspects of the United States shows a tendency for those students who see the United States as being similar to their home country in terms of a given characteristic to like that aspect of the United States, while those who see it as different from their country tend to dislike it. However, the strength of this relationship varies with different aspects of national life. (Probably it varies, too, from individual to individual.) On questions of democratic social practices, this influence is negligible; regardless of how he sees the state of affairs in his own country, the closer to the democratic end of the scale a student sees the host country as being, the more likely he is to approve of it. This is true of such matters as care of the unfortunate, equality of opportunity for different racial and religious groups, freedom of speech, the frequency or infrequency of undemocratic practices, the extent to which people treat each other as equals in their everyday behavior, the extent to which they participate in civic affairs. It suggests that on matters such as these there is considerable agreement among students from all parts of the world as to what is desirable.

With respect to certain other characteristics, however, there is not so strong a correspondence between beliefs as to the state of affairs in the host country and approval or disapproval of those characteristics of the host country. For example, there is a less strong, though nevertheless clear, tendency for those who see relations between students and professors in the United States as most informal to be the most approving. For still other characteristics there is no relationship between beliefs and approval; for example, there is no consistent relation at all between the belief that in the United States most leisure-time activities are carried on outside the home and approval or disapproval of this state of affairs.

For characteristics where approval of the United States is closely related to belief as to the position of the United States, the extent of perceived similarity between United States and home country has a negligible relation to approval of the United States. For characteristics where the correlation between belief about the United States and approval of this country is less close, perception of the United States as like one's own country or as different from it tends to show a moderate relation to extent of approval of the United States. Especially with respect to friendship and family relations and items about philosophy of life, there are moderate negative correlations between extent of discrepancy seen between the two countries and approval of the United States; that is, the more a student sees the United States as being like his own country, the more likely he is to approve of the United States. However, even with respect to such characteristics, the correlation is far from perfect; in other words, the extent to which the student sees the host country as being similar to or different from his home country is far from being the only determinant of his liking or disliking of the host country.[5]

What about the impact of experiences in the host country? Relatively few classes of experiences have been investigated in detail: attendance at different types of educational institution, participation in an orientation program before the start of the first academic year, shifts in the subjective experience of level of "national status," social relations with members of the host country, and the ease of the student's adjustment or the extent of his satisfaction with his experiences.

Attendance at different types of school seems to have little consistent effect on either beliefs or feelings about the host country. One might expect that foreign students who go to small colleges in small towns would get quite a different view of American life than those who attend large metropolitan universities, but in the first of our studies, where this was a focus of investigation, the few differences between students at different types of institution formed no consistent pattern.

Similarly, one might expect that attendance at a six-week orientation program designed to help prepare students for the adjustments involved in starting their studies at American universities and in meet-the demands of everyday life in an American community would have an effect on attitudes toward the United States. But in our second study, although we found that participation in such a program did lead to greater ease in establishing social relations with Americans, it had almost no effect on the content of beliefs or the favorableness of feelings about the United States.

Several investigators have suggested that a foreign student's reactions to the host country are likely to be strongly influenced by whether he feels he has been treated with the respect due him. An individual who goes abroad can hardly avoid becoming, to some extent, an unofficial representative of his country, and a student is especially likely to find himself in this role. Groups in the host country may ask him to talk about his home country; the student himself may feel an obligation to try to explain his country to the people of the host country. The student's nationality becomes an important aspect of his personal identity. To the extent that he finds in the host country respect for his home country, he is likely to feel that he personally is accepted and respected; to the extent that he sees the people of the host country as contemptuous of his home country, he is likely to believe that they look down on *him*. Indian students have been described as being strongly critical of many aspects of American life; Scandinavian and French students, on the other hand, have been described as responding more dispassionately, appreciating some aspects and criticizing others. It has been suggested that the rather hostile criticisms of Indian students are a defensive reaction to their feeling that Americans look down on their country, while the more "objective" reactions of the French and Scandinavian students have been attributed in part to the fact that these students feel secure about the position of their home countries, both in their own eyes and in those of Americans.[6]

This hypothesis formed the major focus of a study by Morris (1960) and was examined, though in less detail, in the Research Center studies. Morris predicted that students who gained in "national status" by coming to the United States would be more favorable in their evaluation of the United States than those who lost in "national status." A student was considered to have "gained in national status" if he believed most Americans would rate his country higher than he himself did, to have "lost in national status" if he believed they would rate it lower than he himself did. (Actually, there were few students who believed most Americans would place their home countries higher than they themselves did; the distinction became one between those students who had lost in national status and those who had not lost, that is, who saw Americans as rating their countries approximately the same as they did.) Morris found that students who had lost in national status evaluated the United States less favorably than those who had not lost. In one of our studies, the same finding appeared. In the other of our studies, there was no difference in favorableness of evaluation between those who had lost in national status and those who had not. Thus it appears that there is a tendency for students who see Americans as having an unjustifiably disparaging view of their countries to react with negative feelings toward the United States, but that there are conditions under which, and groups in which, this does not occur.[7] What these conditions are, and what the characteristics of these groups of students may be, is a matter for further research.

We have noted that, underlying the expectation that exchange-of-persons programs will increase international good will, is an assumption that getting to know the people of another country will lead to liking them. However, we have also noted that not all foreign students become more favorable toward the country in which they have studied. Is the assumption incorrect? Perhaps getting to know people does not necessarily, or even usually, lead to greater liking. On the other hand, perhaps the difficulty is that some, or many, foreign students do not really "get to know" the people of the host country. Probably more than superficial contact is needed to change attitudes, and it may be that not all foreign students have the degree of contact with people of the host country that is likely to produce attitude change. The two Research Center studies focused on this question, comparing the attitudes of students who differed in the extent and nature of their social relations with Americans. This question has also been considered, though in less detail, in other studies (for example, Goldsen, 1955; Morris, 1960).

If we take as a measure of social relations such relatively objective facts as the proportion of free time a foreign student spends with

Americans, the nature and variety of the activities in which he participates with them, and the frequency of such participation, it appears that students who have more extensive interaction with Americans tend to see personal relationships in the United States as being closer than do those who interact less with them, and to be more approving of such aspects of American life as friendship and family patterns and the characteristics of Americans as individuals. Yet even with respect to these aspects differences between students who differ in extent of interaction with Americans are neither clear-cut nor consistent; they do not appear on all the relevant questions, and they are complicated by the fact that students from different parts of the world differ both in extent of interaction with Americans and in their beliefs about American friendship and family patterns. And extent of interaction with Americans seems to have no effect at all on beliefs or feelings about broader social patterns (for example, the treatment of Negroes or the extent of freedom of speech) or about American foreign policy.

If we take as the measure of social relations the student's report of whether or not he has made at least one close friend, the connection with beliefs and feelings about the United States is much stronger. In both of our studies, at the time of the second interview (that is, when most of the students had been in this country about eight or nine months), students who reported having made one or more close American friends described both friendship and family relations in the United States as closer than did those without a close American friend, and expressed greater liking for American friendship and family patterns and greater approval of the traits they saw as characteristic of Americans. They scored higher, too, on a summary measure based on evaluation of a number of different aspects of American life, and they were likely both to describe themselves as more favorable in their feelings toward the United States and to be rated by their interviewers as being more favorable than those who did not have close American friends. In the study by Morris, although no difference was found between those with and without at least one close American friend on a summary measure based on evaluations of a number of different aspects of American life, those who had at least one American friend were more likely than those without American friends to say that they liked the United States "very much," and were more likely to say that their views had become more favorable during their stay.[8] Goldsen (1955) found that students who scored high on a measure based on questions about friendship with Americans differed in their *beliefs* about personal-social relationships among Americans and about American foreign policy, but not in their beliefs about public or formal institutions. When she turned to measures of *approval,* however, she found that those who scored high on the friendship measure were more favorable on almost every question, including those referring to public or formal institutions.

It seems rather clearly established, then, that there is an association between having one or more close American friends and liking American life, especially the aspects involving personal-social relations. However, questions remain about the interpretation of this association. In all of these studies, the reports both of friendship and of attitudes toward the United States were obtained from the students themselves. It is possible that differences in outlook or in style of expression may underlie the apparent relationship; some persons may tend to give expansive or optimistic or favorable answers to all questions, and thus to report that they have made close friends and that they like various aspects of American life, while others, describing not very different relationships and reactions, may not call their associates close friends and may be more restrained in their statements of liking.

A further problem of interpretation has to do with time sequences and causal relationships. In both the Goldsen and Morris studies, the data were gathered at only one point in time, when most of the students questioned had been in this country a year or more. In the Research Center studies, measures of attitudes toward the United States were obtained early in the students' stay as well as toward the end of their first academic year in this country, but here too reports of friendships were obtained at only one point in time, the same as that at which the second measure of attitudes was obtained. While, as indicated, we found that students who reported at this time (the end of the first academic year), that they had at least one close American friend were more favorable in their attitudes toward the United States than those who said they had no close American friends, we found in addition that the former group had also been more favorable than the latter when they were first asked their attitudes, at the beginning of the year. Perhaps some of them had already made friends at that time and had already undergone favorable changes in attitude. But perhaps those who were initially most favorable were the most likely to make friends with Americans, rather than vice versa.

Undoubtedly there are many other factors, besides those discussed here, that influence a foreign student's beliefs and feelings about the country in which he is studying. These may include past experiences and personal characteristics; they may include a wide variety of experiences in the host country; they may include his expectations of how the sojourn will affect his future career; they may include events on the international scene. Although a beginning has been made in understanding what takes place in the process of cross-cultural education and what factors may affect some of its outcomes, much remains to be learned.

Time Stages in Attitudes toward the Host Country

A good deal of evidence suggests that foreign students (at least in the United States) typically go through a cycle in their feelings toward the host country. Starting out with highly enthusiastic reactions, they are likely to become more critical after a few months; a period of relatively negative feelings is likely to be followed by a return to more favorable evaluations, though the initial rosy view may not be recaptured. Sewell *et al.* (1954) and Scott (1956) reported such a pattern among Scandinavian students in the United States, Coelho (1958) among Indian students, and Morris (1960) among students from many different countries. Gullahorn and Gullahorn (1956) noted that American students in France also seem to go through such a cycle. In both of our studies, where the final interview took place at a time that some investigators have suggested is likely to fall within the trough of this "U-curve," a decrease in favorableness toward the United States from first to final interview was consistent with the idea of such a pattern.

It has been suggested that such changes in favorableness of evaluation of the host country may reflect stages in the process of adjustment through which most students go. Early in his stay, the student seems to play the role of an observer. He is excited at being in a new country, pleased that he can find his own way around and make himself understood, and satisfied with relatively superficial social relations. During this stage, he tends to have very favorable feelings about the host country. But after a time, according to this view, he finds the observer role no longer appropriate; he wants to find a place for himself in the life around him (even though he does not intend to stay in the country indefinitely) and to establish more meaningful personal relationships. In trying to do this he encounters problems and frustrations; if he attributes his difficulties to shortcomings of the host country, he may become less favorable in his feelings toward it. Eventually he works out a *modus vivendi;* with the re-establishment of equilibrium in his own life comes a return to a relatively favorable view of the host country.

Sewell (1954) reported parallel cycles following this U-pattern with respect to contact with Americans, adjustment during the stay, and attitudes toward the United States. However, Lysgaard (1954) found such a trend with respect to reported ease of establishing personal contact with Americans and with respect to some of his adjustment measures, but found no consistent time pattern with respect to negative or positive characterizations of the "typical American" nor with respect to whether Americans as people or American democracy were found to be "better" or "worse" than the student had expected. And in our studies, although there was a negative shift in attitudes that fit the first half of a U-pattern, there was no corresponding shift on measures of adjustment. Thus it would appear that stages of adjustment and shifts in attitudes do not necessarily proceed *pari passu*.

One might expect that changes in feeling toward the host country would be accompanied by complementary changes in feeling toward the home country; that is, one might expect the student to be relatively unfavorable toward his home country when he is most enthusiastic about the host country, and most favorable toward his home country when he is least favorable toward the host country. However, there is some indication that the contrary may be the case. Coelho (1958) found shifts in evaluation of the host country roughly paralleled by corresponding shifts in evaluation of the home country (in this case, India). Limited data from our studies showed positive correlations between changes in evaluation of the United States and changes in evaluation of the home country. On the other hand, Bennett *et al.* (1958), in their discussion of Japanese who have studied in America, note a "polarity" in images of America and Japan—a tendency to see the two countries as antitheses, and to have an "all or none" attitude of favorableness toward one or the other.

After the student returns home, his views and feelings about the host country may change again; in fact, the end result may have little resemblance to his attitudes while he is in the host country. Few studies of returned foreign students have been concerned with changes in attitudes toward the host country *after* the student has returned home, and even fewer have attempted to analyze factors that may influence post-sojourn changes in attitudes. However, from studies of returned foreign students and from anecdotal reports, it is possible to draw some clues as to factors that may be important, though it does not seem possible to estimate their relative influence.

Some students have reported that the host country "looks better" after they return home.[9] As time passes, the minor irritations that are an almost inevitable part of everyday living in any setting are forgotten, leaving the pleasant and admirable aspects to dominate the picture. Instead of the minor irritations of everyday life in the host country, the student is now faced with those of the home country, which he may have forgotten while he was abroad; by contrast, the recollection of the host country, from which these details have tended to drop out, may seem especially pleasant.

We do not mean to suggest that shifts in attitude toward the host country after the student returns home are likely to be predominantly favorable, or that those students whose reaction has become favorable while they are in the host country will necessarily continue to view it favorably after they return home. Riegel (1953), in a study of Belgians who had been in the United States on grants, found that those who had been back in Belgium only a short time before they were interviewed were more favorable toward the United States than those whose American sojourn was farther behind them. He concluded that the student is likely to be most favorable toward the host country immediately after his return, and that his attitudes gradually revert to those commonly held in the groups of which he is a member.

Other investigators have also stressed the importance of the attitudes toward the host country that are current in the home country when the student returns.[10] If he finds that the dominant view is critical or even hostile, he may find it easier to re-establish himself in his own country if he does not appear too favorable toward the host country. If he finds that his foreign experience, rather than helping his career, seems for some reason to hinder it, this may lead him to become negative toward his foreign experience, whatever his feelings about the host country may have been during his stay there.

Watson and Lippitt (1955), in one of the very few investigations in which students have been interviewed both during their foreign sojourn and after their return home, considered, not attitudes toward the host country, but the development of an international point of view, democratic values, and interest in changes in the home country and belief in the possibility of such changes. They found that a group which had showed considerable positive change in these respects during a stay in the United States experienced a good deal of difficulty in readjusting after their return home and tended to shift back toward their original attitudes after a few months at home, while a group which had been·in the United States for a shorter time and showed little change during the stay showed positive changes after their return home. These investigators suggested that the most productive stay, from the point of view of the outcomes with which they were concerned, may be one that is just long enough to challenge old assumptions and suggest new ones but not long enough to permit the new ideas to "jell," so that the re-thinking and re-evaluation may be carried out in the setting where the results are to be applied.

Note on Future Research

Investigations of the effects of a period of study in a foreign country on attitudes toward that country have so far yielded some measure of agreement on a few aspects, some stimulating hypotheses, and many questions. Much more research is needed before the total picture can even be sketched. There is room for many different types of studies, focused on many different questions: the effects of differences in past experience or in other characteristics of the students, the effects of different experiences in the host country, the effects of situations and events after the student returns to his own home country. Whatever the focus of investigation, review of studies carried out to date suggests that, in order to make possible clear-cut interpretation of the findings, data of the following sorts are needed: (1) evidence about preconceptions, gathered if possible before the visit, as a baseline from which to measure change; (2) follow-up after students have returned home, to assess long-term effects on attitudes; (3) comparable investigations of foreign students in countries other than the United States, to check the extent to which findings represent general phenomena of cross-cultural education or the extent to which they represent responses to the specific experience of studying in a particular country. Data such as these are, of course, difficult and expensive to gather from a research base in a single country; perhaps what is needed is collaboration among research groups in a number of countries.

Notes

[1] The first of these studies was supported by the Committee on Cross-Cultural Education of the Social Science Research Council, under a grant from the Carnegie Corporation of New York, the Ford Foundation, and the Rockefeller Foundation. The second was supported jointly by the International Educational Exchange Service of the State Department, the Ford Foundation, and the Rockefeller Foundation. A grant from the Foundation for Research in Human Behavior made possible additional analysis of the data and preparation of the book reporting the findings.

[2] We are using "attitudes" to refer to students' statements of beliefs, feelings, and evaluations.

[3] These statements are based on a number of studies: Sewell et al. (1954), Lambert and Bressler (1956), Selltiz (1956), Morris (1960), and Selltiz et al. (1963).

[4] These statements are based on our own studies and on data kindly made available to us by Dr. Richard T. Morris.

[5] Again, these statements are based on our studies and on data made available by Morris.

[6] These statements about Indian students are based on Lambert and Bressler (1956); about Scandinavians, on Sewell et al. (1954); about French visitors, on Selltiz (1956).

[7] The method of computing "national status" was slightly different in the study where no relationship to favorableness was found from the method used in the two studies where such a relationship was found. However, it does seem likely that the difference in scoring could be responsible for the difference in the findings.

[8] These statements are based on analysis by us of data supplied by Morris.

[9]Sewell *et al.* (1954) report that those students in their study who were in the United States for the second time were "quite in agreement" that such is the case. This phenomenon has also been mentioned to us in personal communications from several foreign students after their return home.

[10]See, for example, Useem and Useem (1956) and Bennett, Passin, and McKnight (1958).

References

Bennett, John W., Herbert Passin and Robert K. McKnight. *In Search of Identity: The Japanese Overseas Scholar in America and Japan.* Minneapolis, University of Minnesota Press, 1958.

Buchanan, William and Hadley Cantril. *How Nations See Each Other: A Study in Public Opinion.* Urbana, Ill., University of Illinois Press, 1953.

Coelho, George V. *Changing Images of America: A Study of Indian Students' Perceptions.* Glencoe, Ill., Free Press, 1958.

Goldsen, Rose. Unpublished memorandum on study of foreign students at Cornell University, May 13, 1955.

Gullahorn, John T. and Jeanne E. Gullahorn. "American Students in France." University of Kansas, 1956. Unpublished.

Lambert, Richard D. and Marvin Bressler. *Indian Students on an American Campus.* Minneapolis, University of Minnesota Press, 1956.

Lysgaard, Sverre. "A Study of Intercultural Contact: Norwegian Fulbright Grantees Visiting the United States." Institute for Social Research, Oslo, 1954. Unpublished.

———. "Adjustment in a Foreign Society: Norwegian Fulbright Grantees Visiting the United States." *International Social Science Bulletin,* 1955, VII, 45–51.

Morris, Richard T. *The Two-Way Mirror: National Status in Foreign Students' Adjustment.* Minneapolis, University of Minnesota Press, 1960.

Riegel, O. W. "Residual Effects of Exchange of Persons." *Public Opinion Quarterly,* 1953, **17**, 319–327.

Scott, Franklin D. *The American Experience of Swedish Students: Retrospect and Aftermath.* Minneapolis, University of Minnesota Press, 1956.

Selltiz, Claire. "As Others See Us: Factors Influencing the Image of the United States Held by Nationals of Other Countries." Unpublished Master's Thesis, Department of Psychology, Graduate School of Arts and Sciences, New York University, 1956.

Selltiz, Claire *et al. Attitudes and Social Relations of Foreign Students in the United States.* Minneapolis, University of Minnesota Press, 1963.

Sewell, William H., Richard T. Morris and Oluf Davidsen. "Scandinavian Students' Images of the United States: A Study in Cross-Cultural Education." *Annals of American Academy of Political and Social Science,* 1954, **295**, 126–135.

Useem, John and Ruth Hill Useem. *The Western-Educated Man in India: A Study of His Social Roles and Influence.* New York, Dryden Press, 1955.

Watson, Jeanne and Ronald Lippitt. *Learning across Cultures: A Study of Germans Visiting America.* Ann Arbor, University of Michigan Press, 1955.

21
Indian Students
and the United States

The emergence of India as a major world power, sympathetic but uncommitted to the West, has created a measure of self-conscious curiosity, sometimes anxiety, in many Americans concerning the reactions of Indian leadership and public opinion to the United States. It is inevitable that the image of the United States conveyed to the Indian public should be somewhat selective and distorted, inasmuch as the Indian media of mass communication concern themselves largely with American foreign policy and neglect broader sociocultural aspects of the American scene. Such information on the United States as is exported characteristically fails to provide a substantial corrective—neither the superficial frivolities emanating from Hollywood nor the excessively grim realities of the protest novel are capable of transmitting a representative picture of the United States.

The nature of this picture formed at a distance is illustrated by the preconceptions entertained by Indian students upon arrival in the United States—a stereotypical, indistinct, and limited image composed of uncorrelated fragments. They had anticipated that the United States would be a land endowed with abundant natural resources and wealth, whose inhabitants worked feverishly and constantly to command a whole host of mechanized wonders, whose cities were dominated by skyscrapers, whose ethos was scientific and rationalistic to the neglect of the spiritual, whose social relations were marked by casualness, rudeness, and violence, frequently institutionalized in the

Richard D. Lambert and Marvin Bressler, "Indian Students and the United States: Cross-Cultural Images," *The Annals* (American Academy of Political and Social Science), Vol. 295 (September, 1954), pp. 62–72.

person of the gangster, whose social system was equalitarian except for discriminatory practices directed against colored peoples; and whose labor force contained a disproportionate number of cowboys. The students were aware that some of these images were over-simplified, bordering on caricature, but in essence these grotesqueries constituted almost the whole of their expectations.

One expression of official concern with this naïve and unflattering stereotype takes the form of encouraging Indian students to attend American institutions of higher learning with the expectation that these foreign visitors, having observed the "American way of life," will return to their home country prepared to convey a more favorable image of the United States. The exchange-of-persons program reflects a basic confidence in the capacity of American institutions to arouse admiration: there seems to be some assumption that the sustained and intimate scrutiny implied in the process of guided culture contact will foster accurate perceptions which confirm the excellence of American institutions and thereby create the basis for favorable atti-tudes to the United States.

The actual mechanism of image formation and the development of favorable attitudes toward the United States appear to be consid-erably more complex. It is quite obvious that at the very minimum the student's personality, life history, preconceptions, experiences en route and in the United States, and anticipation of return all con-tribute to the content of his perceptions and to a generally favorable or unfavorable appraisal of the United States. However, our data in-dicate that the primary determinant of image formation involves a process by which American institutional areas are perceived and inter-preted in the context of their relevance to Indian culture, history, and aspirations. This mechanism of cultural reference is operative among all students and is applicable to all institutional areas over all points of time, whether or not images of American life are derived from the media of mass communication or from direct observation. Other personality and behavior dimensions not specific to the Indian culture usually assumed their chief significance as superimpositions on this basic process. The emphasis of this article, therefore, is upon cross-cultural links; how the "Indianness" of the student affects his image of the United States.

We have chosen three important areas of American life illustrating three different types of cultural reference which the Indian student brings to bear on his American experiences: family practices, political behavior, and race relations.

The Indian student's perception of American family practices indicates the operation of two basically antithetical frames of reference among Indian intellectuals: the traditional family of India's ideal culture and the Western liberal-humanitarian ethic with its strong emphasis on the emancipation of women and suppression of status inequalities. Political behavior is perceived and measured by the extent to which a given political philosophy implicitly suggests sympathetic kinship to doctrines justifying India's struggle for freedom and her current political policy. The perception of American race relations not only occurs within a context of historically rooted racial grievances, but also includes strong individual involvement arising out of fear of personal discrimination and status deprivation. This image is accordingly much more complex, personality oriented, and subject to gross distortions of perceptions.

It should be emphasized that an over-all orientation to a foreign culture is more than a simple summation of discrete images. The concluding section will be devoted to a brief discussion of an additional set of processes resulting from the students' confrontation with Americans' image of India, and the way in which these processes influence his over-all assessment of America.

The Family

The comments of the Indian student about the American family system tended to cluster around three areas: (1) the family's restricted function and interaction; (2) the role and status of its various members; and (3) family emphasis upon the gratification of personality needs rather than societal ends, with a resulting general orientation of capriciousness and frivolity in family institutional practices.

Restricted function and interaction

The Indian joint family is a unit comprising several degrees of kinship and several generations organized communally and usually living in the same household. It is an economic unit, a graduated status system with clearly defined roles, a vehicle for ritual and the observance of religious practices, a common commensal unit, a dormitory arrangement, and a sphere of relationships within which primary psychological needs are met.

Family roles are hierarchically stable, clearly defined, and reciprocal duties and obligations take precedence over individual motives. The effect of any act on other members of the family may be anticipated and therefore conflicts can be kept to a minimum. To be sure, intra-family clashes do occur, but many of these are institutionalized, culturally acceptable, and thus do not constitute a serious disruptive force. For instance, quarrels between the sisters-in-law and between mother-in-law and daughter-in-law are a culturally required part of joint family living, even though the outcome is predictable and the victors never vary. These and other sporadic conflicts can be resolved by a final arbiter, the patriarchal figure. The individual spends his life in some joint family. If for any reason a joint family splinters it breaks into segments, but seldom involves the departure of isolated individuals. The occasional mobile member, not essential to the family welfare at the moment, can leave to pursue his own ends, but the price of his freedom is a willingness to return in the event of family need.

The joint family so described was widely admired among the Indian students for ensuring stability and performing most of the functions necessary to individual members, and for providing a satisfactory, conflict-free psychological setting. The admiration persisted in spite of the fact that none of the students identified his own family as fulfilling all the requirements of the ideal type.

In contrast to the satisfying and benevolent despotism of the joint family the Indian students perceived in America a loosely knit structure providing for limited interactions and restricted functions. The simple quantitative fact of a three-, four-, or five-person household limited to two generations provides striking contrast to the emphasis on the intimate relationships among the members of the joint family. While several commented that the complexity inherent in large numbers is reduced in the American small family, the net effect is diminution of the responsibility, warmth, and serenity associated with the orderly relationship of the extended group. From the standpoint of the Indian student, there is ample evidence of the lesser importance of the home in American life. For example, lack of elaborate family ritual at meal time, restrained rather than demonstrative greetings at family reunions, the brittle casualness of the chic middle-class mother in dealing with her children, ready divorce, serial monogamy, and the increasing vogue of the psychiatric couch and the marriage clinic.

Role and status

The Indian student is not likely to become sufficiently intimate with any one American family to observe the subtle interplay of "real" family relationships. Few American families can resist the temptation to display the "typical American family at home," a dramatization which frequently results in an exaggerated caricature of the official norms. Consequently, the perceptions of Indian students tend to be influenced by consistently overplayed family roles. The specific roles which impress themselves most upon Indian students are the role of women and the role of the aged — those most markedly different from the Indian pattern. The traditional literature, current folklore, songs, and moving pictures depict a vast number of heroines who embody an ideal role for women which is widely accepted by all segments of Indian society. She is to be docile, patient, submissive, a paragon of housewifely virtues, but at the same time full of charm, a companion, and wise in the ways of beauty. Above all, she should be modest and show continued awareness of the double standard by observing rituals of inferior status, and by exhibiting proper embarrassment and constraint in interactions with men. While in actual practice, of course, woman's role is considerably more complex and ambivalent, nevertheless this ideal image served as one standard by which all women, and consequently American women, could be judged.

In addition, the Western liberal-humanitarian system of values which is opposed to all immutable status distinctions, including those pertaining to women, has been internalized to a varying extent by all of the Indian students. In general the inferior role assigned to women jars against the Western ideals of equality of individuals and greater emphasis on achieved rather than ascribed status. Indians apply the emancipation ethics fully to certain isolated women — brilliant women in the professions, arts, and politics — and favor such lesser commitments to emanicipation as disapproval of "cruelties to women" such as suttee, prohibition of remarriage, complete dependence upon males.

In view of these contradictory philosophies — the Indian ideal woman and the Western emancipation ethic — the student sometimes finds himself in favor of the role-status structure of the American family when he perceives it in equalitarian terms, but opposed to the same characteristics when he views them in the context of the ideal role assigned to Indian women. However, American family life is presumably characterized by so much of this allegiance to the humanitarian individualistic ethic that it excludes cherished values still present in the Indian social framework and still held by our subjects. It would be possible to marshal an impressive array of quotations to illustrate this feeling among the students, but the following passage will suffice to show the attempt to reconcile the contradictory philosophies.

I might say something regarding the social life of the people, absolute equality among the two sexes and how the women also help the family by supplementing the income, how these ladies are also educated, they can talk on public affairs. . . .

I mean it has its advantages to some extent, I thought, that the woman is independent and she can look after herself. If she has some work or something important and if the husband is not at home or nobody is at home, she could do it herself. Now in our society she wouldn't know what to do because she wouldn't have been taught.

I should say the freedom you allow your women, I was very much struck by it. I should say that in my experience it is more than what the woman deserves. Women we consider to be something delicate and feminine. She must distinguish herself in dress, manners, and everything, which is not the case here. She wears blue jeans and walks like a tractor truck. In that case I can't appreciate the femininity of women.

Old people

There were considerably fewer data indicating contradictory feelings concerning the role of the aged in the American family. All Indian students who had occasion to speak to this subject disapprovingly noted the comparatively inferior status of old people. As they recalled India, it seemed to them that:

. . . there is greater affection and love between father and son, because there they regard that it is the sacred duty of the father to look after his son during his infancy and it is the sacred duty of the son to look after their older parents.

By contrast:

Here we find that people have greater individuality, and they will not like the fathers or grandfathers to live with them because that interferes with the development of individual personality.

There was very little disposition to dismiss this particular status pattern as one of those inevitable cultural differences which are likely to distinguish one nation from another. Characteristically, the student felt obliged to determine the causes of the relegation of the aged to an inferior status—it was seldom mentioned without accompanying analysis. Those students who were troubled by this question, but whose tact or approval of the United States forbade wholesale condemnation, struggled to explain it by appealing to the authority of some larger, more acceptable value, such as individual responsibility. More commonly, so fundamental a violation of what they consider to be a basic and universal ethical imperative implied deeper revelations about the spiritual basis of the entire social structure. The lack of respect for age sometimes confirmed latent suspicions that the student was observing a culture which was devoid of real ethical principles and which was dominated by a complete and all-embracing utilitarian complex.

Self-gratification and capriciousness

The supremacy of group values as a governing principle in Indian family life leads the Indian students to consider American emphasis on individual gratification and sexual compatibility to be misguided. They perceive in the American institutional pattern an acceptance of hedonistic pursuits unrestrained by the "higher ideals" which alone are capable of ennobling the marriage relationship.

Critical statements included not only disparagement of American family values but also the paradoxical assertion that even individual happiness is not so well achieved as by the Indian model, whose social arrangements provide personal satisfactions only as a peripheral by-product. So even though in India

> . . . the marriage takes place before you are independent enough to think of selecting your own partner. . . . I think I am very happy, and these marriages are generally happier than the marriages which are by choice of the partner.

Closely related to the contention that there were defects both in the dominant value system and in the familial institutional structure is a less clearly defined, but apparently intense feeling that Americans as individuals have a common failing; namely, they lack the proper high moral seriousness in their approach to family life. The Indian students discerned an element of light-headed frivolity and capriciousness in courtship and family behavior. This view was sometimes expressed in the sternest moralistic terms as in "embracing and kissing and these things I take to be just the road for going into debauchery or the lack of morals." At other times it was contained in the assertion that the slightest irritation or weariness was apt to be accompanied by divorce in contrast with the Hindu practice where, in the higher castes, divorce is forbidden, and where in fact it is largely unnecessary, "because the girl who marries a boy is very much faithful to the boy . . . she is always so much devoted to the husband and the husband to the wife." On still other occasions this feeling is implied in the discovery of such terms as "boy friend," which is not as one might expect, "that one whom she would actually marry, but she would at any time drop him too . . . if she comes across someone later whom she likes better." Or to summarize the complex more explicitly, "I mean, to me it is not bad at all to go with a girl, but the only thing is that I think to go you must be serious. It shouldn't be just one of those things."

The impression should not be conveyed that the Indian students perceive American family life as entirely uniform or that their reactions were wholly unfavorable. The "what were your first impressions" or "what struck you most" type of question which is inevitably present even in the most nondirective interviews tends to bias responses toward generalizations emphasizing perceived differences rather than toward those elements mutually present and approved in both cultures. The interviews indicate that the students are sometimes aware that although there may be customary patterns and practices which tend to distinguish the entire social structure, various social strata and groups in the United States exhibit pronounced differentials in their behavior. Thus there were some comments on the greater simplicity, refinement, and spirituality of family life in religious homes, especially among the Society of Friends. There was also some recognition of rural-urban and regional differences. Nevertheless, the differences were perceived as minor variations on a common pattern, and it was the common pattern which figured in comparisons with India.

Political Background

Indian students are much more attentive to politics than are their American counterparts. The political intricacies of a long nationalist struggle made complex political ideas and parliamentary practices commonplace knowledge among Indians. The visiting students are thoroughly conversant with detailed political histories of a vast number of Indian political figures and recall as part of their shared experience years of highly emotional political involvement. The Indian student's image of American political processes is best understood against the background of the nationalist movements which have engaged the energies of Indians and other Asian peoples throughout this century. The logic which underlies nationalist movements demands that the aspirations of the struggle include more than the mere transfer of power and authority from a set of foreign functionaries to their native counterparts. Slogans of liberation included more than opposition to "imperialism" and "foreign oppressors." They also promised that with liberation would come redress of domestic inequities and grievances. Consequently the Indian intellectual tended to be identified both in foreign and domestic affairs with intense humanitarian sympathy. Except for the special interest groups such as the landlords and princes, there is now virtually no vocal conservative group in matters economic and political. Conservatism in India takes the form of urging the return to a pristine religious state. There is no significant segment among the Indian intelligentsia which feels the need to resolve the conflict between individual liberties and governmental planning implied in the term "creeping socialism." Among those who are politically effective the extreme rightist position is somewhat left of center in the normal liberal-conservative continuum.

It follows that as members of the intellectual class at home the Indian students in the United States tend to respond sympathetically to political movements which seem to be dedicated to the interests of the "masses" and the "common man." They perceive in terms of a symbolic vocabulary which makes generous use of slogans carrying strong emotional connotations in India. Their general approach is often supported by detailed knowledge. Nevertheless, the students are judging American political processes in terms of an abstract liberal ethic which is concrete and relevant in its reference to India, where political necessity at this stage of development demands emphasis upon nation building, uplift of the masses, social planning, and an educated electorate. It is in this context that the liberal-humanitarian standard applied to American political life should be understood.

American Politics: What the Students Said

The images described in the following sections are brief composite summaries of common sentiments revealed in student responses. Those sections outside of the quotation marks are paraphrases of statements in the interviews; those within quotes are the actual words of the students.

Interest groups

Ideally the democratic process should give every individual equal access to power — the greater the diffusion of power in a society the more nearly does it approach the democratic model. The United States deviates considerably from this ideal because there is "control by a party, rather than an individual — and when it comes to elections you have to please every boss. It is not exactly on principles." The existence of lobbies accentuates the concentration of power because legislative bodies are sensitive to the wishes of small groups which do not represent the wishes of the people as a whole. The small groups with the greatest influence are likely to be "financially strong interests" because they can "organize themselves better."

The one restraining influence on irresponsibly wielded power is the recognition on the part of the bosses and lobbyists that ultimate veto power resides in the people, whose dormant disaffections may occasionally be translated into effective political protests against the more cynical practices. This consideration requires a continuous assessment of the limits of public patience and some concessions to the popular will. However, such restraint should not obscure the fact that the American political structure is characterized by dominant power groups whose existence "is not consonant with the spirit of democracy."

Mass communications in politics

On the whole the American people are reasonably well informed on current affairs because they have ready access to information media such as the press, radio, and television. On the other hand, news is presented in a provincial and superficial manner, overemphasizing trivia and matters of local interest. Moreover, the media of mass communication are concentrated in the hands of the "wealthy section," who control public opinion for the benefit of right-wing political elements. As a result the universal literacy of Americans is not always a guarantee of a high level of information or of a considerable degree of political sophistication. The American is especially untutored in foreign affairs, and his ignorance of India is "no less than colossal."

Political parties

It is frequently difficult to discern the differences "between the so-called Democrats and the so-called Republicans." They do not disagree on fundamentals, and there are men in each party who seem ideologically more appropriate to the other. However, the Democrats more nearly "symbolize the close identity with the great mass of people, with the laboring class, with the farmers, with the Negroes . . . it symbolizes more a party for the common man than the Republican party." Likewise in the sphere of foreign policy the party of Roosevelt and Truman can be expected to be more ungrudgingly internationalist in outlook than the Republicans. The Republican party by contrast tends to be dominated by the wealthy and the powerful, who have an excessive allegiance to anachronistic conceptions of laissez-faire capitalism. If they pursued their own inclinations, they would transform government into a subsidiary of "big business." The selection of candidates in the presidential election of 1952 was indicative of Republican-Democratic party orientations. It is unfortunate for the United States that Mr. Stevenson did not become the President, for his administration would have been more humanitarian and more germane to twentieth-century realities than Mr. Eisenhower's.

Political atmosphere of the United States

The predominant fact of current American political life is an excessive fear of Communism.

I mean, the fear of Communism, it is a sort of craze . . . I mean sort of hysteria in this country, and actually, as a matter of fact, I didn't think that this American society is being threatened by Communism. Communism can never ruin this society, I mean for many years to come.

Obsessive anti-Communism has unfortunate social consequences because in its name even gradualistic social changes are assailed. While
the implementation of welfare measures under government aegis may
depart from traditional capitalist practice, "a certain degree of socialism is healthy," or at least inevitable. However, capitalism as it exists in the United States modified by the New Deal philosophy is
basically healthy and has produced "economic wonders." American
capitalism is by no means decadent nor has it reached "maturity."
In view of the essential soundness of the American socioeconomic
structure there are no compelling domestic reasons to justify the
prevalent anti-Communist preoccupation in the United States.

In foreign affairs there should be no fear of direct Communist military aggression against the United States. Moreover, Communism is
making fewer inroads in other nations than Americans suppose. In
India, only a very small percentage of the population is cordial to
Soviet doctrine. Hence the existence of "anti-Communist hysteria"
may best be interpreted as an opportunistic attempt to find a scape-
goat, "something like Hitler or Pakistan," and as a capitulation to the
most irresponsible elements in American politics.

The chief victims of the current political climate are "liberals."
When even General Marshall is publicly maligned it is obvious that
less influential men will be reluctant to engage in free discussion of
controversial social issues. Militant anti-Communism constitutes as
great a threat to democracy as do the few adherents of the Communist
party.

I oppose Communism because it represents fear, curtailment of political freedom, and so on. I cannot see any difference between McCarthyism and Communism in this respect. It is, however, encouraging to see that some of the
greatest intellectuals and biggest newspapers are rallying against McCarthy.

Negroes in America

The area of white-Negro relations tends to elicit images which once
again seem to lie within the anticipated and familiar context of the
liberal-humanitarian orientation. However, this element of the liberal
syndrome differs from other expressions of humanitarian good will and
outrage in the degree of intensity with which it is held, in the extent
of the personal involvement which it entails, and the fullness of the
preconceptions about this area prior to the arrival of the students in
the United States.

Most Indian students were not conspicuously well read on American
life upon arrival, yet a surprising number of them were conversant
with Myrdal's multivolumed *American Dilemma,* were shocked by its

contents, and sympathetic to its thesis. Several revealed detailed knowledge of the legal niceties connected with the approaching Supreme Court ruling on educational segregation in the South, while one or two knew of isolated cases of racial violence in several small American communities.

Personal experiences of discrimination

Much of the intensity of interest and feeling concerning the role of the Negro in the United States is in part a result of the latent and sometimes overt color tension which lay beneath the surface of British-Indian relations prior to Indian independence and which still exists between Western and Asian nations. A more immediate explanation lies in the fact that of all the values incorporated in the American social structure the existence of discriminatory practices based on color was most capable of jeopardizing the status of the Indian students during their stay in the United States. Color was a potential disqualifying factor in the acquisition of desirable housing arrangements, in comfortable tourist mobility, and the accessibility of desired social contacts.

There were in point of fact a number of instances in which students experienced situations in which they reported personal inconvenience and embarrassment. One student was advised by a friend not to visit a New York night club because he might not be served. Another was served with a separate set of utensils at a restaurant. Still another sensed that he was giving offense when he "danced with a white girl." Such incidents did not occur frequently but they were constant reminders of the possibility of recurrent humiliations.

It is not surprising that certain individuals departed from an otherwise balanced approach to America to display a color sensitivity and a distortion of experience almost pathological in nature. To cite one of many examples: a student who was not selected to accompany a tour to Hyde Park sponsored by his orientation center gave this account of the incident:

There was a competition between a number of candidates for going to Hyde Park and there was a limited number of tickets. I went to the place from which we were to leave for Hyde Park right on time, I think before the time, but I was not selected for being taken. I don't know what criterion was adopted and, rightly or wrongly, it led me to the feeling that it might have been prejudice against the colored people since they are not taking me and they are taking people from other lands.

However, the greater number of the Indian students never experienced any manifestations of real or fancied discrimination because much of their time was spent in the company of fellow nationals, American students, and Americans especially sympathetic to foreign students. This circumstance may contribute to the fact that for the most part the Indian students' perception of race relations in the United States lacks anecdotal substance and is generally vague and symbolic. The students are seldom indignant about general economic deprivation, poor housing, and dirty neighborhoods; they reserve their most bitter remarks for "the white man's complex," "social discrimination," "white chauvinism"—all presumably artificial barriers to social intercourse unworthy of the American creed.

Race and caste

One may suspect that the existence of the alleged "white superiority complex" provides some sense of gratification for the Indian students. The recognition of what seemed to them an indisputable vulnerability in the American ethic seemed to mitigate criticisms of practices in India. If American treatment of the Negro is so conspicuously poor then it must follow that India, faced with problems of greater proportions, should not be condemned for her failure to solve them.

Negroes follow your dress. They follow your manner. I mean they are not much different. They may be inferior mentally in some cases, but they are not given an equal chance. So I said naturally you must take less time to wipe off the differences; whereas we must take relatively more time to do away with the caste system. But we are progressing better than you have progressed.

Whatever the merits of this line of reasoning it appears clear that from the perspective of the Indian student an America which countenances differential treatment of the Negro must forfeit much of its claim to the moral superiority which should characterize the most powerful leader of the democratic West.

The Sensitive Area Complex

It is difficult to determine the extent to which perceptions of major but segmental aspects of American life contribute to the development of an over-all "favorable" or "unfavorable" attitude toward the United States. Elsewhere[1] we have advanced the thesis that visitors from low-status countries develop their attitudes towards the United States not so much on the basis of their reactions to American life, but rather as an end product of a "looking-glass" process based on their perception of the American image of their home countries. The process of temporary international migration characteristically impels the visitor to reappraise his own culture appreciatively and is usually marked by a heightened identification with his own country and an increased sensitivity to its status. Very early in his visit the Indian student perceives an American image of India which contains elements appearing to him to imply low status for his home country and by extension for him. Americans, in talking with him about India, allude to certain specific subjects (such as caste, untouchables, population expansion) which are associated with colonial status and reactive nationalism and thus have become "sensitive." The mere mention of these subjects even in a neutral or favorable context will cause the visitor to feel that Americans are hostile to India, a condition which will in turn predispose him to a general negative view of the United States.

If confirmed by subsequent research, the implication of this thesis is that so long as Indian students and visitors from other "low-status" countries correctly or incorrectly perceive that Americans hold an unfavorable image of their home countries even extravagantly favorable assessments of American life will be largely irrelevant to the formation of "friendly" attitudes toward the United States. Therefore, our foreign policy and public pronouncements with respect to countries recently emerged from colonial status must carefully avoid these emotion-laden areas of cultural conflict.

For amity, contact is not enough, especially if protracted contact serves only to accumulate a series of assaults on the self-esteem of nationals of low-status countries. Among other things, friendliness is a function of both personal and cultural security, and only after the viewer has a minimal feeling of security can the hostile elements of an image surrender to a more objective assessment.

Note

[1] Richard D. Lambert and Marvin Bressler, "The Sensitive Area Complex: A Contribution to the Theory of Guided Culture Contact," *The American Journal of Sociology,* Fall, 1954.

22
Scandinavian Students' Images of the United States

During the past two years an investigation of visiting students from Scandinavia has been carried out at the University of Wisconsin. The central purpose of this study was to explore the processes involved in cross-cultural interchanges of students and to attempt to arrive at a more adequate understanding of the effects of foreign educational experiences. The following presentation of selected aspects of findings which have emerged from this investigation will center around the students' perceptions of various major areas of American society. Since many of these perceptions are expressed comparatively, a brief sketch of Scandinavian culture will precede the description of the students' impressions of the American personality and norms, the American educational system, family life, politics, and economics. Following this, certain characteristics of the Scandinavian students' reactions to the American experience will be discussed. Two major patterns of orientation will be described, and phases in the students' orientation toward America as well as attitude mechanisms employed in dealing with the new environment will be identified. Finally, one aspect of the anticipated effects of the foreign visit will be briefly discussed.

The study is based mainly on intensive interviews with 38 students from Norway, Sweden, and Denmark. This group, which varies in age from eighteen to about forty, is made up of 34 male and 4 female

William H. Sewell, Richard T. Morris and Oluf M. Davidson, "Scandinavian Students' Images of the United States: A Study in Cross-Cultural Education," *The Annals* (American Academy of Political and Social Science), Vol. 295 (September 1954), pp. 126–135.

students. Twenty-one of the visitors came from Norway, 8 from Sweden, and 9 from Denmark. Most of them are here on individually planned and privately financed study programs. Nine out of the 38 are engaged in the study of engineering, while of the rest 8 are studying one of the physical sciences and 21 are working within the fields of the liberal arts or social sciences. Of the total, 16 are doing graduate work and the others are undergraduates.

In spite of the fact that the Scandinavian countries under study are three politically independent constitutional monarchies with detectable cultural differences, the results of the present investigation indicate that, in regard to the students' images of America, they can properly be treated as a unit. Also by virtue of their linguistic similarities, their common traditions, and cultural homogeneity, they appear as an entity in the eyes of many Americans.

The desire on the part of each country to remain independent is strong, and attitudes of nationalism or patriotism are very common. Far from being militaristic or isolationist in nature, or taking the form of fear of disunity or subversion, these attitudes manifest themselves in great pride in accomplishments within cultural, social, and technical fields of human endeavor. They are continuously being passed on to the younger generation and reinforced through a variety of direct and symbolic means.

The preconceptions of America which the Scandinavian students bring with them form a picture which is by no means a clear one. It is however quite apparent that attention and interests have been guided to certain aspects of American culture more than to others. For this reason, the students are more aware of American technological developments and popular music, for example, than they are of religion, moral orientation, or patterns of social interaction.

Since in physical appearance the visiting Scandinavian student is not especially foreign-looking, and since his English-speaking facility is comparatively great, he is generally able to move around in the community without being detected as a native of a foreign country. At the same time, he makes no attempt to hide his identity as such, and he may even be observed to exhibit conspicuously his Scandinavian background by wearing certain kinds of clothing. This finding is compatible with our observation that the Scandinavian student comes to the United States with feelings of very high national status. In no way does he as a representative of Scandinavia feel inferior to his American fellow men. He is quite confident that the standing of Scandinavia in the United States is very good.

Images of American Personality

One of the striking impressions resulting from interviewing Scandinavian students is that they all consider Americans rather immature in one respect or another, whether their general attitude toward America is favorable and tolerant or impatient and antagonistic.

The positive interpretation consists, first of all, in admiring the warm friendliness and spontaneity of Americans, the informality of dress and address, the quick acceptance of the stranger into the group and the family. This admiration is tempered, sooner or later, by the feeling that much of this warmth and acceptance is merely skin-deep.

The superficial nature of American friendliness may be positively appreciated. Several of the Scandinavian students felt that the ease of social relationships here, the emphasis on social activity, joining, and party going had been beneficial for them personally — that it had made them able to get along better with others and to know others more quickly, had reduced their shyness and improved their social graces. One student remarked after a considerable stay in this country:

I now feel the urge to associate with people — to call up somebody to go out and have a beer or something. . . . I have never felt that way before. I spent a lot of time alone while at school in Scandinavia, just alone with a book. I don't think I can go back to that now; it would bother me quite a bit. . . .

A large number of the students have expressed a desire to see some of the American informality and spontaneity in social relationships transferred to their own culture.

On the other hand, the discovery of the seeming shallowness of friendships may come as an unpleasant shock and bring with it accusations of hypocrisy: the charge that informality is in itself merely a formality to cover up a lack of real concern for the other individual. Americans are said to have hundreds of acquaintances but no true friends:

They are not deeply interested in you as a person (which is reflected in their general lack of interest — and knowledge — about your country) and are apt to resent it if you are frank with them, or look too closely into their personal affairs.

There is another set of American personality characteristics which is commonly perceived as immature by the Scandinavian students, but which again may draw forth opposite reactions: Americans are happy-go-lucky, self-confident, exuberant, fresh, careless, reckless, uninhibited, flippant, wasteful, noisy, inconsiderate. These adjectives seem to have some sort of common descriptive base, but carry with them varying interpretations and evaluations of such behavior. On the opposite side, the ebullience of the American spirit is seen as one of the strong motivating forces for the tremendous technical and commercial advances typical of America. The American emphasis upon constant activity and motion—the intense drive of the businessman, the bustling sales personality—fits in the same syndrome. It is admired by many of the students, who compare it with the relatively more stable, tradition-bound, and restricted distribution and consumption patterns found at home.

Negatively, this carefree, self-confident nature is detected by the visitors in the excessive spending and installment-plan buying in this country, which they feel give a false impression of the standard of living. The happy-go-lucky attitude toward life often turns into inconsiderate behavior, which the students see reflected in a lack of concern for community property. One of the first impressions of several of the students, which came as something of a shock to them, was the dirtiness and sloppiness found in the cities and on the campus itself:

It would be inconceivable at home for the students to throw papers around the way they do . . . and not to bother even to pick them up. . . . Do they like to live in a pigsty? Or do they think somebody else will pick up after them? It's disgraceful!

Intellectual and aesthetic immaturity

There is a rather different set of perceptions which touches upon another facet of the over-all image of America, namely, the general intellectual and aesthetic immaturity of Americans. This perception is common to almost all the students in the study and, unlike the characteristics previously discussed, brings forth a common, unfavorable reaction. The chief focus here is upon the inability of Americans to carry on a serious conversation or discussion: they not only are ignorant of the serious affairs going on in the world, but they are not even interested in finding out. The reasons for this superficiality are assigned in several directions—the overemphasis on material, practical events, the lack of tradition in America, isolationism, rigidity of values, excessive emotionality, conformity—but the perceptions of the presence of this intellectual immaturity are constant:

Americans do not think deeply enough; they have no intellectual curiosity; they have no real opinions on serious topics; politics here is all emotion, not intellectual; there are no books on the bookshelves in the homes; they can't think logically.

The image of America as aesthetically immature or uncultured carries with it a general assumption that causes may be found in the very heavy stress placed on the technical, materialistic aspects of life:

Americans don't know what they want except money; there are hardly any pictures on the walls; American jazz is their only cultural export; students here learn art, music, and architecture without sentiment; emphasis on the technical makes them forget art and nature.

Some of the students also see the lack of artistic tradition as a cause of the immaturity. The negative reaction to America's cultural standards is reinforced in the criticism of mass media:

Advertisements spoil the radio; movies are inferior to European products; TV is low-grade vaudeville; burlesque shows and the worship of movie idols are symbols of American cultural attainment.

Reactions to the image

It should not be inferred from some of the rather scathing comments quoted that even the typical negative reaction to the perceived American personality is bitter, angry, or resentful. The general tone is quite different, and can be best summarized by another quotation from a Scandinavian student:

I realized that I would dislike many things here but I tried to tell myself that I must not judge Americans according to European standards of judgment but that I had to judge them by other measurements because America is a young country and Europe is old.

Conversely, a favorable attitude toward American character does not necessarily mean that the student wishes to be like the American or that he wishes to take back American ways to his own country. An illustrative comment here is:

I would not want a child of mine to go through an American public school— not because I worry that he would learn less but because I know it would make him an American and I want my children to be Danish. . . . We do things one way in Denmark—Americans do differently—I like Danish ways better because I am a Dane. An American would like the American ways better because he is an American. . . . Everyone likes his own country better than any other country.

All in all, there seems to be a common set of perceptions which are then interpreted and evaluated differentially in a rather detached fashion, with generally more light than heat. As one student put it: "I figure a country is a country; if other people can live there, I can live there."

Images of American Norms

The visiting Scandinavian students all claim that the numerous pioneer novels, Indian stories, and Wild West movies which they read or saw before coming to this country had little direct effect upon their preconceptions of America. They do, however, concede that these sources of information have undoubtedly aided in building up in their minds a picture of America as a country where individualism flourished, where strong opinions were strongly voiced, and where mobility and lawlessness were pronounced.

To their surprise, and sometimes to their dismay and disappointment, they find quite the opposite in many areas of American life. They perceive a mass culture which implacably forces every individual into a mold of conforming behavior. In art, in dating behavior, in sports, in clothes, in party behavior, and even in the use of swear words, there is a definite lack of variety, a hesitance to express originality. Generally this fear of appearing different is not seen as a result of any lack of intelligence or creativity, but as careful conformity to a set of externally imposed rules, for fear of being disliked. It is undesirable to behave differently as an individual. The American code seems to the Scandinavian student to be: Do not be different, but if you have to, be different together.

The consistent conforming of Americans to norms of the group or the organization is seen by many of the Scandinavian students as a form of superficiality in values. For example, one of the students observed:

At home an act is more apt to be moral or amoral depending upon its consequences in each situation for human happiness and well-being, not because it follows or violates some rule.

The perceived low incidence of individually reached moral judgments in America is evidenced in several ways:

There are too many laws here, and too little control. Police interfere in too many spheres of private life.

Political ideas all come from newspapers. Americans are like a flock of sheep. They don't think for themselves.

Religion is external. They go to church, but they aren't really religious in the way they choose to act.

Boy-girl relations are artificial and based on popularity. Too many moral restrictions have to be obeyed according to a rigid sex code, not the way they really feel about it. . . . It is all false modesty based on what the other person might think of you.

The students' negative reactions to conformity are most marked in the areas of sports and social recreation. There is an almost universal criticism of American commercialized, spectator sports, which provide so little in the way of physical exercise for the majority of those involved and which impose such a rigid seasonal restriction on sports conversation and participation. The contrast with the many individually oriented sports of Scandinavia, such as skiing, hiking, and the like, is continually, and unflatteringly, brought out. In response to the question "What about your own country have you missed the most while here?" practically all of the students mentioned fresh air and natural facilities for non-organized recreation as the deprivation felt most strongly. A main objection to social gatherings, and to the few individual sports in which Americans are engaged, is the overemphasis on planning and organizing the activities:

You can't just go on a walk or sit down and talk with people in your own way, you always have to *do* things, in just such an order and in just such a way, one after another . . . always a program, always prearranged. . . .

The pressures for conformity are seen to be reinforced by the Americans' fear of being alone:

Americans like to have many friends, but with no reason for making them. . . . People want to be popular with everybody. . . . You have to be a social animal and belong to all sorts of social organizations to be respected here. . . . Americans value social contacts highly and get lonely without them.

It must be stated, however, that at least one of the students was able to interpret his own perception of American conformity as partially a function of his unfamiliarity with subtle differences in the new culture:

Americans and American ways all look alike, but maybe that's just because they are different from us. They are probably just as different to each other as they seem alike to us.

Images of American Institutions

In the case of practically all the students of our sample, attendance at an American university was the primary reason for their visit to this country. Also, the great majority of them had attended a university or other institution of higher learning at home prior to coming here. This means not only that their educational experiences in this country represent roughly comparable shared activities but also that these experiences contain a relatively high degree of psychological meaningfulness in the sense that the students have been exposed to two different university environments in the same sequence. Their contacts with other aspects of American culture are so varied that comparability is often very difficult.

Preparatory to entering a Scandinavian institution of higher learning the students went through four years of secondary school or Gymnasium. During these years they were held to a very rigid schedule of classwork with almost no freedom of choice in selection of courses. Attendance was required, the competition was keen, and with three or four hours of homework daily, little time was left over for social or other extracurricular activities. The continuation of study at a university marked a definite break in the type of schooling. At this point they were considered intellectually and socially mature and sufficiently independent to pursue specialized study with little supervision. They were free to attend lectures or to stay away and took their exams when they felt ready to do so.

American universities

It is against this background of previous experience that the Scandinavian students' reaction to the American university system should be seen. Only by so doing may one understand the reasons why the topic of supervision of students elicits more unfavorable responses in an unstructured interview than any other aspect of American university education. They say that "required class attendance is childish" and that "frequent exams interfere with studying." While they find the physical facilities excellent and generally favor the student-teacher relationships, which are closer than at home, they are not impressed with the standards of education in America, particularly at the high school and undergraduate levels. They attribute this especially to the less rigid selection procedures and to the considerable amount of time spent by American students in social activities. In this connection the Scandinavian students are greatly surprised about the lack of distinction between work and recreation which their American fellow students exhibit. The sight of a group of young scholars engaged in studying midst half-empty Coca-Cola bottles and blaring radios or phonographs never ceases to amaze them. It is perhaps significant that every Scandinavian student who initially lived in a dormitory soon moved out.

Family life

The opportunity for contacts with American family life varies widely among the group of visiting students. In spite of this, their evaluation of this phase of the American culture shows a certain consistency which no doubt derives from the fairly uniform background of family life and customs in Scandinavia with which the students compare it. They come to see the American home as one in which "the family bonds are not very strong," where "recreation is not family centered," and where "the wife dominates the family picture too much." They also find that "there is not enough control over smaller children." It is worthwhile noting that these observations are related to the interviewer with special emphasis and conviction by those students who come from rural areas in Scandinavia where family life is relatively more patriarchal and autocratic, and where, in the absence of many commercial recreational facilities and convenient means of transportation, family life is comparatively close.

Religion

Perhaps no other aspect of the American culture puzzles the Scandinavian students so much as does religion. Their first impression is one of great diversity and much competitive activity in interdenominational relations. In view of the religious homogeneity of Scandinavia this could perhaps be expected. The students are further amazed by the large number of people in America who go to church on Sundays. Their surprise in this respect could also be anticipated, because the proportion of people in Scandinavia who go to church more than a few times every year is quite small. However, the visiting students also come to a conclusion which is less readily comprehended: they are quite in agreement that Americans are hypocritical. As one said: "They go to church but they aren't really religious; their religion is external and not so deep." Perhaps this impression should be seen against the background of a rather common belief in religious circles in Scandinavia to the effect that true religiosity is incompatible with any excessive or conspicuous concern for worldly goods or money. The students feel that "churches in America are too money oriented" and that "collection of money in churches is undesirable." While in this country, only one out of the 38 students attended church regularly. The majority never went, or on occasion attended mainly to "see what it was like." With one exception, the students all claimed to be fairly or very liberal in their orientation toward religion.

Political issues

The students as a group considered themselves somewhat to the right of center politically at the time when they arrived in the United States. At that time their knowledge of and interest in American political matters were very limited, and, in general, the group can be said to be a politically unalert and uninterested one. They rarely avail themselves of the opportunities offered by the various campus organizations to hear lectures or participate in the discussion of domestic or foreign political issues. Perhaps this is the reason why their impressions of politics in America show little pattern. On the other hand, the students often point out that they find it difficult to get into a discussion of political or social issues with Americans in informal social settings, and if they succeed in initiating such discussions, the conversation very seldom goes much beyond casual observations of current happenings.

One may detect a considerable degree of concern in the students' evaluation of freedom in America. Responses such as "America is losing her freedom" or, more specifically, "Freedom of speech in America is curtailed" are not uncommon. Nor are the visitors impressed with the standards of political behavior in this country. Those who were here during the last presidential campaign and conventions are especially prone to make this known. On the further question of equality in human relations as it relates to the students' perception of American democracy, the visitors find more equality in professor-student and employer-employee relationships than they are used to. They completely approve of this and often express a desire for adoption of such practices in Scandinavian industries and institutions.

Prior to coming here the Scandinavian students had heard about discrimination against Negroes in America. However, they believed that it was largely a problem of the past and almost exclusively confined to the South. While they find little evidence of discrimination against Negroes after coming to this country, they are quite surprised by the tensions here between gentile and Jewish people.

In regard to the question of postwar American foreign policies in general and foreign aid programs specifically, it is surprising to these students to find in America a considerable degree of disregard for the United Nations and disapproval of the foreign aid programs. It obviously irritates them that "many Americans think Europe ought to be very grateful for this aid, when, in effect, it is really good business for America."

The picture which the Scandinavian students develop of economic matters in the United States is a much more favorable one. They commend the American people for their industriousness and efficiency and attribute much of the credit for the high standard of living to these qualities. It also pleases them to see that private enterprises in this country have maintained a comparatively high degree of independence from governmental influence, but in the same vein they disapprove of having their own countries labeled with "the American interpretation of socialism." Those who have held jobs here, in particular, are favorably impressed by the efficient methods of production in America. They would like to see these methods transferred to their home countries.

Impact of Stay

Reports from studies of students from other cultures reveal that, by comparison, the Scandinavian visitors approach America in an objective and practical manner. In their appraisal of this country they do not often feel compelled to judge in terms of ultimate pros and cons, but instead direct their evaluation to fairly specific areas or incidents. The preponderance of remarks during the interview which were critical of the United States should not necessarily be interpreted as a sign of dissatisfaction with the sojourn. Rather, such criticism should be seen in the light of the fact that the Scandinavian students generally do not consider the conditions under which they live and study in America superior to those available in their own countries. Consequently they do not deem it necessary to refrain from criticizing these conditions. It is quite obvious, also, that the Scandinavian visitors feel under no obligations to express feigned niceties about America in front of the interviewer, who is considered by them as a representative of their own culture. [All of the interviewing was done by Oluf M. Davidsen.] Furthermore, they readily admit that a good share of their criticism is nothing but banter. While the national awareness of the Scandinavian students is naturally heightened by their presence in a foreign country, they do not seem to consider their experiences here as a threat to their national status, and emotional reactions are largely confined to situations where they feel curtailed in their effort to accomplish the specific purposes for which they come. In general, by comparison with other foreign students, the Scandinavian visitors seem to adjust to the American scene with remarkable ease.

Two patterns of orientation

Relying on those findings that emerge most clearly from our data, we can distinguish certain differences between Scandinavian students in their orientation and adjustment to the new environment. At the risk of making unfounded generalizations at a point when our material has not been exhaustively analyzed, we may differentiate between two major patterns of orientation.

We have been dealing with one group of students whose social and academic adjustment has been relatively easy, who have associated extensively with Americans, and whose attitudes toward the new culture are comparatively favorable. More often than not, the English facility of these students is high, they have previously had contacts with other cultures, and their prior knowledge of the United States is relatively broad. Transferring into the American university was a smooth process for this group, involving no academic prestige or credit loss. While here, these students have been relatively free from financial worries, and their behavior has indicated a comparatively high degree of personal flexibility.

This orientation pattern contrasts with one which is manifested by a group of students whose attitudes toward America at the end of their stay are relatively unfavorable, who have experienced varying degrees of difficulty in academic adjustment, and whose social contacts in this country have not extended far outside of the Scandinavian student subculture on campus. Typically, this group uses the English language with relatively limited proficiency, and their rate of improvement in this respect is slow. They have had no or few previous contacts with other cultures, and their prior knowledge of America is slight. Personal rigidity, occasionally to the point of stubbornness, is likewise characteristic of these individuals. Upon entering the university here, these students have often encountered difficulties in the process of transfer of credits, or they have interpreted the transfer experience as constituting a loss in academic prestige. Financial worries and dissatisfaction with their educational experience here also typify this group. The group is, however, decidedly in the minority.

This attempt to distinguish in the sample of visiting Scandinavian students between the two sets of attitudinal and behavioral patterns contains striking omissions. It is anticipated that more sharply focused and further differentiated pictures will result when the analysis of data has been completed.

Time changes

Our interviews with each student have been spread out over a period of time ranging anywhere from a few months to almost two years. This has provided opportunity to observe the students' orientation to the United States as a process in time. At the present stage of our analysis there is beginning to emerge a certain relationship between the students' reactions to their experiences here and the length of time they have spent in this country. With a considerable degree of clarity, our data point to three such orientation phases which seem to indicate a U-shaped curve of favorability toward America. The initial stage is characterized by fascination and by many superficial social contacts with Americans. During the intermediate phase, the number of social contacts with Americans appears to decrease, and the students seem to become increasingly critical in their evaluation of America. Finally, in the case of students whose sojourn extends beyond eighteen to twenty-four months, a much more relaxed attitude in matters pertaining to social relations is observed, and their judgments about the new culture become more favorable and differentiated. Among the numerous factors which influence the duration of each of these stages, language facility, social ease, and personal flexibility seem to be of special importance.

The relationship between the reactions to social and educational experiences in America with which foreign students leave this country and their orientation toward America after they have returned to their own countries is one about which very little is known and also one about which doubtful assumptions have been made. Careful follow-up studies would be required to bring this relationship completely to light. However, it seems appropriate to point out certain types of behavior on the part of our sample of visiting Scandinavian students which pertain to this issue. As has been stated previously, these students come to America with feelings of high national status. These feelings manifest themselves in surprise about the ignorance of Americans about Scandinavia and in annoyance when attempts at overcoming this ignorance are limited to casual and superficial questions and inquiries. They also show up in the form of a high degree of identification with the home culture and in the students' anxiety to convey information about the Scandinavian countries. In the presentation of such information many of the students seem to be somewhat selective in favor of those aspects of their own culture which they deem desirable. While the operation of this attitude mechanism is perhaps a common phenomenon, it is felt that in the case of the Scandinavian students it is used more as an offensive than a defensive mechanism. Whatever its nature, it is significant that our data point to a reversal of this attitude mechanism after the students have returned. Those of our sample who are in this country for the second time are quite in agreement that such is the case. "Once you are home, everything over here looks brighter," or, "When you get home, you forget the bad things and remember only the good things about America," are statements frequently made by such students. They also maintain that they are much more prone to defend America when home than while here. Even the students who are here for the first time expect to experience this same reversal.

Significance of the Investigation

The principal aim of the present investigation was to develop leads and researchable hypotheses pertaining to the area of cross-cultural education. The exploratory nature of the methods and techniques used in pursuing this aim clearly requires that the generalizations about Scandinavian students' reactions to the American experience should be thought of as suggestive contributions to a widening field of scientific interest rather than final judgments or established facts.

23
The American
Goes Abroad

The attitudes of Americans toward foreign countries, and particularly toward foreign study, have changed significantly over the past 150 years. In the eighteenth century, the liberal and broad-minded Thomas Jefferson expressed the opinions of many Americans of that period when he said:

Let us view the disadvantages of sending a youth to Europe. To numerate them all would require a volume. I will select a few. If he goes to England he learns drinking, horse racing, and boxing. These are the peculiarities of English education. . . . He forms foreign friendships which will never be useful to him. . . . It appears to me that an American coming to Europe for education loses in his knowledge, in his morals, in his health, in his habits and in his happiness.

The contrast between Jefferson's viewpoint and that of current political leaders was dramatically demonstrated in the 1960 presidential campaign. Both Mr. Kennedy and Mr. Nixon, in the platforms of both political parties and in their speeches, strongly supported programs of educational exchange and emphasized particularly the necessity of sending larger numbers of young Americans abroad. President Kennedy advocated as a major new contribution to foreign policy the establishment of a Peace Corps, which would make it possible for large numbers of young Americans to work in educational and technical development programs throughout the world, especially in the nations of Africa, Asia, and Latin America.

No one who reads the daily newspapers can doubt that each year

Donald J. Shank, "The American Goes Abroad," *The Annals* (American Academy of Social and Political Science), Vol. 335 (May, 1961), pp. 99–110.

increasing thousands of Americans are going abroad for various reasons. It is significant that, in the recent discussions of the problems of United States gold reserves, both the Eisenhower and Kennedy administrations have, in different ways, proposed control of dollar expenditures in other nations by United States citizens. American tourists, military personnel, businessmen, students, and others have suddenly become a factor in our international trade policy.

Although very large numbers of United States citizens annually go to other countries, the Passport Division of the State Department supplies unfortunately inadequate figures regarding the exact flow; and even scantier information is available on the purposes of foreign travel. Of some 10,000 Americans in United States Government service overseas, we know that more than 5,500 are in the diplomatic service and some 1,200 in the United States Information Agency. More than 400,000 United States citizens are either serving in or employed by the armed services in foreign countries. We know that at least 28,000 United States missionaries are working throughout the world. It is estimated that many hundreds of thousands of business men and their families spend all or part of each year in a foreign country. Added to these are some 1,300,000 United States tourists who are said to go to another country each year.

The Impact Abroad

Today many Americans, as well as nationals of other countries, are reported to be troubled about the impact abroad of tourists and representatives of United States Government, the military, business, and even church groups. This is not a new concern. Mark Twain obviously antedated *The Ugly American* when he described the American tourist in *Innocents Abroad.* Twain said:

The peoples of those foreign countries are very ignorant. They looked curiously at the costumes that we had brought from the wilds of America. They observed that we talked loudly at table sometimes. . . . In Paris, they just simply opened their eyes and stared when we spoke to them in French. We never did succeed in making these idiots understand their own language.

. . . .

Statistics regarding United States citizens who go abroad on educational projects are, unfortunately, almost as difficult to pin down as those of Americans who go for other purposes. . . . The United States collegiate registrar, with his passion for neat and exact educational statistics, has no counterpart in other countries. There are, however, some interesting clues. In 1960, the State department reports, 90,130 passports were issued to Americans who listed themselves as students.

This is not a very useful figure, since we know nothing of the age of the travelers or their definition of education. The Institute of International Education, through strenuous efforts, secured reports from a large number of—but by no means all—foreign institutions which indicated that 13,651 United States students were in foreign universities in 1958–1959. Edward Weidner and his colleagues at Michigan State University, in their interesting survey, *The International Programs of American Universities,* reported that 7,000 students and faculty were abroad on United States-sponsored university programs in 1957–1958. None of these statistics except those of the Passport Division attempts to measure the numbers of American students and teachers who go abroad each year on summer "educational" projects. It is in this undefined area that most American students go overseas.

Variety of Programs

In trying to box the compass of Americans in educational exchange, one is immediately bewildered by the heterogeneity of programs as well as the variety of individuals who participate in them. Although there is not yet an organized program to send United States nursery school pupils to Nigeria or Switzerland for a summer or year of education, it is safe to assume that some eager internationalist is plotting one. Existing exchange programs stretch almost from the cradle to the grave.

Education is usually loosely defined in international exchange of people. If exposure to any new experience is education, then all sponsors who arrange to move bodies from one country to another are educators. Travel is broadening is an old saw, and Paris is undoubtedly more interesting and exciting than Punxatawney, Pennsylvania. This in itself may well be a valid reason for going to another country, but it is not what many people here and abroad have traditionally considered to be education.

Although many sponsors say they promote educational exchange in order to build international understanding and peace, they are usually forced to include more specific objectives for participants. In attempting to analyze why a given individual or group of individuals choose to go to another country, at least five stated objectives can easily be identified. First, many Americans admit that they go abroad simply to see other countries. This has a long and distinguished history in the cultures of many nations. Discounting Mr. Jefferson, the Grand Tour of the last century can be defended for young Americans. A second justification is that the individual or group goes to learn something about the people and culture of another country. This implies that the young man or woman is doing more than seeing the great monuments and the night clubs of any given city. A third reason is that the individual goes to learn a foreign language. In view of the discouraging history of the study of other languages by Americans, the goal of such programs is to be lauded, although one may question how effectively many American participants in exchange programs achieve it. A fourth clearly stated objective is the desire to acquire knowledge or skill in some specific field. And, finally, there are a relatively small number of Americans who go abroad to teach or to help in the development of foreign institutions.

If these goals are accepted, the question may well be raised as to how effectively they are achieved. There is little objective evidence based on impartial studies of United States citizens who go to other countries. Little enough is known about the impact on foreign students and visitors of their experience in the United States. Almost nothing is known about the foreign experiences of Americans. The Social Science Research Council, as well as individual scholars of the United States, have, however, in recent years analyzed the cross-cultural impact of foreign educational exposure. From these studies, it is clear that any individual who goes to another country passes through certain phases of adjustment. When he first arrives he is a spectator. That is, he observes what is going on about him. He may compare what he sees to the ways of his own people, but he does not participate. The second phase comes when the student begins to get personally involved in the life of the other country. He is trying to work out a place for himself and is coming to grips with another culture. This phase, according to the social scientists, usually represents the low point of personal adjustment in the individual's experience. Usually at this time he is most likely to be unhappy, to have difficulties, and to be difficult. Then, having struggled through this slough of despond, he moves into the third stage when he feels that he has mastered the situation and can get along in the new setting. According to the studies, not much real learning occurs until the student is in the last stage.

If the analysis by the Social Science Research Council of the impact on the individual of a foreign experience is correct, it is interesting to approach the question of Americans going abroad in terms of the length of their stay and the kind of program in which they are participating.

Summer Programs

The summer foreign educational project of eight to ten weeks now attracts the largest number of Americans. The range of so-called educational tours is staggering. The casual reader of the travel sections of popular magazines and newspapers finds almost countless tours which advertise "academic credit available," "study and travel," "learn and earn credit," "lectures by distinguished foreign scholars," and so on without limit. These programs vary from a ten-week visit to a dozen or more countries to an intensive concentration on the study of Russian in a Soviet city. The sponsors of programs range from well-established commercial travel agencies and special groups with apparent or real educational connections to individual professors who, in their advertising, imply official college or university sponsorship. The serious American student, teacher, or parent must realize that, in the summer educational tour business, the old warning, caveat emptor, has real meaning.

Obviously, study tours claim a wide variety of educational content, offering every type of foreign experience. These vary along such lines as the following.

Travel programs

Bicycle tours present the interesting spectacle of a small army of knapsacked young Americans wheeling along the roads, checking out historic sites, having occasional conversations with the natives if their language is up to it, meeting other young people from many countries under the broad roof of the hostel. There is usually a tour leader or guide who stimulates discussion and keeps the youngsters out of trouble. It appears that the boys and girls get plenty of outdoor exercise—an esteemed value in our society; that they capture at least a glimmer or a sense of the past—which so few Americans have; and that they learn something about the United States by realizing that many things they take for granted are not common abroad. Other than this, one wonders whether we should expect much more. The young people do not necessarily discard their previous stereotypic notions about the countries they visit. They simply exchange them for others; and these may be no more valid than the ones they cherished before.

From the bicycle, American groups advance to the bus, the de luxe train, or the chartered plane. These programs are designed for the less hearty. The supposed advantage is that they usually cover a greater number of countries. The group leader is perhaps more learned and certainly less muscular. On the other hand, the group is more likely to stay at the better hotels and to miss the valuable contact with other young people that the hostel offers. The contacts of these Americans with foreign persons are likely to be brief, reminding one of the English ladies in innumerable novels who "do" Florence and Rome, never straying from the society of other English travelers of similar class and economic status.

Residence and project programs

Another quite different type of summer educational program is that offered by an extended stay with a family in another country. This experience has the advantage of making it almost imperative that the American go through the spectator phase quickly, since he is thrust into a family situation and the language problem must be dealt with immediately. It has the obvious further advantage of keeping the American in one place for a month, which is a necessity if any real impact on learning or attitude is to result. Assuming the ideal participant – a bright-eyed, intelligent, well-adjusted fellow, open-minded, eager to learn, with a basic command of the language – and the ideal family, the individual can certainly undergo considerable personal development as a result of his experience. He must certainly throw out some of his preconceived opinions and replace them with new ones.

A fourth type of summer travel project is reflected in the attempt of a group of individuals or an institution to bring together a homogeneous group, with special training, to undertake a specific summer project. A few organizations, and a number of imaginative college and university students working with experts in various subject-matter fields and with experience in various parts of the world, have set up a year-long orientation program on the campus which culminates in extended field experience in another country. The participants devote themselves to advance serious study of the country, establish in advance meaningful contacts in the country to which they are going, and bring back to the United States campus continuing projects of co-operation with the foreign country. In recent years, such groups have gone to Asia, Africa, and Latin America, and some have concentrated in esoteric languages and in such fields as anthropology, international relations, music, and so on.

A fifth type of summer program involves a work experience in another country. These again usually involve careful advance preparation, some orientation, and close working relations with nationals of the host country. Although these programs have traditionally been centered in Western Europe and certain Latin-American countries, in recent years the work-project approach has been extended to Africa and Asia. Some work camps have youngsters from many countries, so that the American is exposed to people with diverse cultural backgrounds.

A sixth type of program is the summer school abroad. A survey by the Institute of International Education (IIE) reports 174 summer schools for 1961 and indicates that some 10,500 Americans enrolled in 118 foreign summer schools last year. Summer schools in the United States offer the United States student a chance to continue his regular study, to accelerate his program, and to make up courses. The concept of the foreign summer school is quite different. In most foreign countries there are few if any national students in residence. Courses at universities in France, Italy, Austria, Spain, and Mexico, for example, are designed exclusively for students from other nations. These sessions, which usually combine language training and a special set of courses for foreigners dealing with the civilization of the country, do not provide the same program of academic competence which we consider necessary for summer schools in the United States. The summer sessions, for example, at the British and French universities usually concentrate on one or more subject fields. The contact that the American student has with the foreign community depends largely on the individual. The opportunity is there to meet people of the other country, but there are usually no students of the host nation in attendance.

This heterogeneity of approach to summer programs is typical of most educational activities of United States students and teachers in foreign countries.

Summer educational projects have so far been subjected to almost no critical analysis. Few have asked what the objectives of such programs are and how effectively the educational goals of the programs are being achieved. The interest of individual students in seeing foreign countries has been capitalized upon by travel promoters on and off the campus who have held out the lure of academic credit to persuade individuals and parents to sign up. Some colleges and universities have accepted summer experiences of dubious quality for credit toward a degree. This situation must be corrected by United States educational institutions if sound summer educational projects in other countries are to be developed and strengthened.

Graduate Programs

Study abroad during the regular academic year historically has been considered chiefly the domain of graduate students. During the nineteenth century, many individual American scholars, chiefly in science and medicine, went to Germany and other Western European countries for advanced work. The impact of their experience substantially influenced the shape and standards of our graduate and professional education. The fellowship programs of the American Association of University Women, established in 1890, and the Rhodes Trust, in 1903, encouraged graduate study by Americans in other countries. The distinguished tradition of these and other pioneering efforts was so well established that more recent programs for Americans to go abroad have been planned at the postbaccalaureate level. The Fulbright program, the largest international scholarship project in our history and the only major program now supported by the United States Government, is essentially for graduate students. Scholarships for Americans offered by foreign governments and foreign universities are also primarily limited to graduate students.

There are obvious reasons why United States graduate students, rather than undergraduates, have usually been thought to be the best qualified participants in a formal academic program in another country. Since the United States undergraduate college is unique, a graduate student usually fits more easily into a foreign university. In other nations there are, of course, (1) limited curricular offerings, (2) different classroom procedures and faculty-student relationships, and (3) no grades, credits, counseling, extracurricular activities, or dormitories to which the United States student is usually accustomed. The American who goes abroad to enroll in a foreign university must have language skill, imagination, drive, ability, and the willingness to work on his own if he is to have a worthwhile experience. Enrolling officially and selecting appropriate courses is an education in itself. The student must be able to work on his own and be able to make decisions without the aid of a faculty adviser, for whom no foreign counterpart really exists.

American graduate students today evidently have limited pioneer spirit when they consider foreign study. Although complete statistics are not available, IIE's *Open Doors* reported that in 1958–1959, of the 13,651 students reported in 520 foreign institutions, 1,832 found their way to France. Graduate students, like American tourists and summer educational travelers, are evidently intrigued by the Left Bank of Paris.

Distribution problems

Although the United States desperately needs able young people who know the culture and people of all areas, it is discouraging to note that graduate students seem not to be much interested in many parts of the world. A hasty look at the applications which IIE receives for the large government-sponsored programs—Fulbright, Inter-American Cultural Convention and Smith-Mundt—proves this. In the fall of 1960, IIE received 4,015 applications for some 750 places in thirty-four countries in these three programs. It is not surprising that 907 applications were for ninety-two places in the United Kingdom, in view of the dismal lack of language competence among American students. The lure of Western Europe accounts for the fact that there were 704 applications for 154 places in France and 608 for 151 places in Germany. For four fellowships in Korea, only one United States graduate student indicated that this country was his first choice; for two places in Iceland, only one; for six places in Guatemala, only one. It is disheartening to record that for fellowships in Honduras, Nicaragua, and Panama, not a single United States candidate indicated a desire to study there.

Although United States graduate students who go abroad usually have some association with a foreign university, this is not the only pattern. Campuses or centers in other countries are increasingly being established by United States colleges or universities to provide an educational program as much like that in the United States as possible. The largest such enterprise is the University of Maryland Overseas Program, which now operates in twelve countries ranging from Ethiopia and the Ryukyuan Islands to France, Germany, and the United Kingdom. The Maryland program was established to serve the educational needs of the United States military forces in foreign countries. More than 32,000 United States citizens, either members of the military service or civilians associated with the military service and their children, are enrolled in these centers throughout the world, where credits can be obtained toward the degree of the University of Maryland.

In addition, of course, an unknown number of American graduates and undergraduates take off each year on their own to "study" in a foreign country. Most of these young people vaguely hope to receive academic credit later at their home institutions, but there is little evidence of careful planning or productive experience for many of them. The largest foreign hegira of individual Americans in history consisted, of course, of the GI's who settled in droves in the more attractive centers of Western Europe following World War II. The unfortunate —and, in some cases, disastrous—impression which many of these GI "students" left abroad continues to bedevil the more serious students who have followed them during the past fifteen years.

Undergraduate Programs

United States undergraduates have gone to Europe under the sponsorship of an American college for more than a quarter of a century. The so-called Junior Year Abroad traditionally was considered a more or less esoteric experience for a limited number of well-to-do young people, chiefly female, who went abroad to advance their knowledge of a foreign language. This situation has changed drastically in the last five years. In 1956–1957, according to IIE statistics, twenty-two United States colleges and universities made it possible for 542 United States undergraduates to spend all or a part of the regular academic year in another country earning credit toward the baccalaureate degree. Three years later, in 1959–1960, the number of institutions had grown to sixty-four and they sent 2,405 students abroad. This new dimension of foreign study is the most striking phenomenon of the decade.

No one can ever wisely predict what will happen in any aspect of United States higher education. It is, however, clear that a growing number of colleges and universities are determined to make it possible for their undergraduates to have the experience of living and perhaps studying in another nation. Almost every day one hears of another college embarking upon a program. A discerning observer of United States experience in foreign countries, Dr. Harlan Cleveland, former Dean of the Maxwell School of Syracuse University and now an Assistant Secretary of State, has predicted that in the next few years every United States student will have the live option of spending part of his undergraduate program in another country. The potential implications of such a movement are staggering. To find places for even a small percentage of the almost four million students in our 1,800 postsecondary colleges in the relative handful of foreign universities would require the ability to transfer the contents of a huge vat to a thimble. In thinking of the movement of hundreds of thousands of United States college students to foreign countries, we must recognize how limited formal educational resources are abroad. We must realize how crowded these institutions are. The population bulge inundating United States colleges is not a uniquely American characteristic. Thousands of nationals are pounding at the doors of foreign universities, competing for places in crowded classrooms and libraries. In addition, most foreign institutions, particularly in Western Europe, are now accepting, relatively, a much larger percentage of students from foreign countries than is the case in the United States. Last year about 1.6 per cent of all students enrolled in United States colleges were foreigners. In some countries of Western Europe, the percentage of foreign students is already as high as 20 per cent.

As is the case with summer study projects, there is tremendous variety in the approach and objectives of undergraduate programs abroad. United States colleges and universities are sending their students in increasing numbers to half a dozen countries of Latin America and to a few places in Asia. No longer is it only the junior who goes abroad; many programs now include freshmen, sophomores, and seniors. Length of stay varies from three months to a year or more. The author of this article visited some twenty-five programs in Europe and Latin America during the past six months and tried to characterize the variations in an article in the October 1960 IIE *News Bulletin:*

Fordham allows only its honor students to go to Europe; a brother Jesuit institution, Georgetown, allows no honor students to go. Sweet Briar requires at least two years of pre-college French and two years of college French; Hollins sends many students to France who have had no training in the French language. Stanford students and their Stanford professors live and study on a lovely hill near the town of Beutelsbach, many miles from a German university; Heidelberg College in Ohio sends it students to Heidelberg University, where they take all their courses in the university and stay without a U. S. faculty supervisor during the second semester. . . . The only safe generalization that can be made about present undergraduate programs abroad is that it is not safe to generalize.

An honest observer of present programs must admit that most United States undergraduates are not really enrolled in foreign universities in the same way that nationals of the country are enrolled. This is to be expected. Even if the American student has excellent language competence, the course of study in most foreign universities involves a series of interrelated lectures upon which a degree candidate is examined when he has completed his studies. The injection of an American undergraduate into this program is neither feasible nor desirable. The American seeking a course in history finds, for example, that the only offering is a detailed study of the life of Bismarck, although the visitor probably has not had even a survey course in European history. The literature student finds herself limited to a semester's series of lectures on one play of a relatively obscure French poet, even though she may not have had a survey of French literature. For these reasons, most United States undergraduates either take special courses arranged for foreigners, such as the *Cours de Civilisation,* or special courses taught either by United States or foreign faculty members for the United States student group. Although many of these may be excellent, they are not the same courses with the same standards expected of students of the country.

Evaluation

Even with these caveats, certain positive values can be discerned in present undergraduate programs:

(1) Almost all Americans who study abroad as undergraduates believe that it is the richest educational experience in their lives. It is not surprising that young people feel that a stay in a foreign country, particularly when they get credit for it, is worthwhile and exciting. Podunk and Siwash are clearly not as interesting and exciting as Florence, Paris, Delhi, Kampala, and Mendoza.

(2) Most American students testify that major educational growth abroad is in general education rather than in their subject fields. Obviously students in language, literature, and the arts find a foreign experience very rich in terms of their major. Students in the social sciences, the natural and physical sciences, and other areas cannot really claim to be making significant progress in their fields of concentration. United States colleges might well consider, therefore, gearing future undergraduate foreign study to the sophomore level, since in our present system general education is thought to be completed at the junior year.

(3) Every student who goes abroad during the regular academic year claims with some justification that overseas experience has given him greater language competence than he could have achieved at home. This again is to be expected, since motivation to learn a language is a decisive factor. Students want to talk with natives, read the newspapers, listen to the radio. In addition, most present programs devote much more time to language study than is the case in United States institutions. In their enthusiasm for learning the language of a foreign country, undergraduates usually bitterly criticize language teaching methods at home. At the same time, most of them recommend higher standards of language preparation as prerequisite to foreign study in order to increase the educational benefits of the foreign experience.

Study abroad in itself does not insure the establishment of close relations with foreign nationals. Living with a foreign family is rightly considered to be highly desirable, but it does not guarantee the establishment of close personal relationships. This obviously is determined by the character and interests of both the United States student and the foreign family. Many American undergraduates abroad live as a group either in a hostel or hotel. Their contacts with nationals, and particularly with students, are severely handicapped. Ideally, United States undergraduates should be housed with students of the host country in university residence halls; this is impossible, since dormitory accommodations are limited in all parts of the world.

Most United States students who go abroad do not have adequate orientation for the experiences which they face. Many young men and women know almost nothing about the educational systems to which they are to be exposed and nothing at all about the social or political environment in which they will be expected to live. Even more tragic is the fact that many students know little about the social problems and developments in the United States. Young and naive Americans are suddenly faced with mature, politically sophisticated individuals in a foreign country. This is a disturbing reality of exchange. If increasing numbers of Americans are to go abroad, we must find ways to prepare them for the experience which they face. This involves not only providing basic information about the country to which they are to go but, more importantly, broadening their understanding of the political and economic issues in the United States with which they will be confronted by students and other foreigners who know more about the United States than do our own students.

If additional thousands of undergraduates are to go to other countries in the early future, United States colleges and universities must plan with great care. Although many foreign scholars and citizens of other countries criticize the approach of the University of Maryland and Stanford University, which have established either special educational institutions or resident centers for Americans, it is probable that this may increasingly be the pattern for the future. As has already been pointed out, foreign universities are already overcrowded; courses and faculty are not easily available of the type which American colleges want for their students; housing is limited in many major cities. United States colleges and universities may, therefore, have to face seriously the problem of providing or arranging for themselves much of the education for their students who go abroad. Courses will need to be arranged, taught either by United States faculty or by qualified scholars of the foreign country; housing arrangements will need to be made. The opportunity for exposure to foreign cultures and foreign peoples will depend upon the ingenuity and experience of Americans.

Any American educator who goes abroad knows that United States higher education is not highly regarded in many parts of the world. Although few will doubt that well-planned educational experiences in another country can contribute greatly to the training of young college students, the impact of undergraduate and graduate programs in other nations cannot be underestimated. Whatever a United States college or university arranges must be honest education. The United States institution must set realistic and obtainable goals and spend the time and money necessary to arrange the courses and experience which assure progress toward stated objectives. Anything less will further undermine the standing of United States higher education in other nations.

Teachers and Professors

Unfortunately, data regarding United States public school teachers and college and university faculty members who go abroad for a serious educational project are also inadequate. IIE reports for 1959–1960 that 1,777 faculty members from 339 United States colleges and universities were on research or teaching assignments in eighty-seven countries. This represented a drop over the preceding year, although a number of educational institutions did not report data. As in the case of students, most faculty who went abroad went to Europe — 52.4 per cent. Twenty per cent went to the Far East and only 10 per cent to Latin America. Only fifty-nine faculty members were located in Africa.

Little is now known about how college and university teachers or administrators can be used most effectively in another country. It is probably true that most United States faculty who go abroad do so to advance their own scholarly interests on a sabbatical or research project. However, increasing numbers are being called upon to help in the educational development projects of the United States Government, international organizations, or foundations. Many faculty members find it as difficult as students do to find useful and rewarding places for themselves in foreign universities.

Lower school and, particularly, secondary school teachers are now being recruited for new demands in the growing establishment of schools in developing nations, especially in East and West Africa. Hundreds if not thousands of teachers from the United States are needed. This demand will throw new problems into the exchange process. Can American teachers be found who are willing to spend a year or more in the Congo, Mali, Rhodesia, or Tanganyika? Can they be given the special training that will be required to make them useful in these new areas?

PART VI

*The Response
of the United States — The New
International Education Program*

*T*here has been considerable dissatisfaction with the scope and organization of United States international educational affairs. For this reason, President Lyndon B. Johnson's remarks at the Smithsonian Institution on the occasion of its bicentennial celebration were received with great interest and wide support. These remarks became the springboard for the passage of the International Education Act by both House and Senate on October 21, 1966. With the passage of the Act, educators across the country and around the world began to speak of a bright new era for international education in the United States. In the ensuing months, however, these bright hopes have been dimmed by the repeated failure of the United States Congress to provide adequate funding for the Act. At the moment, the story of the International Education Act is one of unkept promises and increased ill feeling between the public and the private sectors.

This section contains selected excerpts from some of the major public documents related to the International Education Act: the President's Message on International Education, the Senate Report, and the House Report. The section concludes with an article by William Marvel, President of Education and World Affairs, that assesses the implications of the Act for international education in the years ahead.

President's Message on International Education

In a special message to Congress on February 2, 1966, the President proposed a broad program for action in the fields of international education and health.

Last year the Congress by its action declared: the nation's number one task is to improve the education and health of our people.

Today I call upon Congress to add a world dimension to this task.

I urge the passage of the International Education and Health Acts of 1966.

We would be shortsighted to confine our vision to this nation's shorelines. The same rewards we count at home will flow from sharing in a worldwide effort to rid mankind of the slavery of ignorance and the scourge of disease.

We bear a special role in this liberating mission. Our resources will be wasted in defending freedom's frontiers if we neglect the spirit that makes men want to be free.

Half a century ago, the philosopher William James declared that mankind must seek "a moral equivalent of war."

The search continues—more urgent today than ever before in man's history.

Ours is the great opportunity to challenge all nations, friend and foe alike, to join this battle.

We have made hopeful beginnings. Many of the programs described in this message have been tested in practice. I have directed our agencies of government to improve and enlarge the programs

Reprinted from *International Education Program, 1966* (New York: Education and World Affairs, 1966), pp. 22–31.

already authorized by Congress.

Now I am requesting Congress to give new purpose and new power to our efforts by declaring that:

- programs to advance education and health are basic building blocks to lasting peace.
- they represent a long-term commitment in the national interest.
- the Department of Health, Education, and Welfare is charged with a broad authority to help strengthen our country's capacity to carry on this noble adventure.

Education

Education lies at the heart of every nation's hopes and purposes. It must be at the heart of our international relations.

We have long supported UNESCO and other multilateral and international agencies. We propose to continue these efforts with renewed vigor.

Schooled in the grief of war, we know certain truths are self-evident in every nation on this earth:

- Ideas, not armaments, will shape our lasting prospects for peace.
- The conduct of our foreign policy will advance no faster than the curriculum of our classrooms.
- The knowledge of our citizens is one treasure which grows only when it is shared.

International education cannot be the work of one country. It is the responsibility and promise of all nations. It calls for free exchange and full collaboration. We expect to receive as much as we give, to learn as well as to teach.

Let this nation play its part. To this end, I propose:

- to strengthen our capacity for international educational cooperation.

- to stimulate exchange with students and teachers of other lands.

- to assist the progress of education in developing nations.

- to build new bridges of international understanding.

I.

To strengthen our capacity for international educational cooperation

Our education base in this country is strong. Our desire to work with other nations is great. But we must review and renew the purpose of our programs for international education. I propose to:

1. Direct the Secretary of Health, Education, and Welfare to establish within his Department a Center for Educational Cooperation.

This Center will be a focal point for leadership in international education. While it will not supplant other governmental agencies already conducting programs in this field, it will:

— Act as a channel for communication between our missions abroad and the U.S. educational community;

— Direct programs assigned to the Department of Health, Education, and Welfare;

— Assist public and private agencies conducting international education programs.

2. Appoint a Council on International Education.

Our commitment to international education must draw on the wisdom, experience, and energy of many people. This Council, to be composed of outstanding leaders of American education, business, labor, the professions, and philanthropy, will advise the Center for Educational Cooperation.

3. Create a Corps of Education Officers to serve in the United States Foreign Service.

As education's representatives abroad, they will give sharper direction to our programs. Recruited from the ranks of outstanding educators, they will report directly to the Ambassador when serving in foreign missions.

4. Stimulate New Programs in International Studies for Elementary and Secondary Schools.

No child should grow to manhood in America without realizing the promise and the peril of the world beyond our borders. Progress in teaching about world affairs must not lag behind progress made in other areas of American education.

I am directing the Secretary of Health, Education, and Welfare to earmark funds from Title IV of the Elementary and Secondary Education Act of 1965, so that our regional education laboratories can enrich the international curricula of our elementary and secondary schools.

5. Support Programs of International Scope in Smaller and Developing Colleges.

Many of our nation's institutions have been unable to share fully in international projects. By a new program of incentive grants administered through HEW these institutions will be encouraged to play a more active role.

6. Strengthen Centers of Special Competence in International Research and Training.

Over the past two decades, our universities have been a major resource in carrying on development programs around the world. We have made heavy demands upon them. But we have not supported them adequately.

I recommend to the Congress a program of incentive grants administered by HEW for universities and groups of universities —

(a) to promote centers of excellence in dealing with particular problems and particular regions of the world.

(b) to develop administrative staff and faculties adequate to maintain long-term commitments to overseas educational enterprises.

In addition, I propose that AID be given authority to provide support to American research and educational institutions, for increasing their capacity to deal with programs of economic and social development abroad.

II.

To Stimulate Exchange with the Students and Teachers of Other Lands

Only when people know about — and care about — each other will nations learn to live together in harmony. I therefore propose that we:

1. Encourage the Growth of School-to-School Partnerships.

Through such partnerships, already pioneered on a small scale, a U. S. school may assist the brick-and-mortar construction of a sister school in less developed nations. The exchange can grow to include books and equipment, teacher and student visits.

To children, it can bring deep understanding and lasting friendships.

I recommend a goal of 1,000 school-to-school partnerships.

This program will be administered by the Peace Corps, in cooperation with AID, particularly its Partners of the Alliance Program. The chief cost will be borne by the voluntary contributions of the participating schools.

2. Establish an Exchange Peace Corps.

Our nation has no better ambassadors than the young volunteers who serve in 46 countries in the Peace Corps. I propose that we welcome similar ambassadors to our shores. We need their special skills and understanding, just as they need ours.

These "Volunteers to America" will teach their own language and culture in our schools and colleges. They will serve in community programs alongside VISTA Volunteers. As our Peace Corps Volunteers learn while they serve, those coming to the United States will be helped to gain training to prepare them for further service when they return home.

I propose an initial goal of 5,000 volunteers.

3. Establish an American Education Placement Service.

We have in the United States a reservoir of talent and good will not yet fully tapped:

— school and college teachers eager to serve abroad;

— professors and administrators who are retired or on sabbatical leave;

— Peace Corps volunteers who desire further foreign service.

To encourage these men and women to assist in the developing nations and elsewhere, I recommend that we establish an American Education Placement Service in HEW.

It will act as an international recruitment bureau for American teachers, and will provide supplemental assistance for those going to areas of special hardship.

In time, I hope this Service will lead to the development of a World Teacher Exchange — in which all nations may join to bring their classrooms into closer relationships with one another.

III.

To Assist the Progress of Education in Developing Nations

To provide direct support for those countries struggling to improve their education standards, I propose that we:

1. Enlarge AID Programs of Education Assistance.

In my message on Foreign Assistance, I directed AID to make a major effort in programs of direct educational benefit. These will emphasize teacher training — vocational and scientific education — construction of education facilities — specialized training in the United States for foreign students — and help in publishing badly needed textbooks.

2. To Develop New Techniques for Teaching Basic Education and Fighting Illiteracy.

Our own research and development in the learning process can be adapted to fit the needs of other countries. Modern technology and new communications techniques have the power to multiply the resources available to a school system.

I am calling on HEW to support basic education research of value to the developing nations.

I am requesting AID to conduct studies and assist pilot projects for applying technology to meet critical education shortages.

3. Expand United States Summer Teaching Corps.

The Agency for International Development now administers programs for American teachers and professors who participate in summer workshops in less developed countries. They serve effectively to support teacher-training in these countries. They also enrich their own teaching experience.

I propose this year that AID double the number of U.S. participants in the Summer Teaching Corps.

4. *Assist the Teaching of English Abroad.*

Many of the newer nations have a vital need to maintain English as the language of international communication and national development. We must help meet this demand even as we extend the teaching of foreign languages in our own schools.

I have directed AID, supported by other agencies, to intensify its efforts for those countries which seek our help.

5. *Establish Bi-National Educational Foundations.*

We have at our disposal excess foreign currencies in a number of developing nations. Where conditions are favorable, I propose that significant amounts of these currencies be used to support Bi-National Educational Foundations. Governed by leading citizens from the two nations, they would have opportunities much like those afforded major foundations in the United States to invest in basic educational development.

To the extent further currencies are created by our sales of agricultural commodities abroad, I propose that a portion be earmarked for educational uses, particularly to assist technical training in food production.

IV.

To Build New Bridges of International Understanding

The job of international education must extend beyond the classroom. Conferences of experts from many nations, the free flow of books and ideas, the exchange of works of science and imagination can enrich every citizen. I propose steps to:

1. Stimulate Conferences of Leaders and Experts

I have directed every department and agency to support a series of seminars for representatives from every discipline and every culture to seek answers to the common problems of mankind.

We are ready to serve as host to international gatherings. I have therefore called on the Secretary of State and Attorney General to explore ways to remove unnecessary hindrances in granting visas to guests invited from abroad.

2. Increase the Flow of Books and Other Educational Material.

I recommend prompt passage of legislation to implement the Florence Agreement and thus stimulate the movement of books and other educational material between nations. This Agreement was signed by representatives of the U.S. Government in 1959 and ratified by the Senate in 1960. This necessary Congressional action is long overdue to eliminate duties and remove barriers for the importation of educational materials.

I also recommend that Congress implement the Beirut Agreement to permit duty-free entry of visual and auditory materials of an educational, scientific or cultural nature.

Finally, we must encourage American private enterprise to participate actively in educational exchange. I urge the Congress to amend the United States Information and Educational Exchange Act of 1948 to permit improvements in the Informational Media Guarantee Program.

3. Improve the Quality of U.S. Schools and Colleges Abroad.

We have a potentially rich resource in the American elementary and secondary schools and colleges overseas assisted by the Department of State and AID.

They should be showcases for excellence in education.

They should help make overseas service attractive to our own citizens.

They should provide close contact with students and teachers of the host country.

I request additional support to assist those institutions which meet these standards.

4. Create Special Programs for Future Leaders Studying in the United States.

There are some 90,000 foreign students now enrolled in U.S. institutions. Many of them will someday play leading roles in their own countries. We must identify and assist these potential leaders.

I recommend that HEW and AID provide grants to enrich their educational experience through special courses and summer institutes.

The Choice We Must Make

We call on rich nations and poor nations to join with us — to help each other and to help themselves. This must be the first work of the world for generations to come.

For our part, the programs in International Education and Health I am recommending this year will total $524 million:

— $354 million in the foreign assistance program.

— $103 million in the Health, Education, and Welfare Department program.

— $11 million in the Peace Corps program.

— $56 million in the State Department cultural and education program.

As I indicated in my message on Foreign Assistance yesterday, these programs will be conducted in a manner consistent with our balance of payments policy.

We must meet these problems in ways that will strengthen free societies — and protect the individual right to freedom of choice.

Last Fall, speaking to a gathering of the world's scholars at the Smithsonian Institution, I said: ". . . We can generate growing light in our universe — or we can allow the darkness to gather."

In the few months since then, forty-four million more children have come into the world. With them come more hunger — and more hope.

Since that time the gross national product of our nation has passed the $700 billion mark.

The choice between light and darkness, between health and sickness, between knowledge and ignorance is not one that we can ignore.

The light we generate can be the brightest hope of history. It can illuminate the way toward a better life for all. But the darkness — if we let it gather — can become the final, terrible midnight of mankind.

The International Education and Health Acts of 1966 present an opportunity to begin a great shared adventure with other nations.

I urge the Congress to act swiftly for passage of both measures.

Our national interest warrants it.

The work of peace demands it.

Lyndon B. Johnson

Senate Report

On October 12, 1966 the Committee on Labor and Public Welfare submitted to the Senate a Report to accompany H.R. 14643 and recommended that the bill as amended be passed. The following extracts from the Report provide a short analysis of the principal provisions of the bill as finally passed by both the House of Representatives and the Senate.

The committee notes with pleasure that it has received the assurances of the administration that the primary goal of this legislation is building, in this country, a strong base at the graduate level for international research and studies and, on the undergraduate level, giving a wide segment of our students a chance to learn more about the world and the cultures, customs, and values of other countries.

Section 103 requires the Secretary of Health, Education, and Welfare to publish in full in the Federal Register all written agreements with other agencies in carrying out the provisions under this act. This formalizes in the statute the assurances given by the administration, and accepted by the committee, that in the operation of the program the principles of academic freedom and full publication of scholastic endeavor will be followed.

It is for this reason also that the Federal control prohibitions were strengthened to assure that there be complete freedom of publication of research findings funded by grants under this title and to preclude any attempt to direct or limit the library resource materials acquisition programs developed by the institutions of higher education.

It is the intent of the committee that the programs authorized under this title be those which represent the best judgment of the higher education community, broadly representative of all segments of higher education, including not only graduate, undergraduate, and two-year institutions, private and public, but also the educational resources to be found in the professional associations of each of the scholastic and ancillary disciplines as well as that of informed individuals representing the public such as business, labor, government, and the professions.

The committee, further, believes that the independence of the Advisory Committee from the Department of Health, Education, and Welfare should be most helpful to the Secretary in organizing and following the

Senate and House excerpts from *International Education Act of 1966* (New York: Education and World Affairs, 1966), pp. 19–26, 33–49.

many projects and activities which could be supported under this legislation. To strengthen further the Advisory Committee, funding authority to hire an independent staff has been provided. Again, this provision will allow for the development of a resource to the Advisory Committee consisting of outside expertise and permit the committee to give guidance in formulating the long-range goals of this legislation to the Secretary and to advise him on a continuing basis on the administration of the program.

SHORT SUMMARY OF THE PRINCIPAL PROVISIONS OF THE BILL

TITLE I

If enacted as amended by the committee, H.R. 14643, following the findings and declaration of section 2, would:

(1) In section 101 authorize grants to universities, or groups thereof, for graduate centers of research and training in international studies. These centers might focus on a geographic area or on particular fields or issues in world affairs, or on both;

(2) In section 102 authorize grants to universities and colleges or groups thereof, to assist them in planning and carrying out comprehensive programs to strengthen and improve undergraduate instruction in international studies. It is intended to encourage programs involving not only those departments traditionally concerned with area and international studies, such as political science, international relations, history, and languages (including programs of English language training for foreign teachers, scholars and students), but also other parts of the institution — particularly the professional schools, in which over 60 percent of the United States undergraduates are enrolled. These sections also provide for grants to public and private nonprofit agencies and organizations including professional and scholarly associations, as well as the Library of Congress and the Smithsonian Institution, when such grants will make an especially significant contribution to attaining the objectives of the respective section. This authority is provided specifically because of the important role which such groups have played in the development of international education;

(3) In section 103 prescribe methods of payments and permit the Secretary to utilize the services and facilities of any agency

of the Federal Government and of any public or nonprofit agency or institution in accordance with written agreements between the Secretary and the head of the institution when the text of such agreements have been published in the Federal Register;

(4) In section 104 provide the standard provisions against Federal control of education by any Federal official, department or agency. In addition, the committee strengthened the prohibition against Federal control by specifying that no control could be exercised over the selection of library resources by any educational institution and by prohibiting any Federal control over the content of any material developed or published under any program assisted under the act;

(5) In section 105 authorize the appropriation of $1 million in in the current fiscal year and limit the expenditure for this fiscal year to report preparation of the statutory Advisory Committee provided in section 106. For fiscal year 1968, $40 million was provided for the required annual reports and for program operation and the sum of $90 million was provided for fiscal year 1969. **The Secretary with the advice of the National Advisory Committee on International Studies is directed to prepare for the President and the Congress a report to be received not later than April 30, 1967, which will contain specific recommendations for the carrying out of the program under this title of the act together with recommendations for amendment to the title and other acts amended by this act;**

(6) **In section 106 establish in the Department of Health, Education, and Welfare a National Advisory Committee on International Studies consisting of the Chairman and 15 members. The Assistant Secretary of Health, Education, and Welfare for Education is named as the Chairman and a majority of the other members shall consist of a broad representation of higher education in the United States. The remainder of the Committee shall include members of the general public and individuals experienced in foreign affairs.**

TITLE II

Title II of H.R. 14643 consists of amendments made to other statutes related to the International Education Act.

Section 201 broadens and strengthens title VI of the National Defense Education Act of 1958 by removing the requirement in existing law that precludes instruction in languages such as French, German, Spanish, and Italian. The section also authorizes grants as well as contracts for language and area centers and, finally, it vests the authority for carrying out the language and area programs of title VI with the Secretary of Health, Education, and Welfare instead of the Commissioner of Education.

Section 202 broadens the institute coverage of title XI of the National Defense Education Act of 1958 by providing for international affairs institutes for secondary school teachers and authorizing the appropriations for fiscal year 1967 of $3.5 million and for fiscal year 1968 of $6 million.

Section 203 modifies the Mutual Educational and Cultural Exchange Act of 1961 to permit foreign students from less developed countries, where the United States does not have a surplus of local funds, to exchange their currencies for U.S. dollars to finance their study in the United States. The committee placed a limitation on United States currency of not to exceed $10 million for fiscal year 1968 and not to exceed $15 million for fiscal year 1969, and a limitation of not more than $3,000 in any one academic year for any one student.

Section 204 extends the benefits of the loan insurance program provided under title IV-B of the Higher Education Act of 1965 to American students studying abroad. . . .

House Report

On May 17, 1966 the Committee on Education and Labor submitted to the House of Representatives a Report to accompany H.R. 14643, along with a recommendation that the bill be passed. The following extensive extracts from the Report provide the background to the legislation as well as the insights of the Task Force on International Education on the significance of the bill:

Once an almost completely neglected aspect of American higher education, training in the cultures, languages, and current affairs and problems of other countries — especially in non-Western regions — is now receiving considerable attention on campuses across the Nation.

Only 15 years ago, students had hardly any opportunity to learn about the larger part of the world's peoples and cultures. American higher education was based almost entirely on the Western European culture brought here by immigrants to the United States. Textbooks and teaching materials for international studies were either inadequate or nonexistent, and library resources in the relevant subjects were severely limited.

Only a handful of universities gave courses on Asia or the Middle East which emphasized the contemporary world; still fewer offered courses on Africa. A Ford Foundation study in 1953, for example, found that there were at least 20 Asian languages, each spoken by millions of people, for which the most elementary learning materials were not available in the United States.

Moreover, not many university faculty members or graduate students went abroad to study foreign cultures. Those who did go overseas more often went for advanced training in a particular specialty, such as medicine, than to study any aspect of the life of the countries to which they went.

The effort to remedy the imbalance in international studies in the 1950's and 1960's has been initiated and supported almost entirely by private resources, particularly those of the major private foundations and a relatively few universities and colleges, some of which are publicly supported. These efforts have been stimulated by the many changes — economic, political, scientific — following World War II. The Nation's new international activities included foreign aid, first in Western Europe and Japan. Then, from an increasing number of newly independent nations came requests for trained manpower to assist in economic and social development programs. Membership in the United Nations and the location of international organizations in the United States further heightened the interest of American people in the events and changes in the rest of the world. American business investment abroad climbed from less than $12 billion in 1950 to more than $40 billion in 1965, a year when some 35,000 executives, engineers, and other personnel were working overseas. And scholarly research on foreign areas, some of which had proved extraordinarily valuable during the war, was becoming recognized as a continuing need in governmental and private relations with the rest of the world.

The growing international focus of American higher education today can be measured in part from the following:

In 10 years, foreign-area programs stressing training and research on the languages and cultures of non-Western regions more than doubled, and by 1964 there were 153 such programs at universities across the Nation.

Almost 4,000 college and university faculty members were abroad in 1965 to study, engage in research, or apply their skills to the problems of emerging nations. In addition, some 18,000 American students went abroad to take part of their studies at foreign institutions.

In 9 years, the number of foreign faculty and scholars at American campuses for research or visiting professorships increased more than tenfold, and in 1964 totaled almost 9,000.

Foreign student enrollment in 1965–66 reached 90,000 and included representatives of 159 countries and territories.

This rapid growth in international education programs has placed a
substantial burden on the universities and colleges involved. Yet
there is wide agreement that their present resources fall far short of
meeting national needs.

The response of the universities of the United States to the challenge of world affairs is as varied as the institutions themselves.
Each institution has evolved in its own way—in response to the interests of its faculty, the opportunities presented, the leadership given,
and the needs to which it reacts most strongly. This response has emphasized, in a wide variety of patterns and combinations, such elements as non-Western and intercultural curriculum elements at the
undergraduate level, graduate area study centers, programs for foreign
students, functional and problem-oriented research programs, general
and specialized library development, training of United States nationals for service abroad, travel, study, and research overseas individually and in institutional settings, cooperative programs with
other institutions at home and abroad, and programs in educational
assistance with the support of private foundations or Government
agencies. Our publicly supported universities have retained the traditional dual concerns with teaching and scholarship and have added a
third dimension: service to the society beyond the campus.

As our people and our Government have entered into ever growing
international commitments and activities, it has been a natural development for our universities to become more involved in both teaching
and studying about the world beyond our borders. Similarly, it has
been a natural development for the American public university, and
in some measure the private university as well, to develop a service
function extending to a "community" beyond the borders of its local
constituency, even beyond the borders of the State and Nation. . . .

Federal reliance on university resources

The record is clear that in the past two decades the Federal Government has come to rely heavily on the colleges and universities of the
United States for personnel, knowledge, and institutional expertise in
relation to activities in international education and in other fields as
well. It is generally agreed that this reliance has not brought with it
adequate Federal support to strengthen these institutions as resources
for the future. Perhaps the most important influence in shaping the
relationship in this manner has been the fact that the Federal agencies
active in international education have been primarily concerned with

the various problems and challenges in foreign affairs for which they were primarily responsible, and only secondarily concerned with the welfare of the educational institutions upon which they were drawing. Of the four Federal agencies primarily charged with overseas activities in international education, none has education as a primary concern, still less the strength and balanced development of our higher educational institutions here at home: in the budget of the Agency for International Development and its predecessor agencies, for example, educational activities have never accounted for more than 4 percent of the total annual appropriation.

The result has been that the Federal agency in question has generally come to the university in question with a request which was short-term, often to be carried out on a crash basis, and nearly always conceived and planned according to the foreign policy objectives and purposes of the agency in question rather than according to any of the needs or desires of the university. This has generally been true even with overseas educational assistance projects where the experience of the university would have been a valuable asset in Government planning. Because it is usually brought into the project only after project plans have been crystallized according to Government needs, the university has all too frequently been forced to assume responsibility for operation of a project which it has not planned and can only change with difficulty. It is not given leeway to assimilate the project to its home needs by maximizing the benefits from its participation. Because of this lack of university participation in planning, and still more because of Government concern with paying only for activities for which direct overseas "payoff" could easily be envisioned, there have rarely been provisions allowing even for follow-up studies to evaluate the total effectiveness of the project over time.

It has unfortunately become clear that Government-supported overseas educational assistance projects have proven of primary benefit to the Government and only secondarily beneficial to the university or individual professor involved. It is significant in this respect that service abroad has not yet become a normally accepted element of an academic career, in large part because of the lack of opportunity for research or other recognized professional development.

In his message of February 2, 1966, President Johnson for the first time in the history of this Nation established greater effectiveness of our efforts in international education as one of our major national policy objectives. He also made clear that to implement this new program, the Federal Government will have to rely more heavily than ever on the resources of United States higher education. The Center for Educational Cooperation, which the President announced would be established in the Department of Health, Education, and Welfare, will serve as a central point of overview and leadership for the total United States effort in both the domestic and foreign aspects of international education. The Center will serve as a central point of reference within the Federal Government for the colleges and universities of the United States in their concern with international education; of necessity, the Center must draw heavily on their resources both for personnel and for expertise.

The President also proposed the creation of a corps of education officers who will serve in selected embassies abroad, providing central guidance for all aspects of official American educational relationships with the host country. If these positions are to be filled by those best equipped to handle this important job, the Government will have to turn to the academic community in most cases to fill them.

Other programs proposed by the President will place an even heavier drain on our present supply of educational talent. The President directed AID "to make a major effort in programs of direct educational benefit" to developing nations, by assisting other countries in increasing their own capacities to educate their people, to do research, and to produce the resources on which an excellent educational system can be built. As part of this effort, the President recommended, under existing legislative authority, a significant increase in the number of Americans teaching abroad, including a stepped-up and improved program of English teaching; a general upgrading of U.S. schools and colleges overseas; and evaluation and improvement of the education and services provided to foreign students studying in this country.

In addition to these aspects of international education, which would aid the United States through aiding the peoples of other countries, the President laid particular stress on strengthening the education of Americans as knowledgeable citizens and for specialized work with international implications.

Federal support

The committee concludes that the Federal Government has a clear responsibility to support and strengthen the capabilities of our colleges and universities for international studies and research. The testimony before the Task Force established the magnitude of the need and the importance to our Nation of an educational system with high competence in world affairs. Private sources, particularly the foundations and the universities themselves, have made heavy commitments to the support of international programs. It is now apparent, however, that if our colleges and universities are to meet the demands placed upon them in the field of international affairs, we must provide additional support from Federal funds. However valuable the financial support provided by State, local, and private sources for international studies and research programs in colleges and universities, such financing is no longer adequate.

Many of the capabilities which this bill would support constitute a national responsibility. As Chancellor Franklin Murphy, of the University of California at Los Angeles, said in his testimony:

"At UCLA we have graduate programs in which five different African languages are taught. Quite clearly we are not teaching those languages in order to solve the problems of California; these are not really very germane to the interests of the California citizen. This is in the national interest because it is one of the few places in the world where this concentration can be found, and students come from all over the United States for this experience."

The record of past experience with governmental and private support of international studies in our universities and colleges persuades the committee that Federal grants under the International Education Act of 1966 will not result in reliance upon Federal financing; on the contrary, several witnesses testified that the enactment of H.R. 14643 is likely to stimulate rising levels of support for these programs from the resources of the recipient institutions themselves, from State and local governments, and from private sources. The committee notes particularly the possibility and desirability of greatly increased support by private business. Witnesses testified before the Task Force that programs contemplated under the International Education Act of 1966 would produce the knowledge and the personnel required by American business both to compete in international markets and to play an effective role in assisting the economic development of the emerging nations. In this connection, it is apparent that American business and industry have unique resources which can strengthen the activities of our country in many aspects of international education at home and abroad.

The Opportunity
and the Responsibility

The world is full of challenges and we tend to be reminded of so many of them that the word sometimes seems to lose its ring. There is no need to overdramatize the situation we confront with the International Education Act. But it is important that we recognize the essential meaning of what has now happened.

The new legislation is almost certainly the most significant federal move ever made in the field of international education. In passing the Act, however, Congress has not authorized the responsible agency (Department of Health, Education, and Welfare) to go directly into grant-making, but instead has called for an initial period of consulting, assessing and planning. Instead of approving $10,000,000 for grants to educational institutions in FY 1967, as provided in the version of the bill as first passed by the House, the final Act authorizes $1,000,000 for planning purposes. And equally significant, it calls for a full report to Congress in the spring of 1967 to justify appropriation of the $40,000,000 authorized for grant-making use during the next fiscal year. Clearly, it is the intent of Congress that the remainder of the 1967 fiscal year be a time of further preparation, a period when the foundations of a substantial new program must be carefully built.

In the nature of international education, this assigns a considerable measure of responsibility to the private educational community. The government can stimulate, give shape and direction, and provide large-scale financing. But the ideas and activities that make up international education are mainly the province of the schools, colleges and universities of the nation. And the Congress has essentially confirmed this

William W. Marvel, President, Education and World Affairs. From *International Education Act of 1966* (New York, Education and World Affairs, 1966), pp. 50–56.

relationship by insisting—through several provisions of the new Act—
that the academic community be promptly geared into the planning
process as a fully equal partner with the government.

So the responsibility is fully upon the private sector to make a decisive contribution to the further shaping of the new initiatives in
international education. What happens under the Act in the years
ahead depends significantly on how the academic community now re-
sponds. The fact that Congress has not yet appropriated the
$1,000,000 authorized in the Act for this year complicates the prob-
lem, but it does not relieve the academic community of the responsibility to respond—and to respond creatively and constructively.

The response that must be made will have to depend in part on the
relevant government agencies for stimulation and leadership. While
that is being organized, however, we in the private sector can make
some advance by gaining familiarity with and understanding of the
now-established framework of the new international education program. To contribute directly to that end is, of course, the purpose of
this collection of relevant documents and interpretative material.

With respect to the legislation itself, some of the changes incorporated into the final version are of sufficient importance to warrant
special highlighting. Here the academic community can find clues to
the ways it must respond if its role is to be meaningful.

Watchwords: planning and consultation

If there is any single theme that runs through the Act and its legislative history, it is the call for careful planning on several fronts:
by HEW as the responsible department of government; between HEW
and the academic community; within the academic community; and
within the individual institutions. Widespread consultation among
the many interested parties is clearly implied. One of the major Senate
changes in the Act, scaling down the previous authorization of
$10,000,000 for grants to $1,000,000 for planning, clearly reveals
this intent. Future grant-making, now contingent on a full and further
justification to Congress of what will be done with the first $40,000,000,
is in any event postponed until FY 1968. For all practical purposes,
taking into account the calendar of the normal legislative year, the
first grants to colleges and universities can scarcely occur before the
end of calendar year 1967.

Strengthened advisory council

The final version of the Act establishes a National Advisory Committee on International Studies, a considerably strengthened version

of the advisory body previously intended by the House (which was to be established by Executive Order and appointed by the Secretary of Health, Education, and Welfare). Not only will the new committee be appointed by the President, but it will also be intimately concerned with the broad reporting functions assigned to the Secretary of HEW. In a provision that has few precedents, the committee is authorized to have its own staff appointed independently of Civil Service regulations and GS salary levels. From the Act itself, and especially from the legislative history, we find that Congress intends it to be made up of high-level expert and professional members. In addition to the Assistant Secretary of HEW for Education, who will serve as chairman of this committee, "a majority shall constitute a broad representation of higher education in the United States and the remainder shall include representatives of the general public and individuals experienced in foreign affairs."

An advisory committee cast in this form has several important implications for the future. It can be a source of high-level counsel and support for the future Center for Educational Cooperation in HEW as the CEC emerges as the federal government's "focal point for leadership in international education." It can help stimulate and sustain the continuing dialogue between the academic community and the government. It can serve as "general watchdog" over the administration of the Act and the government's efforts in international education generally. In this connection, Section 106 (b) of the Act assures the Advisory Committee of direct access to the Congress by directing that any recommendations of that committee "shall be included in the report(s) provided for . . ." in the different relevant sections of the Act. It can function as a buffer between the Center in HEW, as administering agency for the Act, and whatever incompatible or improper pressures might develop from the private sector or from various agencies within the government.

Broad legislative authority

In view of the absence of formulae circumscribing HEW's grant-making power and of the "openness" of the language, the Act can be considered an almost unprecedentedly broad legislative authority. The absence of guidelines and criteria worried key members of Congress and led to the incorporation of certain provisions which signaled that Congress would be paying especially close attention to the development of programs under the Act. One of these new provisions was, of course, the concept of a greatly strengthened Advisory Committee. Another was the action already mentioned: postponement of grant-making authority until FY 1968, and requirement of a report justifying the projected FY 1968 expenditure of $40,000,000. This obviously gives the Congress another opportunity to review in detail plans for the first grant programs. Finally, in authorizing use of the "services and facilities of any agency of the Federal Government" to carry out the purposes of the Act, it is required that written agreements between the Secretary of HEW and the head of any other such agency be published in the Federal Register three weeks prior to the date on which any such agreement is to become effective. This seems to be a safeguard primarily against the improper involvement in any activities funded under the International Education Act of the foreign affairs, military or intelligence agencies, a potential danger over which several members of Congress expressed special concern.

Focus on broad strengthening of institutions

A moment's reflection makes it clear that the International Education Act is predominantly an "institutional type" of legislation. It is not designed in the first instance to channel funds to individual scholars or small *ad hoc* research groups. It is for the broad, general strengthening of universities, colleges, other higher educational institutions, and the related non-profit organizations and associations that work with them in the pursuit of common purposes. It seems probable that even the disciplines, area studies institutes, international centers, professional groups and other subdivisions of the scholarly and research community will increasingly be called on to orient their programs through the universities and colleges in order to qualify for support under the International Education Act.

Cooperative planning: intra-institutional and inter-institutional

Both explicitly and implicitly, the Act stresses the importance of intensive institutional planning and inter-institutional cooperation and consultation. The explicit call for such planning has been mentioned several times previously.

To place this kind of demand on any institution, but especially to make this requirement of newer, "developing" colleges and universities, is in the last analysis to insist on a substantial measure of collaboration and consultation among them. They often cannot effectively undertake such planning on a wholly independent, one-for-one basis. Furthermore, the explicit authorization of grants to ". . . combinations of such institutions . . .," in both sections 101 and 102 of the Act, and the further authorization in section 103 of grants for use of the services and facilities ". . . of any other public or nonprofit agency or institution . . ." — all of this seems to bring within the scope of the new programs various types of consortia, regional groupings, and other associations, organizations and bodies which are in a position to assist individual institutions to realize the purposes of the Act.

The place of professional and disciplinary interests

An important footnote to the emphasis on institutions as the recipients of grants is the significance of the Act as far as the disciplinary fields and the professions within higher education are concerned. The net effect may well be that certain professional schools and departments in the arts and sciences complex will for the first time begin to look to the education part of the Department of Health, Education, and Welfare. The education sphere within HEW has not tended to be the rallying ground for a number of the leading professions and disciplines. But now, within the broad framework of university and college participation in the Act, they are likely to start looking to HEW. In both the language and the legislative history of the Act, the achievement of a strong international dimension in the professional schools is included among the intended purposes. As a result of developments along this line the education sector of HEW will probably begin to build the kind of understanding and rapport with the university and college world which it so far has enjoyed mainly with secondary and elementary level educators.

Making a one-sentence general assessment of progress to date in translating the Smithsonian address into action, one might fairly conclude that many significant things have been achieved while certain other important matters have slipped from view. Attention has focused on the legislative side of the program, on an act to strengthen the international aspects of *American education at home.* There has consequently been less emphasis on the major *international, intercultural meaning* of the full program. We have thought less about the compelling terms in which the Smithsonian speech was framed — a call on all the nations of the world to join together in cooperation to advance education everywhere. There has been highly uneven progress with respect to the several features of the President's full International Education Program — as announced in the February 2nd message to Congress — aside from those incorporated into the Act itself.

And there remains a list of highly important unattended problems. These problems are as follows:

— The *serious manpower problem* that affects the entire area of international education. Where will the people come from — and how will new recruits be found and trained — to staff all the positions here and abroad implied by the expanded international education program?

—The *flow of federal money* into the private sector *in support of research relating to international education,* especially the tangle of problems involved for American scholars seeking to conduct social science field research overseas.

—The need to base our international educational efforts increasingly on full collaboration with educators, scholars, and other leaders of the host countries, including *the absolute necessity of more systematic bi-national cooperative planning of major programs.*

—The fact that the *much-discussed and ever-mounting 'foreign student problem'* in the United States does not seem to be disappearing, and the urgent necessity of providing better means to assist colleges and universities in this country to do a more effective job not only in educating those students, but initially in evaluating, screening and selecting them for admission to United States institutions.

—The need for a *careful review of the present condition of the Fulbright Program,* in light of many related developments over the twenty years since it was first established, looking toward the possible revision and general modernization of this important instrument of educational exchange.

—The necessity to take a *new look at the whole apparatus of governmental and quasi-governmental boards and bodies that have evolved over the last two decades for various specific purposes related to international education.* Is there a solid rationale for their continued existence? What should be their relationship to each other, to the new Center and to the other agencies that will continue to have a role in international education?

The only reason for reviewing this list of problems still ahead is to suggest the magnitude of the nation's future agenda in international education. It is another way of stating the challenge that faces the academic community—a challenge that is capable of absorbing our greatest wisdom, our best efforts, and our long-continuing attention.

PART VII

*A Selected
Bibliography*

The purpose of this bibliography is to represent the variety of international educational relations that are currently being explored in professional publications, in the popular press, and at public forums and professional conferences. The literature on international education can be divided into two broad categories: technical assistance and cultural relations. Although the programs in these separate areas are quite distinct in terms of purpose, they overlap considerably when examined from the point of view of function. For instance, both types of programs use exchange-of-persons activities in implementing their goals. However, in this bibliography exchange-of-persons activities are listed only under cultural relations because most of the literature on exchange-of-persons activities deals with questions that relate to cultural relations. There is practically no literature on the relationship of technical assistance as such and the exchange of persons.

In this bibliography, the publications on technical assistance are divided into (1) those that describe multilateral and bilateral governmental and nongovernmental assistance programs; (2) those that analyze the political and economic dynamics of development in the aided countries; (3) those that examine the cultural factors that influence aid programs; and (4) those that deal with the recruitment, selection, and training of personnel for overseas work.

Most of the publications on multilateral and bilateral governmental and nongovernmental assistance programs that are descriptive in nature are written by individuals who have participated in the programs they discuss. Another important source of material in this area is government publications. For the most part, the publications on this topic are produced by practitioners rather than theoreticians.

The theoreticians come to the fore in the literature on the political and economic dynamics of development aid. Although some of the most highly respected literature in the field of international education has grown out of the interest that political scientists and economists have recently shown in the problems of education and development, the literature is not without its limitations. One frequently heard complaint is that few of the proposals found in this literature are based upon rigorous empirical research.

The next category under technical assistance deals with the role of culture in the transfer of learning across national boundaries. What is discussed here is how culture affects the acquisition of new learnings, especially those related to modernization. The writings of anthropologists, sociologists, and, in some instances, psychologists, increasingly are being numbered among the important works in this area. This has resulted in the questioning of many of the old clichés about how individuals from various cultures interact when they work together on common problems.

Finally, there is the literature on the recruitment, selection, and training of personnel for overseas work. Few would deny that the single most important factor in the success of overseas programs is the type of personnel selected to work in these programs; however, the literature in this area is sparse and provides few guidelines that are useful. If nothing else, this makes the area a most promising one for young scholars who are interested in pioneering new frontiers in the field of international education.

Two topics figure prominently in the publications on cultural relations programs. The first concerns the purposes and the functions of these programs, particularly as they relate to education, diplomacy, and propaganda. The fact that the question of the interrelationship of these seemingly diffuse elements is even raised reflects the new and expanded role that cultural relations has assumed since World War II. A striking example of this change is evidenced in the phenomenal growth in the number of American libraries and English training centers abroad.

The second topic under cultural relations is the exchange of persons. The literature in this area is extensive and includes some of the finest empirical research studies in the field of international education. These research studies were coordinated by the Committee on Cross-Cultural Education of the Social Science Research Council. The Committee concentrated upon exchange of persons activities because it felt that these activities are at the very heart of international education.

The last major section of the bibliography deals with the role of the school in promoting international understanding. The stated purpose of activities in this area is to promote world peace and a full understanding of other nations. Most of the references contain practical suggestions on how and what to teach children about other nations. Currently, these sources do not command the respect of scholars in the field of international education. This respect would be forthcoming if educationists and area specialists would form more cooperative relationships to produce these materials. However, there is little likelihood that this will happen in the immediate future.

The greater part of this bibliography is based upon references found largely at Teachers College, Columbia University, and Widener Memorial Library, Harvard University. Both libraries have outstanding collections in the field of international education. Hopefully, in addition to the sources listed, scholars will find the organizational schema of this bibliography of value in gaining fresh insights into the field of international education. A word about the schema is in order at this point. The schema was developed to systematize the literature in the field. As such it represents a compromise between the intrinsic nature of the field and the areas of the field that are currently being examined in the literature. Thus, it is quite possible that important areas of the field are slighted or ignored altogether in this bibliography.

Primarily, the bibliography was compiled as a resource for scholars in the field of international education. However, it should prove valuable as well for librarians who need a guideline to evaluate their holdings and to laymen who want to familiarize themselves with the field of international education.

UNESCO and General References on International Education

Books, Pamphlets, and Government Publications

Ascher, Charles S. *Program Making in UNESCO, 1946–1951: A Study in the Processes of International Administration.* Chicago, Public Administration Service, 1951. 84 p.

Barker, H. Kenneth, ed. *AACTE Handbook of International Education Programs.* Washington, D. C., American Association of Colleges for Teacher Education, 1963. 72 p.

Bodenman, Paul S. *American Cooperation with Higher Education Abroad: A Survey of Current Programs.* U.S. Department of Health, Education and Welfare; Office of Education; Bulletin 1957. No. 8. Washington, D.C., Government Printing Office, 1957. 211 p.

Education and World Affairs. *The U.S. Office of Education: A New International Dimension.* New York, Education and World Affairs, n.d. 72 p.

Flack, Michael J. *Sources of Information on International Educational Activities.* Washington, D.C., American Council on Education, 1958. 114 p.

Fraser, Stewart, ed. *Governmental Policy and International Education.* New York, John Wiley & Sons, 1965. 373 p.

Havighurst, Robert J. and Bernice L. Neugarten. *Society and Education,* 2nd ed. Boston, Allyn and Bacon, 1962, p. 433–56.

Laves, Walter H. C. and Charles A. Thomson. *UNESCO: Purpose, Progress, Prospects.* Bloomington, Ind., Indiana University Press, 1957. 469 p.

Michigan State University, Institute of Research on Overseas Programs. *The International Programs of American Universities: An Inventory and Analysis.* East Lansing, Mich., Michigan State University, 1958. 323 p.

Pillsbury, Kent. *UNESCO Education in Action.* International Education Monographs No. 4. Columbus, Ohio, Ohio State University Press, 1963. 106 p.

Scanlon, David G., ed. *International Education: A Documentary History.* New York, Teachers College Press, 1960. 196 p.

Shuster, George N. *UNESCO: Assessment and Promise.* New York, Harper & Row, 1963. 130 p.

Thomas, Jean. *U.N.E.S.C.O.* Paris, Gallimard, 1962. 266 p.

Unesco. *What is UNESCO?* Paris, Unesco, 1962. 62 p.

U.S. Congress, House Committee on Government Operations. *Government Programs in International Education,* Forty-Second Report. Washington, D.C., Government Printing Office, 1959. 251 p.
Wright, Quincy. *The Study of International Relations.* New York, Appleton-Century-Crofts, 1955, p. 307–320.

Articles and Periodicals

Brickman, William W. "A Course in International Education." *The Journal of Teacher Education,* 5:141–44, June 1954.
Brickman, William W. "International Education." *Encyclopedia of Educational Research,* rev. ed. New York, Macmillan, 1950, p. 617–27.
Caldwell, Oliver J. "Education Provides a New Approach to Diplomacy." *Nation's Schools,* 53:43–47, February 1954.
Cotner, Thomas E. "Responsibilities of the Bureau of International Education in U.S. Educational Foreign Policy." *Higher Education,* 19:3–7+, April 1963.
Gross, F., ed. "International Education." *Journal of Educational Sociology,* 20:1–64, 1946.
Holland, G. K. "Education, International." *Encyclopedia Britannica.* Chicago, Encyclopedia Britannica, Inc., 1963. Vol. 7, p. 1015–16.
Jackson, Mae L. "The Reporting on International Education in American Press." *Comparative Education Review,* 8:344–46, December 1964.
Katz, Joseph. "Canada and the International Cooperation Year in Education." *Comparative Education,* 1:79–88, March 1965.
Kneller, George F. "Comparative Education." *Encyclopedia of Educational Research,* 3rd ed. New York, Macmillan, 1960, p. 316–23.
Parker, Franklin. "UNESCO at 15: Young Adam in Troubled Eden." *School and Society,* 89:431–33, December 16, 1961.
Quattlebaum, Charles A. "International Education." *Encyclopedia Americana,* 1966 ed. New York, Americana Corporation, 1966. Vol. 15, p. 237–39.
Shuster, George N. "The Trials and Triumphs of UNESCO." *Saturday Review,* February 24, 1962, p. 21–22+.
Tripp, Brenda M. H. "UNESCO in Perspective." *International Conciliation,* 497:321–83, March 1954.
UNESCO Chronicle. Paris, Unesco, 1948 to date. Monthly.

Technical Assistance: Education and Development

Multilateral, Bilateral, and Nongovernmental Assistance Programs

Books, Pamphlets, and Government Publications

Adams, Velma. *The Peace Corps in Action.* Chicago, Follett Publishing Co., 1964. 318 p.
Adams, Walter and John A. Garraty. *Is The World Our Campus?* East Lansing, Mich., Michigan State University Press, 1960. 180 p.

Albertson, Maurice, *et al. New Frontiers for American Youth: Perspectives on the Peace Corps.* Washington, D.C., Public Affairs Press, 1961. 212 p.

American Council of Voluntary Agencies For Foreign Service. *The Role of Voluntary Agencies in Technical Assistance.* New York, The Council, 1953. 176 p.

American Council on Education. Committee on Institutional Projects Abroad. *Conferences on University Contracts Abroad.* Washington, D.C., The Council, 1955, 66 p.; 1958, 68 p.; 1959, 114 p.; 1960 70 p.

Bass, Lawrence W. *The Management of Technical Programs with Special Reference to the Needs of Developing Countries.* New York, Frederick A. Praeger, 1965. 138 p.

Behrman, Daniel. *When the Mountains Move: Technical Assistance and the Changing Face of Latin America.* Paris, Unesco, 1954. 69 p.

Benham, Frederic C. *The Colombo Plan, and Other Essays.* London, Royal Institute of International Affairs, 1956. 89 p.

Bingham, Jonathan B. *Shirtsleeve Diplomacy: Point 4 In Action.* New York, John Day Co., 1954. 303 p.

Bock, Edwin A. *Fifty Years of Technical Assistance: Some Administrative Experiences of U.S. Voluntary Agencies.* Chicago, Public Administration Clearing House, 1954. 65 p.

British Information Services. *Community Development: The British Contribution.* New York, The Services, 1962. 37 p.

——. *United Kingdom Technical Assistance for Overseas Development.* New York, The Services, 1961. 25 p.

——. *University Education, the U.K. Dependencies.* New York, The Services, 1960. 12 p.

Brown, William A. and Redvers Opie. *American Foreign Assistance.* Washington, D.C., The Brookings Institution, 1953. 615 p.

Butts, R. Freeman. *American Education in International Development.* New York, Harper & Row, 1963. 138 p.

Cerych, Ladislav. *Problems of Aid to Education in Developing Countries.* New York, Frederick A. Praeger, 1965. 226 p.

Coffin, Frank M. *Witness for AID.* Boston, Houghton Mifflin, 1964. 273 p.

Colombo Plan Bureau. *Progress of the Colombo Plan, 1959.* Colombo, The Bureau, 1960. 115 p.

Committee on Educational Interchange Policy. *Military Assistance Training Programs of the U.S. Government.* New York, Institute of International Education, 1964. 28 p.

Council for Technical Cooperation in South and Southeast Asia. *Technical Cooperation under the Colombo Plan: Report.* London, H. M. Stationery Office, 1950–51. Annual.

Curti, Merle. *American Philanthrophy Abroad: A History.* New Brunswick, N.J., Rutgers University Press, 1963. 651 p.

Curti, Merle and Kendall Birr. *Prelude to Point Four: American Technical Missions Overseas 1838–1938.* Madison, Wis., University of Wisconsin Press, 1954. 284 p.

Davis, Russell and Brent Ashabranner. *Point Four Assignment: Stories From the Records of Those Who Work in Foreign Fields for the Mutual Security of Free Nations.* Boston, Little, Brown and Co., 1959. 246 p.

Der Ostblock und die Entwicklungsländer. *The Soviet Bloc and the Developing Countries.* Hanover, Germany, Verlag für Literatur und Zeitgeschehen, 1964. 47 p.

Domergue, Maurice. *Technical Assistance: Definition and Aims, Ways and Means, Conditions and Limits.* Paris, Organization for Economic Cooperation and Development, 1961. 51 p.

Dreier, John C., ed. *The Alliance for Progress: Problems and Perspectives.* Baltimore, Johns Hopkins Press, 1962. 146 p.

Educational Policies Commission. *Point Four and Education.* Washington, D.C., The Commission, 1950. 27 p.

Ellender, Allen J. *A Report on United States Foreign Operations in Africa.* 88th Congress, 1st Sess. Senate Document no. 8. Washington, D.C., Government Printing Office, 1963. 803 p.

Esman, Milton J. *Needed: An Education and Research Base To Support America's Expanded Commitments Overseas.* Pittsburgh, Pa., University of Pittsburgh Press, 1961. 46 p.

Espy, Willard R. *Bold New Program.* New York, Harper & Row, 1950. 273 p.

Ford Foundation. *Design for Pakistan: A Report on Assistance to the Pakistan Planning Commission by the Ford Foundation and Harvard University.* New York, The Foundation, 1965. 36 p.

France. Ambassade, U.S. Service de Presse et d'Information. *France, Aid and Cooperation.* New York, The Ambassador's Office, 1962. 56 p.

Gardner, John W. *AID and the Universities.* New York, Education and World Affairs, 1964. 51 p.

Glick, Philip M. *The Administration of Technical Assistance: Growth in the Americas.* Chicago, University of Chicago Press, 1957. 390 p.

Great Britain. Department of Technical Cooperation. *Technical Cooperation: A Progress Report by the New Department.* London, H. M. Stationery Office, 1962. 18 p.

Great Britain. Treasury. *Assistance From the United Kingdom for Overseas Development.* Cmnd. 974. London, H. M. Stationery Office, 1960. 19 p.

Hoopes, Roy. *The Complete Peace Corps Guide.* New York, The Dial Press, 1961. 180 p.

Hutchinson, Sir Joseph B. *Britain's Contribution to Development in the Tropics.* Hull, Yorkshire, University of Hull Publications, 1961. 20 p.

Japan. Ministry of Foreign Affairs. *Some Features of Japan's Development Assistance.* Tokyo, The Ministry, 1961. 12 p.

Kreinin, Mordechai E. *Israel and Africa: A Study in Technical Cooperation.* New York, Frederick A. Praeger, 1964. 206 p.

Lawson, Ruth C. *International Regional Organizations: Constitutional Foundations.* New York, Frederick A. Praeger, 1962. 387 p.

Loeber, Thomas S. *Foreign Aid: Our Tragic Experiment.* New York, W. W. Norton, 1961. 139 p.

Mack, Robert T. *Raising the World's Standard of Living: The Coordination and Effectiveness of Point Four, United Nations Technical Assistance, and Related Programs.* New York, Citadel Press, 1953. 285 p.

Maddox, James G. *Technical Assistance by Religious Agencies in Latin America.* Chicago, University of Chicago Press, 1956. 139 p.

McNeill, William H. *Greece: American Aid in Action, 1947–1956.* New York, Twentieth Century Fund, 1957. 240 p.

Millikan, Max. F. and Donald L. M. Blackmer, eds. *The Emerging Nations: Their Growth and United States Policy.* Boston, Little, Brown and Co., 1961. 171 p.

Montgomery, John D. *The Politics of Foreign Aid: American Experience in Southeast Asia.* New York, Frederick A. Praeger, 1962. 336 p.

National Planning Association. *The Role of Universities in Technical Cooperation.* Washington, D.C., The Association, 1955. 23 p.

Pentony, DeVere E., ed. *United States Foreign Aid: Readings in the Problem Area of Wealth.* San Francisco, Chandler Publishing Co., 1960. 148 p.

President's Committee on Foreign Aid. *European Recovery and American Aid.* Washington, D.C., The Committee, 1947. 286 p.

Rivkin, Arnold. *Africa and the West: Elements of Free-World Policy.* New York, Frederick A. Praeger, 1962. 241 p.

Robock, Stefan H. *Brazil's Developing Northeast: A Study of Regional Planning and Foreign Aid.* Washington, D.C., The Brookings Institution, 1963. 213 p.

Rosen, Seymour M. *Soviet Training Programs for Africa.* U.S. Office of Education. Bulletin 1963, no. 9. Washington, D.C., Government Printing Office, 1963. 13 p.

Rubin, Jacob A. *Your Hundred Billion Dollars: The Complete Story of American Foreign Aid.* New York, Chilton Books, 1964. 299 p.

Saccio, Leonard J. *The Educational Challenge in Underdeveloped Areas.* Department of State Publication 6793. International Information and Cultural Series 65. Washington, D.C., Department of State, 1959. 7 p.

Scheyven, Louis. *Belgium's Assistance to the Developing Countries.* Memo from Belgium, no. 28. Brussels, Ministry of Foreign Affairs and External Trade, 1963. 8 p.

Scigliano, Robert G. and Guy H. Fox. *Technical Assistance in Vietnam: The Michigan State University Experience.* New York, Frederick A. Praeger, 1965. 78 p.

Sharp, Walter R. *International Technical Assistance: Programs and Organization.* Chicago, Public Administration Service, 1952. 146 p.

Shields, James J., Jr. *Education in Community Development: Its Function in Technical Assistance.* New York, Frederick A. Praeger, 1967. 150 p.

Shriver, Sargent. *Point of the Lance.* New York, Harper & Row, 1964. 240 p.

Smith, Bruce L. *Indonesian-American Cooperation in Higher Education.* East Lansing, Mich., Institute of Research on Overseas Programs, Michigan State University, 1960. 133 p.

Southeast Asia Treaty Organization. *SEATO, 1954–1959.* Bangkok, The Organization, 43 p.

Steuber, Fritz A. *The Contribution of Switzerland to Economic and Social Development of Low-income Countries.* Winterthur (Switzerland), Keller, 1961. 62 p.

Sutton, Francis X. *The Ford Foundation Program in Africa.* New York, The Ford Foundation, n.d. 10 p.

Sweden. Finansdepartementet. *Swedish Development Assistance.* Stockholm, Iduns Tryckeriaktiebolag Esselte, 1962. 44 p.

Thomas, Ann Van Wynen and A. J. Thomas, Jr. *The Organization of American States.* Dallas, Tex., Southern Methodist University Press, 1963. 530 p.

United Nations. Technical Assistance Board. *Report.* New York, United Nations. Annual.

_____. Economic and Social Council. *United Nations Development Decade: Activities of the United Nations and Related Agencies in the Immediate Future.* Thirty-sixth Session, Agenda Item 6(a). New York, United Nations, 1963. 189 p.

U.S. Agency for International Development. *The AID Program.* Washington, D.C., The Agency, 1964. 54 p.

_____. *Building on Experience: A Report of AID in Action.* Washington, D.C., The Agency, 1964. 28 p.

_____. *Principles of Foreign Economic Assistance.* Washington, D.C., Government Printing Office, 1963. 49 p.

_____. *Private Enterprise in International Development.* Washington, D.C., The Agency, 1963. 9 p.

_____. *Report to Congress. The Foreign Assistance Program.* Washington, D.C., The Agency. Annual.

_____. *The Story of AID.* Washington, D.C., The Agency, n.d. 28 p.

_____. *A Task to Share: AID Participant Training Programs for Foreign Nationals.* Washington, D.C., The Agency, n.d. 18 p.

_____. *Training for Development.* Washington, D.C., The Agency, 1963. 20 p.

_____. *A Two-Way Street: Benefits Accruing from the International Training Programs of AID.* Washington, D.C., The Agency, 1963. 48 p.

U.S. Department of State. *The United States and Africa.* Department of State Publication 7710. African Series 40. Washington, D.C., Government Printing Office, 1964. 15 p.

U.S. International Cooperation Administration. *Americans on a New Frontier: U.S. Technicians Lend a Hand Abroad.* Department of State Publication 6921. Economic Cooperation Series 55. Washington, D.C., Government Printing Office, 1960. 29 p.

_____. *ICA: What It Is and What It Does.* Department of State Publication 6803. Economic Cooperation Series 51. Washington, D.C., Government Printing Office, 1959. 13 p.

_____. *Participants in Technical Cooperation.* Washington, D.C., The Administration, 1959. 20 p.

_____. *Report of Progress in Teacher Education.* Washington, D.C., The Administration, 1960. 101 p.

———. *Technical Cooperation in Education*. Department of State Publication 7024. Economic Cooperation Series 58. Washington, D.C., Government Printing Office, 1960. 31 p.

———. *Technical Cooperation: The Dramatic Story of Helping Others to Help Themselves*. Washington, D.C., Government Printing Office, 1959. 59 p.

———. *Working with People: Examples of U.S. Technical Cooperation*. Department of State Publication 6942. Economic Cooperation Series 56. Washington, D.C., Government Printing Office, 1960. 31 p.

Warne, William E. *Mission for Peace—Point 4 in Iran*. Indianapolis, Ind., Bobbs-Merrill, 1956. 320 p.

Westerfield, H. B. *The Instruments of America's Foreign Policy*. New York, T. Y. Crowell, 1963. 538 p.

White, Lyman C. *International Non-Governmental Organizations: Their Purposes, Methods and Accomplishments*. New Brunswick, N.J., Rutgers University Press, 1951. 325 p.

Wingenbach, Charles E. *The Peace Corps—Who, How, and Where*. New York, John Day Co., 1961. 154 p.

Wolf, Charles. *Foreign Aid: Theory and Practice in Southern Asia*. Princeton, N.J., Princeton University Press, 1960. 442 p.

Articles and Periodicals

"Aiding Underdeveloped Areas Abroad." *The Annals* (American Academy of Political and Social Science), 268:1–187, March 1950.

Anderson, P. Nyboe. "Danish Aid to Developing Countries." *The New Era*, 46:88–90, April 1965.

Andrus, J. Russell. "Technical Assistance through Inter-University Contracts." *Higher Education*, 12:75–80, January 1956.

Bell, David E. "The University's Contribution to the Developing Nations." *Higher Education*, 20:5–8, March 1964.

Benveniste, Guy. "Five Areas of Controversy: New Problems in Aid to Education." *International Development Review*, 7:20–24, June 1965.

Bertelsen, P. H. "Folk High Schools for West Africa." *International Development Review*, 3:28–31, October 1961.

Bigelow, Karl W. "Teachers for Africa." *Overseas*, 3:18–22, November 1963.

Bowles, Frank. "International Cooperation in Education." *The Journal of Teacher Education*, 17:61–64, Spring 1966.

"Community and Regional Development: The Joint Cornell-Peru Experiment." *Human Organization*, 21:107–124, Summer 1962.

Cordier, Andrew W. "Association in Growth: International Assistance." *Teachers College Record*, 64:553–58, April 1963.

———. "The Service of American Education to the Developing Countries." *Social Education*, 29:137–41, March 1965.

Edwards, Mike. "Teachers in the Peace Corps." *Saturday Review*, July, 20, 1963, p. 42–44+.

James J. Shields, Jr.   381

Enarson, Harold L. "The Successes and Failures of AID." *Phi Delta Kappan,* 47:188–92, December 1965.

———. "United States Commitment to Education in Developing Societies." *National Elementary Principal,* 44:12–19. February 1965.

———. "The Universities Stake in the Developing Nations." *Educational Record,* 45:27–32, Winter 1964.

Finch, Rogers B. "The Peace Corps and Higher Education—Two Years of Partnership." *Higher Education,* 19:3–6+, June 1963.

"Focus on Foreign Aid." *Intercom* (Foreign Policy Association), 5:11–72, July 1963.

"Formulating a Point Four Program." *The Annals* (American Academy of Political and Social Science), 270:1–149, July 1950.

Frank, Isaiah. "Foreign Aid and the Liberal Dissent." *The New Republic,* January 23, 1965, p. 17–22.

Fulbright, J. W. "Foreign Aid? Yes, But with a New Approach." *The New York Times Magazine,* March 21, 1965, p. 27+.

Hamblin, F. N. "Western Nigeria Modernizes Teacher Education: The Ohio University Contract." *Changes in Teacher Education: An Appraisal.* Official Report of the Columbus Conference, 1963. Washington: National Commission on Teacher Education and Professional Standards, 1964, p. 479–88.

Hill, F. F. "Education: the Need for Constructive Ideas—Key Issues for Policy Makers." *International Development Review,* 4:4–7, December 1962.

Holland, Kenneth. "A Catalyst for Inter-American Higher Education." *Teachers College Record,* 64:687–92, May 1963.

"International Assistance in Educational Planning." *International Review of Education,* 7:444–47, 1961.

"International Co-operation for Social Welfare—A New Reality." *The Annals* (American Academy of Political and Social Science), 329:1–153, May 1960.

Korbonski, A. "COMECON." *International Conciliation,* 549:1–62, September 1964.

Leavitt, Howard B. "U.S. Technical Assistance to Latin American Education." *Phi Delta Kappan,* 45:220–25, January 1964.

Moran, H. O. "Canada's Educational Aid Programs." *Canadian Education and Research Digest,* 1:5–12, December 1961.

Neff, Kenneth L. "Education and the Forces of Change—How Meet the Immense Challenge of Southeast Asia?" *International Development Review,* 4:22–25, March 1962.

Ohly, John H. "Planning Future Joint Programs." *Human Organization,* 21:137–53, Summer 1962.

"Partnership for Progress: International Technical Co-operation." *The Annals* (American Academy of Political and Social Science), 323:1–159, May 1959.

Porter, Willis P. "America's First Peace Corps." *Saturday Review,* July 20, 1963, p. 45.

Roucek, Joseph S. "Is South America Making Progress?" *Phi Delta Kappan*, 47:210–14, December 1965.

Ruffner, Ralph W. "American Educational Aid for National Development." *Teachers College Record*, 62:348–55, February 1961.

Shields, James J. "Technical Aid in Education and International Understanding." *The Year Book of Education*, 1964:344–53.

Snyder, C. Kenneth. "Africa's Challenge to American Higher Education." *Higher Education*, 19:7–19, June 1963.

Spence, R. B. "Teacher Education in Afghanistan." *Educational Forum*, 26:143–53, January 1962.

Stone, Donald C. "The Peace Corps: Caveats." *Overseas*, 1:6–10, December 1961.

"The Peace Corps." *The Annals* (American Academy of Political and Social Science), 365:1–146, May 1966.

Thurber, Clarence E. "Training Administrators for Developing Countries." *International Development Review*, 3:34–38, June 1961.

"Understanding Foreign Aid." *Headline Series* (Foreign Policy Association), 160:3–60, July–August 1963.

Vent, Myron H. "AID and AUB: Partners in Middle East Development." *Higher Education*, 19:8–12, April 1963.

Politics, Economics, and Development

Books, Pamphlets, and Government Publications

Adams, Don, ed. *Educational Planning.* Syracuse, N.Y., Syracuse University, 1964. 152 p.

Agarwala, A. N. and S. P. Singh, eds. *The Economics of Underdevelopment.* New York, Oxford University Press, 1961. 510 p.

Almond, Gabriel and James S. Coleman, eds. *The Politics of the Developing Areas.* Princeton, N.J., Princeton University Press, 1960. 591 p.

Anderson, C. Arnold and Mary Jean Bowman. *Education and Economic Development.* Chicago, Aldine Publishing Co., 1965. 430 p.

Apter, David. *The Politics of Modernization.* Chicago, University of Chicago Press, 1965. 481 p.

Asher, Robert E., *et al. Development of the Emerging Countries: An Agenda for Research.* Washington, D.C., The Brookings Institution, 1962. 239 p.

Bauer, P. T. and B. S. Yamey. *The Economics of Under-developed Countries.* Chicago, University of Chicago Press, 1957. 271 p.

Benham, Frederic C. *Economic Aid to Underdeveloped Countries.* London, Oxford University Press, 1961. 121 p.

Burns, Hobert W., ed. *Education and the Development of Nations.* Syracuse, N.Y., School of Education, Syracuse University, 1963. 112 p.

Coleman, James S., ed. *Education and Political Development.* Princeton, N.J., Princeton University Press, 1965. 620 p.

Committee on Educational Interchange Policy. *Educational Exchange in the Economic Development of Nations.* New York, The Committee, 1961. 25 p.

Conference of African States on the Development of Education in Africa,
Addis Ababa, 1961. *Final Report.* Paris, Unesco, 1961. 127 p.

Cowan, L. Gray, James O'Connell and David G. Scanlon, eds. *Education and
Nation-Building in Africa.* New York, Frederick A. Praeger, 1965. 403 p.

Curle, Adam. *Educational Strategy for Developing Societies: A Study of
Educational and Social Factors in Relation to Economic Growth.*
London, Tavistock, 1963. 180 p.

_____. *Planning for Education in Pakistan.* Cambridge, Mass., Harvard University Press, 1966. 208 p.

Deutsch, Karl W. and William J. Foltz, eds. *Nation-Building.* New York,
Atherton Press, 1963. 167 p.

Emerson, Rupert. *From Empire to Nation: the Rise to Self-Assertion of Asian
and African Peoples.* Cambridge, Mass., Harvard University Press, 1960.
466 p.

Expert Working Group on Social Aspects of Economic Development in Latin
America. *Social Aspects of Economic Development in Latin America.*
Paris, Unesco, 1963. 2 v.

Frankel, S. Herbert. *The Economic Impact on Underdeveloped Societies.*
Cambridge, Mass., Harvard University Press, 1955. 179 p.

Geiger, Theodore and Leo Solomon, eds. *Motivations and Methods in Development and Foreign Aid.* Washington, D.C., Society for International
Development, 1964. 152 p.

Hanson, John W. and Cole S. Brembeck, eds. *Education and the Development of Nations.* New York, Holt, Rinehart and Winston, 1966. 529 p.

Harbison, Frederick and Charles A. Myers. *Education, Manpower and Economic Growth: Strategies of Human Resource Development.* New
York, McGraw-Hill, 1964. 229 p.

Hirschman, Albert O. *The Strategy of Economic Development.* New
Haven, Conn., Yale University Press, 1960. 217 p.

Hunter, Guy. *Education for a Developing Region: A Study in East Africa.*
London, George Allen and Unwin, 1963. 119 p.

Kautsky, John H., ed. *Political Change in Underdeveloped Countries:
Nationalism and Communism.* New York, John Wiley & Sons, 1962.
347 p.

Lewis, L. J. *Education and Political Independence in Africa, and Other
Essays.* Edinburgh, Thomas Nelson and Sons, 1962. 128 p.

Massachusetts Institute of Technology. Center for International Studies.
Economic, Social, and Political Change in the Underdeveloped Countries and Its Implications for United States Policy. Cambridge, Mass.,
The Institute, 1960. 207 p.

Meier, Gerald M. *Leading Issues in Development Economics.* New York,
Oxford University Press, 1964. 572 p.

Organization for Economic Cooperation and Development. *Economic Development of Overseas Countries and Territories Associated with OEEC
Member Countries.* Paris, The Organization, 1958. 272 p.

_____. *Development Plans and Programmes.* Paris, The Organization,
1964. 224 p.

————. *The Flow of Financial Resources to Developing Countries in 1961.* Paris, The Organization, 1963. 88 p.

Organski, A. F. K. *The Stages of Political Development.* New York, Alfred A. Knopf, 1965. 229 p.

Paddock, William and Paul Paddock. *Hungry Nations.* Boston, Little, Brown and Co., 1964. 344 p.

Piper, Don C. and Taylor Cole, eds. *Post-primary Education and Political and Economic Development.* Durham, N.C., Duke University Press, 1964. 238 p.

Powelson, John P. *Latin America: Today's Economic and Social Revolution.* New York, McGraw-Hill, 1964. 303 p.

Pye, Lucian W. *Politics, Personality and Nation Building: Burma's Search for Identity.* New Haven, Conn., Yale University Press, 1962. 307 p.

Riddleberger, James W. *Development Assistance Efforts and Policies in 1961.* Paris, Organization for Economic Cooperation and Development, 1962. 46 p.

Rostow, Walter W. *The Stages of Economic Growth.* New York, Cambridge University Press, 1960. 178 p.

Schultz, Theodore W. *The Economic Value of Education.* New York, Columbia University Press, 1963. 92 p.

Shannon, Lyle W., ed. *Underdeveloped Areas: A Book of Readings and Research.* New York, Harper & Row, 1957. 496 p.

Shils, Edward A. *Political Development in the New States.* The Hague, Mouton, 1965. 91 p.

Singer, Hans W. *International Development: Growth and Change.* New York, McGraw-Hill, 1964. 295 p.

Staley, Eugene. *The Future of Underdeveloped Countries.* New York, Frederick A. Praeger, 1961. 483 p.

Theobald, Robert. *The Challenge of Abundance.* New York, C. N. Potter, 1961. 235 p.

————. *The Rich and the Poor: A Study of the Economics of Rising Expectations.* New York, C. N. Potter, 1960. 196 p.

Thorp, Willard L. *Development Assistance Efforts and Policies.* Paris, Organization for Economic Cooperation and Development, 1964. 114 p.

United Nations. Economic Commission for Asia and the Far East. *Problems of Social Development Planning with Special Reference to Asia and the Far East.* New York, United Nations, 1964. 71 p.

————. Secretary-General. *Technical Assistance for Economic Development.* Lake Success, United Nations, 1949. 328 p.

————. *Science and Technology for Development.* Vol. 2. New York, United Nations, 1963. 197 p.

Unesco. *Economic and Social Aspects of Educational Planning.* Paris, Unesco, 1964. 264 p.

Vaizey, John. *The Economics of Education.* New York, The Free Press of Glencoe, 1962. 165 p.

Wallerstein, Immanuel M. *Africa, the Politics of Independence: An Inter-*

pretation of Modern African History. New York, Vintage Books, 1961. 173 p.

Ward, Robert E. and Dankwart A. Rustow. *Political Modernization in Japan and Turkey.* Princeton, N.J., Princeton University Press, 1964. 502 p.

Articles and Periodicals

Adams, Don. "Education and the Wealth of Nations," *Phi Delta Kappan,* 47: 169–74, December 1965.

Anderson, C. Arnold. "Educational Planning in the Context of National Social Policy." *Phi Delta Kappan,* 47: 180–84, December 1965.

Blaise, Hans C. "Education and Development: A Literature Survey and Comment." *International Development Review,* 6: 7+, September 1964.

Bowman, Mary Jean. "Converging Concerns of Economists and Educators." *Comparative Education Review,* 6: 111–19, October 1962.

Brembeck, Cole S. "Education for National Development." *Comparative Education Review,* 5: 223–31, February 1962.

Caldwell, L. K. "Universities and International Technical Assistance: The Uses of Government Contracts." *The Journal of Higher Education,* 36: 226–73, May 1965.

Curle, Adam. "Social and Economic Problems of Increasing Human Resources in Under-developed Countries." *The Year Book of Education,* 1962: 528–38.

———. "Some Aspects of Educational Planning in Underdeveloped Areas." *Harvard Educational Review,* 32: 292–300, Summer 1962.

De Witt, Nicholas. "Investment in Education and Economic Development." *Phi Delta Kappan,* 47:197–99, December 1965.

"Economics of Education." *International Social Science Journal,* 14:619–718, 1962.

Edding, Friedrich. "Economics of Educational Planning." *International Review of Education,* 8:93–97, 1962.

Gideonse, Harry D. "Economic Growth and Educational Development." *College and University,* 38:421–33, Summer 1963.

Hamblin, F. N. "Education and National Development." *Higher Education,* 18:7–10, September 1961.

Hanna, Paul R. "Education as an Economic and Social Instrument in the Newly Developing Nations." *Phi Delta Kappan,* 43:354–56, May 1962.

Laska, John A. "The Stages of Educational Development." *Comparative Education Review,* 8:251–63, December 1964.

"New Nations: The Problem of Political Development." *The Annals* (American Academy of Political and Social Science), 358:1–179, March 1965.

Porter, Willis. "Education for Economic Development in India and Pakistan." *Phi Delta Kappan,* 47:200–04, December 1965.

Schultz, Theodore W. "Capital Formation by Education." *The Journal of Political Economy,* 68:571–83, December 1960.

Singer, H. W. "International Aid for Economic Development: Problems and Tendencies." *International Development Review,* 6:16–21, March 1964.

"Symposium on Education and Development." *Comparative Education Review,* 8:5–47, June 1964.

"Technology and Economic Development." *Scientific American,* 209:52–244, September 1963.

Vaizey, John. "Comparative Notes on Economic Growth and Social Change in Education." *Comparative Education Review,* 5:7–12, June 1961.

————. "Education as Investment in Comparative Perspective." *Comparative Education Review,* 5:97–104, October 1961.

Cultural Factors and the Process of Innovation

Books, Pamphlets and Government Publications

Arensberg, Conrad M. and Arthur H. Niehoff. *Introducing Social Change; A Manual for Americans Overseas.* Chicago, Aldine Publishing Co., 1964. 214 p.

Bascom, William R. and Melville J. Herskovits, eds. *Continuity and Change in African Cultures.* Chicago, University of Chicago Press, 1959. 309 p.

Bennis, W. G., K. D. Benne and R. Chin, eds. *The Planning of Change.* New York, Holt, Rinehart and Winston, 1961. 781 p.

Braibanti, Ralph J. and Joseph J. Spengler, eds. *Tradition, Values and Socio-Economic Development.* Durham, N.C., Duke University Press, 1961. 305 p.

Byrnes, Francis C. *Americans in Technical Assistance: A Study of Attitudes and Responses to their Roles Abroad.* New York, Frederick A. Praeger, 1965. 168 p.

Doob, Leonard W. *Becoming More Civilized: A Psychological Exploration.* New Haven, Conn., Yale University Press, 1960. 333 p.

Ellingsworth, Huber, ed. *Communications and Change.* Washington, D.C., International Cooperation Administration, 1960. 27 p.

Foster, George M. *Traditional Cultures and the Impact of Technological Change.* New York, Harper & Row, 1962. 292 p.

Ginzberg, Eli, ed. *Technology and Social Change.* New York, Columbia University Press, 1964. 158 p.

Hagen, Everett E. *On the Theory of Social Change: How Economic Growth Begins.* Homewood, Ill., Dorsey Press, 1962. 557 p.

Hall, Edward T. *The Silent Language.* Garden City, N.Y., Doubleday, 1959. 240 p.

Hayes, Samuel P. *Measuring the Results of Development Projects: A Manual for the Use of Field Workers.* Paris, Unesco, 1959. 100 p.

Herskovits, Melville J. *The Human Factor in Changing Africa.* New York, Alfred A. Knopf, 1962. 500 p.

Mead, Margaret, ed. *Cultural Patterns and Technical Change.* New York, New American Library, 1955. 294 p.

Nida, Eugene A. *Customs and Culture: Anthropology for Christian Missions.* New York, Harper & Row, 1954. 306 p.

Spicer, Edward H., ed. *Human Problems in Technological Change: A Casebook.* New York, Russell Sage Foundation, 1952. 301 p.

Ward, Barbara E. *The Rich Nations and the Poor Nations.* New York, W. W. Norton, 1962. 159 p.

Wilson, John. *Education and Changing West African Culture.* New York, Teachers College Press, 1963. 125 p.

Articles and Periodicals

Beaglehole, E. "Evaluation Techniques for Induced Technological Change." *International Social Science Bulletin,* 7:376–86, 1955.

"Contours of Culture Change in South Asia." *Human Organization, 22:* 1–104, Spring 1963.

"Dimensions of Cultural Change in the Middle East." *Human Organization,* 24:1–104, Spring 1965.

Foster, Philip J. "Status, Power, and Education in a Traditional Community." *The School Review,* 72:158–82, Summer 1964.

Hanks, L. M. "Indifference to Modern Education in a Thai Farming Community." *Human Organization,* 17:9–14, Summer 1958.

Jelliffe, Derrick B. and F. John Bennett. "Cultural Problems in Technical Assistance." *Children,* 9:171–77, September–October 1962.

Luke, K. D. "U.S. Influence on East African Education." *Overseas,* 3:4–9, October 1963.

"A Meeting on Criteria and Techniques of Evaluation of Technical Assistance for Economic Development." *International Social Science Bulletin,* 7:443–58, 1955.

Papanek, Gustav F. "Framing a Development Program." *International Conciliation,* 527:305–372, March 1960.

Ramos, Carlos P. "Problems of Evaluating Technical Assistance in a Developing Country." *Philippine Journal of Public Administration,* 8:303–07, October 1964.

U.S. Agency for International Development. *The Multiplier in International Development.* Washington, D.C., The Agency. Bi-monthly.

Useem, John, John D. Donoghue and Ruth Hill Useem. "Men in the Middle of the Third Culture: The Roles of American and Non-Western People in Cross-Cultural Administration." *Human Organization,* 22:169–79, Fall 1963.

Ward, Barbara. "We May Be Rich But They Are Happy." *The New York Times Magazine,* May 5, 1963, p. 22–3+.

The Recruitment, Selection, and Training of Personnel for Overseas Work

Books, Pamphlets, and Government Publications

Cleveland, Harlan and Gerard J. Mangone, eds. *The Art of Overseasmanship.* Syracuse, N.Y., Syracuse University Press, 1957. 150 p.

Cleveland, Harland, Gerard J. Mangone and John Clarke Adams. *The Overseas Americans.* New York, McGraw-Hill, 1960. 316 p.

Committee on Foreign Affairs Personnel. *Personnel for the New Diplomacy.* Washington, D.C., Carnegie Endowment for International Peace, 1962. 161 p.

Council on Social Work Education. *Interprofessional Training Goals for Technical Assistance Personnel Abroad.* Ithaca, N.Y., The Council, 1959. 198 p.

Dustan, Jane. *Training American Businessmen for Work Abroad.* New York, Council for International Progress in Management, 1961. 36 p.

Fuller, C. Dale. *Training of Specialists in International Relations.* Washington, D.C., American Council on Education, 1958. 145 p.

Lederer, William J. and Eugene Burdick. *Sarkhan.* New York, McGraw-Hill, 1965. 307 p.

————. *The Ugly American.* New York, W. W. Norton, 1958. 285 p.

Organization for Economic Cooperation and Development. *Catalogue of Training Institutions in the Field of Economic Development.* Paris, The Organization, 1962. 164 p.

Thurber, Clarence E. and Richard E. Spencer. *American Professions and Overseas Technical Assistance.* University Park, Pa., The Pennsylvania State University, 1965. 114 p.

Torre, Mottram, ed. *The Selection of Personnel for International Service.* Geneva, World Federation for Mental Health, 1963. 161 p.

Articles and Periodicals

Barton, Robert D. "Global Careers — A Program." *Overseas,* 1:7–10, January 1962.

Griffith, Ernest S. "The Challenge of International Education: Five Years of the School of International Service." *The Journal of Higher Education,* 36:32–7, January 1965.

Hall, Edward T. "Orientation and Training in Government for Work Overseas." *Human Organization,* 15:4–10, Spring 1956.

Hollis, W. Peter and Eswin R. Henry. "Key to Better Selection and Training: Measuring Successful Performance Overseas." *International Development Review,* 3:8–12, October 1961.

Shields, James J. "5 Criteria for Teaching in East Africa — Guidelines for the Novitiate." *International Development Review,* 4:27–9, June 1962.

Smith, M. B. "A Factorial Study of Morale Among Peace Corps Teachers in Ghana." *Journal of Social Issues,* 19:10–32, 1964.

Winslow, Anne. "The Technical Assistance Expert." *International Development Review,* 4:17–24, September 1962.

Cultural Relations and Education

Cultural relations programs: diplomacy, education, and propaganda

Books, Pamphlets, and Government Publications

Adams, Richard N. and Charles C. Cumberland. *United States University*

Cooperation in Latin America. East Lansing, Mich., Michigan State University, 1960. 264 p.

American Assembly. *Cultural Affairs and Foreign Relations.* Robert Blum, ed. Englewood Cliffs, N.J., Prentice-Hall, 1963. 184 p.

American Council for Nationalities Service. *European Beliefs Regarding the United States.* New York, The Council, 1949. 134 p.

Barghoorn, Frederick. *The Soviet Cultural Offensive: The Role of Cultural Diplomacy in Soviet Foreign Policy.* Princeton, N.J., Princeton University Press, 1960. 353 p.

_____. *Soviet Foreign Propaganda.* Princeton, N.J., Princeton University Press, 1963. 329 p.

Barnett, Vincent M., ed. *The Representation of the United States Abroad.* Rev. ed., New York, Frederick A. Praeger, 1965. 251 p.

Buchanan, William. *How Nations See Each Other, A Study in Public Opinion.* Urbana, Ill., University of Illinois Press, 1953. 220 p.

Carnegie Endowment for International Peace. *Annual Report.* New York, The Endowment. Annual.

Choukas, Michael. *Propaganda Comes of Age.* Washington, D.C., Public Affairs Press, 1965. 299 p.

Claude, Inis L. *Swords into Plowshares: The Problems and Progress of International Organization.* 3rd ed. rev. New York, Random House, 1964. 458 p.

Colligan, Francis J. *Twenty Years After: Two Decades of Government Sponsored Cultural Relations.* Department of State Publication 6689. International Information and Cultural Series 59. Washington, D.C., Government Printing Office, 1958. 20 p.

Coombs, Philip H. *The Fourth Dimension of Foreign Policy: Educational and Cultural Affairs.* New York, Harper & Row, 1964. 158 p.

Dizard, Wilson P. *The Strategy of Truth: The Story of the U.S. Information Service.* Washington, D.C., Public Affairs Press, 1961. 213 p.

Dulles, Foster R. *Americans Abroad: Two Centuries of European Travel.* Ann Arbor, Mich., University of Michigan Press, 1964. 202 p.

Elder, Robert E. *The Foreign Leader Program.* Washington, D.C., The Brookings Institution, 1961. 115 p.

Ellul, Jacques. *Propaganda: The Formation of Men's Attitudes.* New York, Alfred A. Knopf, 1965. 320 p.

Frankel, Charles. *The Neglected Aspect of Foreign Affairs: American Educational and Cultural Policy Abroad.* Washington, D.C., The Brookings Institution, 1966. 156 p.

Holt, Robert T. and Robert W. van de Velde. *Strategic Psychological Operations and American Foreign Policy.* Chicago, University of Chicago Press, 1960. 243 p.

Hovet, Thomas. *Bloc Politics in the United Nations.* Cambridge, Mass., Harvard University Press, 1960. 197 p.

Hughes, Lloyd H. *The Mexican Cultural Mission Programme.* Paris, Unesco, 1950. 77 p.

Joseph, Franz M., ed. *As Others See Us: The United States Through Foreign Eyes.* Princeton, N.J., Princeton University Press, 1959. 360 p.

Isaacs, Harold R. *Emergent Americans: A Report on "Crossroads Africa."* New York, John Day Co., 1961. 158 p.

Kandel, Isaac L. *Intellectual Cooperation: National and International.* New York, Teachers College Press, 1944. 78 p.

————. *United States Activities in International Cultural Relations.* Washington, D.C., American Council on Education, 1945. 102 p.

Klineberg, Otto. *Tensions Affecting International Understanding: A Survey of Research.* New York, Social Science Research Council, 1950. 227 p.

Laves, Walter H. C. *Toward a National Effort in International Educational and Cultural Affairs.* Department of State Publication 7238. International and Cultural Series 78. Washington, D.C., Government Printing Office, 1961. 82 p.

MacLaurin, John. *The United Nations and Power Politics.* New York, Harper & Row, 1951. 468 p.

McMurry, Ruth and Muna Lee. *The Cultural Approach: Another Way in International Relations.* Chapel Hill, N.C., University of North Carolina Press, 1947. 280 p.

Meyerhoff, Arthur E. *The Strategy of Persuasion: The Use of Advertising Skills in Fighting the Cold War.* New York, Coward-McCann, 1965. 191 p.

Murray, Gilbert. *From the League to U.N.* London, Oxford University Press, 1948. 217 p.

Peters, William. *Passport to Friendship: The Story of the Experiment in International Living.* Philadelphia, J. B. Lippincott Co., 1957. 286 p.

Plimpton, Ruth T. *Operation Crossroads Africa.* New York, Viking Press, 1962. 142 p.

Quattlebaum, Charles A. *Current Educational and Cultural Relations of the United States with Foreign Countries.* Washington, D. C., The Library of Congress, Legislative Reference Service, 1947. 82 p.

Schwantes, Robert S. *Japanese and Americans: A Century of Cultural Relations.* New York, Harper & Row, 1955. 380 p.

Snyder, Harold E. *When Peoples Speak to Peoples.* Washington, D.C., American Council on Education, 1953. 206 p.

Thomson, Charles A. and Walter H. C. Laves. *Cultural Relations and U.S. Foreign Policy.* Bloomington, Ind., Indiana University Press, 1963. 227 p.

U.S. Department of State. *Educational and Cultural Diplomacy—1963.* Department of State Publication 7765. International Information and Cultural Series 87. Washington, D.C., Government Printing Office, 1964. 141 p.

————. Bureau of Public Affairs. *Department of State 1963: A Report to the Citizen.* Washington, D.C., Government Printing Office, 1963. 150 p.

U.S. Information Agency. *Review of Operations.* Washington, D.C., Government Printing Office. Semi-annual.

_____. *VOA.* Washington, D.C., Government Printing Office, 1965. 8 p.

U.S. Senate. Committee on Foreign Relations. *Overseas Information Programs of the United States.* Washington, D.C., Government Printing Office, 1958. 208 p.

Walters, F. P. *A History of the League of Nations.* London, Oxford University Press, 1952. 833 p.

Whitaker, Urban G., ed. *Propaganda and International Relations.* Rev. ed. San Francisco, Chandler Publishing Co., 1962. 246 p.

Articles and Periodicals

"America through Foreign Eyes." *The Annals* (American Academy of Political and Social Science), 295:1–145, September 1954.

Bauer, Raymond A. "Accuracy of Perception in International Relations." *Teachers College Record,* 64:291–99, January 1963.

Brickman, William W. "The Meeting of East and West in Educational History." *Comparative Education Review,* 5:82–9, October 1961.

Cole, Wayne S. "The United States in World Affairs, 1929–1941." National Council for the Social Studies *Thirty-first Yearbook,* 1961: 282–95.

Crane, Robert E. L. "International Teacher Development Programs." *Higher Education,* 19: 7–8+, January 1963.

Dillon, Wilton S. "Afro-American Interchange: Proposals for a Two-way Flow." *Teachers College Record,* 67:1–9, October 1965.

"International Congresses of Education," in Paul Monroe, ed., *A Cyclopedia of Education.* New York, Macmillan, 1912. Vol. 3, p. 477–78.

"International Frontiers in Education." *The Annals* (American Academy of Political and Social Science), 235:1–134, September 1944.

Moravia, Alberto. "When Art Becomes Propaganda." *Saturday Review,* April 17, 1965, p. 23–25+.

Murrow, Edward R. "America's Intellectual Image Abroad." *Educational Record,* 43:29–37, January 1962.

"National Programs of International Cultural Relations." *International Conciliation,* 462:297–336, June 1950.

Sands, Theodore. "Propaganda vs. Diplomacy." *The Nation,* 188:288–89, May 30, 1959.

Weintal, Edward. "Our Link to Moscow," *Overseas,* 1:12–16, November 1961.

Exchange of Persons — The Promise and the Reality

Books, Pamphlets, and Government Publications

Adams, Effie K. *Experiences of a Fulbright Teacher.* Boston, Christopher Publishing House, 1956. 215 p.

Aydelotte, Frank. *The American Rhodes Scholarships: A Review of the First Forty Years.* Princeton, N.J., Princeton University Press, 1946. 208 p.

Beebe, George A. *The Foreign Student in the New York City Area.* New York, Greater New York Council of Foreign Students, 1955. 144 p.

Bennett, John W., *et al. In Search of Identity: The Japanese Overseas Scholar in America and Japan.* Minneapolis, University of Minnesota Press, 1958. 369 p.

British Council. *Overseas Students in Britain.* London, The Council, 1962. 39 p.

British Information Services. *Marshall Scholarships.* New York, The Services, 1953. 4 p.

Cieslak, Edward C. *The Foreign Student in American Colleges: A Survey and Evaluation of Administrative Problems and Practices.* Detroit, Wayne University Press, 1955. 175 p.

Coehlo, George V. *Changing Images of America: A Study of Indian Students' Perceptions.* Glencoe, Ill., The Free Press, 1958. 145 p.

Committee on Educational Interchange Policy. *Academic Exchanges with the Soviet Union.* New York, The Committee, 1958. 28 p.

———. *College and University Programs of Academic Exchange.* New York, The Committee, 1960. 36 p.

———. *Hungarian Refugee Students and United States Colleges and Universities.* New York, The Committee, 1957–58. 2 v.

———. *Twenty Years of United States Government Programs in Cultural Relations.* New York, The Committee, 1959. 30 p.

Conference Board of Associated Research Councils. Committee on International Exchange of Persons. *Educational Exchanges: Aspects of the American Experience.* Washington, D.C., National Academy of Sciences, 1956. 74 p.

Cormack, Margaret. *An Evaluation of Research on Educational Exchange.* Washington, D.C., Department of State, Bureau of Educational and Cultural Affairs, 1962. 137 p.

———. *She Who Rides A Peacock: Indian Students and Social Change.* New York, Frederick A. Praeger, 1961. 264 p.

Cummings, Ivor and Ruth C. Sloan. *A Survey of African Students Studying in the United States.* New York, The Phelps-Stokes Fund, 1949. 78 p.

Davis, James M., Russell G. Hanson and Duane R. Burnor. *Survey of the African Student: His Achievements and His Problems.* New York, Institute of International Education, 1961. 171 p.

Dawes, Norman. *A Two Way Street.* New York, Asia Publishing House, 1962. 180 p.

Dayo, Olugboji. *The Problem of Nigerian Overseas Students.* Lagos, Nigeria, C.M.S. Press, 1959. 28 p.

DuBois, Cora. *Foreign Students and Higher Education in the United States.* Washington, D.C., American Council on Education, 1956. 221 p.

Education and World Affairs. *The Foreign Student: Whom Shall We Welcome.* New York, Education and World Affairs, 1964. 35 p.

Garraty, John A. and Walter Adams. *From Main Street to the Left Bank. Students and Scholars Abroad.* East Lansing, Mich., Michigan State University Press, 1959. 216 p.

Hevi, Emmanuel J. *An African Student in China.* New York, Frederick A. Praeger, 1963. 220 p.

Institute of International Education. *Foreign Study for U.S. Undergraduates: A Survey of College Programs and Policies.* New York, The Institute, 1958. 45 p.

_____. *IIE Services to Colleges and Universities.* New York, The Institute, [1963?]. 19 p.

_____. *Open Doors.* New York, The Institute. Annual.

_____. *Annual Report of the Director.* New York, The Institute. Annual.

International Education Assembly. *International Education through Cultural Exchange.* New York, The School Executive, 1945. 46 p.

Lambert, Richard D. and Marvin Bressler. *Indian Students on an American Campus.* Minneapolis, University of Minnesota Press, 1956. 122 p.

League of Nations. International Institute of Intellectual Cooperation. *University Exchanges in Europe.* Paris, The League, 1929. 240 p.

Métraux, Guy S. *Exchange of Persons: The Evolution of Cross Cultural Education.* New York, Social Science Research Council, 1952. 53 p.

Morris, Richard T. *The Two-Way Mirror: National Status in Foreign Students' Adjustment.* Minneapolis, University of Minnesota Press, 1960. 215 p.

Neumann, Franz L., *et al. The Cultural Migration: The European Scholar in America.* Philadelphia, University of Pennsylvania Press, 1953. 156 p.

Pan American Union. *OAS Fellowship Program.* Washington, D.C., The Union, 1958. 11 p.

Redding, J. Saunders. *An American in India: A Personal Report on the Indian Dilemma and the Nature of Her Conflicts.* Indianapolis, Bobbs-Merrill, 1954. 277 p.

Selltiz, Claire, *et al. Attitudes and Social Relations of Foreign Students in the United States.* Minneapolis, University of Minnesota Press, 1963. 434 p.

Scott, Franklin D. *The American Experience of Swedish Students: Retrospect and Aftermath.* Minneapolis, University of Minnesota Press, 1956. 129 p.

Unesco. *Report on the Indian Study.* UNESCO/SS/COM/7. Paris, Unesco, 1965. 57 p.

_____. *Report on the United Arab Republic Study.* UNESCO/SS/COM/6. Paris, Unesco, 1964. 21 p.

U.S. Advisory Commission on International Educational and Cultural Affairs. *A Beacon of Hope – The Exchange-of-Persons Program.* Washington, D.C., Government Printing Office, 1963. 65 p.

_____. *A Sequel to A Beacon of Hope – The Exchange-of-Persons Program.* Washington, D.C., Government Printing Office, 1964. 34 p.

U.S. Department of State. *American Students Abroad.* Washington, D.C., Government Printing Office, 1957. 30 p.

————. *International Educational Exchange Program 1948–1958.* Publication 6647. Washington, D.C., Government Printing Office, 1958. 65 p.

————. Board of Foreign Scholarships. *Experiment in International Understanding: A Report. . .with a Close-up of the U.S. Educational Exchange Program with Italy.* Washington, D.C., Government Printing Office, 1963. 75 p.

————. Bureau of Educational and Cultural Affairs. *Foreign Visitor Programs.* Department of State Publication 7631. International Information and Cultural Series 86. Washington, D.C., Government Printing Office, 1964. 11 p.

————. Bureau of Educational and Cultural Affairs. *International Educational, Cultural and Related Activities for African Countries South of the Sahara.* Washington, D.C., The Department, 1961. 321 p.

Useem, John and Ruth H. Useem. *The Western-Educated Man in India; A Study of His Social Roles and Influence.* New York, Dryden Press, 1955. 237 p.

Watson, Jeanne and Ronald Lippitt. *Learning Across Cultures: A Study of Germans Visiting America.* Ann Arbor, Mich., Institute for Social Research, University of Michigan, 1955. 205 pp.

Articles and Periodicals

Altbach, Philip G. "The International Student Movement." *Comparative Education Review,* 8:131–37, October 1964.

"America Through Foreign Eyes." *The Annals* (American Academy of Political and Social Science), 295:1–145, September 1954.

Bailyn, Lotte and Herbert C. Kelman. "The Effects of a Year's Experience in America on the Self-Image of Scandinavians." *Journal of Social Issues,* 18:30–44, 1962.

Bennett, John W. "The Innovative Potential of American-educated Japanese." *Human Organization,* 21:246–51, Winter 1962–63.

Bens, Allis and John Bens. "Orientation Afloat." *Overseas,* 3:20–3, February 1964.

Bjerstedt, A. "Ego-involved World-mindedness, Nationality Images, and Methods of Research." *The Journal of Conflict Resolution,* 4:185–92, 1960.

————. "Reduction of 'Barrier Tendencies' During Experience of International Co-living." *Acta Psychologica,* 13:329–46, 1958.

Carter, William D. "UNESCO's Exchange of Persons Programme." *The Year Book of Education,* 1954:362–68.

Coehlo, George V., ed. "Impact of Studying Abroad." *Journal of Social Issues,* 18:1–89, 1962.

Cook, Donald B, and J. Paul Smith. "The Philosophy of the Fulbright Programme." *International Social Science Bulletin,* 8:615–28, 1956.

Coombs, Philip H. "International Educational Exchange: A Work for Many Hands." *Higher Education,* 18:3–6+, September 1961.

Cormack, Margaret L. "Three Steps to Better Orientation," *Overseas,* 3:11–15, September 1963.

Cotner, Thomas E. "Buenos Aires Convention Fellowship Program, 1939–1951." *Higher Education,* 7:209–13, May 1951.

_____. "International Teacher Exchange Contributes to World Understanding." *World Affairs,* 121:12–15, March 1959.

_____. "Student and Teacher Exchange Between the United States and Countries of the Caribbean," in Alva C. Wilgus, ed. *The Caribbean: Contemporary International Relations.* Gainesville, Fla., University of Florida Press, 1957, p. 235–81.

Davis, James M. "Some Trends in International Educational Exchange." *Comparative Education Review,* 8:48–57, June 1964.

"Effectiveness of the Educational and Cultural Exchange Program of the U.S. Department of State." *Overseas,* 2:22–5, April 1963.

Feraru, Arthur. "Home Base for Foreign Students." *Overseas,* 1:5–7, November 1961.

Forstat, Reisha. "Adjustment Problems of International Students." *Sociology and Social Research,* 36:25–30, September–October 1951.

French, John R. P. and Robert B. Zajonc. "An Experimental Study of Cross-Cultural Norm Conflict." *Journal of Abnormal and Social Psychology,* 54:218–24, 1957.

Gardner, John W. "Foreign Students in America." *Foreign Affairs,* 30:637–50, July 1952.

Goldsten, Rose K., *et al.* "Factors Associated with the Development of Cross-Cultural Social Interaction." *Journal of Social Issues,* 12:26–32, 1956.

Gullahorn, John T. and Jeanne E. Gullahorn. "American Students in France: A Perspective on Cultural Interchange." *French Review,* 32:254–60, January 1959.

Henderson, Gregory. "Foreign Students: Exchange or Immigration?" *International Development Review,* 6:19–21, December 1964.

Herman, Simon N. and Erling Schild. "Contexts for the Study of Cross-cultural Education." *The Journal of Social Psychology,* 52:231–250, November 1960.

_____. "Ethnic Role Conflict in a Cross-cultural Situation." *Human Relations,* 13:215–28, August 1960.

Kizilbash, Mehdi. "The Employment of Returning U.S. Educated Indians." *Comparative Education Review,* 8:320–26, December 1964.

Laing, A. "They Came From Many Lands." *Overseas,* 1:11–15, January 1962.

Lippitt, Ronald and Jeanne Watson. "Some Special Problems of Learning and Teaching Process in Cross-cultural Education." *International Social Science Bulletin,* 7:59–65, 1955.

Loomis, Charles P. and Edgar A. Schuler. "Acculturation of Foreign Students in the United States." *Human Organization (Applied Anthropology),* 7:17–34, Spring 1948.

Lysgaard, Sverre. "Adjustment in a Foreign Society: Norwegian Fulbright Grantees Visiting the United States." *International Social Science Bulletin,* 7:45–51, 1955.

Maurer, I. A. "Fulbright Act in Operation." *Far Eastern Survey,* 18:104–47, May 4, 1949.

Mendelsohn, Harold and Frank E. Orenstein. "A Survey of Fulbright Award Recipients: Cross-Cultural Education and Its Impacts." *Public Opinion Quarterly,* 19:401–07, Winter 1955–56.

Morris, Richard T. "National Status and Attitudes of Foreign Students." *Journal of Social Issues,* 12:20–5, 1956.

Riegel, O. W. "Residual Effects of Exchange-of-Persons." *Public Opinion Quarterly,* 17:319–27, Fall 1953.

Sasnett, Martena T. "Foreign Student Problems on American Campuses: A Report on Observations Across the Country." *College and University,* 26:93–101, October 1950.

Sloan, Ruth C. "Educational Exchange with Africa: Fallacies of Generalization." *News Bulletin* (Institute of International Education), 25:23–6, November 1949.

Smith, Howard P. "The Effects of Intercultural Experience – A Follow-Up Investigation." *Journal of Abnormal and Social Psychology,* 54:266–69, 1957.

Smith, M. Brewster. "Evaluation of Exchange of Persons." *International Social Science Bulletin,* 7:387–97, 1955.

————. "Some Features of Foreign-Student Adjustment." *The Journal of Higher Education,* 26:231–41, May 1955.

Stone, Donald C. "Some Research and Action Needs in International Educational Exchange." *Educational Record,* 39:374–81, October 1958.

"The Rising Demand for International Education." *The Annals* (American Acadamy of Political and Social Science), 335:1–165, May 1961.

Zajonc, Robert B. "Aggressive Attitudes of the 'Stranger' as a Function of Conformity Pressures." *Human Relations,* 5:205–16, 1952.

Zimmerman, Claire and Raymond A. Bauer. "The Effect of an Audience upon What is Remembered." *Public Opinion Quarterly,* 20:238–48, Spring 1956.

International Understanding: The Role of the School

Books, Pamphlets, and Government Publications

Adams, Thomas R. *Education for International Understanding.* New York, Institute of Adult Education, Teachers College, Columbia University, 1948. 181 p.

Arndt, Christian O. *Programs and Projects for International Understanding.* Oneonta, N.Y., American Association of Colleges for Teacher Education, 1956, 160 p.

Arndt, C. O. and S. Everett, eds. *Education for a World Society: Promising Practices Today.* New York, Harper & Row, 1951. 273 p.

Bereday, George Z. F. and Joseph A. Lauwerys. *Education and International Life: The Year Book of Education 1964.* New York, Harcourt, Brace & World, 1964. 493 p.

Bidwell, Percy W. *Undergraduate Education in Foreign Affairs*. New York, King's Crown Press, 1962. 215 p.

Committee on the College and World Affairs. *The College and World Affairs*. New York, The Hazen Foundation, 1964. 74 p.

Committee on the University and World Affairs. *The University and World Affairs*. New York, The Ford Foundation, 1960. 84 p.

Everett, Samuel. *Teaching and World Affairs*. Washington, D.C., N.E.A., Educational Policies Commission, 1954. 41 p.

Everett, Samuel and Christian O. Arndt, eds. *Teaching World Affairs in American Schools*. New York, Harper & Row, 1956. 270 p.

Hill, C. P. *Toward World Understanding: Suggestions on the Teaching of History*. Paris, Unesco, 1953. 117 p.

Houle, Cyril O. and Charles A. Nelson. *The University, The Citizen and World Affairs*. Washington, D.C., American Council on Education, 1956. 179 p.

Kenworthy, Leonard S. *International Understanding through the Secondary Curriculum*. Washington, D.C., National Association of Secondary School Principals, 1956. 303 p.

———. *Introducing Children to the World in Elementary and Junior High Schools*. New York, Harper & Row, 1956. 268 p.

———. *World Horizons for Teachers*. New York, Teachers College Press, 1952. 141 p.

Lauwerys, Joseph A. *Toward World Understanding – History Textbooks and International Understanding*. Paris, Unesco, 1953. 84 p.

Morehouse, Ward. *The International Dimensions of Education in New York State*. Albany, N.Y., University of the State of New York, 1963. 47 p.

National Education Association. Committee on International Relations. *Education for International Understanding in American Schools*. Washington, D.C., The Association, 1948. 241 p.

———. Educational Policies Commission. *American Education and International Tensions*. Washington, D.C., The Commission, 1949. 54 p.

Preston, Ralph C., ed. *Teaching World Understanding*. New York, Prentice-Hall, 1955. 207 p.

Quillen, Isaac J. *Textbook Improvement and International Understanding*. Washington, D.C., American Council on Education, 1948. 78 p.

Sayres, William C. *The Non-Western World in New York State Higher Education*. Albany, N.Y., University of the State of New York, 1961. 63 p.

Spicer, Dorothy G. *Windows Open to the World: A Handbook of World Fellowship Projects*. New York, The Woman's Press, 1946. 127 p.

Strong, Charles F. *Teaching for International Understanding: An Examina- of Methods and Materials*. London, H. M. Stationery Office, 1952. 95 p.

Swift, Richard N. *World Affairs and the College Curriculum*. Washington, D.C., American Council on Education, 1959. 194 p.

Taba, Hilda. *Cultural Attitudes and International Understanding: An Evaluation of an International Study Tour*. New York, Institute of International Education, 1953. 84 p.

Unesco. *Education for International Understanding: Examples and Suggestions for Class-room Use.* Paris, Unesco, 1959. 116 p.

———. *Toward World Understanding: A Handbook of Suggestions on the Teaching of Geography.* Paris, Unesco, 1951. 101 p.

———. *Toward World Understanding In the Classroom with Children under Thirteen Years of Age.* Paris, Unesco, 1952. 63 p.

U.S. Office of Education. *Education for Freedom and World Understanding.* Washington, D.C., Government Printing Office, 1962. 62 p.

———. *How Children Learn about Human Rights.* Bulletin 1951. No. 9. Washington, D.C., Government Printing Office, 1960. 16 p.

Weidner, Edward W. *The World Role of Universities.* New York, McGraw-Hill, 1962. 366 p.

Willcock, J. B., ed. *Preparing Teachers for Education for International Understanding.* Hamburg, Unesco Institute, 1962. 100 p.

Wilson, Howard E. *American College Life as Education in World Outlook.* Washington, D.C., American Council on Education, 1956. 195 p.

Wilson, Howard E. and Florence H. Wilson. *American Higher Education and World Affairs.* Washington, D.C., American Council on Education, 1963. 158 p.

Articles and Periodicals

Bowles, Chester. "Education for World Responsibility." *Department of State Bulletin,* 46:206–10, February 5, 1962.

Byrnes, Robert F. "Teaching Materials for Foreign Area Instruction." *Phi Delta Kappan,* 47:223–27, December 1965.

Cajoleas, Louis P. "International Understanding: A Theoretical Analysis of a Goal in Education." *Teachers College Record,* 61:188–94, January 1960.

Caldwell, Oliver J. "A Case for Polycultural Education." *Phi Delta Kappan,* 47:193–96, December 1965.

Cousins, Norman. "The World, the Individual, and Education." *NEA Journal,* 49:10–12, April 1960.

Eggertsen, Claude. "International Education and Teacher Training." *Education Digest,* 26:50–52, November 1960.

Eisenhower, D. D. "The Role of the Teacher in Promoting Peace and Understanding." *Department of State Bulletin,* 41:479–81, October 5, 1959.

Gould, Sir Ronald. "An East-West Bridge for a New Generation." *National Parent–Teacher,* 54:28–30, October 1959.

Hechinger, Fred M. "Foreign Languages Stage A Comeback." *Saturday Review,* February 16, 1963, p. 64–6+.

Hoffman, Paul G. "Teaching in an Interdependent World." *NEA Journal,* 49:10–12, December 1960.

Long, Harold M. "Improving the Teaching of World Affairs." *NEA Journal,* 49:39–40, May 1960.

Melady, Thomas P. "Catholic Colleges and the Emerging New Nations." *Bulletin* (National Catholic Educational Association), 59:160–63, August 1962.

Robbins, John. "The New Asia and American Education." *Teachers College Record,* 62:339-47, February 1961.

Rosenhaupt, Hans. "Waging Peace in the Schools." *NEA Journal,* 49:14-16, November 1960.

Smith, Paul E. "How to Teach About the U.N." *NEA Journal,* 49:47-8, April 1960.

"Special Feature—Education in the International Scene." *NEA Journal,* 50: 16-35, May 1961.

"Teaching International Understanding." *School Life,* 39;7-9, March 1957.

Wesley, Edgar B. "American Studies in British Universities." *Comparative Education Review,* 5:182-88, February 1962.

Bibliographies

Cotner, Thomas E. *International Educational Exchange: A Selected Bibliography.* U.S. Office of Education. Bulletin 1961, no. 27. Washington, D.C., Government Printing Office, 1961. 117 p.

Great Britain. Ministry of Overseas Development. Library. *Technical Cooperation: A Monthly Bibliography.* London, The Library, 1964-. Monthly.

Katz, Saul M. and Frank McGowan. *A Selected List of U.S. Readings on Development.* Prepared for the United Nations Conference on the Application of Science and Technology for the Benefit of Less Developed Areas. Washington, D.C., Agency for International Development, 1963. 363 p.

Pan American Union. Department of Technical Cooperation. *Exchange of Persons.* No. 2. Washington, The Union, 1960. 66 p.

Unesco. *Teaching About the United Nations and the Specialized Agencies: A Selective Bibliography.* Paris, Unesco, 1959. 60 p.

U.S. Office of Education. *Bibliography: Publications in Comparative and International Education.* Washington, D.C., The Office, 1956-. Annual.

U.S. Department of State. Bureau of Educational and Cultural Affairs. Policy Review and Research Staff. *International Educational and Cultural Exchange—A Selective Bibliography of Materials on Both Governmental and Private Programs.* Washington, D.C., The Bureau, 1963. 15 p.

_____. Division of Library and Reference. *Overseas Information Programs of the United States Government—A Bibliography of Selected Materials with Annotations.* Washington, D.C., Government Printing Office, 1951. 34 p.